Boys' Love Manga

Boys' Love Manga

*Essays on the Sexual Ambiguity
and Cross-Cultural Fandom
of the Genre*

Edited by Antonia Levi,
Mark McHarry *and*
Dru Pagliassotti

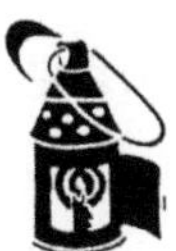

McFarland & Company, Inc., Publishers
Jefferson, North Carolina, and London

LIBRARY OF CONGRESS CATALOGUING-IN-PUBLICATION DATA

Boys' love manga : essays on the sexual ambiguity and cross-cultural
fandom of the genre / edited by Antonia Levi,
Mark McHarry and Dru Pagliassotti.
p.   cm.
Includes bibliographical references and index.

ISBN 978-0-7864-4195-2
softcover : 50# alkaline paper ∞

1. Comic books, strips, etc. — History and criticism. 2. Homosexuality — Comic
books, strips, etc. 3. Women cartoonists. 4. Popular culture — Japanese influences.
I. Levi, Antonia, 1947– II. McHarry, Mark, 1951– III. Pagliassotti, Dru.
PN6710.B67 2010   741.5'952 — dc22   2010002971

British Library cataloguing data are available

On the cover: Heise, *Red Lover*, digital illustration, 8½" × 11", 2008

Manufactured in the United States of America

*McFarland & Company, Inc., Publishers
Box 611, Jefferson, North Carolina 28640
www.mcfarlandpub.com*

Dedicated to 米澤 嘉博 (Yonezawa Yoshihiro) 1953–2006,
the co-founder and president of Japan's Comic Market.
From its inception it has provided a safe place for fans
to buy and sell *dōjinshi*, much of it boys' love.
In its growth over thirty-five years to become one of
Japan's largest conventions, it has helped nurture
BL into a worldwide phenomenon.

Table of Contents

Introduction

Antonia Levi

Drawn in Japanese manga (comic book) style, the two androgynous young men on the bed are impossibly beautiful. Only their bare chests indicate their masculinity. They are joined in a passionate embrace, their naked bodies entwined, their long hair flying. One young man's wrists are loosely bound with silken ropes. His partner holds him down as they gaze rapturously into one another's eyes. Although their genitals are hidden by the tangled sheets, the eroticism of the scene is palpable. This is not, as many westerners might assume, gay erotica. It is an example of boys' love manga — same-sex male romances and erotica written mostly by and for women.

In Japan, boys' love is simply one of many genres that make up the artistic/literary form called manga. Like other manga genres, boys' love stories appear in professional publications, as well as in self-published (*dōjinshi*) formats which may include characters borrowed from other authors' manga, anime, video games and other products. Boys' love runs the gamut from complex graphic novels dealing with serious issues to light-hearted, erotic short pieces in which neither plot nor theme play significant roles. Boys' love themes and conventions are often found as subplots in other Japanese cultural forms.

At the peak of the manga boom in the early 1990s, Mark McLelland estimated that manga comprised approximately 40 percent of all print publications in Japan.[1] That is nothing new in Japan. Antecedents of the genre may be found as long ago as seventh-century picture scrolls (*e-makimono*). Adam Kern traces the origins of modern manga to illustrated tales that were the predominant literature during the Edo period (1603–1868 CE), such as the *kibyōshi* (yellow-cover books) of Santō Kyōden (1761–1816 CE). These texts fluidly combined images and writing and sold more than 30,000 copies each in Edo — then the world's largest city.[2]

The content of boys' love stories is not terribly shocking or even surprising to the Japanese audiences for which they were originally intended. Male same-sex romances and erotica intended for a wider, often at least partially female audience, have a long tradition in Japan. Even Lady Murasaki's usually heterosexual hero Genji indulges in a same-sex affair in the eleventh-century novel *Tale of Genji*. Stories of same-sex relationships between Buddhist priests and their acolytes (*chigo*) were common during the feudal era, as were stories about same-sex relationships among samurai. Woodblock prints (*ukiyo-e*) further illustrated and celebrated such relationships. Kabuki theatre was patronized by women as well as men. The erotic desirability of adolescent male actors (*wakashugata*), as well as male actors playing female roles (*onnagata*), was described in widely circulated theatrical critiques (*hyōbanki*) sold in major cities.[3] This advanced the tradition of same-sex male romances and what can only be described as a fascination with androgyny and the liminal possibilities of gender.

In the nineteenth century, the West brought homophobia to Japan, but it never completely eclipsed the older traditions. Kabuki theater survived, even though many plays treating male-male love were dropped from its repertoire, and in the early twentieth century, the all-female Takarazuka theater, with its impossibly beautiful male role actors (*otokoyaku*), added another layer to the cult of androgyny and gender-bending. Boys' illustrated magazines in the 1920s and 1930s continued the beautiful boy (*bishōnen*) tradition, albeit with only implied same-sex erotica.

A Short History of Boys' Love Manga

When manga emerged in the postwar era, they brought this tradition with them, along with a plethora of other artistic and literary traditions. Some elements were apparent even before female artists became dominant in writing stories, many of them boys' love stories, for women and girls in the 1960s. Tezuka Osamu's *Ribon no kishi* (*Princess Knight*; 1953), about a cross-dressing princess with a male soul and the male friend who falls in love with her without realizing she is female, was not exactly boys' love, but it did introduce many of the gender-bending issues that would become standard in the boys' love tradition. Certainly *Ribon no kishi* was an influence on Hagio Moto, whose *Tōma no shinzō* (*Heart of Thomas*; 1974), a tragic tale of love and suicide in a German boys' school, is often considered to be one of the founding works of the boys' love genre. It was also a favorite of Yamagishi Ryōko, who tied boys' love more fully into Japanese contexts with *Hi izuru tokoro no tenshi* (*Heaven's Son of the Land of the Rising Sun*; 1980), about the same-sex romances of Shōtoku Taishi, the eighth-century prince who is credited with bringing Buddhism to Japan. In 1978, *Comic Jun* became one of the first monthly manga to specialize in boys' love stories, selling, at its peak, 150,000 copies a month.[4] By comparison, in 2003, *BeXBoy* and *BeXBoy Gold*, published alternately each month, had a monthly circulation of about 250,000 copies distributed throughout Japan.

Coinciding with the rise of commercially produced boys' love manga was the development of fan-created and published works called "yaoi." The term was coined as a sardonic acronym for *yama-nashi, ochi-nashi, imi-nashi* (no climax, no point, no meaning) by a group of fans who titled their 1979 *dōjinshi Rappori yaoi tokushū gou* (*Rappori*: Special Yaoi Issue). They coined the acronym because their work was usually comprised of a collection of scenes and episodes lacking any overarching structure. There were yaoi parodies of *Gundam* (War Story) in the early 1980s, but it was the popularity of *Captain Tsubasa* in 1985, a *dōjinshi* based on a popular manga about boys' football (soccer), and the *Saint Seiya* manga boom of 1987 that put the acronym into the Japanese vernacular.[5] By then, yaoi, expressed mostly in *dōjinshi*, began showing the characteristics identified by Kazuko Suzuki that gave impetus to the boys' love/yaoi fan movement. They were (1) amateur publications that were outside mass media restrictions (2) read by teenagers, who comprise the majority of boys' love readers and who encouraged other teens to create yaoi works (3) premised on widely known characters and settings, and (4) they featured characters depicted as ordinary teenage boys or men in their twenties, the same age group as many of its fans.[6]

Today yaoi and boys' love are widely read genres in Japan. Commercial boys' love manga are displayed on the main floors of mainstream bookstores in large cities as well as sold in small-town convenience stores. The Otome Road district of Tokyo has buildings with billboards of *bishōnen*— older *seme* and younger *uke*— in erotic embraces, enticements to the *dōjinshi* sold in the area's book stores. In August 2007, more than 550,000 people, a majority of them young women and teenage girls, attended Tokyo's Comic Market (Komiket), a twice-yearly fan-organized event held since 1975, to buy and/or sell yaoi-themed *dōjinshi* created by small circles of friends. The sales of boys' love *dōjinshi* and other BL products at the Comic Market may have been more than $200 million U.S. dollars in 2008. *Dōjinshi* markets also exist in cities such as Osaka and Niigata that attract tens of thousands of consumers, and informal fan networks exist whose participants exchange *dōjinshi* via postal mail.

Boys' Love in the West

Today, boys' love manga are part of the popular culture landscape in Japan. They are an accepted part of growing up female and are less accepted, but nonetheless sought out, by some young men who read them, a number estimated at ten percent of readers in 2003, according to a *BeXBoy* editor.[7] That, however, was not the case when boys' love manga and a few animated films left their native land and found new audiences among people who knew little if anything about the traditions that had contributed to its creation. As Ien Ang's 1985 pioneering study of globalizing popular culture, *Watching Dallas*, revealed, the responses of audiences viewing material never designed for them can be surprising.

Yaoi and, subsequently, boys' love reached North America and Europe on a large scale via the broadcast on commercial television of anime that would become canonical for fans creating yaoi works. In North America, watershed events included the broadcast of the anime series *Gundam Wing* on the Cartoon Network in 2000[8] and the development of the World Wide Web, which had begun its swift trajectory to widespread adoption about five years earlier.

The arrival of boys' love in the West was affected by two significant factors: marketing and existing fan practices. Although some boys' love manga appeared earlier, the first boys' love anime to be distributed in North America was *Kizuna* (*Bonds*; 1994). The distributor, Ariztical, described the anime as "the first gay male anime to be released on DVD in the U.S."[9] and marketed it to a gay male audience.

Another major factor was the coterminous existence of a Western fan tradition known as "slash." The term is not as violent as it sounds. It refers to the forward slash on a keyboard, which is used by slash writers to indicate which characters from popular culture they are rewriting as a homoerotic couple, a "pairing"; the first such pairing to be described as "slashed" was Kirk/Spock (pronounced Kirk-slash-Spock). By the time boys' love arrived, slash was well established in the West and understood to refer to homoerotic writing and artwork created almost exclusively by women that features male characters from popular media.[10]

Unlike slash, however, boys' love and yaoi attracted a surprising number of gay male fans. That was no doubt partly caused by early marketing efforts, but marketing is not the only reason. Content also plays a role. Because yaoi and boys' love works originated in a different historical milieu, depictions of gender and sex in yaoi and boys' love works are different from those in slash stories. Given gender theorist Judith Butler's contention that real-life sex and gender identities are inherently unstable, boys' love products may suggest different theoretical implications for cultural expressions of sex and gender than those of slash.

One significant difference may well be the greater lability of gender and sex, which has been a topos of Japanese literature since at least the Heian period (794–1185 CE) and which is fully expressed in boys' love manga and anime. That lability is an accepted part of Japanese fictional understandings and, in boys' love, this often leads to depictions of fictional worlds in which same-sex relationships and gender shifting are presented as givens without explanation or excuses. This is the case, for example, in *Yami no matsuei* (*Descendants of Darkness*) where the same-sex preferences of most of the characters are taken for granted as part of the fictional world portrayed.

Slash, on the other hand, developed out of Western concepts of sex and gender and contrasts more dramatically against other Western mainstream cultural works. Western popular culture has become a bit more open to portraying same-sex relationships and challenging the unchanging nature of sex and gender, but there is, as yet, no systematic commercial production of slash or slash-like romances or erotica, no same-sex Harlequin romances. Slash remains very much the domain of amateur fan fiction writers, almost all of them women.

Slash also utilizes mostly characters drawn from live action films and television series and portrayed by adult actors. As a result, the youthful teen look that so easily translates into androgyny in boys' love manga, and allows for so many layered interpretations of sex and gender, is much harder for slash writers to achieve. Despite its subject matter, slash tends to be far more explicitly heterosexual in its assumptions and in the worlds it portrays. This is perhaps best exemplified in the slash sub-genre known as INGB, which stands for "I'm not gay but...." In INGB fanfics, the characters assure one another that although they are passionately attracted to each other, same-sex relationships are not the norm for them. Such scenarios are not unknown in boys' love, but they are far from being as pervasive as they are in slash.

It is important, however, not to overstate the differences between boys' love and slash. There are also similarities and even connections. Boys' love is often considered to have developed independently of slash, and that is to some degree true. However, both genres emerged as important trends in the 1970s, a time marked by a global questioning of gender and sex. Moreover, early boys' love creators in Japan such as Hagio Moto or Takemiya Keiko admit to being influenced by Western works, and many slash enthusiasts were at least aware of boys' love manga before it became commercially available in the West. More recently, a plethora of Harry Potter–inspired slash and *dōjinshi* have revealed the extent to which the two fan subcultures (yaoi/boys' love and slash) are influencing one another.

Currently boys' love and yaoi have an increasingly visible presence in the West. Boys' love began to boom in the U.S. in 2005, after the success of popular manga series like *Kizuna, FAKE,* and *Eerie Queerie!* Panels about yaoi at mainstream anime and comic-book conventions; the enthusiasm of fans at conventions such as Comic-Con International, Sakura-Con, and Yaoi-Con who were vocal about the need for imported and translated titles; the success of the few boys' love series already licensed and translated; and the profusion of bootleg online scanlations indicated an existing audience hungry for more material.

Fan Practices in the West

When anime and manga reached the West, they brought with them not only the fictional products (written and drawn materials), but a variety of fan practices such as holding conventions devoted to the celebration and distribution of anime and manga, and "cosplay," derived from the English words "costume" and "play." Cosplay involves dressing up as a fictional character or at least as a person who exists in a fictional world. Conventions and cosplay were certainly not unknown to western science fiction and comic book fans who referred to them as "cons" and "masquerades" respectively. It didn't take long for anime cons and cosplay to become a part of popular culture fandom in the West or for the traditions to become intertwined. Science fiction fans, for example, often use "cosplay" instead of "masquerade," while anime cosplayers often pride themselves on remaining in the character whose costume they wear for the duration of the convention and interacting with others only as that character, a tradition that does not obtain in Japan.

Boys' love, however, poses a problem for cons and cosplay in the West. Although science fiction, comic book, and anime cons are designed to create liminal spaces for interests that society at large finds odd or shocking, boy's love and slash fans still often stand out, especially when in costume and role-playing. As anime became more mainstream, boys' love fans' cross-dressing and acting out of same-sex sexual fantasies and scenarios found themselves increasingly restricted. At many cons, even scholarly discussions of boys' love were often scheduled late at night, sometimes with the added proviso that all participants must be over the age of eighteen. In several cases, monitors were placed at the door to check IDs. At Toronto's Anime North convention in 2007, a separate area was set aside called "Yaoi North." "A guy dressed up as Pikachu called me a freak," complained one boys' love fan at Seattle's 2006 Sakura-Con. "To the mundanes, everyone at this con is a freak, but we're pariahs even to the other freaks."[11]

As a result of such experiences, boys' love fans in the West have found it necessary to create their own spaces where homophobic and other attitudes hostile to or dismissive of their interests are eliminated. More and more, they have begun to hold their own cons, separate events where they can feel free from the disapproval of others. The largest of these is Yaoi-Con, held annually in or near San Francisco. Although most of the attendees are female (as far as anyone can tell, given the cosplay going on), between fifteen and twenty percent are male. Many are costumed as *bishōnen*, the beautiful, androgynous boys who are the embodiment of the boys' love genre. There is even a *bishōnen* auction at which women bid for their favorite "beautiful boy."

Even Yaoi-Con is not quite free from mainstream pressures, however. The con is, of necessity, limited to those eighteen and older. The con organizers must know that many boys' love fans are younger than that. An online survey I conducted in 2003 revealed that over one third of the boys' love fans who responded were eighteen or younger.[12] For legal reasons, however, the con must remain closed to them.

What Does It All Mean?

In this book, scholars from a wide variety of disciplines discuss the topic of boys' love outside Japan.

In Part One, three authors, Hope Donovan, Paul M. Malone and Yamila Abraham, address economic, social and cultural issues related to global publishing.

Hope Donovan argues, in "Gift Versus Capitalist Economies: Exchanging Anime and Manga in the U.S.," that boys' love fans and publishers are united by a common culture but divided by their respective economic practices. Taking an anthropological approach,

Donovan analyzes the ways in which boys' love fandom engages in a form of ritualized gift-giving that both challenges and is challenged by the capitalist economy of boys' love publishers in the U.S.

Paul M. Malone looks at the manga boom in Germany in "From *BRAVO* to Animexx.de to Export: Capitalizing on German Boys' Love Fandom, Culturally, Socially and Economically." He considers how mechanisms of growth, such as the Web site Animexx, which has been a hub for the commercialization of German fandom, and boys' love, which encourages a passionate level of involvement, have helped turn fans into producers and independent entrepreneurs.

Yamila Abraham's chapter "Boys' Love Thrives in Conservative Indonesia" looks specifically at the challenges Indonesian boys' love artists and readers face in a culture that is becoming increasingly intolerant of erotic works and homosexuality. Abraham, who commissions boys' love works from artists in Indonesia, fears that they will never be free to see their works published within their home country.

In Part Two, Dru Pagliassotti, Mark John Isola, Marni Stanley, M. M. Blair and Tan Bee Kee address questions of genre, both from the point of view of literary theory and from the responses of the readership.

Although yaoi and slash are often addressed in academia as substantially different from mainstream, heterosexual romances, Dru Pagliassotti's chapter "Better Than Romance? Japanese BL Manga and the Subgenre of Male/Male Romantic Fiction" points out their similarities and argues that they are, in most ways, identical in form and function. Moreover, while male/male romances offer some relief from the plot conventions and gender stereotypes criticized in mainstream, heterosexual romances, they raise new questions and potential criticisms with regard to their often sexually explicit content and their problematic relationship to queer politics.

In "Yaoi and Slash Fiction: Women Writing, Reading, and Getting Off?" Mark John Isola examines how yaoi and slash challenge established theories of the gaze in complicating the critical reception of yaoi and slash narratives, particularly as they pose a challenge for contemporary theory regarding the narrative production and consumption of (homo)sexual narratives.

Disagreeing with assertions that women create and enjoy yaoi and slash texts as a form of compensation for social and psychological disempowerment, Marni Stanley analyzes authors' direct comments to the reader to show how they address the reader and sexuality in playful, celebratory terms. Her chapter "101 Uses for Boys: Communing with the Reader in Yaoi and Slash" argues that boys' love texts offer women a chance to subvert the dominant narratives of female sexuality and liberate their own sexual fantasies.

M. M. Blair addresses the curious phenomenon of boys' love female readership expressing often violent dislike for the female characters within the genre in "'She Should Just Die in a Ditch': Fan Reactions to Female Characters in Boys' Love Manga." By analyzing fan comments to BL manga posted in LiveJournal's Yaoi Daily community, Blair shows that this apparent misogyny is not a characteristic of the reader but, instead, a product of the text.

In "Rewriting Gender and Sexuality in English-Language Yaoi Fanfiction," Tan Bee Kee also uses fan commentary, fiction, and art from a LiveJournal community devoted to the series *Weiss Kreuz* (*Knight Hunters: Weiss Kreuz*) to discuss the internal contradictions regarding sex, gender and sexual orientation implicit in such works. She argues that despite such mixed messages, fans ultimately do challenge gender norms through creating such works and participating in such a community.

The third part contains essays by Neal K. Akatsuka, Mark McHarry, Mark Vicars and Kim Senior, Alexis Hall, Alan Williams, and Uli Meyer dealing with perceptions of queerness in the boys' love genre.

In "Uttering the Absurd, Revaluing the Abject: Femininity and the Disavowal of Homosexuality in Transnational Boys' Love Manga," Neal K. Akatsuka critically examines the ways in which boys' love opens up a space that both subverts and strengthens heteronormative, patriarchal discourses. Boys' love's transnational popularity with, especially, female readers, he argues, is due to its affirmation of feminine agency; however, this affirmation is reached by disengaging homosexuality from its real social and personal consequences.

Using an early BL manga, Takemiya Keiko's *Kaze to ki no uta*, Mark McHarry also takes on the question of the abject in "Boys in Love in Boys' Love: Discourses West/East and the Abject in Subject Formation." McHarry describes discourses in twentieth-century France that were influential in the foundation of boys' love and discourses in Edo-period Japan that may be influential in boys' love's elaboration of the subjectivity of the *uke* (younger partner). Looking at Takemiya's use of borders and time, he employs the western psychoanalytic idea of abject in the formation of subject to suggest reasons why *Kaze* and boys' love generally depict adolescent males as erotic objects and why that can be valuable.

Mark Vicars and Kim Senior, in "Queering the Quotidian: Yaoi, Narrative Pleasures and Reader Response," focus on how yaoi is used by "Western" readers (a gay man from working class United Kingdom and a straight woman from middle class Australia) to resist and (re)perform heterogendered pedagogies in everyday life. In their social, cultural and sexual position in relation to texts they attempt to re-experience unimagined significances and to re-imagine the effects between "proper" and "improper" ways of being and doing gender and sexuality.

Alexis Hall engages many of the same questions using "realness" rather than propriety in "Gay or Gei? Reading 'Realness' in Japanese Yaoi Manga." Using interviews conducted at Yaoi-Con in October 2006, Hall notes how perceptions of "realness" in the romantic fantasy worlds of boys' love is primarily related to depictions of gayness and sexuality in ways that reveal the basic assumptions of the readers, and often ignore complexities in how sexuality is perceived and expressed in both Japan and the U.S.

In "Raping Apollo: Sexual Difference and the Yaoi Phenomenon," Alan Williams discusses competing narratives in recent studies of yaoi, pointing to where these narratives reach their ethical impasses, in asking whether yaoi in its current transnational form may speak to aspects of human desire that are beyond a single gender and culture.

Uli Meyer continues that line of questioning in "Hidden in Straight Sight: Trans*gressing Gender and Sexuality via BL," analyzing boys' love through the lens of "creative transvestitism" and boys' love fans as variations on the concept of the "girlfag." Meyer also offers insights into the origins of boys' love both in Japan and Europe and presents a compelling argument for including *yuri* (same-sex female romances) as part of the same phenomena that produce boys' love.

Notes

1. Mark McLelland, "Manga," in *Encyclopedia of Erotic Literature*, ed. Gaëtan Brulotte and John Phillips (New York: Routledge, 2006), 849.

2. Adam L. Kern, *Manga from the Floating World: Comicbook Culture and the Kibyōshi of Edo Japan* (Cambridge, MA: Harvard University Asia Center, 2006), 53.

3. Gregory Plugfelder, "Strange Fates: Sex, Gender, and Sexuality in Torikaebaya Monogatari," *Monumenta Nipponica* (47) 3 (2000), 58.

4. Hervé Brient, "Une petite histoire du yaoi," in *Manga 10,000 images: Homosexualité et manga: le yaoi* (Versailles, France: Éditions H., 2008), 8; McLelland, "Manga," 850.

5. Mark McHarry, "Yaoi: Redrawing Male Love," *The Guide* 23 (2003), http://www.guidemag.com/content/index.cfm?id=225.

6. Kazuko Suzuki, "Pornography or Therapy? Japanese Girls Creating the Yaoi Phenomenon," in *Millennium Girls: Today's Girls Around the World*, ed. Sherrie Inness (London: Rowman & Littlefield, 1998), 252.

7. McHarry, "Yaoi: Redrawing Male Love."

8. Mark McHarry, "Identity Unmoored: Yaoi in the West," *Queer Popular Culture: Literature, Media, Film, and Television*. Ed. Thomas Peele. New York: Palgrave Macmillan, 2007), 193 n. 5.

9. Ariztical Entertainment: Building Bridges. http://www.ariztical.com/corporate/about.html.

10. Camilla Decarnin, "Slash Fiction," in *Encyclopedia of Erotic Literature*, 1233.

11. Interview by Antonia Levi, Seattle, WA, March 25, 2006.

12. Antonia Levi, "North American Reactions to Yaoi," in *The Japanification of Children's Popular Culture: From Godzilla to Miyazaki*, ed. Mark I. West (Lanham, MD: Scarecrow, 2009), 153.

Bibliography

Ariztical Entertainment. "About Us." http://www.ariztical.com/corporate/about.html.

Brient, Hervé. "Une petite histoire du yaoi." In *Manga 10,000 images: Homosexualité et manga: le yaoi*. Versailles, France: Éditions H., 2008.

Decarnin, C.M. "Slash Fiction." In *Encyclopedia of Erotic Literature*, edited by Gaëtan Brulotte and John Phillips, 1233–35. New York: Routledge, 2006.

Kern, Adam. *Manga from the Floating World: Comicbook Culture and the Kibyōshi of Edo Japan*. Cambridge, MA: Harvard University Asia Center, 2006.

Levi, Antonia. "North American Reactions to Yaoi." In *The Japanification of Children's Popular Culture: From Godzilla to Miyazaki*, edited by Mark West, 147–73. Lanham, MD: Scarecrow, 2009.

McHarry, Mark. "Yaoi: Redrawing Male Love." *The Guide* (2003). http://www.guidemag.com/temp/yaoi/a/mcharry_yaoi.html.

______. "Identity Unmoored: Yaoi in the West." In *Queer Popular Culture: Literature, Media, Film, and Television*, edited by Thomas Peele, 183–95. New York: Palgrave Macmillan, 2007.

McLelland, Mark. "Manga." In *Encyclopedia of Erotic Literature*, edited by Gaëtan Brulotte and John Phillips, 849–51. New York: Routledge, 2006.

Plugfelder, Gregory. "Strange Fates: Sex, Gender, and Sexuality in Torikaebaya Monogatari." *Monumenta Nipponica* 47 (2000): 347–68.

Suzuki, Kazuko. "Pornography or Therapy? Japanese Girls Creating the *Yaoi* Phenomenon." In *Millennium Girls: Today's Girls Around the World*, edited by Sherrie Inness, 243–67. London: Rowman & Littlefield, 1998.

PART ONE

Boys' Love and Global Publishing

1

Gift Versus Capitalist Economies

Exchanging Anime and Manga in the U.S.

HOPE DONOVAN

In a panel titled "Fansubs: The Death of Anime" at Anime Expo 2008, industry and fan representatives met to discuss the elephant in the room. Industry representatives from FUNimation, Right Stuf, the Society for the Promotion of Japanese Animation, Anime News Network, and Bandai spent the better part of an hour ensconced in a discussion that got at the heart of anime distribution in America — the claim that fansubs and scanlations eat away industry profits, leading to "the death of anime."

The panel was timely. In 2008, the profits of anime and manga licensing companies dropped while attendance at conventions skyrocketed. That year saw the bankruptcy of Iris Print and Broccoli Books, a freeze on some or all releases at Drama Queen, BLU and Yaoi Press, and lay-offs at others — while major U.S. conventions such as Anime Expo, Otakon, and Sakura-Con reported no decline in attendance, and in the case of some, record attendance. Yaoi-Con, the major boys' love convention, saw stable attendance.[1]

Neither the anime and manga industry nor its fandom in the United States is very old. For that matter, neither are their Japanese counterparts — *Shōnen Jump* magazine celebrated its fortieth anniversary in 2008. Anime fandom in the U.S. grew from a few interested science fiction fans in the 1970s to a full-fledged fandom community of its own, able to support hundreds of regional conventions by 2008. Anime and manga companies grew from a cottage industry in the 1990s to a multimillion-dollar-a-year industry by 2008. With the industry's infancy behind it, consumers and providers now seek to deal with the old bone of contention between them. The aforementioned bone is content distribution, in particular the topic of discussion at the "Death of Anime" panel: fansubs and scanlations. To anime and manga companies, these acts are illegal; to fans, they are a labor of love.

From forums on company sites to industry members cosplaying at conventions, the borders between fandom and industry have never been distinct. My own positions as a manga editor for TOKYOPOP and as a BL fan have allowed me to traverse the social landscapes of both cultures. I can assure you that they are one community, united by a cultural commons. However, one of the central sources of the conflict in this commons lies in the respective economic practices of industry versus fan community. Anthropologically speaking, anime and manga companies operate on capitalist terms, which clashes with anime and manga fans' longstanding participation in a gift-giving economy.

Origins

The economic framework of free, gift-based exchange has been a hallmark of manga and anime's development for some time. "Borrowing" each culture's aesthetics took place as early as the 1800s, when French and Dutch Impressionists coveted Japanese woodblock prints. Sometimes making their way to the West as packing material, the influence of Japan's "whimsical pictures" can be seen in the flat color planes of Fauvist works such as Matisse's *The Joy of Life* (1905). During the same period, Japanese artists were exposed to American, French, and British cartoons and found themselves inspired by the publications released by these early colonists.

Japanese cartoonists continued to be influenced by Westerners into the twenties, borrowing word balloons and the art of sequential strips. In Japanese strips, words were written horizontally, rather than the classic Japanese vertical, to fit into Western-style balloons. Round heads, windowshade eyes, and anthropomorphic characters came right out of Western comics. Attention to the "eight lengths" Greek proportions of the human body was observed. Even into the era of moving pictures, Japan's comics absorbed Western aesthetics. Legendary artist Osamu Tezuka "found that a Caucasian look, with dewey saucer-shaped eyes, was extremely popular among readers."[2] Because manga frequently serves as anime source material, the stylistic aesthetics of comics developed over the first century of cultural exchange between the West and East fed directly into anime. "By the mid–1960s the industry had assumed its present configuration," states Schodt in *Manga! Manga!* "Television and comics were firmly intertwined in a symbiotic relationship."[3]

Anime

Also in the 1960s, the first anime began to trickle over to the U.S. The very early titles, like *Astro Boy* and *Speed Racer,* gained popularity and were commercially released as re-dubbed, localized TV shows. In the 1970s, *Space Battlecruiser Yamato* came over as *Star Blazers.* In the 1980s, *Robotech* inspired a new generation of fans. And in the 1990s, *Pokémon* snatched the youth imagination, while Cartoon Network christened Toonami — a two-hour all-anime block for teens. Throughout the 2000s, Cartoon Network continued to air anime programming, as did Sci-Fi. Anime Network, the first all-anime television network, launched on selected providers.

In exchange for whatever edits the TV stations made to localize anime, viewers received free anime. Some of these viewers became fans. But obtaining more material was no easy task before the Internet. As *Star Blazers* fan and future EDC (Earth Defense Command) member Dave Merill put it, "I would have joined the Masons, a clown college or the Communist Party if they'd promised me *Star Blazers* fandom."[4] Joining an EDC or Cartoon/Fantasy Organization fanclub was a good idea — not only was procuring new materials without fanclub connections difficult, it was expensive. Figures from a 1984 Books Nippon Catalog reveal how prohibitive it was for an individual to get source material: it cost $170 for a VHS copy of the first *Space Battlecruiser Yamato* movie — or for *Urusei yatsura: Only You—* also $170. In fact, fans had to pay over $100 for just about anything, even fifty-seven minutes of *Ultraman.*[5]

Being an anime fan in the 1970s and 1980s meant being a "Trekkie with an extra hobby," observed manga creator Tavisha Wolfgarth-Simons.[6] Anime viewing began popping up at science-fiction conventions. Fandom ethnographer Camille Bacon-Smith relates her exposure to viewing rooms at More Easterly Con in 1985: "Friday night, I followed the directions posted on the convention bulletin board to a room where about twenty fans, mostly women, were watching British television. One woman had brought a PAL system and she played tapes that she had received in trade from Australia."[7] Although the video material in question was a live-action TV drama, the same held true for anime. Distribution at limited viewings at cons was the only way for some fans to see a show, or at least a decent-quality reproduction of the show. The earliest anime fan groups borrowed this semi-formal distribution system. In his comprehensive history of fansub distribution, "Progress Against the Law: Fan Distribution, Copyright, and the Explosive Growth of Japanese Animation," Sean Leonard reports, "starting in 1980, [the Gamelans] would show anime programs in one of their hotel rooms at science fiction conventions. [They] put out fliers throughout these conventions, reading, 'If you want to see Japanese animation come up to room XYZ,' and, 'We're going to be showing it all night long.'"[8]

A few fanclubs came to be extremely well-known among fans, including the aforementioned Cartoon/Fantasy Organization. "These clubs all had chapters in a number of cities; the theory behind them was that they could promote anime much more efficiently, and could get more anime for the chapters in different cities to watch, if the chapters united through a central organization," Leonard writes.[9] The C/FO fanclub, with its numerous chapters, required members to pay dues. In exchange, fans gained access to the C/FO library, from which they could request materials. But despite mimicking a capitalist system of exchange, the fans' dues weren't enough to keep the fanclub system afloat.

The head of the C/FO, Fred Patten, stepped down in 1989, leaving a power vacuum. Meanwhile, the distribution system began to collapse, with the central command in San Antonio sluggishly responding to requests for material, eventually abandoning that core duty fully. By July 1989, the C/FO splintered into individual chapters. Though no longer centralized, fanclubs continued to be an important distribution system through the nineties.[10] Anime goods continued to be available in the specialty stores of metropolitan areas, such as Nipponmachi in San Francisco or Little Tokyo in Los Angeles.[11]

The explosion of the Internet into homes during the 1990s forever changed the distribution of anime. It was also in the 1990s when boys' love began to reach a larger audience. Fans could directly connect to others with the same passion, rather than obtaining anime through a club where a wide range of tastes had to be taken into account. Editor Gaby Maya realized that "the Internet helped all the Fujoshi [female fans] to come out of the 'Boys' love closet'" and make warmly communal what before had been "mouth to mouth."[12] Fledgling distributors took note. As the video market expanded, and personal home viewing became possible, BL titles such as *FAKE* were distributed. The stories and art styles so fascinating to fans gained ground in the market.

What had once been a fan interest demonstrated the potential to generate an industry.

Manga

Manga did not enjoy so rich a distribution history. Unlike a film, which can be viewed by as many as the screening room will accommodate, a *tankōbon* (collected edition of manga, or "graphic novel" in the West) cannot be read by many at once. Nor was there a dedicated group of existing science-fiction comic-book fans to proselytize and translate it.

Tavisha Wolfgarth-Simons, creator of the manga *ShutterBox* with husband Rikki Simons, entered manga fandom at an early age. Living in Southern California, she had access to Japanese bookstores and manga, something most fans did not. But as far as conventions went, in 1985, "If you found manga it was only one dealer and it wasn't translated."[13]

The late 1980s saw the beginning of licensed manga's debut. Viz was the biggest player on the block, releasing some of the first titles that would be associated with the manga pre-millennium boom. *Mai the Psychic Girl* (1987) and *Akira* (1988, released by Marvel's imprint Epic Comics) succeeded early. Viz also began translating Rumiko Takahashi's works, with *Lum*Urusei Yatsura* (1989), *Ranma 1/2* (1993), *Maison Ikkoku* (1994) and *Return of Lum* (1995).

"They used the American comic format which was pamphlet 8 × 10 size and they 'flipped the pages,'" recalls Wolfgarth-Simons of these early releases.[14] At the time, the logical place for manga to be sold was comic book shops and other such specialty stores. After the comics distribution consolidation of 1996, where Diamond Distributors gained a monopoly on comics distribution for Marvel, DC, Dark Horse and all mainstream U.S. comics, manga was distributed mostly to comic book retailers. They were printed as floppies (thirty-two page comics, traditionally released monthly) and occasionally *tankōbon*. Floppies persisted into the new millennium but were not as economically viable as *tankōbon*.

However, ground zero of the manga boom was not the comic book stores, but retail bookstores. Some *tankōbon*, like Viz's *Battle Angel Alita* and TOKYOPOP's *Sailor Moon*, made their way into the big retail chains Barnes & Noble and Borders. Aided at the turn of the millennium by the presence of *Sailor Moon, Gundam Wing, Tenchi Muyo* and *Dragonball Z* on the Cartoon Network, Japanese anime style was gaining recognition. And thanks to the standardization pioneered by TOKYOPOP in 2002, the unflipped, 5 × 7.5", $9.99 format proved a hit. TOKYOPOP's production figures began to steeply increase, from an estimated 85 new volumes released in 2002, to 230 new volumes released in 2003, to 449 volumes released in 2004. As general manga sales rose, so too lifted BL manga sales.

Boys' love has always been a robust manga genre in the U.S. for industry distributors. Partially this was due to the delayed commercial release of BL in the U.S., as compared to other genres. Not only did a more mature market situation exist as compared to Viz's early titles, fans often were aware of a series pre-release. Another factor was the mass of material available in Japan from which to select quality titles. Japan experienced a BL boom in the early 1990s, when male-male love, which began in the heart of the illegal market as *dōjinshi* at Comiket, became commercialized. In 1994, nine magazines sold boys' love. Just four years later, the number was up to thirty manga anthologies, releasing thirty *tankōbon* a month. By 2003, the number of anthologies had not risen, but the monthly output had risen to ninety volumes.[15] If those thirty volumes in 2003 had been released by TOKYOPOP instead, they would have represented approximately one third of all the publisher's books.

American fans recognized the glut of BL in Japan versus its relative scarcity in the U.S. and helped each other to the surplus. In 2003, the first BL scanlation groups were forming. Scanlation groups did exist before 2003, of course. A scanlator who wished to remain anonymous at Nakama, a group founded in 2003, identified in an instant-messaging conversation at least five BL scanlation groups already in existence at that time.[16]

The years 2004–2008 saw a rise and fall of BL publishers in the U.S., their pattern mirroring the general trend of manga publishing. Yaoi Press, DMP's June and 801 lines, Deux, Drama Queen, and BLU all arose during this period. Each of these lines enjoyed success on par with mainstream U.S. manga publishers. In Yaoi Press's case, their original English-language books surpassed the success of other original English-language manga, such as TOKYOPOP's floundering effort. Still, BL companies were hit hard by the economic downturn in 2008, and like the rest of the industry, sought survival.

Capitalist vs. Gift Economies

U.S. anime and manga companies developed out of a communal history of exchange between Japan and the U.S., exchange between fans and, eventually, between fans and industry. This last relationship developed as fans purchased anime and manga from retailers. But their interests having achieved commercial "success," fans refused to fade into the background and become traditional consumers. Instead, anime fans negotiated their gift-based economy with the industry's capitalist system, in a manner consistent with the compromises between other closely related capitalist and gift-based economies.

French ethnographer Maurice Godelier writes, "Human society drew on two sources for its emergence: contractual exchange on the one hand, and non-contractual transmission on the other. And it continues to advance on these two legs, to rest on these two bases, both of which are equally necessary and exist only by means of one another."[17] Though a culture may practice the capitalist exchange of money for goods—"contractual exchange"— at the same time, another form of exchange may exist within that culture — gift-giving.

Capitalism, in which money is exchanged for goods and services, is familiar to Westerners. But in the absence of capitalist exchange, as in pre-capitalist societies, a flow of gifts ensures the distribution of wealth. A number of scholars have chronicled gift-giving cultures around the world, from the *kula* exchange in New Guinea to the potlatch of the Kwakiutl of the American Northwest. These collected ethnographies are not a complete catalogue of the world's various gift-giving practices. Although Godelier's objects of study were pre-capitalist cultures in Australia, Africa, Indonesia and America, nearly all cultures practice gift economies even into the present day. For example, in the United States, Christmas and birthdays center around the exchange of gifts. Similarly, in Japan, on Valentine's Day, girls gift chocolate to boys they like. The boy accepts or rejects her chocolate and returns a counter-gift of equal or greater value on White Day.

In a like manner, fandom, although engaged with capitalism, is also structured around a pre-capitalist, gift-giving economy, especially driven by fansubbers and scanlators. Although many anime and manga fandoms operate in this fashion, boys' love fandom provides a particularly relevant case because of the tight focus of its fans and its relatively new introduction to the U.S.

Cooperative Exchange

Marcel Mauss describes two types of gift-giving in his landmark ethnography of the gift, "Essai sur le don" (1922); forms which I will term cooperative gift-giving and competitive gift-giving.

Cooperative exchange is the most prevalent form in the West. In cooperative exchange, a gift is given freely and without respect to compensation. Though the gift necessarily enhances the social status of the giver, agonistic gift giving doesn't attempt to crush the receiver with indebtedness. Instead, gift-giving strengthens the bonds between the participants. The eventual reciprocity between the giver and the receiver forges their bond. It's hard to see free gift-giving molding a culture, but "[r]eciprocity is a form of exchange," writes scholar Marvin Harris, "that is primarily adapted to conditions in which the stimulation of intensive extra productive effort would have an adverse effect upon group survival."[18] In other words, giving gifts balances society. It keeps a society functioning by preventing the build-up of wealth, a sort of booster shot against the hoarding endemic of capitalism. Instead, wealth is always in flux, woven through a community's personal relationships. One of the reasons continual gifting is assured is because a gift, if kept, imprisons the receiver with a debt. In a capitalist society, money can be given to repay this debt. In a pre-capitalist society, the debt is instead passed along, but along with it, the wealth of the gift itself.

Opportunities for cooperative exchange arise constantly in fan communities. American fans of BL in particular form thriving Internet communities based around communication and free exchange. One popular exchange center is the Web site Aarinfantasy. This massive hub with 160,000 members houses *dōjinshi*, games, manga, anime and anything downloadable and related to BL. The exchange of materials is situated in the site's forums, where fans can upload their materials directly to the forum or link off-site for others to download. The off-site links are particularly communal. Fans in possession of source material have the option of uploading it to a maximum number of file-hosting sites (such as Megaupload, YouSendIt, or many others). Fans who download this first source file have the option to upload the file to yet another file-hosting site and advertising the new download right alongside the original. In this manner, fans are "giving back" the gift that they've been given.

Although seemingly pointless, this re-gifting enhances social bonds. As observed by Godelier, "the nearly immediate reciprocation of the object given is perhaps the clearest illustration of the implicit logic of gifts which create debts that are not cancelled by a counter-gift. For the object which returns to its original owner *is not 'given back' but 'given again.'*"[19] Or, as Lewis Hyde writes of a Maori hunting ritual in his book on gift-giving, *The Gift*: "the forest gives to the hunters, the hunters to the priests and the priests to the forest. At the end, the gift moves back from the third party back to the first."[20]

In each exchange of the cycle, a gift is given without regard to receiving anything back; yet, since a gift was given, one is assured of receiving something back so long as the circle of exchange remains unbroken. That exchange of three is expanded to millions when applied to a community. A flurry of gifts is exchanged in the form of fanfiction, fanzines, fanart — all free gifts to other members of the community. On Aarinfantasy, fans have the option to "thank" the poster by clicking a "Thanks" button in the post. On the surface, this looks like a way for consumers to cancel their debt. Their username even becomes attached to the post in a list of users who "Say Thank You." But there are three parts to a reciprocal exchange: giving, acknowledgement/acceptance, and returning the gift. In the example of Japanese Valentine's Day, that's the giving of the chocolate, the acceptance or rejection of it, and the return gift made on White Day. But the third stage is not necessarily a direct return to the giver. For fans who don't re-upload the same material to a new host, the eventual return gift goes to the community in the form of other fan labors.

Aarinfantasy's Web site offers several areas for fans to give back — whether this is sharing fanart in the Member's Gallery or offering support, discussion or interaction in the general forums. These gifts strengthen the communal bonds. "[A] gift establishes a feeling-bond between two people," states Hyde.[21] Evidence of a more reciprocal form of exchange and bonding in the media fan circles is described by Camille Bacon-Smith in *Enterprising Women*: "Each circle has a core of two to four members. A typical group will include an editor or editorial team, several writers, a graphic artist, a video artist, one or two photo-copyists and one or more specialists in linking with sources of materials, including information and the products of other groups."[22] She cites the ideal number at no more than fifteen. Of these individuals, *not one* is a pure consumer. Whether writing fanfics, doing manual labor of photocopying or maintaining communications, every member of the media fan circle is both a consumer and producer — an active participant in an economy. And they are involved in each others' lives, too. She writes, "[T]he fan women travel extensively to visit with one another in small groups. They maintain long-term intense friendships,"[23] concluding some of these fans "find in the community of enterprising women their only source of social relationships and communal support."[24]

Besides Aarinfantasy, other Web hubs currently provide large-scale sharing of BL works, with a greater emphasis on fan participation than distribution. Y!Gallery, a site dedicated to sharing original works, Fanfiction.net, where BL fiction writers can post their stories, and the Web sites LiveJournal and DeviantArt, whose customizable spaces encourage the development of niche communities— all have been colonized by BL fandom communities. Of particular interest is the site LiveJournal, where fans can create in miniature much the same hub as Aarinfantasy, but tailored to their particular fandom or pairing. Role-playing, where fans can act out adventures as their favorite characters, can also be located on LiveJournal. Lastly, there are scanlation Web sites, the homes and original distribution centers of translated scans. These sites function less like a marketplace than Aarinfantasy, although they provide the products to be exchanged.

Lewis Hyde suggested that an object must keep circulating to be a gift. "[A] gift must always be used up, consumed, eaten. The gift is property that perishes."[25] Peer-to-peer file sharing ensures that even though one person "consumes" a copy, they are also passing it to another. The circulation of fan creations invigorates the fandom into both consuming and creating further. Hyde notes, "[W]hen a part of the self is given away, the community appears."[26] In other words, the "debt" incurred when fans "invest" in their work is passed along when the work is consumed. By continually distributing the work, the debt, and wealth, is also passed along.

Competitive Exchange

Though less familiar to the West, an extreme form of gift-giving exists in economies based around competitive exchange. The Kwakiutl of the American Northwest offer a classic example of competitive exchange. The wealthy tribes of the sea coast developed an extreme form of competitive gift-giving called the potlatch. Important chiefs threw potlatches to cement their status, literally throwing away their riches to establish their wealth. During an impressive feast, the chief gave away untold riches. Blankets and foodstuffs were distributed to the guests, and in some potlatches, the chief even burned his house down to shed his material possessions. By creating such a large debt for the beneficiaries of his charity, the ostentatious chief maintained his status. Though he lost many material possessions in the gift-giving, he gained prestige and with it his wealth returned. Until another chief gave away even more, the giver held the highest status.

The same status-oriented, competitive-exchange mindset can be said to be at work among the early fans whose connections in Japan, or whose Japanese language skills, gave them more access to the material. On the surface, the early fan laborers who bothered with postage to get tapes from overseas, or who painstakingly translated movies or episodes and distributed photocopies at cons for a few dollars, were magnanimous souls. But below the surface, as fan historian Leonard writes, "Authors of these booklets were interested in more than the $3 a book: they wanted the prestige within the anime fan community of publishing something that all American fans would want."[27]

By the mid–1990s, both anime and manga had birthed fledging industries in the U.S. Fans founded and staffed the companies; for example, scanlator Alexis Kirsch became TOKYOPOP's acquisitions editor, and Toren V. Smith, an early translator, founded Studio Proteus. Far from being a peculiar phenomenon in anime, Camille Bacon-Smith observes of science fiction culture: "with the exception of two or three people who began reading in college, all those I interviewed for this book, including every industry worker ... were reading science fiction avidly by the time they were fourteen."[28] For many early anime fans, this was a realization of their dream to distribute anime to the world. That goal was still first and foremost in their minds— but running a successful business was hardly secondary. It could be said that these fans had traded in fan prestige and gift-giving economies to move into a capitalist system.

The fact is, however, that although for some a fan hobby matured into a job, the internal hierarchy of the fan community itself did not change. Fans did not seek to become professionals in order to give back, or to gain prestige, even while adopting the new system of buying anime at Best Buy and manga at Borders. The idea of giving back became encapsulated in the concept of "promotion." In the early days of the fandom, promotion consisted of exposing as many people as possible to anime. Early fan distributor James Renault recalls of the 1980s, "Back then, the motivation was just to get anime to the masses."[29] The C/FO, too, wanted mass distribution: "C/FO chapters only sent material to people who really wanted anime and who would share it with other close friends.... Show it to all of your friends in order to promote Japanese animation."[30]

The Society for the Promotion of Japanese Animation, the council that operates Anime Expo, explicitly states "promotion" in its name and further explicates the non-profit nature of the board and the council's goals in their mission statement: "The Society for the Promotion of Japanese Animation (SPJA) is a non-profit organization with a mission to popularize and educate the American public about anime and manga, as well as provide a forum to facilitate communication between professionals and fans."[31]

Scanlation sites tout the rhetoric of "promotion" as well. Consider the introductions of these BL scanlation sites:

> Our main purpose is to promote manga to the English speaking community that doesn't have access to them.— Aku Tenshi[32]

> Our aim in providing these scanlations is to introduce you to the author's work and hopefully interest you.— Obsession[33]

> We're only scanlating manga to promote them and to make them more known.— Game Over or Continue[34]

> *Sakura-Crisis* is a non-profit scanlation site dedicated to bringing lesser-known manga to the attention of the English speaking community.— Sakura-Crisis[35]

> We are a group dedicated to introducing works in Japanese women's oriented adult comics to the English speaking community in the form of translations set into hand-edited scans.... [U]ltimately our projects will encourage visitors to support the mangaka by buying their own copies of their works.— Shi-Ran[36]

> Through the unique and varied interests of our talented staff, we hope our choices continue to expose the English-speaking Yaoi Fan Community to new, provocative and hard-to-find unlicensed work.— Nakama[37]

> Our goal is to bring attention and manga that otherwise would go unknown to the English-speaking world.— Beautiful Soup[38]

Although enthusiasm surrounds these proclamations of promotion, the core may have more to do with self-promotion. Each consumer of the group's wares ends up in their debt. Like the Kwakiutl chiefs, the distributors of anime, manga and scanlations give away gifts that the recipients are incapable, or rarely capable, of repaying. Without similar translation or material-gathering abilities, the consumers cannot overcome their lower status. An example of an unpaid debt can be seen in Papua New Guinea.

The people of the Madang coast exhibit a seemingly bizarre behavior. Year after year, decade after decade, they wait for cargo planes to arrive. The airstrip is built, but shipments of food, clothing and modern amenities have yet to arrive. In his book *Cows, Pigs, Wars and Witches,* Marvin Harris argues that this behavior is a corruption of the gift-giving system. In Papua New Guinea, the natives were enslaved by waves of conquest — Russian, German, Australian — who sought to keep the natives they enslaved docile with gifts. The island's people worked hard and expected to be rewarded. They are waiting this day for the cargo planes to bring them their reward.

Just as the Papua New Guinea natives consider themselves owed a debt, fansubbers also consider a debt to be owed to them. They believe they labored promoting anime and deserve "cargo." *However, they don't ever want the cargo to arrive.* If fansubbers' gifts were to be reciprocated, and the debt to them cancelled, it would mean the end of their status and prestige. If an unpaid debt is a sign of great prestige, as it is in the case of the Kwakuitl chieftains, then the best way to maintain status is to keep others indebted. This is where the economics of fans clash with the economics of industry, because industry is returning the gift. It has taken "promotion" to such a level that it is achieving the widespread conversion of new fans. The former givers are being placed in the position of consumer.

Fans who do not want to acknowledge their gift of manga repaid by industry find fault with the products the industry provides. For example, among the many possible faults in manga reproduction — poor image reproduction, sub-par paper or binding quality, shoddy copyediting — the trait that fans most often target is "authenticity." In 2002, TOKYOPOP began stamping all their books with "100% Authentic Manga." In this way, it severed ties to the companies in the past that "butchered" anime, lending itself legitimacy. But it left itself open to fan criticisms about translations and over-reaching adaptations. One "inauthentic" practice is name Anglicization. For example, *Robotech*'s Misa Hayase became Lisa Hayes, and Hikaru Ichijyo became Rick Hunter. In another example, TOKYOPOP caught flak from fans in 2002 for Anglicizing the names of *Initial D* characters, generating a fan fiasco and subsequent corporate letter of explanation in defense.[39] Another practice is language adaptations that cater too closely to Western tastes, in particular those that evoke Western pop culture. Though many U.S. fans cannot read Japanese, it takes only cursory knowledge to realize Japanese teenagers aren't likely to shop at popular American stores and eat typical American foods. Such blatant edits no longer exist, for the most part, and so fans concentrate on smaller infractions, such as overly slangy speech. For purists, anime and manga must be free of these localization techniques to be "authentic."

Reciprocity

Despite this common criticism, during the "Fansubs: Death of Anime" panel, the concept of "authenticity" was primarily absent from the discussion. Instead, the industry and fan representatives cited lag time between an episode's release in Japan and its release in the U.S. as the major engine powering fansubs. In the case of manga, some scanlation groups have retouched and uploaded chapters from *Shōnen Jump* the same day the material went on sale. It was possible in 2008 to have near-instantaneous access to Japan's fresh content.

Industry representatives weren't quite prepared to absolve their debt to fan promoters, but their words were less than supplicating. "Back when there were, you know, when nothing was out here, it spread the word," said Lance Heiskell of FUNimation. "Groups would promo anime, but now the fansubbers have become more of a status project. It had a use in the 80s, but that use has pretty much ran its course." Adds Justin Sevakis of Anime News Network, "From an industry standpoint, fansubs have not been useful since the VHS days."[40]

Begrudgingly or not, fans and industry are adapting to today's participatory and multi-platform media culture. For instance, two million signed up the first year when Viz rolled out their affordable download-to-own program in 2008. FUNimation and Bandai also began streaming and download-to-own programs, which have met with success. "I think kids generally wanna obey the law," states Axis Entertainment's Jeff Conner.[41] The fact that legal distribution systems in the U.S. have gained a foothold at all is the best evidence towards this assertion. In countries like Korea in the 1990s, manga libraries seriously eroded profits, to the degree that manga creators entreated readers in their author's notes to purchase books rather than borrow them. And in 1980s, "if [anime] went to China, it was more often than not on a 'pirate ship' or through a tape dungeon" writes Leonard.[42] Despite the availability of free anime and manga, Americans still buy what they can, heeding to the true spirit of the fansubbers' disclaimer, "Cease distribution when licensed in your area."

Thanks to technology, the landscape of distribution has changed greatly since the first days of fandom. To borrow a term from Henry Jenkins, fans today live in a "convergence culture." Episodes of new popular anime can be viewed on Hulu, company Web sites, YouTube channels, iTunes, Xbox and television. Manga is on cell phones. Fans can find and participate in communities with a few clicks of a mouse. Industry's current challenge is to pinpoint and catch the attention of "migratory media audiences who will go almost anywhere in search of the kinds of entertainment experiences they want," as Jenkins writes.[43] Technology is finally catching up to the point where devices can support the web of interactivity that anime and manga fans have long practiced. For boys' love fans, specifically, the growth of Internet hubs like Aarinfantasy ensures that boys' love fans are still on the cutting edge of negotiating the limits of participatory culture. As options for expressions increase through technology, the passion for promotion and continued gifting long exemplified by anime and manga fans will only grow along with it.

Notes

1. "History," Sakura-Con, http://www.sakuracon.org/aboutus/history.php; "History: Stats," Otakon, http://www.otakon.com/history_stats.asp; "FAQ," Anime-Expo, http://www.anime-expo.org/general-info rmation/faq/; "Yaoi-Con," Wikipedia, http://en.wikipedia.org/wiki/Yaoi-Con.

2. Frederik Schodt, *Manga! Manga! The World of Japanese Comics* (Japan: Kodansha, 1983), 61.

3. Ibid., 67.

4. Dave Merill, "Star Blazers Chronicles: Anime Fandom Texas Style. The History of the EDC," The Official Website of the Star Blazers Animated Series, http://www.starblazers.com/html.php?page_id=235.

5. Dave Merill, "Let's Buy Anime Stuff — 80s Style!" Let's Anime, http://letsanime.blogspot.com/.

6. Tavisha Wolfgarth-Simons, email message to author, November 12, 2008.

7. Camille Bacon-Smith, *Enterprising Women* (Philadelphia: University of Pennsylvania Press, 1992), 116.

8. Sean Leonard, "Progress Against the Law: Fan Distribution, Copyright and the Explosive Growth of Japanese Animation," http://mit.edu/seantek/www/papers/, 8.

9. Ibid., 10.

10. Ibid., 17.

11. Ibid., 14.

12. Wolfgarth-Simons, email message to author, November 16, 2008.

13. Wolfgarth-Simons, email message to author, November 9, 2008.

14. Ibid.

15. Mizoguchi Akiko, "Male-male Romance by and for Women in Japan: A History and the Subgenres of Yaoi Fictions," *U.S.–Japan Women's Journal* 25 (2003): 57.

16. Nakama Manga, instant-messaging correspondence, November 13, 2008.

17. Maurice Godelier, *The Enigma of the Gift* (Great Britain: University of Chicago Press, 1999), 36.

18. Marvin Harris, *Cows, Pigs, Wars and Witches: The Riddles of Culture* (New York: Vintage Books, 1989), 126.

19. Godelier, *The Enigma*, p. 44.

20. Lewis Hyde, *The Gift: Imagination and the Erotic Life of Property* (New York: Vintage Books, 1983), 18.

21. Ibid., 56.

22. Bacon-Smith, *Enterprising Women,* 27.

23. Ibid., 284.

24. Ibid., 285.

25. Hyde, *The Gift*, 8.

26. Ibid., 92.

27. Leonard, *Progress Against the Law*, 11.

28. Camille Bacon-Smith, *Science Fiction Culture* (Philadelphia: University of Philadelphia Press, 2000).

29. Leonard, *Progress Against the Law*, 15.

30. Ibid., 16.

31. "About," Society for the Promotion of Japanese Animation, http://www.spja.org/about/.

32. "Aku Tenshi FAQ," Aku Tenshi, http://www.aku-tenshi.com/faq.php.

33. "Frequently Asked Questions," Obsession, http://ob-session.blogspot.com/2005/08/frequent-asked-questions-what-are.html.

34. "Disclaimer," Game Over or Continue, http://gooc.susanne-wenzel.de/index2.php?site=disclaimer.

35. Sakura-Crisis homepage, http://sakuracrisis.ukepile.com/.

36. "Mission Statement," Shi-Ran, http://shi-ran.cjb.net/.

37. Nakama homepage, http://nakamanga.com/.

38. "Information," Beautiful Soup, http://soup.umi-sora.com/?page_id=194.

39. "Tokyopop Open Letter regarding Initial D," Anime News Network, http://www.animenewsnetwork.com/news/2002-07-13/tokyopop-open-letter-regarding-initial-d.

40. "Fansubs: Death of Anime." Panel at Anime Expo, July 2008. http://www.animenewsnetwork.com/convention/2008/anime-expo/industry-roundtable-fansubs-the-death-of-anime.

41. "Fansubs: Death of Anime."

42. Leonard, *Progress Against the Law*, 26.

43. Henry Jenkins, *Convergence Culture: Where Old and New Media Collide* (New York: New York University Press, 2008), 2.

Bibliography

"About." Society for the Promotion of Japanese Animation. http://www.spja.org/about/ (accessed Nov. 13, 2008).

"Aku Tenshi FAQ." Aku Tenshi. http://www.aku-tenshi.com/faq.php (accessed Nov. 14, 2008).

Bacon-Smith, Camille. *Enterprising Women*. Philadelphia: University of Pennsylvania Press. 1992.

_____. *Science Fiction Culture*. Philadelphia: University of Philadelphia Press. 2000.

"Disclaimer." Game Over or Continue. http://gooc.susanne-wenzel.de/index2.php?site=disclaimer (accessed Nov. 14, 2008).

"Fansubs: Death of Anime." Panel at Anime Expo, July 2008. http://www.animenewsnetwork.com/convention/2008/anime-expo/industry-roundtable-fansubs-the-death-of-anime (accessed April 19, 2009).

"FAQ." Anime-Expo. http://www.anime-expo.org/general-information/faq/ (accessed April 30, 2009).

"Frequently Asked Questions." Obsession. http://ob-session.blogspot.com/2005/08/frequent-asked-questions-what-are.html (accessed Nov. 14, 2008).

Godelier, Maurice. *The Enigma of the Gift*. Great Britain: University of Chicago Press, 1999.

Harris, Marvin. *Cows, Pigs, Wars and Witches: The Riddles of Culture*. New York: Vintage Books. 1989.

"History." Sakura-Con. http://www.sakuracon.org/aboutus/history.php (accessed April 30, 2009).

"History: Stats." Otakon. http://www.otakon.com/history_stats.asp (accessed April 30, 2009).

Hyde, Lewis. *The Gift: Imagination and the Erotic Life of Property*. New York: Vintage Books. 1983.

"Information." Beautiful Soup. http://soup.umi-sora.com/?page_id=194 (accessed Nov. 14, 2008).

Jenkins, Henry. *Convergence Culture: Where Old and New Media Collide*. New York: New York University Press. 2008.

Leonard, Sean. "Progress Against the Law: Fan Distribution, Copyright and the Explosive Growth of Japanese Animation." http://mit.edu/seantek/www/papers/ (accessed Aug. 12, 2008).

Merill, Dave. "Let's Buy Anime Stuff — 80s Style!" Let's Anime. http://letsanime.blogspot.com/ (accessed Oct. 28, 2008).

_____. "Star Blazers Chronicles: Anime Fandom Texas Style. The History of the EDC." *The Official Website of the Star Blazers Animated Series*. http://www.starblazers.com/html.php?page_id=235 (accessed Nov. 10, 2008).

"Mission Statement." Shi-Ran. http://shi-ran.cjb.net/ (accessed Nov. 14, 2008).

Mizoguchi, Akiko. "Male-male romance by and for women in Japan: a history and the subgenres of Yaoi fictions." *U.S.–Japan Women's Journal 25* (2003): 49–75.

Nakama homepage. http://nakamanga.com/ (accessed Nov. 14, 2008).

Sakura-Crisis homepage. http://sakuracrisis.ukepile.com/ (accessed Nov. 14, 2008).

Schodt, Frederik. *Manga! Manga! The World of Japanese Comics*. Japan: Kodansha. 1983.

"Tokyopop Open letter regarding Initial D." Anime News Network. http://www.animenewsnetwork.com/news/2002-07-13/tokyopop-open-letter-regarding-initial-d (Accessed October 12, 2008).

"Yaoi-Con." Wikipedia. http://en.wikipedia.org/wiki/Yaoi-Con (accessed June 29, 2009).

2

From *BRAVO* to Animexx.de to Export

Capitalizing on German Boys' Love Fandom, Culturally, Socially and Economically

Paul M. Malone

The worldwide craze for manga came late to Germany. Translated manga first appeared in German in the 1980s—one volume of Nakazawa Keiji's *Barefoot Gen* (originally *Hadashi no Gen*) appeared as *Barefoot through Hiroshima: A Picture-Story Against War*, and Ishinomori Shōtarō's *Japan, Inc.* (*Manga Nihon keizai nyūmon*) was also translated[1]—but they were published for their political or economic messages by presses with little or no connection to Germany's small comics industry or its audience, and they failed to make much of an impression. The appearance of the first volume of Ōtomo Katsuhiro's *Akira* also initially failed to attract a large German readership, although the publisher, comics-oriented Carlsen Verlag, at least continued to publish succeeding volumes of the series until sales improved. During this same period, by comparison, other European countries, such as France, Italy and Spain, were already importing and translating manga and giving birth to lively fan communities.[2]

Only in the late 1990s did the German market finally open up to manga, thanks to two concurrent developments: first, the arrival of private, commercial television networks in Germany, with programming hours to fill and advertising time to sell—as opposed to the previously established non-commercial, state-run broadcasters—led to a huge influx of relatively cheaply imported foreign programming, including dubbed versions of Japanese anime cartoon series, which quickly became popular with young viewers. As had previously happened in other countries, these series were often linked to collateral merchandise in the form of toys, costumes, games, collectibles—and ultimately the manga comics that had inspired the television series in the first place. On this basis, manga now entered German cultural consciousness as a category distinct from Western-style comics, with its own aesthetic expectations, and "manga" was adopted into the German language as a loan-word.[3] Thus the RTL 2 network's acquisition of the series *Sailor Moon* and *Dragon Ball*, which began airing in spring of 1997 and late 1998 respectively to become runaway hits, led in turn to the success of the licensed versions of the original manga series, Naoko Takeuchi's *Sailor Moon* and Akira Toriyama's *Dragon Ball*—the latter of which was also the first imported manga to be printed in Japanese-style, right-to-left reading order, which quickly became the norm as a sign of manga authenticity.[4] So, too, despite the fact that Carlsen's *Akira* had appeared as larger-size paperbacks similar to American graphic novels or French *bande dessinée* albums, the usual format of publication rapidly settled on a small paperback digest format similar to the Japanese *tankōbon*.

23

The second important development at the end of the 1990s was the virtual collapse of the German domestic comics market: over-rapid expansion and market glut, combined with the lingering recession in a post-reunification Germany and the small, aging (and over-whelmingly male) readership of traditional Western comics, led to a sudden downturn in sales that bankrupted several smaller publishers and left the surviving larger firms struggling for lifelines.[5] The only growth area in the market was manga, which drew a generally younger demographic and appealed to girls as much as to boys; and so the remaining publishers, chiefly the "big three," Carlsen Verlag, Egmont Ehapa Verlag and Panini Verlag,[6] capitalized heavily on this new territory to create a German manga boom that quickly grew into millions of euro in sales per year.

Manga: Foundation of a New Indigenous Comics Scene

In order to keep the industry afloat, it would have been sufficient in the short term, and certainly cheaper, merely to license and import Japanese manga. However, a significant weakness of the German comics industry had always been its historical dependence on properties from abroad; there had never been a critical mass of successful indigenous comics artists, and thus the German publishers had a long tradition of licensing material from the U.S. (first Disney, and later superhero comics) and from other European countries (primarily Franco–Belgian comics, but also including Italian and Spanish properties), with little or no ability to export German comics in return.[7] Seeing an opportunity to redress this imbalance, the major publishers that have the most stake in the long-term health of the German comics industry, Egmont and Carlsen — and, since 2004, the German branch of TOKYOPOP[8] — have invested in their future by capitalizing on the strongly participatory nature of manga fandom: using contests and internships, they began nurturing local German manga artists and offering them opportunities to publish their work professionally. (The Italian-owned Panini Verlag, in contrast, has instead concentrated on imported material alone under its Planet Manga imprint, and on its American licenses for the DC and Marvel superheroes, as well as *The Simpsons*.)

The first home-grown German manga artists were men, such as Jürgen Seebeck, Robert Labs, and Sascha Nils Marx; however, for a variety of reasons, neither Seebeck's two-volume *Bloody Circus*, Labs's two prematurely canceled series *Dragic Master* and *Crewman 3*, nor Marx's single completed volume of *Naglaya's Heart*, scripted by Stefan Voss, were able to capture their intended *shōnen* readership. Seebeck's work, despite the pedigree of being previously published in Japan, was too different from what was seen as authentic Japanese manga, while Labs's and Marx's series, over and above their inability to maintain consistent quality while meeting deadlines, were too derivative of the large number of imported *shōnen* manga, which made the difference in quality that much more apparent.[9]

The German publishers then turned to embrace the growing new female readership that manga had attracted, and began fostering young women artists. As a result, the majority of the small group of German manga artists now consists of women in their late teens or early twenties, most of whom follow the conventions of popular *shōjo* manga.[10] This strategy has thus led to a miniature home-grown *shōjo* boom: though it may be small relative to the amount of imported Japanese manga, the result is that there are now more female German comics artists in print than ever before in history. A side-effect has been the promotion as artists of first- and second-generation immigrants to Germany, mostly of either Asian or Eastern European background, and so home-grown German manga have become an even more conspicuously multicultural product.[11] The unprecedented economic and cultural importance of this small group of artists is underlined by a statement by Martin Jurgeit, curator of an exhibition on German comics history at the Wilhelm Busch Museum in Hannover: "These artists, with their sales and the chord they've struck among readers, have the best economic conditions that the coming generation of comics in Germany have ever had."[12] The corollary of this importance, however, is that despite the immense popularity of a small group of imported *shōnen* manga, the German comics industry is currently dependent specifically upon *shōjo* manga, whether imported or home-grown, to a degree virtually unique in the West.

Boys' Love, Yaoi and the Fantasy of Egalitarian Romance

One conventional aspect of the *shōjo* manga phenomenon that arrived in the wake of this manga boom is the small but important subgenre variously described as "boys' love," "BL," yaoi, or *shōnen-ai* (the last two being the most commonly used terms in Germany): the depiction of homoerotic relationships between androgynous *bishōnen* or "beautiful boys," who—particularly in their contemporary Japanese cultural context—combine traditionally male social freedoms with a stereotypically feminine appearance and sensitivity. This subgenre had arisen in Japan in the 1970s, when a newly emerging generation of female manga artists (including Hagio Moto, Ikeda Riyoko, Takemiya Keiko) turned to such depictions in order to permit female authors and readers alike to project themselves into the roles of the stories' male protagonists, thus sharing a fantasy of "perfect romance," supposedly unclouded by the power differential between men and women in real Japanese society.[13] Nonetheless, the homosexual relationships in boys' love manga, as well as those in the later and more explicit yaoi manga, are seldom if ever entirely even-handed, thanks to the complex structure of Japanese society and its social notions of power differentials based on age as well as gender.

Yaoi developed among Japan's *dōjinshi*, or amateur comics, circles in the late 1970s, when boys' love had lost its novelty. *Dōjinshi* often appropriate characters from established manga to parodic ends, and yaoi parodied the romantic and idealized nature of boys' love by concentrating on homosexual sex at the expense of plot; hence its name, a contraction of the Japanese *yama nashi, ochi nashi, imi nashi* ("No climax, no resolution, no meaning").[14] By cutting the character constellation of boys' love down to its bare essentials, yaoi emphasized the fact that within these couples, "the idea that sex is necessarily something that the dominant partner 'does' to the submissive partner is carried over from depictions of sex between men and women or senior and junior men in mainstream and gay media"; this relationship is codified by referring to the older and more aggressive partner as the *seme* (derived from a verb meaning "to attack") and the younger, more submissive partner as the *uke* (literally, the "receiver").[15] Generally, in the West, including Germany, yaoi is now regularly used to distinguish more sexually explicit representations of homoeroticism from *shōnen-ai*, which focuses more on romance, regardless of the material's status as fan-produced or professional; both terms are now somewhat outdated in Japanese usage.[16]

Yaoi in its original, parodic form bears obvious similarities to the erotic fan-fiction produced by Westerners known as "slash" (from the mark that both separates and binds, for instance, "Kirk/Spock"), in which already established fictional worlds such as those of

Star Trek, Starsky and Hutch, or Harry Potter serve as the backdrop for their characters to play out scenarios of open homoeroticism.[17] Indeed, the major difference between slash and yaoi, as both Matthew Thorn and Andrea Wood have pointed out, lies less in their conditions of production and consumption — both tend to be created and read primarily by women — than rather in the fact that while the former remains generally both legally and culturally marginalized in the West, the latter has evolved into a commercially published mainstream mass cultural form in Japan.[18] This difference aside, it hardly seems unwarranted to conclude that despite stereotypes of Japan as a more hidebound and repressive society than the West in terms of gender relations, many young women, Westerners and Japanese alike, share a strong sense of "discontent with the standards of femininity to which they are expected to adhere," and even "despair of ever achieving equal relationships with men in a sexist society."[19] These feelings, among others, help motivate them to create and consume material featuring idealized men in relatively egalitarian homosexual relationships.[20]

BRAVO, *Sexual "Enlightenment," and Romanticized Homosexuality*

It would be surprising if young women in Germany were to be exceptional in terms of their experience of the social gender dynamic, and indeed a 1997 study by Mareike Herrmann found that "German girls suffer similarly, if not more, from unequal, discriminatory treatment in schools and widespread low self-esteem as do American girls," and are well aware that they are under constant social "pressure to 'do the right thing'" in terms of behavior (ideally, "good") and achievement (usually, mediocre and inferior to that of boys).[21] Unlike American girls, however, German girls had for years had access to an outlet in the media that performed some, though crucially not all, of the functions of boys' love or yaoi manga: the girls' magazine *BRAVO.*

BRAVO, founded in August 1956 as a weekly devoted to film and television news, soon expanded its focus to popular music, which eventually came to dominate its entertainment pages and fill half the magazine. Although *BRAVO* thus came superficially to resemble American magazines such as *Tiger Beat* (founded in 1965), the German magazine is in fact "unique in its content and, more important, in its long history and the immense popularity it continues to enjoy among teenagers, especially girls."[22] This is because from 1961 on, *BRAVO* devoted ever more space to advice columns and questions of *Aufklärung* (literally, "enlightenment," but often used in German as a synonym for "sex education"), becoming increasingly frank in its discussion of sexuality. Despite *BRAVO*'s obvious status as a mainstream media product and its essential conservatism in espousing traditional gender roles and norms of heterosexual romance, its sexual explicitness has made it controversial for much of its existence; and for many readers, including Herrmann herself as a girl, reading *BRAVO* represented and still represents "a subversive strategy of rebellion against ... parents (and other authority figures)."[23] At the same time, the magazine's coverage of the popular music scene has often allowed readers "to experience power vicariously through famous pop stars" in a manner that "might also explain why girls prefer androgynous types of men or boys: it is easier for them to identify with boys who bear feminine characteristics than with those who exhibit their sexual difference through a more manly appearance."[24]

Kimberly S. Gregson, describing American girls who are fans of *shōjo* anime, similarly observes, "Male pop stars, especially those with feminine features, can serve as practice love objects as young girls begin to think about being in a romantic relationship"; she then draws a direct connection between these girls' attraction to pop stars and their interest in the *bishōnen* of *shōjo* anime.[25] Particularly in the case of the latter topic, Gregson's subjects parley their accumulation of knowledge about cultural background, plots and favorite characters into "cultural capital" within anime fandom (here Gregson makes use of concepts developed by John Fiske), and putting that capital "on display" in the form of their Web sites.[26] Note, however, that the girls in Gregson's study — all twenty-one or younger, and thus slightly older than the German *BRAVO*'s target readership — are portrayed as exclusively "interested in romance, not sex," and "grossed out" by the mere thought of sexually explicit material, which is only referred to in terms of "pornography" or the Japanese equivalents, *hentai* or *ecchi*.[27]

The sex education material in *BRAVO*, by contrast, over three decades ago began including illustrative photographs of "half-naked young people in love-making poses" which regularly depict partial or full female (but not male) nudity.[28] As the magazine's readership crystallized mainly to include girls between the ages of ten and seventeen, many young German girls came to look to *BRAVO* for most or even all of their sexual education, whether against their parents' will or with their tacit agreement — although nominally aimed at all young people, in fact *BRAVO* is generally read by boys only surreptitiously, and usually with somewhat different motivations.[29] These facts would seem to indicate that at the turn of the twenty-first century, there may have been a significant difference, on average, between the tastes, experience and expectations of young American female readers and those of their German counterparts.

This difference is equally, but slightly differently, evident in terms of material dealing with homosexuality. In Gregson's study, *bishōnen* are described solely in the context of their heterosexual romantic relationships with their respective anime series' heroines, and with the equally heterosexual dynamic of the American fans' interest in the boy characters, which incidentally seems to far outweigh any identification on the fans' part with the "kind, sweet" girl protagonists.[30] Homosexuality is passed over in complete silence; though the themes of rape and incest that underlie some *shōjo* anime, such as *Revolutionary Girl Utena*, are mentioned as being both perceived and openly discussed among fans, neither Gregson nor her informants evidence any awareness of boys' love themes (unless they are silently subsumed under the concept of *hentai*).[31]

In contrast, *BRAVO* has indeed dealt with male homosexuality, if relatively rarely — lesbianism, meanwhile, is virtually absent as a subject of "enlightenment." The magazine has nonetheless tended to be comparatively reticent in its treatment: instead of softcore depictions of lovemaking, which are common in the magazine's portrayal of heterosexual relationships, the reader is shown pictures of kissing and cuddling, "making use of and evoking the feminine codes of romance" in a fashion "meant to appeal to a female readership" while still reinforcing heterosexual norms.[32] This idealized, affectionate and egalitarian representation of homosexual relationships, however, not only anticipates aspects of the romanticized power dynamic in boys' love manga, but — in conjunction with the manufactured accessibility of the androgynous, "sensitive" pop stars whose images are offered throughout the magazine — also stands in marked contrast to the cynical messages that *BRAVO* sends regarding heterosexual love in both its fictional stories and advice columns, "where girls are often advised to make themselves attractive and available for men to prevent them from philandering; it is implied that it is their fault if this should happen."[33]

BRAVO's *Failure: Escapism Instead of Activism*

Where *BRAVO* fails its readers most, however, in Herrmann's argument, is in its apparently programmatic "lack of involvement in the development of its readers' talents and interests;" they are allowed to "experience power vicariously" by reading about pop stars, but they are not themselves empowered thereby.[34] Remembering her own youthful experience as an avid reader of *BRAVO* (which was forbidden in her household due to its "bourgeois consumer ideology" and "pornographic content"), Herrmann recalls the magazine as "a companion that helped me escape into a world of fantasy":

> Although this was ultimately a lonely world, my fascination with it was a shared one, connecting me with girlfriends who also collected clippings and posters of favorite stars, arranged them in scrapbooks, and hung them on the walls of their rooms. Just as *BRAVO* alienated us from aspects of each other's realities, it also connected us on the level of fantasy.[35]

Herrmann's "loneliness" springs in part from the relative isolation of her activities: although *BRAVO* gave her the opportunity to engage in what Fiske calls "semiotic productivity" (the reception and personal reinterpretation of popular culture), and she derived some sense of community from being able to engage in "enunciative productivity" (face-to-face discussion of such culture), Herrmann had—or perceived—no opportunity to move beyond an extremely localized fan community by engaging in "textual productivity," or the production of texts that appropriate elements of popular culture in a manner that emulates the artistic (or scholarly) productions of "official culture" and their dissemination.[36]

The difference between the young Mareike Herrmann's experience of being a fan and that of the young girls studied by Kimberly Gregson is not explained simply by the fact that in Herrmann's youth, there was no World Wide Web that would have allowed her to display her cultural capital beyond the walls of her room. Though *BRAVO* has its own Web site nowadays, to a great extent it functions as though the Internet had never been invented[37]; its readers are offered popular culture information, but they are not prompted to leverage this information into cultural capital by means of the kind of active "textual productivity" exemplified by the Web sites of Gregson's American girls.[38] They are addressed as fans but given little motivation to participate actively in a fandom, which in Fiske's definition "offers ways of filling cultural lack and provides the social prestige and self-esteem that go with cultural capital."[39] Only the sexual information that they are given in abundance is meant to be implemented; and that only in order to appeal to men, who are portrayed as the really active and productive members of society, and to stave off other women who might compete for attention.[40] As a result, in questioning her present-day informants, Herrmann found that they were generally completely nonplussed and alienated by the question, "What are you good at?" In a manner that Herrmann recognized from her own childhood, these girls had almost never been encouraged, either by the adults around them or by "their" popular culture magazine, to cultivate hobbies or interests for their own pleasure and satisfaction, or to imagine future careers outside a narrow spectrum of traditionally "feminine" and self-sacrificing occupations. This was particularly true of working-class girls in trade-oriented high school programs; middle-class students from *Gymnasien* (academic high schools) had slightly broader and more optimistic—though in some ways, also more naïve—outlooks.[41]

Nonetheless, Herrmann argues, many young German women continue to take pleasure in reading *BRAVO* as an escape from a dreary reality. And in many respects, given its focus on androgynous pop stars and its dreamy romanticization of homosexuality, it seems quite possible that Germany's most popular teen magazine — at its height of popularity in the mid–1990s, during Herrmann's study, with sales of 1.26 million issues a week and issues usually swapped among several readers after sale, *BRAVO*'s circulation exceeded that of Germany's leading newsmagazine *Der Spiegel*[42] — may inadvertently have played a significant role in "priming" a large German female readership for the acceptance of the themes of boys' love and yaoi manga to a degree unthinkable in the Anglophone countries.

"From Tokyo with Love": Early Reactions to Boys' Love in Germany

The fact that such a receptive audience did exist in Germany became evident very quickly: as early as July 2002 — even as German comics publishers were just beginning to recruit local manga artists— the liberal-leaning *Der Spiegel*, in a cover story in its cultural supplement *KulturSpiegel*, drew its readers' attention to the fact that manga had become extremely popular among young women and girls. Moreover, the article emphasized that Japanese comics could be extremely direct in their portrayal of violence and sex ("The spectrum runs from lifted skirts through to S/M," as one headline put it[43]), and particularly of homoerotic themes. It would be extremely naïve, of course, to believe that comics in the West, and especially in Europe, had never shown violence, sex or homosexuality; the shocking element was apparently the new readership, as implied by one of the article's rather plaintive opening sentences: "Comics were always men's business (*Männersache*)."[44] This sense of shock may explain why, although the article itself does make an attempt to contextualize manga fairly, to explain the cultural roots of their frankness, and to draw attention to their frequent psychological and philosophical complexity, the issue's cover nonetheless screams: "Liebesgruss aus Tokio: Deutsche Mädchen sind ganz wild auf japanische Sex-Comics" ("From Tokyo with Love: German Girls are Totally Wild for Japanese Sex Comics"); while the illustrations, taken out of context and uncredited from several manga, emphasize heterosexual making out and female nudity in a manner that would hardly be out of place in *BRAVO*.

Boys' love had clearly already begun to penetrate the German market; the *KulturSpiegel* article mentions by name Ozaki Minami's *Zetsuai*, the first *shōnen-ai* manga to appear officially in German translation, thanks to Carlsen; and competitor Panini had eventually followed suit with Ragawa Marimo's *New York New York*. Egmont would soon publish Ōkami Mineko's *Gekka kajin*, as *Lumen Lunae*.[45] Despite the somewhat alarmist tone of the *KulturSpiegel* report, however, it would be a grave overstatement to suggest that the major publishers were rushing headlong into publishing boys' love stories. Even as late as spring 2006, in an interview with the fan Web site animePRO, Egmont's managing editor Georg Tempel admitted that until recently, boys' love had not been a major focus of either his own or his competitors' publishing strategies— in part because Japanese *shōnen-ai* manga are usually put out by smaller presses that are harder to track down and negotiate with, and in part because comics publishers, who generally also produce books aimed at children, have to be circumspect in dealing with erotic material, and it was difficult finding boys' love manga that were not too "hard-core": "Whether it's Mickey Mouse at Egmont or Harry Potter at Carlsen, it's always unpleasant if a publisher that puts out products for children lands in the headlines on account of pornography."[46]

Nonetheless, all of the major publishers were increasing their small output of boys' love manga, perhaps spurred by the recent arrival on the scene of further competition, in the form of the German branch of TOKYOPOP, which had been founded in 2004 well-armed with connections to Japanese publishers and their licenses. Relatively unfettered by any pre-existing image as a purveyor of children's literature, TOKYOPOP had already begun both recruiting local German manga artists and publishing Japanese *shōnen-ai*, starting with Takanaga Hinako's *Little Butterfly*.[47] From 2005 on, all four major German publishers have thus steadily maintained a stable of boys' love properties—though Panini has dropped to a distant fourth in terms of the size of its manga catalog, regardless of genre, leaving the field largely to Carlsen, TOKYOPOP and Egmont, in roughly that order. At the same time, however, unlike their American counterparts, German manga publishers have hardly attempted to cultivate readership among boys' love fans by setting up separate imprints comparable to Central Park Manga's "Be Beautiful" line in the U.S.,[48] or by marking categories that would appeal to such an audience, other than the more generic "romance" or "adult"—though both Carlsen and Egmont have a separate heading on their manga Web sites for "*shōnen-ai*" or "boys' love" (Carlsen uses the English term), allowing an easy overview of their offerings.[49]

If for the last few years the German readership of manga, including the genre of boys' love, have nonetheless been relatively well served by the majors as consumers, the same cannot be said for home-grown creators of boys' love manga, whose opportunities to publish with the larger publishers have so far been few and far between. Among German-produced manga, boy's love was initially conspicuous by its absence, which was made even more obvious by strategies such as explicit exclusion: Korean-German Judith Park's *shōjo* romantic comedy *Y Square*, for example, features a gay male protagonist, Yagate, who admits to finding his schoolmate Yoshitaka attractive. Park, however, inserts a note in the same panel: "Nonetheless, *Y Square* isn't going to become a *shonen-ai*!"[50] And sure enough, since Yoshitaka is straight but oafish, Yagate selflessly pitches in to help him woo a young woman, Ju-Jin.

Boy's love was also played for laughs, as in Lenka Buschová's *Freaky Angel*, whose protagonist is Hikari, a rather scatterbrained angel charged with helping people who have romantic problems. Her first case is the nerdy Satoshi, whose romantic fixation on "Mr. Scrubber," the broom he uses to clean his school classroom, is revealed to be a sublimation of his crush on a female classmate named Ren. When Ren is unmasked as a boy in drag, Satoshi is unperturbed; but their embrace prompts Hikari to vomit, complaining, "Does this have to be so kitschy?"[51] In the case of both strategies, it is clear that readers are expected already to possess the necessary cultural capital to know what *shōnen-ai* means and what its conventions are, whether those conventions are about to be ignored or parodied.

Egmont Ehapa Verlag was ultimately the first to publish a serious original German *shōnen-ai*, Chinese-born Cheng Ying Zhou's *Shanghai Passion*, in 2005. In contrast—if not in response—to Park's declaration in *Y Square*, which had appeared only three months earlier, the characters of *Shanghai Passion* openly acknowledge that they are living out a *shōnen-ai* manga; an anachronistically tongue-in-cheek comment, since the plot is set in 1930s China.[52] It took almost a year, however, before rival TOKYOPOP responded with its own local talent, *In the End* by Pink Psycho, a team of two young men individually named Heath and Nheira.[53] The two publishers have since then taken turns: Diana Liesaus's tale of Cambridge students in love, *Musouka*—the first ongoing German boys' love manga—began appearing as an Egmont manga almost a year later again, and the second continuing tale, Anna Hollmann's *Stupid Story*, was published by TOKYOPOP another six months after that.[54] Carlsen, meanwhile, largest of the major publishers, has yet to release a home-grown boys' love manga, though its Web site has announced Franziska Steffen and Tina Lindhorst's *Chouchin* and two other titles for February 2009.[55]

Animexx, the German Verein *Tradition and Social Capital*

This does not mean, however, that aspiring German manga artists, particularly those who are interested in boys' love, lack outlets for their creativity. On the contrary: as Gregson has pointed out in connection with the American *shōjo* fans she describes, "The Web makes it possible for ... fans to be part of the bigger and supportive online fan base."[56] And in Germany, a major online locus of both manga and anime fandom is Animexx, the Association of Friends of Anime and Manga (*Verein der Anime- und Mangafreunde e.V.*). Animexx was established in January 2000 as an *eingetragener Verein* (plural *Vereine*), or registered voluntary association, under German law in order to promote Japanese popular culture, in particular manga and anime.[57]

The association thus builds on a tradition of German popular culture with roots in the 1840s, the *Vereinswesen* or "citizen's right to voluntary association." In the nineteenth century, the *Vereinswesen* often referred primarily to membership in male bourgeois groups, at least nominally united by athletic, cultural or religious interests—before 1848, many German territories severely restricted association for overtly political purposes; though afterwards, Germany's political parties in fact essentially grew out of the *Vereine*.[58] The *Verein* was an important part of the process of political liberalization and of the broadly based public impetus to transform the fragmented and largely still absolutist German monarchies into a unified, constitutional modern European state (a project that was only partially successfully realized by German unification in 1871).

During the twentieth century, however, the *Vereinswesen* expanded to include not only women and men, and political groups of every stripe, but also all manner of popular interests, such as sports or celebrity fans, amateur dancers, hobby gardeners, car collectors, model train enthusiasts, and so on. As a result of this widespread expansion through all levels of society, Germany is "reputed to be the world champion in *Vereinsmeierei*,"[59] which might be roughly translated as "joining to keep up with the Joneses." Although modern statistical analyses do not quite bear out this stereotype—people in the United States in fact appear to hold more memberships in voluntary associations per capita, as do all the Scandinavian countries[60]—the prevalence of this image among Germans themselves is an important indicator of the central importance of the *Verein* in German history and society.

This importance is due not least to the fact that *Vereine* are crucial generators of "social capital," which Robert Putnam has described as "features of social organization such as networks, norms, and social trust that facilitate coordination and cooperation for mutual benefit."[61] These features were vital for creating a politically active middle class in Germany during the 1800s, and are thought to remain important factors in maintaining democratic civil societies today.[62] The idea of mutual benefit is still a significant element in the constitution of *Vereine*: when Animexx officially declares itself to be *gemeinnützig*, which is conventionally translated as "non-profit," is in fact literally describing itself as "useful to the community" or "serving the public good." The nature of this service is made clear on the association's Web site under the rubric, "What is Animexx?":

> It is our goal to offer anime and manga fans the opportunity to exchange views, to publish and publicize their own works, and to improve their skills. This occurs both via our Web site, Animexx.de, and by means of the many fan meetings and conventions that we organize and support.[63]

Despite Putnam's fears that "the technological transformation of leisure" has contributed to the disruption of "many opportunities for social-capital formation," and a similar sense on Michael Mertes's part that, in the specifically German context, "modernity ... means a loosening of ligatures, including a withering away of the committed *citoyen*,"[64] it is nonetheless apparent that the arrival of the Internet tremendously facilitated the formation and maintenance of *Vereine*, which were originally small, regional organizations, yet can now extend their reach to any computer terminal, at least in theory. Animexx has exploited this technology to create one of Germany's largest manga/anime-oriented Web sites, Animexx.de, which counts over 130,000 online members—one hundred times larger than the core membership of the *Verein* itself, though still far less than the current circulation of *BRAVO*, which has settled just below half a million[65]—and includes information about the *Verein*, sections for news about the German manga/anime market, user blogs and forums, help for organizing events, an Animexx-wiki, a shop for Animexx-related merchandise, and plentiful space for fans to communicate and upload their own fan fiction, cosplay and convention photos, and *dōjinshi*. Several hundred sketches, pictures and comics are added to the Web site as a whole every day.[66] This last function has made Animexx.de in turn not only a significant training ground for aspiring local German manga artists, and particularly for those interested in boys' love, but also an accessible medium for them to make use of their cultural capital to engage in Fiske's "textual productivity."

Within the catalogue of themes listed on Animexx.de's *dōjinshi* pages, "*Shōnen-ai*" is one of the larger categories, with more than 2,700 *dōjinshi* available for viewing out of more than 10,000. (At least three other categories, "Romantik," "Fantasy" and "Alltag"—"everyday life"—are larger, but most *dōjinshi* are also listed under more than one heading.[67]) Many artists also increase their cultural capital on display by linking to additional artworks available on their personal pages on other sites, such as MySpace or deviantART. By thus making available German *dōjinshi* of all kinds, Animexx.de not only advertises these works to interested print publishers, but also serves as a mechanism for quality control and vets material for its legal acceptability, since site rules are detailed and strictly formulated regarding what kind of *dōjinshi* may be uploaded and then, after inspection, made available to the public—in contrast to American practice, for instance, where Web sites generally do not inspect uploaded material beforehand, and take action to remove content only after the fact, if a complaint is made.

In addition to forbidding sloppily drawn, plagiarized or photography-based works—which might be considered issues not only of aesthetic quality, but also of professionalism—Animexx.de also expressly forbids certain types of content. Images that do not belong to the artist, for example, cannot be integrated into *dōjinshi* in any manner, for reasons of copyright, nor can works drawn by friends or acquaintances be uploaded under an artist's name. Libel laws also have to be respected, and in addition "real-person slash," meaning the depiction of real people in fictive romantic or sexual relationships, is forbidden to prevent damaging the subjects' reputations; moreover, for reasons of good taste, depictions of gore, extreme violence (or its victims), sodomy and necrophilia are very unlikely to be sanctioned.[68]

Most importantly, because German child pornography and child abuse laws forbid representation of children as sexual objects, there is a complete ban on *shota* or *lolicon. Shota* is defined on Animexx.de as "the depiction, whether unambiguous or ambiguous, of very young characters (under 14 years old) engaging in sex or games of violence or domination, with the participation of an adult or with children of the same age." Although this description nowhere specifies the sex of the characters in question, it is assumed that they are male — perhaps because this distinction is built into the Japanese word as used in the West, or possibly because of the popularity of boys' love — since the next sentence tersely defines *lolicon* as "the feminine equivalent." The text goes on:

> Sexual abuse of children is a punishable offense, forbidden in Germany, as you certainly know. Stories in which children are recognizable as "sexual objects" will be treated as *shota* and deleted, and the artists will be warned. Your characters may not look like children if you draw *hentai* or the like (giving their ages in the text is no help — only the apparent age counts!).[69]

Note that erotic material, or *hentai*, is not itself forbidden — pornography is legally available in Germany, and Animexx.de accordingly has a *hentai dōjinshi* section, open to works that clearly depict only adult sexual activity, and accessible only to registered Animexx members who have provided proof that they are eighteeen or older. By this means, the cultural capital on display on the Web site is policed, so that it conforms as nearly as possible to the values of the official culture.

From Animexx to the Publishers — and Beyond

The *dōjinshi* pages of Animexx.de have introduced to a wide readership many artists who have gone on to publish their works in Germany's manga market. Although home-grown manga still serves as only an ancillary market for Germany's major manga publishers, Carlsen, Egmont and TOKYOPOP, it forms an important market segment for the smaller Verlag Schwarzer Turm, which in addition to its own comics line specializes in publishing only manga by German artists.[70] Publisher Michael Möller, one of Schwarzer Turm's proprietors, soon discovered that Animexx.de was a perfect tool for recruiting fresh talent.[71] As a result, Schwarzer Turm has published a variety of manga anthologies in partnership with Animexx, most notably *Paper Theatre*, whose stories have often begun as online *dōjinshi*.[72] One of these stories was Anna Hollmann's abovementioned *Stupid Story*, the first two chapters of which had originally appeared on Animexx.de in 2004, under one of Hollmann's online nicknames, "Lynea," and indexed under "*Shōnen-ai*," "Romantik" and "Humor."[73] Installments of *Stupid Story* then appeared in the first three volumes of *Paper Theatre*, before Hollmann was signed to a contract with TOKYOPOP.[74] Hollmann's first paperback volume appeared in March of 2008, and in October of the same year won a Sondermann Comics Prize at the Frankfurt Book Fair, guaranteeing the continuation of the story, which has also been licensed to appear in translation in 2009 by the French publisher Taïfu Comics.[75] Hollmann is thus the first boys' love manga artist to play a role in the German publishers' long-term strategy of using home-grown manga to "move to the other end of the value-added chain," as TOKYOPOP chief editor Joachim Kaps put it in a 2006 interview, "namely, to sell licenses abroad."[76]

In this manner, the German comics industry can finally for the first time become an exporter, as well as an importer, of product; and Hollmann's series has moved well beyond being the kind of cultural capital of fandom that most of the textually productive material posted on Animexx.de represents. Indeed, *Stupid Story* has become a form of social capital, insofar as it serves to create and institutionalize relationships between larger and more extended groups between fandom and the publishing industry, both nationally (in the form of interaction between Animexx, Schwarzer Turm and TOKYOPOP) and internationally (in the form of interaction between TOKYOPOP Germany, the French Taïfu, and the prospective French readership). It is by no means incidental that the creation of these new networks has serious implications for the creation and exchange of economic capital as well — not only across national borders and between corporate entities, but also for Hollmann as an individual, since in keeping with German publishing practices she maintains a stake in the copyright to the material and the profits it generates.

In addition to *Paper Theatre*, Schwarzer Turm has continued to publish other, more specialized anthologies, particularly the series *Hungry Hearts*, focusing on erotic manga stories with both heterosexual and homosexual themes, which has appeared twice so far, with at least two more volumes forthcoming. Since an important part of Schwarzer Turm's remit as a niche publisher has always been the publication of various Western-style erotic comics series for adults only, the manga in *Hungry Hearts* are accordingly often much more explicit in their depictions of sexuality than those published by the larger concerns.[77]

Following the lead of Schwarzer Turm, several newer and even smaller specialized publishers have now arisen to cater exclusively to the boys' love market: both Fireangels Verlag and The Wild Side Verlag license and import material from abroad — chiefly the U.S., France and Italy — but they also publish home-grown German-language boys' love manga.[78] All of the German artists currently publishing with Fireangels and The Wild Side also have a presence on the Animexx.de Web site, so that the initial chapters of both Martina "Chiron-san" Peters' boys' love science-fiction thriller *K-A-E 29th Secret* and Makiko "Zombiesmile" Ponczeck's sexually less explicit but more violent *Lost and Found*, for example, were once available on their respective personal *dōjinshi* pages. Ponczeck's page still links to the first chapter of her book, with information and a convenient link to help the reader buy the published manga in its entirety.[79] Peters' page, however, no longer links to the beginning of her story, since two volumes have now appeared from Fireangels; instead, in addition to links to shops where these volumes can be purchased (including Amazon.de), there is a synopsis of their content and a link to the continuation of the story, which has not yet been collected into a print volume.[80]

These two approaches to textual productivity have become marketing strategies, whose difference cannily reflects the fact that Ponczeck's work is a single, self-contained volume, while Peters' is an ongoing series; what they have in common, however, is a partnership in their small publishers — Peters and Ponczeck are art directors at Fireangels and The Wild Side respectively. As a result, though outside of the corporate paradigm, like Hollmann they have exceeded the boundaries of fan culture, which, because it is not profit-oriented, "makes no attempt to circulate its text outside its own community,"[81] and are now leveraging their work into both social and economic capital. Note that an important part of this process of leveraging is the transformation from an original electronic medium of dissemination into hard copy print form; none of the publishers mentioned markets electronic texts in place of old-fashioned physical, shippable — and thus exportable — books.

One final example of this process is the work of Fahr Sindram, which falls on the periphery of the boys' love genre, but certainly owes its existence to that genre's popularity. Sindram, whose Animexx.de nickname is "Fahr-chan," but who usually employs the nickname "FahrLight" instead, entered the German manga scene by way of the Internet and was eventually "discovered" turning out sketches at the 2005 Leipzig Book Fair, after which Schwarzer Turm publisher Michael Möller tracked her down using the Animexx.de Web site.[82] Sindram then worked organizing and setting up the *Paper Theatre* series, several volumes of which carried her own one-page humorous stories; but she also previewed her own manga series, which was already contracted to another publisher, in the anthology's second volume.[83] Sindram's "Gothic drama" *Losing Neverland* (the title refers indirectly to *Peter Pan* by parodying the title of the 2004 film *Finding Neverland*[84]) is set in Victorian London; its story concerns motherless fourteen-year-old Laurence V. Laurence, whose crippled sailor father prostitutes him to middle-class men in order to pay the bills. The undernourished, elfin "Laurie," continually dressed in a kind of anachronistic Lolita drag when he is dressed at all, appears hardly more than ten years old; his otherwise ethereal beauty is marred by cankers around his mouth. In a world in which every adult male is apparently an eager pederast, Laurie's life is a litany of endless exploitation and suffering, relieved only by the catty camaraderie of his fellow hustlers— including his would-be lover Maurice— and the companionship of his "conscience," a moldering fox-skin stole named Fanny, who speaks to him when nobody else is around.[85]

Sindram's deft drawings and sense of humor leaven the otherwise rather morbid proceedings; but though it is not sexually explicit, this rather absurd mélange of elements from *Oliver!*, *The Boys in the Band*, *Midnight Cowboy*, *Calvin and Hobbes* and the Marquis de Sade would nonetheless likely be a risky undertaking— even under the laws in effect before November 2008— if both she and her publisher, the German-run but British-based Butter & Cream Verlagsgesellschaft, did not continually remind the reader, within and without the text as well as in interviews, that Sindram's intention in *Losing Neverland* is to use some of the conventions of boys' love to raise awareness of child abuse and to protest the dissemination of *shota* materials.[86] As Sindram has forcefully put it, while she is an avid reader of *shōnen-ai* and has nothing against yaoi and *hentai*— and anyone who says that manga in general portray too much sex and violence "needs to be smacked"—child pornography is a different matter altogether: "There are boundaries being transgressed, and they're sacred."[87]

On this basis, somewhat paradoxically, material that very possibly would not have passed muster for uploading onto the Animexx.de Web site— the pages of "Fahr-chan" contain only a *Losing Neverland* side story, thus once again acting as advertising, and of course providing a link to Butter & Cream— has not only been socially accepted, but indeed praised, with an honorable citation from Germany's Council for Sustainable Development (*Rat für Nachhaltige Entwicklung*), whose mandate extends beyond environmental issues to facilitating positive communication and networking in the interests of "social coherence"— in other words, to the creation and maintenance of social capital.[88] In the case of Sindram's work, its now officially acknowledged value as social capital— proclaimed on a sticker on the first volume's cover— has come to far outweigh its potential to shock as "mere" cultural capital within fandom.

As the cornerstone of Butter & Cream's manga output, *Losing Neverland* is now also being capitalized upon for export; thus, despite the fact that Sindram recommends the series only for readers fourteen and older, the intention is to expand the readership internationally, with an English edition already available and French and Japanese translations in preparation. Moreover, since Sindram is contracted to produce eight volumes of the series, *Losing Neverland* is positioned to become the longest-running home-grown German manga yet—if all goes according to plan.[89] Even if Sindram fails to complete the series, *Losing Neverland* nonetheless demonstrates that Germany has developed the necessary infrastructure for aspiring manga artists to move from fandom to a professional career as a producer of officially sanctioned, if still mass, culture. The fact that Sindram's work is in many ways even more transgressive of social norms than a great deal of boys' love manga may actually clear the way for even more artists to take up the genre—possibly in ways that Sindram will find distasteful.

Animexx: Hub for the Commercialization of Fandom

Notably, when artists are contracted to the three major publishers, they tend overwhelmingly to be credited only under their real name; by contrast, artists who publish with the smaller presses almost always make use of one of their online nicknames or usernames, either in conjunction with their real name (as Anna "Cross" Hollmann does for her contributions to Schwarzer Turm's *Paper Theatre*, but not for the TOKYOPOP edition of *Stupid Story*; and as Martina "Chiron-San" Peters does on the covers of her series *K-A-E 29th Secret*, published by Fireangels—but not on her single all-ages volume for Carlsen, *E-Motional*[90]) or as a pseudonym instead of their real name (as Ponczeck does on *Lost and Found*). This practice not only refers back to the original online presence of both author and work, as brokered by Animexx.de, but also maintains a sense of community among the artists. At the same time, however, it cannot be overlooked that the exposure of these artists' cultural capital under their nicknames on the Web site and in their published works serves well to create a kind of "branding" or name recognition than can easily be turned to the generation of economic capital as well, while also maintaining the artists' "civilian identities" for other projects, since most of the manga artists described here clearly want to have artistic careers beyond a specialty in boys' love or even in manga in general.

As a result of their multiple functions as meeting place, talent scout, clearing house, and arbiter/censor, the Animexx *Verein* and its Web site have clearly become not only a major influence in German manga and anime fandom, but arguably the single most important force in catering both to German fans' growing interest in home-grown manga and to German manga creators' sense of community and self-identification not only as a subculture, but also as a viable profession. Although this observation can be made at the level of manga and its fandom in general, where Animexx.de plays a pivotal role in the ongoing recruitment of artistic talent by the German comics industry and the entry of aspiring artists into professional careers, it is particularly in the area of boys' love—which despite its niche status, encourages an especially passionate level of involvement—that the *Verein* and its Web site have been vital in turning fans into producers and even into independent entrepreneurs. Thus, textual production that once might have reached only a relatively small circle of fans as cultural capital, is increasingly being turned into both social and economic capital, with the explicit intention of reviving and expanding the German comic industry and redressing the traditional imbalance of trade with other comics-producing nations. Given the overwhelming number of young women involved in these activities, Animexx is clearly making great strides in counteracting the long-term legacy of conservative corporate mass entertainment vehicles such as *BRAVO*; whether the current period of economic uncertainty and recession will undercut this progress, however, in what remains an extremely small and precarious market still largely dominated by corporate interests, cannot be foreseen.

Notes

1. Nakazawa Keiji, *Barfuß durch Hiroshima: Eine Bildergeschichte gegen den Krieg* (Reinbek: Rowohlt Verlag, 1982); Ishinomori Shōtarō, *Japan GmbH* (Bonn: Verlag Norman Rentrop, 1989).

2. Ōtomo Katsuhiro, *Akira*, 19 vols. (Hamburg: Carlsen Verlag, 1991–6); Heike Jüngst, "Japanese Comics in Germany," *Perspectives: Studies in Translatology* 12.2 (2004): 87–89; Bernd Dolle-Weinkauff, "The Attractions of Intercultural Exchange: Manga Market and Manga Reception in Germany." *Mobile and Popular Culture in Asia*. Asia Culture Forum 2006. 1. URL: http://www.cct.go.kr/data/acf2006/mobile/mobile_0402_Bernd%20Dolle-Weinkauff.pdf. Last accessed 10 March, 2009; Paul M. Malone, "Manga in Europe," in *Manga: An Anthology of Global and Cultural Perspectives*, ed. Toni Johnson-Woods (New York: Continuum, forthcoming).

3. German nouns are gendered; loan-words are assigned a gender through consensus. This does not always lead to universal agreement: German Japanologists treat "manga" as a neuter noun (*"das Manga"*), presumably by morphological analogy with the many neuter nouns ending in *a* derived from Greek. The general public, however, including comics scholars, have embraced it as masculine (*"der Manga"*), presumably by functional analogy with the loan-word *"der Comic."* Jaqueline Berndt, *Phänomen Manga: Comic-Kultur in Japan* (Berlin: Edition q, 1995), 12.

4. Takeuchi Naoko, *Sailor Moon*, 18 vols. (Mannheim: Reiner Feest Verlag, 1998–2000); Toriyama Akira, *Dragon Ball*, 42 vols. (Hamburg: Carlsen, 1997–2000); Malone, "Manga in Europe," forthcoming; Jüngst, "Japanese Comics," 87–91.

5. Andreas C. Knigge, *Alles über Comics: Eine Entdeckungsreise von den Höhlenbildern bis zum Manga* (Hamburg: Europa Verlag, 2004): 69–70.

6. "CARLSEN MANGA! Startseite." URL: http://www.carlsen.de/web/manga/index. Last accessed 14 April, 2009; "Manganet" [EGMONT Verlagsgesellschaften mbH; Egmont Manga & Anime]. URL: http://www.manganet.de/index.php. Last accessed 14 April, 2009; "Comic, Comics, Manga, Anime bei PaniniComics.de." URL: http://www.paninicomics.de/?s=serie&gs_gruppe=8. Last accessed 14 April, 2009.

7. Paul M. Malone, "*Mangascape* Germany: Comics as Intercultural Neutral Ground," in *Comics as Nexus of Culture*, ed. Mark Berninger and Gideon Haberkorn (Jefferson, NC: McFarland, forthcoming).

8. "TOKYOPOP — Manga, Manhwa, Manhua und Cine-Manga." URL: http://www.tokyopop.de/. Last accessed 14 April, 2009.

9. Jürgen Seebeck, *Bloody Circus*, 2 vols. (Hamburg: Carlsen, 2001); Robert Labs, *Dragic Master*, 2 vols. (Hamburg: Carlsen, 2001, 2005); Robert Labs, *Crewman 3*, 2 vols. (Hamburg: Carlsen, 2003–4); Sascha Nils Marx and Stefan Voss, *Naglayas Herz* (Cologne: Egmont, 2002); Steffi Holzer, Martin Jurgeit and Sascha Krämer, "Es muss nicht immer Japan sein: *Mangas* aus deutschen Landen," *Comixene* 78 (2004): 7; Heike Jüngst, "Manga in Germany: From Translation to Simulacrum," *Perspectives: Studies in Translatology* 14.4 (2006): 251–2; 259.

10. Jörg Böckem, "Sind die süüüß!," in *KulturSpiegel* 9 (2006): 11. The difference between *shōnen* and *shōjo* manga is chiefly one of target audience, rather than genre; the former are aimed at young boys and the latter at young girls, though both include a wide variety of genres and themes.

11. Although this boom has also included the import of Korean *manhua* and Chinese *manhwa*, local German artists always follow the conventions of Japanese manga when they differ from those of the other two forms— even when the German artists in question are of Korean or Chinese background. Malone, "*Mangascape* Germany," forthcoming.

12. Stefan Pannor, "*Dragon Ball* und die Folgen," in *Deutschland online* 25 March 2008, URL: http://www.magazine-deutschland.de/de/artikel/artikelansicht/article/dragonball-und-die-folgen.html. Last accessed 3 March, 2009. All translations from German are my own.

13. Midori Matsui, "Little Girls were Little Boys: Displaced Femininity in the Representation of Homosexuality in Japanese Girls' Comics," in *Feminism and the Politics of Difference*, ed. Sneja Gunew and Anna Yeatman (Boulder, Colorado, and San Francisco: Westview Press, 1993): 179.

14. Matthew Thorn, "Girls and Women Getting Out of Hand: The Pleasures and Politics of Japan's Amateur Comics Community," in *Fanning the Flames: Fans and Consumer Culture in Contemporary Japan*, ed. William W. Kelly (New York: State University of New York Press, 2004): 170–1.

15. Mark McLelland, "No Climax, No Point, No Meaning? Japanese Women's Boy-Love Sites on the Internet," in *Journal of Communication Inquiry* 24.3 (2000): 280.

16. McLelland, "No Climax," 277; Kristy L. Valenti, "'Stop, My Butt Hurts!' The Yaoi Invasion," in *The Comics Journal* 269 (July 2005): 122; Andrea Wood, "'Straight' Women, Queer Texts: Boy-Love Manga and the Rise of a Global Counterpublic," in *WSQ: Women's Studies Quarterly* 34.1 & 2 (2006): 394–5.

17. McLelland, "No Climax," 276–7.

18. Thorn, "Girls and Women," 173; Wood, "'Straight' Women," 406.

19. Thorn, "Girls and Women," 180.

20. Suzuki Kazuko, "Pornography or Therapy? Japanese Girls Creating the Yaoi Phenomenon," in *Millennium Girls: Today's Girls Around the World*, ed. Sherrie Inness (Lanham, MD: Rowman & Littlefield, 1998): 244; Henry Jenkins, *Textual Poachers: Television Fans and Participatory Culture* (London: Routledge, 1992): 185–205.

21. Mareike Herrmann, "'Feeling Better' with *Bravo*: German Girls and Their Popular Youth Magazine," in *Millennium Girls: Today's Girls Around the World*, ed. Sherrie Inness (Lanham, MD: Rowman & Littlefield, 1998): 227, 229, 232.

22. Herrmann, "'Feeling Better,'" 218.

23. Herrmann, "'Feeling Better,'" 216.

24. Herrmann, "'Feeling Better,'" 232.

25. Kimberly S. Gregson, "What if the Lead Character Looks Like Me? Girl Fans of *Shoujo Anime* and Their Web Sites," in *Girl Wide Web: Girls, the Internet, and the Negotiation of Identity*, ed. Sharon R. Mazzarella (New York: Peter Lang, 2005): 127.

26. Gregson, "What if," 131–2; Fiske elaborates an idea of cultural capital first developed by Pierre Bourdieu, and extends it to popular culture as well as high culture. John Fiske, "The Cultural Economy of Fandom," in *The Adoring Audience: Fan Culture and Popular Media*, ed. Lisa A. Lewis (London: Routledge, 1992): 30–33.

27. Gregson, "What if," 128–9.

28. Herrmann, "'Feeling Better,'" 221, 233.

29. Herrmann, "'Feeling Better,'" 221–2. While the sexual information itself is generally regarded as valuable or interesting, these illustrations are often the least favorite aspect of the magazine among its female readership, particularly for the younger members, due to a sense that the models in the photographs create unrealistic expectations of female beauty, and the knowledge that "the boys get off on them." On the other hand, the equally graphic "Foto-Love-Stories" in every issue are much more popular: the girls recognize that these are formulaic fictions and accept them, including the pictures, as entertainment; 233–4.

30. Gregson, "What if," 127–8; 136–7.

31. Gregson, "What if," 128.

32. Herrmann, "'Feeling Better,'" 238.

33. Herrmann, "'Feeling Better,'" 231.

34. Herrmann, "'Feeling Better,'" 229, 232.

35. Herrmann, "'Feeling Better,'" 216.

36. Fiske, "Cultural Economy," 37–9.

37. Note that any visit to the *BRAVO* Web site is dominated by relentless pop-up ads; in this respect, at least, the magazine is up to date. URL: www.bravo.de. Last accessed 3 March, 2009.

38. Gregson, "What if," 128–9; Fiske, "Cultural Economy," 39–40.

39. Fiske, "Cultural Economy," 31.

40. Herrmann, "'Feeling Better,'" 229, 233.

41. Herrmann, "'Feeling Better,'" 227–9. Gregson's study, by comparison, takes no account of class differences; however, the very nature of her investigation, which focuses on young women with both Internet access and the leisure time to create Web sites, is likely to exclude certain socio-economic strata; Gregson, "What if," 137–8.

42. Herrmann, "'Feeling Better,'" 220, 239.

43. Jörg Böckem and Christoph Dallach, "Manga Chutney," *KulturSpiegel* 7 (July 2002): 22.

44. Böckem and Dallach, "Manga Chutney," 21.

45. Ozaki Minami, *Zetsuai 1989*, 5 vols. (Hamburg: Carlsen, 2000–2001); Marimo Ragawa, *New York New York*, 4 vols. (Planet Manga, 2002); Ōkami Mineko, *Lumen Lunae*, 5 vols. (Cologne: Egmont, 2002–2003).

46. Christian Könen, "Interview mit Georg Tempel, Verlagsleiter von EMA," *www.animePRO.de* (13 April 2006). Tempel uses the English loan word "hard-core" in German.

47. Takanaga Hinako, *Kleiner Schmetterling*, 3 vols. (Hamburg: TOKYOPOP, 2005–2007). TOKYOPOP Germany does also publish manga for younger readers, however, and is also the current German licensee of Jeff Smith's comic epic for readers ten years old and up, *Bone*, 8 vols. (Hamburg: TOKYOPOP, 2006).

48. Wood, "'Straight' Women," p. 407; Valenti, "'Stop,'" p. 122.

49. "CARLSEN MANGA!" URL: http://www.carlsen.de/web/manga/boys_love. Last accessed 5 January, 2009; "Manganet." URL: http://www.manganet.de/. Last accessed 5 January, 2009.

50. Judith Park, *Y Square* (Hamburg: Carlsen, 2005): 35. Also available in English translation: Judith Park, *Y Square* (New York: Yen Press, 2008).

51. Lenka Buschová, *Freaky Angel* (Cologne: Egmont, 2005): 56.

52. Cheng Ying Zhou, *Shanghai Passion* (Cologne: Egmont, 2005): n.p.

53. Pink Psycho, *In the End* (Hamburg: TOKYOPOP, 2006); on the rather problematic nature of *In the End* as a boys' love story, see Paul M. Malone, "Home-grown *Shōjo Manga* and the Rise of Boys' Love Among Germany's 'Forty-Niners,'" in *Intersections: Gender and Sexuality in Asia and the Pacific* 21 (April 2009): para. 21.

54. Diana Liesaus, *Musouka*, 2 vols. (Cologne: Egmont, 2007); Anna Hollmann, *Stupid Story* (Hamburg: TOKYOPOP, 2008).

55. "CARLSEN MANGA!" URL: http://www.carlsen.de/web/manga/boys_love. Last accessed 5 January, 2009.

56. Gregson, "What if," 130.

57. "Animexx e.V.: der Verein." URL: http://animexx.onlinewelten.com/verein.phtml. Last accessed 5 January, 2009.

58. Oded Heilbronner, "The German Bourgeois Club as a Political and Social Structure in the Late Nineteenth and Early Twentieth Centuries," in *Continuity and Change* 13.3 (1998): 443.

59. Michael Mertes, "Germany's Social and Political Culture: Change through Consensus?" in *Daedalus* 123.1 (1994): 21.

60. According to the study in question, incidentally, the actual world champion "joiners" are the Dutch, while the Japanese rank near the bottom of the scale. James E. Curtis, Douglas E. Baer, Edward G. Grabb, "Nations of Joiners: Explaining Voluntary Association Membership in Democratic Societies," in *American Sociological Review* 66.6 (2001): 791–2, 801.

61. Robert D. Putnam, "Bowling Alone: America's Declining Social Capital," in *Journal of Democracy* 6.1 (1995): 67. Putnam is by no means the inventor of the concept of social capital — in this regard, see Putnam, "Bowling Alone," 77, n. 4 — but he is among the most recent scholars to popularize the concept in the specific context of voluntary associations.

62. Putnam, "Bowling Alone," 65.

63. "Animexx e.V.: der Verein." URL: http://animexx.onlinewelten.com/verein.phtml. Last accessed 5 January, 2009. Animexx is in fact the sponsor of Germany's largest annual fan-organized anime and manga convention, Connichi, held in Kassel every September since 2003, as well as several smaller conventions. Connichi's nearest rival, AnimagiC, is a commercial venture; both are much smaller than comparable events in France, for example.

64. Putnam, "Bowling Alone," 74; Mertes, "Political Culture," 21.

65. "Heinrich Bauer Verlag: BRAVO." URL: http://www.bauerverlag.de/bravo.0.html. Last accessed 6 January, 2009.

66. Stefan Pannor, "Deutsche Mangas: Jung, weiblich, sexy ... Zeichnerin," in *Spiegel Online* (12 Nov. 2007). URL: http://www.spiegel.de/kultur/literatur/0,1518,516148,00.html. Last accessed 8 January, 2009.

67. "Animexx.de: *Dōjinshi*." URL: http://animexx.onlinewelten.com/doujinshi/. Last accessed 5 January, 2009.

68. In modern German usage, *Sodomie* usually refers to sexual intercourse with animals; its use as a synonym for anal sex is outdated.

69. "Animexx.de: Hinweise DJ-Hochladen (Wiki)." URL: http://animexx.onlinewelten.com/wiki/index.php/Hinweise_DJ-Hochladen. Last accessed 5 January 2009. New, EU–mandated legislation prohibiting depictions of sexual activity involving persons between fourteen and eighteen as "youth pornography" (*Jugendpornographie*), has not as yet led to any change in the Animexx.de regulations. It remains to be seen what impact the new laws will have on many branches of the entertainment industry, including *BRAVO*. The new legislation, which took effect on 5 November, 2008, is proclaimed in *Bundesgesetzblatt* 2008, Part 1, No. 50 (4 Nov. 2008): 2149–51. URL: http://www.bgblportal.de/BGBL/bgbl1f/bgbl108s2149.pdf. Last accessed 2 March, 2009.

70. "Verlag Schwarzer Turm." URL: http://www.schwarzerturm.de/. Last accessed 14 April, 2009.

71. Pannor, "Deutsche Mangas."

72. Various editors, *Paper Theatre*, 6 vols. (Weimar: Schwarzer Turm, 2006–9). Animexx also publishes its own *dōjinshi* anthologies independent of Schwarzer Turm; so far six volumes have appeared. Various editors, *Manga-Mixx*, 6 vols. (Buchenberg: Animexx, 2006–8).

73. "Animexx.de: *Dōjinshi*: Lynea." URL: http://animexx.onlinewelten.com/doujinshi/zeichner/40070/. Last accessed 5 January, 2009.

74. Anna Hollmann, "Stupid Story," in *Paper Theatre 1*, ed. Simone Xie and Anna Pätzke (Weimar: Schwarzer Turm, 2006): 177–89; *Paper Theatre 2*, ed. Simone Xie and Anna Pätzke (Weimar: Schwarzer Turm, 2006): 175–91; *Paper Theatre 3*, ed. Anna Pätzke and Vicky Danko (Weimar: Schwarzer Turm, 2006): 79–97.

75. The Sondermann Comics Prize is awarded by popular vote and sponsored by the Book Fair, the Web site www.comicforum.de, *Spiegel* magazine's online division, and the newspaper *Frankfurter Rundschau*. Although the prize is prestigious, due partly to the status of the Frankfurt Book Fair as the world's largest, there is no monetary award. "Comic-Preis Sondermann wird im Comic-Zentrum der Frankfurter Buchmesse verliehen: Die Publikumslieblinge stehen fest," *Frankfurter Buchmesse*, URL: https://de.book-fair.com/fbf/jour nalists/press_releases/fbf/detail.aspx?c20f0587-85d5-44d3-a9a4-eb75d0c6143b=eb0316e3-af29-4156-8bbc-a32fa1417e2c. Last accessed 6 January, 2009; "Taïfu Comics: Voir le sujet — DES AUTEURES ALLEMANDES ET AMERICAINE CHEZ TAÏFU !!!!!," *Taïfu Comics*, URL: http://taifu-comics.com/forum/viewtopic.php?t= 2815. Last accessed 6 January, 2009.

76. Böckem, "Sind die süüüß!," 11. This strategy has already led to the successful translation and export of TOKYOPOP artists Christina Plaka, Anike Hage and Pink Psycho, whose works are now available in English: Christina Plaka, *Yonen Buzz*, 4 vols. (Los Angeles: TOKYOPOP, 2006–8); Anike Hage, *Gothic Sports*, 3 vols. (Los Angeles: TOKYOPOP, 2007–8); Pink Psycho, *In the End* (Los Angeles: TOKYOPOP, 2008). Carlsen's Judith Park is also part of this strategy, with her *Y Square* not only appearing in English, as mentioned earlier, but also in French, Greek, Italian and Russian. Hollmann's manga, however, is both the first clear-cut boy's love case, and the first case in which Animexx.de has played an essential role.

77. Beatrice Beckmann, ed., *Hungry Hearts*, 2 vols. (Weimar: Schwarzer Turm, 2007, 2008).

78. "Fireangels Verlag." URL: http://www.fireangels.net/. Last accessed 14 April, 2009; "Homepage" [The Wild Side]. URL: http://www.thewildside.biz/index2.php. Last accessed 14 April, 2009.

79. "Animexx.de: *Dōjinshi* 'Lost and Found.'" URL: http://animexx.onlinewelten.com/doujinshi/zeich ner/228768/output/24497/. Last accessed 5 January, 2009; Zombiesmile [Makiko Ponczeck], *Lost and Found* (Amberg: The Wild Side, 2007).

80. "Animexx.de: *Dōjinshi* 'K-A-E — Quit / Continue (Band 6).'" URL: http://animexx.onlinewelten.com/ doujinshi/zeichner/4607/output/32489/. Last accessed 5 January, 2009; Martina "Chiron-san" Peters, *K-A-E 29th Secret: Blank File* (Dachau: Fireangels, 2005); *K-A-E 29th Secret: Invisible Sound* (Dachau: Fireangels, 2008).

81. Fiske, "Cultural Economy," 39.

82. "Interview mit Fahr Sindram auf mangaka.de." *Mangaka.de.* URL: http://www.mangaka.de/index. php?page= interview-mit-fahr-sindram;PHPSESSID=1i9ssuosars9dkhvlqc3bbb2r18ng3ft. Last accessed 6 January, 2009; Burkhard Ihme, "Papiertheater im Schwarzen Turm: Ein Interview mit Michael Möller (Mille) und Stefanie Urbig (Schwarze Katze)," in *COMIC!-Jahrbuch 2007*, ed. Burkhard Ihme (Stuttgart: Interessenband Comic e. V. ICOM, 2007): 56.

83. Fahr Sindram, "Losing Neverland," in *Paper Theatre 2*, ed. Simone Xie and Anna Pätzke (Weimar: Schwarzer Turm, 2006): 93–108.

84. No reference to Michael Jackson's Neverland estate in California was intended, but Sindram admits that the coincidence is apt. Fahr Sindram, *Losing Neverland*, Vol. 1 (Berlin: Butter & Cream, 2006): n.p.

85. Fahr Sindram, *Losing Neverland*, Vol. 1 (Berlin: Butter & Cream, 2006): n.p.; "Interview mit Fahr Sindram." *Mangaka.de.*

86. "Butter & Cream." URL: http://www.butter-and-cream.com/butt/faq.htm. Last accessed 6 January, 2009; "Interview mit Fahr Sindram: Comicgate gek-Comicmagazin mit Rezensionen, Interviews, Webcomics und vielem mehr." *Comicgate.* URL: http://www.comicgate.de/content/view/420/76/. Last accessed 6 January, 2009.

87. "AnimeY — Fahr Sindram im AnimeY Interview!" *AnimeY Online Magazin.* URL: http://www.animey. net/specials/ 77. Last accessed 6 January, 2009.

88. "Rat für Nachhaltige Entwicklung: Mandate given to the German Council." *Rat für Nachhaltige Entwicklung.* URL: http://www.nachhaltigkeitsrat.de/en/the-council/mandate-given-to-the-german-council/?blstr=0. Last accessed 8 January, 2009.

89. "Butter & Cream." *Butter & Cream Verlagsgesellschaft.* URL: http://www.butter-and-cream.com/ butt/faq.htm. Last accessed 6 January, 2009; "Interview mit Fahr Sindram auf mangaka.de." *Mangaka.de.* URL: http://www.mangaka.de/index.php?page=interview-mit-fahr-sindram;PHPSESSID=1i9ssuosars9d khvlqc3bbb2r18ng3ft. Last accessed 6 January, 2009.

90. Martina Peters, *E-Motional* (Hamburg: Carlsen, 2007). Note that an artist's preferred nickname is not always identical with the nickname he or she uses on Animexx.de — where Hollmann, for example, is "Lynea" rather than "Cross."

Bibliography

"Animexx e.V.: der Verein." *Animexx.* http://animexx.onlinewelten.com/verein.phtml (accessed 5 January, 2009).

"AnimeY — Fahr Sindram im AnimeY Interview!" *AnimeY Online Magazin.* http://www.animey.net/specials/77 (accessed 6 January, 2009).

Beckmann, Beatrice, ed. *Hungry Hearts.* 2 vols. Weimar: Schwarzer Turm, 2007, 2008.

Berndt, Jaqueline. *Phänomen Manga: Comic-Kultur in Japan.* Berlin: Edition q, 1995.

Böckem, Jörg. "Sind die süüüß!" *KulturSpiegel* 9 (Sept. 2006): 8–11.

Böckem, Jörg and Christoph Dallach. "Manga Chutney." *KulturSpiegel* 7 (1 July 2002): 20–23.

"*BRAVO.*" www.bravo.de (accessed 3 March, 2009).

Bundesgesetzblatt 2008, Part 1, No. 50 (4 Nov. 2008), http://www.bgblportal.de/BGBL/bgbl1f/bgbl108s2149.pdf (accessed 2 March, 2009).

Buschová, Lenka. *Freaky Angel.* Cologne: Egmont, 2005.

"Butter & Cream." *Butter & Cream Verlagsgesellschaft.* http://www.butter-and-cream.com/butt/faq.htm (accessed 6 January, 2009).

"CARLSEN MANGA! Startseite." http://www.carlsen.de/web/manga/index (accessed 14 April, 2009).

Cheng Ying Zhou. *Shanghai Passion.* Cologne: Egmont, 2005.

"Comic, Comics, Manga, Anime bei PaniniComics.de." http://www.paninicomics.de/?s=serie&gs_gruppe=8 (accessed 14 April, 2009).

"Comic-Preis Sondermann wird im Comic-Zentrum der Frankfurter Buchmesse verliehen: Die Publikumslieblinge stehen fest." *Frankfurter Buchmesse.* https://de.book-fair.com/fbf/journalists/press_releases/fbf/detail.aspx?c20f0587-85d5-44d3-a9a4-eb75d0c6143b=eb0316e3-af29-4156-8bbc-a32fa1417e2c (accessed 6 January, 2009).

Curtis, James E., Douglas E. Baer, and Edward G. Grabb. "Nations of Joiners: Explaining Voluntary Association Membership in Democratic Societies." *American Sociological Review* 66, no. 6 (2001): 783–805.

Dolle-Weinkauff, Bernd. "The Attractions of Intercultural Exchange: *Manga* Market and *Manga* Reception in Germany." *Mobile and Popular Culture in Asia.* Asia Culture Forum 2006. http://www.cct.go.kr/data/acf2006/mobile/mobile_0402_Bernd%20Dolle-Weinkauff.pdf (accessed 10 March, 2009).

"Fireangels Verlag." http://www.fireangels.net/ (accessed 14 April, 2009).

Fiske, John. "The Cultural Economy of Fandom." In *The Adoring Audience: Fan Culture and Popular Media,* edited by Lisa A. Lewis, 30–49. London: Routledge, 1992.

Gregson, Kimberly S. "What if the Lead Character Looks Like Me? Girl Fans of *Shoujo Anime* and Their Web Sites." In *Girl Wide Web: Girls, the Internet, and the Negotiation of Identity,* edited by Sharon R. Mazzarella, 121–40. New York: Peter Lang, 2005.

Hage, Anike. *Gothic Sports.* 4 vols. Hamburg: TOKYOPOP, 2006–8.

_____. *Gothic Sports.* 3 vols. Los Angeles: TOKYOPOP, 2007–8.

Heilbronner, Oded. "The German Bourgeois Club as a Political and Social Structure in the Late Nineteenth and Early Twentieth Centuries." *Continuity and Change* 13.3 (1998): 443–473.

"Heinrich Bauer Verlag: BRAVO." http://www.bauerverlag.de/bravo.0.html (accessed 6 January, 2009).

Herrmann, Mareike. "'Feeling Better' with *Bravo*: German Girls and Their Popular Youth Magazine." In *Millennium Girls: Today's Girls Around the World,* edited by Sherrie Inness, 213–42. Lanham, MD: Rowman and Littlefield, 1998.

Hollmann, Anna. *Stupid Story.* 2 vols. Hamburg: TOKYOPOP, 2008–9.

_____. "Stupid Story." In *Paper Theatre 1,* edited by Simone Xie and Anna Pätzke, 177–89. Weimar: Schwarzer Turm, 2006.

_____. "Stupid Story." In *Paper Theatre 2,* edited by Simone Xie and Anna Pätzke, 175–91. Weimar: Schwarzer Turm, 2006.

_____. "Stupid Story." In *Paper Theatre 3,* edited by Anna Pätzke and Vicky Danko, 79–97. Weimar: Schwarzer Turm, 2006.

Holzer, Steffi, Martin Jurgeit and Sascha Krämer. "Es muss nicht immer Japan sein: *Mangas* aus deutschen Landen." *Comixene* 78 (2004): 6–14.

"Homepage." The Wild Side. http://www.thewildside.biz/index2.php (accessed 14 April, 2009).

Ihme, Burkhard. "Papiertheater im Schwarzen Turm: Ein Interview mit Michael Möller (Mille) und Stefanie Urbig (Schwarze Katze)." In *COMIC!-Jahrbuch 2007,* edited by Burkhard Ihme. Stuttgart: Interessenband Comic e. V. ICOM, 2007: 56–60.

"Interview mit Fahr Sindram auf mangaka.de." *Mangaka.de.* http://www.mangaka.de/index.php?page=interview-mit-fahr-sindram;PHPSESSID=1i9ssuosars9dkhvlqc3bbb2r18ng3ft (accessed 6 January, 2009).

"Interview mit Fahr Sindram: Comicgate — Comicmagazin mit Rezensionen, Interviews, Webcomics und vielem mehr." *Comicgate.* http://www.comicgate.de/content/view/420/76/ (accessed 6 January, 2009).

Ishinomori Shōtarō. *Japan GmbH*. Bonn: Verlag Norman Rentrop, 1989.

Jenkins, Henry. *Textual Poachers: Television Fans and Participatory Culture*. London: Routledge, 1992.

Jüngst, Heike. "Japanese Comics in Germany." *Perspectives: Studies in Translatology* 12, no. 2 (2004): 83–105.

______. "*Manga* in Germany: From Translation to Simulacrum." *Perspectives: Studies in Translatology* 14, no. 4 (2006): 248–259.

Knigge, Andreas C. *Alles über Comics: Eine Entdeckungsreise von den Höhlenbildern bis zum Manga*. Hamburg: Europa Verlag, 2004.

Könen, Christian. "Interview mit Georg Tempel, Verlagsleiter von EMA." *AnimePRO*. www.animepro.de (accessed 13 April 2006).

Labs, Robert. *Dragic Master*. 2 vols. Hamburg: Carlsen, 2001, 2005.

______. *Crewman 3*. 2 vols. Hamburg: Carlsen, 2003–4.

Liesaus, Diana. *Musouka*. 2 vols. Cologne: Egmont, 2007.

"Manganet." *EGMONT Verlagsgesellschaften mbH; Egmont Manga & Anime*. http://www.manganet.de/index.php (accessed 14 April, 2009).

Malone, Paul M. "Home-grown *Shōjo Manga* and the Rise of Boys' Love Among Germany's 'Forty-Niners.'" *Intersections: Gender and Sexuality in Asia and the Pacific* 21 (April 2009), http://intersections.anu.edu.au/issue20/malone.htm (accessed 14 April, 2009).

______. "*Manga* in Europe." In *Manga: An Anthology of Global and Cultural Perspectives*, edited by Toni Johnson-Woods. New York: Continuum, forthcoming.

______. "*Mangascape* Germany: Comics as Intercultural Neutral Ground." In *Comics as Nexus of Culture*, edited by Mark Berninger and Gideon Haberkorn. Jefferson, NC: McFarland, forthcoming.

Marx, Sascha Nils and Stefan Voss. *Naglayas Herz*. Cologne: Egmont, 2002.

Matsui, Midori. "Little Girls were Little Boys: Displaced Femininity in the Representation of Homosexuality in Japanese Girls' Comics." In *Feminism and the Politics of Difference*, edited by Sneja Gunew and Anna Yeatman, 177–96. Boulder, Colorado, and San Francisco: Westview Press, 1993.

McLelland, Mark. "No Climax, No Point, No Meaning? Japanese Women's Boy-Love Sites on the Internet." *Journal of Communication Inquiry* 24, no. 3 (2000): 274–91.

Mertes, Michael. "Germany's Social and Political Culture: Change through Consensus?" *Daedalus* 123, no. 1 (1994): 1–32.

Nakazawa, Keiji. *Barfuß durch Hiroshima: Eine Bildergeschichte gegen den Krieg*. Reinbek: Rowohlt Verlag, 1982.

Ōkami Mineko. *Lumen Lunae*. 5 vols. Cologne: Egmont, 2002–2003.

Ōtomo Katsuhiro. *Akira*. 19 vols. Hamburg: Carlsen Verlag, 1991–6.

Ozaki Minami. *Zetsuai 1989*. 5 vols. Hamburg: Carlsen, 2000–2001.

Pannor, Stefan. "Deutsche Mangas: Jung, weiblich, sexy ... Zeichnerin." *Spiegel Online* (12 Nov. 2007). http://www.spiegel.de/kultur/literatur/0,1518,516148,00.html (accessed 8 January, 2009).

______. "*Dragon Ball* und die Folgen." *Deutschland online* (25 March 2008). http://www.magazine-deutschland.de/de/artikel/artikelansicht/article/dragonball-und-die-folgen.html (accessed 3 March, 2009).

Park, Judith. *Y Square*. Hamburg: Carlsen, 2005.

______. *Y Square*. New York: Yen Press, 2008.

Peters, Martina ["Chiron-san"]. *E-Motional*. Hamburg: Carlsen, 2007.

______. *K-A-E 29th Secret: Blank File*. Dachau: Fireangels, 2005.

______. *K-A-E 29th Secret: Invisible Sound*. Dachau: Fireangels, 2008.

Pink Psycho. *In the End*. Hamburg: TOKYOPOP, 2006.

______. *In the End*. Los Angeles: TOKYOPOP, 2008.

Plaka, Christina. *Yonen Buzz*. 4 vols. Hamburg: TOKYOPOP, 2005–8.

______. *Yonen Buzz*. 4 vols. Los Angeles: TOKYOPOP, 2006–8.

Putnam, Robert D. "Bowling Alone: America's Declining Social Capital." *Journal of Democracy* 6, no.1 (1995): 65–78.

Ragawa, Marimo. *New York New York*. 4 vols. Planet Manga, 2002.

"Rat für Nachhaltige Entwicklung: Mandate given to the German Council." *Rat für Nachhaltige Entwicklung*. http://www.nachhaltigkeitsrat.de/en/the-council/mandate-given-to-the-german-council/?blstr=0 (accessed 8 January, 2009).

Seebeck, Jürgen. *Bloody Circus*. 2 vols. Hamburg: Carlsen, 2001.

Sindram, Fahr. "Losing Neverland." In *Paper Theatre 2*, edited by Simone Xie and Anna Pätzke, 93–108. Weimar: Schwarzer Turm, 2006.

______. *Losing Neverland*. 2 vols. Berlin: Butter & Cream, 2006–7.

Suzuki, Kazuko. "Pornography or Therapy? Japanese Girls Creating the *Yaoi* Phenomenon." In *Millennium Girls: Today's Girls Around the World*, edited by Sherrie Inness, 243–67. Lanham, MD: Rowman & Littlefield, 1998.

"Taïfu Comics: Voir le sujet — DES AUTEURES ALLEMANDES ET AMERICAINE CHEZ TAÏFU !!!!!" *Taïfu Comics.* http://taifu-comics.com/forum/viewtopic.php?t=2815 (accessed 6 January, 2009).

Takeuchi, Naoko. *Sailor Moon.* 18 vols. Mannheim: Reiner Feest Verlag, 1998–2000.

Tananaga, Hinako. *Kleiner Schmetterling.* 3 vols. Hamburg: TOKYOPOP, 2005–2007.

Thorn, Matthew. "Girls and Women Getting Out of Hand: The Pleasures and Politics of Japan's Amateur Comics Community." In *Fanning the Flames: Fans and Consumer Culture in Contemporary Japan,* edited by William W. Kelly, 169–87. New York: State University of New York Press, 2004.

"TOKYOPOP — Manga, Manhwa, Manhua und Cine-Manga." *TOKYOPOP.de.* http://www.tokyopop.de/ (accessed 14 April, 2009).

Toriyama, Akira. *Dragon Ball.* 42 vols. Hamburg: Carlsen, 1997–2000.

Valenti, Kristy L. "'Stop, My Butt Hurts!' The *Yaoi* Invasion." *The Comics Journal* 269 (July 2005): 121–25.

Wood, Andrea. "'Straight' Women, Queer Texts: Boy-Love Manga and the Rise of a Global Counterpublic." *WSQ: Women's Studies Quarterly* 34, nos. 1 & 2 (2006): 394–414.

Various, ed. *Paper Theatre.* 6 vols. Weimar: Schwarzer Turm, 2006–9.

Various, ed. *Manga-Mixx.* 6 vols. Buchenberg: Animexx, 2006–8.

"Verlag Schwarzer Turm." *Verlag Schwarzer Turm.* http://www.schwarzerturm.de/ (accessed 14 April, 2009).

Zombiesmile [Makiko Ponczeck]. *Lost and Found.* Amberg: The Wild Side, 2007.

3

———————

Boys' Love Thrives in Conservative Indonesia

Yamila Abraham

In 2004 I started the boys' love graphic novel publishing company Yaoi Press and put out the first call for artist submissions. It was answered by a studio in Indonesia. I recall being very concerned that they would object to the work due to the erotic and homosexual content.

"Before we go any further," I said in my first email reply to them, "you should know that I need artists to draw gay love scenes between two men. I know that Indonesia is a Muslim country. I understand if you want to withdraw your submission."[1]

The studio head Adetyar responded, "Yamilla [*sic*] is not a problem for us. Anything you need we will draw. Some artists will only draw hugging and kissing for you. Some artists will only draw love that's not hardcore. But some will also draw hardcore. We ask you not send contributor copies for hardcore because is illegal here. But all others you send."[2]

In a later email he expanded, "Yes we are Muslim country but lots of yaoi fans here. In studio even there are fans. Lots drawing dojinshi with yaoi."[3]

This was at a time when I still had to explain what BL was to most people I met at fan conventions in the U.S. I was surprised to learn that BL was such a sensation in Indonesia. This was a country that not only did not have any commercial BL products, but had legal and cultural restrictions against them.

I have learned a great deal about BL in Indonesia over the years. I thought I had a good grasp of what was going on there, but in tackling this paper, I found I was still oversimplifying an extremely complex situation. Political, historical, religious, and cultural factors all influence the proliferation of BL in Indonesia.

Indonesia once had a tradition of same-sex relationships before it was colonized by the Dutch. Despite this history, it is becoming increasingly intolerant of homosexuality and erotic works under strengthening Muslim political and social influences. The population of Indonesia is 87 percent Muslim,[4] a religion that condemns homosexuality.[5] Most of the population want the tenets of Islam incorporated into the laws, as was proven on a vote for a morality bill recently.[6] However, Indonesia is no longer a military dictatorship and fights to ensure that it doesn't become one again. Indonesians won't tolerate an oppressive government interfering in their personal lives.

This creates a political and legal dichotomy that has had both direct and indirect effects on BL fans within the country. The Indonesian boys' love artist and fan community has successfully exported BL works out of the country and is enjoying an underground popularity online and at conventions. However, I fear Indonesia's new anti-pornography laws endanger this subculture's future.

Background

I have worked with more than thirty Indonesian artists and writers over the last four years as the publisher of Yaoi Press. Several of these creators I consider close friends. I spend time chatting online with them through the use of Internet Relay Chat. I have acted as an agent on behalf of an Indonesian publisher to attempt to have its *shōjo* graphic novels licensed in English, and I have acted as an agent on behalf of individual Indonesian artists to help them break in with other publishers with whom I am acquainted.

Over the years, I've taken an interest in Indonesian culture. Certain artist friends are happy to see my interest and eagerly tell me about their country.

Among these friends is Rhea Silvan, who assisted me tremendously in researching this paper. Silvan is a Chinese-descended Indonesian who lives in the central island of Java. She is a widely published manga-style artist who has worked for publishers in the U.S. as well as Indonesia.

Silvan was the first Indonesian I got to know who was a passionate BL fan. When she did some screen-toning work for Yaoi Press, I sent her a copy of our graphic novel *Winter Demon* as a gift along with her other contributor copies. She fell in love with this story and insisted that she be given the opportunity to draw a volume of the series. The current artists were kind enough to let her have the project (Fig. 1).

Silvan is the top Indonesian artist with whom Yaoi Press works. Her artwork is nearly indistinguishable from authentic Japanese manga, which appeals to our audience. She is not common among Indonesian artists. In addition to her formal art training she went to a manga art school in Jakarta order to learn the Japanese illustration style.

From Comics to Manga to Boys' Love

The development of BL fandom in Indonesia parallels the way most fans are now discovering the genre in the U.S. Indonesian BL fans began as manga fans.

Just as in the U.S., indigenous comics were the popular sequential art form prior to manga's introduction. These comics were called *cerita bergambar,* "story with pictures," and became prevalent after World War II.[7] The 1960s and '70s are considered the "Golden Age" of comics in Indonesia due largely in part to the development of the comic rental kiosk.[8] This boom was shortened by different government figures who denounced comics as "Western poison" that "fostered laziness." Manga came about at just the right time: there was a vacuum of indigenous comics starting in the 1980s. Hafiz Ahmad, Beny Maulana, and Alvanov Apalanzani explain the problem:

> Older artists from previous generations never passed down his/her ability to the next generation, while at the same time they could no longer catch up with the changes and trends. The second problem was there was no attempts from the publishers to encourage artists' regeneration or local comics, many of them only seemed to care with profit rather than public benefit.[9]

Publisher Elex Media Komputindo brought the first translated Japanese comics to Indonesia in 1990. These works became wildly popular, and eventually ninety percent of all comic imports were coming from Japan.[10]

The comic rental kiosks still exist as several franchises across Indonesia. Artist W. Tony

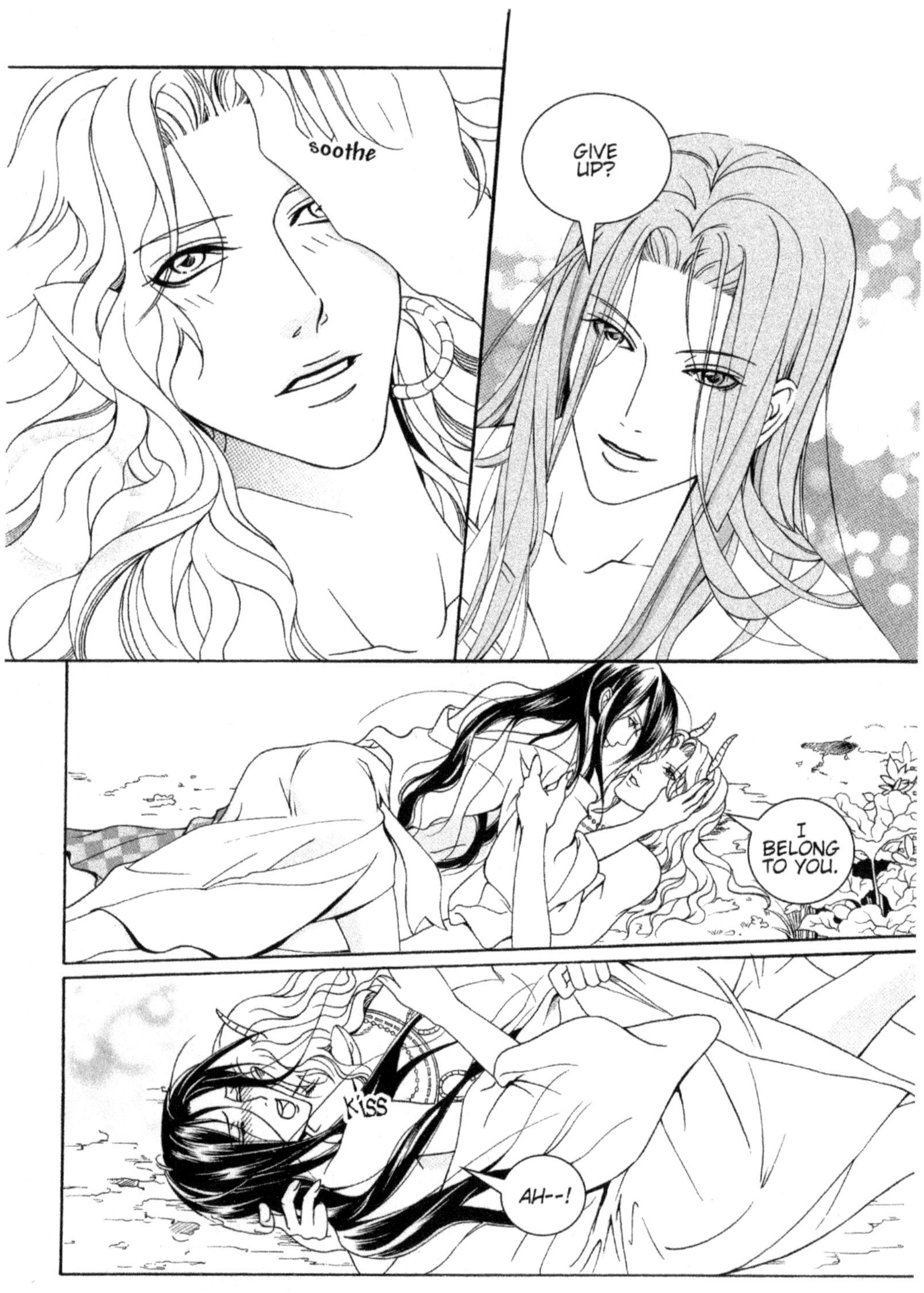

Figure 1. By Rhea Silvan. *Winter Demon 4*, Copyright © 2008 Yaoi Press LLC.

explained to me during an Internet chat session in March 22, 2009, that the shelves are filled with manga now.

"It's very easy to read manga in Java," Tony typed, referring to Indonesia's largest island, where half the total population lives. "You have everywhere to buy if you want, or you can still rent and read all you want at the Starfly lounges. The cost is around rp.12000 ($1.07) to buy a manga graphic novel, or rp.2000 ($.17) to rent."

Manga has been established in Indonesia for over a decade. Television networks started airing anime in earnest in 1996 with *Rurouni Kenshin* on SCTV.[11] This brings us to the current state of Indonesia, where the likes of *Naruto, One Piece,* and *Death Note* have grown into a national obsession among younger people. The indigenous sequential art is now manga-style. Manga art schools are opening on Indonesia's main island.[12]

BL fans were certainly begotten from manga fans. However, no commercial BL is distributed in the country. In a November 6, 2008, email, Silvan described a situation where a publisher "accidentally" put out *Ghost,* a manga that's considered to be "*shōnen-ai,*" having a very tame romance between two male characters.

> It was serialized in few volumes, and had high appreciation from fans. It was only shonen-ai rated, but the editor once said that she often get mail complaints from mothers that were afraid about the contents of a manga where a boy is falling in love with another boy. Even though that wasn't depicted too clear in the story.
> The most that big Indonesian publisher is willing to print is only any books that can be considered safe, such as: *Yami no matsuei* by Matsushita Yoko or *X* by CLAMP.[13]

Manga publishers in Indonesia face a dilemma. They are aware of the demand for BL but are unable to tread even lightly in that direction without an outcry from parents. Publisher Elex Media Komputindo puts out manga-style works by Indonesians. Silvan explained in the same email that these works are where one sees the most hints of *shōnen-ai:* "Even though the characters don't kiss, you know there's something going on because of how they speak and react to each other. It's maybe something a parent wouldn't assume is gay, but fans of yaoi know what the artist is trying to say."

Liberal Democracy/Conservative Religious State

The fact that Indonesia is an Asian country with an extensive trade history with Japan facilitated the successful introduction of manga. The primary reason there are BL fans in Indonesia is because commercial manga and anime is popular there.

It is very telling of Indonesia that frivolous and secular recreational items are tolerated in their popular culture. This is not the same in neighboring Malaysia, for instance, where the Harry Potter novels are banned for their depictions of "magic, sorcery, wizardry, witchcraft, Satanism, occult, and sheer evil."[14]

Do not presume, however, that this means that conservative Muslim politicians have not scored significant wins in the Indonesian Parliament. They have enjoyed great success, along with liberal democrats. Indonesia has a unique history in which the conservative religious party and the liberal democrat party were recently fighting on the same side. According to Nathaniel Myers,

> Both opposed the surviving elements of Suharto's government, distrusted the military's intentions, and sought to tackle the worst legacies of the old regime, like rampant corruption, a bloated bureaucracy, and a politically powerful military.[15]

Democracy took root in Indonesia with tremendous speed after the first truly democratic elections in 2006. U.S. Secretary of State Condoleezza Rice praised Indonesia for its "vibrant democracy" and its "deserved reputation for tolerance and inclusion and for the celebration of diversity [which] is indeed an inspiration to the entire world"; at the same time that Rice visited, however, Indonesia performed ruthless crackdowns on adultery, public displays of affection, and public drinking.[16]

Indonesia is a true democracy, not a theocracy. However, democracy is not the same as liberalism, as Myers points out: "The aspirations of Indonesia's liberals and religious conservatives are inherently competing, and ultimately Indonesians will have to make a choice."[17]

For example, sexuality of any kind is seen as a danger for unwed youths. A non-government organization called Yayasan Pelita Ilmu distributes a monthly magazine to school-aged youths.[18] One issue showed the fate of a pregnant, unwed girl. Her options were to have a dangerous illegal abortion and continue her studies or get married at a very young age and presumably give them up. Unwed women have no access to family planning or reproductive health services. Still, this was more favorable than the scenario the magazine gave for a homosexual boy, described by Brigitte M. Holzner and Dede Oetomo:

> The article reports the story of a 17-year-old boy with homosexual interests who was invited after a cyber chat to a Gay and Lesbian Room, where he met a 25-year-old man who said he would introduce him to the gay world. He was taken to an apartment where he was raped by two men, who tied his feet and covered his mouth with tape. The boy suffocated and died. The perpetrators cut up his body, put the parts in a suitcase and left it in front of a post office.[19]

For now, Indonesia's new democracy proves to be tolerant of frivolous secular diversions so long as they are not pornographic in nature. It is similar to the USA in that the same standards do not apply to violence: gory battles and graphic beheadings are common in Indonesian media.

Law

Vague, long-standing laws have indirectly stifled BL in Indonesia. Sections 281 and 282 of the KUHP[20] restrict prurient materials. Section 281 prohibits the distribution of anything that might arouse a teenager's sexual urges, and Section 282 states that anyone who distributes text or images that violate the "ethical norm" may be punished for up to nine months.

These laws were applied in the banning of *Playboy* magazine from Indonesia in 2006.[21] Two powerful Muslim religious organizations act as lobbyists in Indonesia: the FPI (Front Pembela Islam or Front Defense Islam) and the MUI (Majelis Ulama Indonesia or Ulama Assembly of Indonesia), with the FPI being the more militant of the two.

In an email on November 6, 2008, Rhea Silvan wrote, "These religious organizations are the first heard when there's printed material with pornographic aspects. When there was news of Playboy going to be published in Indonesia, the leader of MUI, Din Syamsuddin, was one of the most vocal in asking the government to stop Playboy distributing their issues. The FPI protest also. The FPI members attacked the Playboy office and threw stones at the workers."

The *Playboy* ban occurred despite the fact that the Indonesian version was not going to include nude pictures and made "[a] promise to respect local values and to limit distribution to avoid sale to minors."[22]

The Indonesian parliament debated for ten years about updating the older laws with a broader anti-pornography bill. One of the parties that pushed for the change was the PKS (Partai Keadilan Sejahtera or the "Prosperous Justice Party"), which is based on the precepts of Islam. A new bill was finally passed on October 30, 2008 that more clearly defined what would be illegal. Peter Gelling of the International Herald Tribune described the bill:

> The bill outlaws pornographic acts and images, broadly defining pornography as "man-made sexual materials in the form of drawings, sketches, illustrations, photographs, text, voice, sound, moving pictures, animation, cartoons, poetry, conversations and gestures." It also makes illegal public performances which could "incite sexual desire."[23]

The protracted battle over the bill shows the deep concern many Indonesians had over Islam dictating state policy.[24] This harkens back to the liberal/conservative tensions referenced earlier. In this most recent instance, the conservative religious parties were clearly victorious.

A form of "freedom of speech" protection does exist in Indonesia through the Undang-Undang Dasar 45 (The Constitution of Indonesia) in section 28: "Freedom for gathering and socializing, pouring out your thoughts in the form of writing and speech, is protected by law." However, "of course this does not protect you if you violate ethical norms," Silvan wrote in her November 2008 email. "It never would apply to pornographic writings and speech." She further expanded on the situation:

> Indonesia is a country with high restriction of pornographic contents, but at the same time the restriction is not strong enough since there are some parts which can be overlooked. The reason is either the cops get bribed enough to let the issue go, or they have difficulties to keep these restricted material distributions at bay. For example, porn videos still exist in the market. Illegal mangas are also distributed free here in Indonesia. Some of it was translated Japanese yaoi mangas. They took the scans directly from various scanning sites in internet, translating it poorly to Indonesian language and printed it out with low quality. I don't know why, but government doesn't seem to have their eyes focused in these illegal mangas. Maybe they're too busy with anything else. The only thing I know though, these yaoi mangas sold much in higher number than other genres.

Culture and Religion

One of the common Western assumptions about Muslim countries is that women living in them have fewer rights than men. Indonesia, however, has surpassed the U.S. in the protection of women's rights. It has built gender equality into its constitution. In addition, Indonesia signed the Convention on the Elimination of All Forms of Discrimination Against Women (CEDAW) in 1980 and ratified it in 1984. CEDAW was a convention established by the UN General Assembly in 1979. Ratifying the convention formalized Indonesia's commitment to ending all forms of discrimination against women, under whatever grounds and reasons.[25] The country elected a female vice president in 1999 who later won the presidency in 2001.

Furthermore, there is no equivalent to Iran's "Morality Police"[26] in Indonesia. Women in Indonesia feel free to pursue their BL interest both in private and at public fan conventions. Yet, despite the large number of women freely producing and enjoying BL, most homosexuals in the country remain closeted. There is nothing to show a correlation between the rise in BL's popularity and the level of acceptance of homosexuality in Indonesia.

Homosexuality was historically accepted in Indonesia until Protestant Dutch settlers came and stigmatized it; same-sex customs still exist in remote Sulewesi villages as the remnants of an ancient, widespread Indonesian tradition, according to Richard Ammon:

> A "warok" is a charismatic conductor of ceremonies who has one or several young male apprentices called "gemblaks." Being a gemblak was considered a privilege since it conveys status as well as the boys' families receiving a dowry. The duties include caring for the warok in his household as well as assisting him in ceremonies, which sometimes require the apprentice to dress as women, in costumes and masks. Sexual intimacy is usually assumed to be part of the arrangement, but not always. After about 17 years of age the boys give up their positions in the esteemed household and eventually go on to marriage — well trained in conjugal matters.[27]

This history does not affect the official modern stance on homosexuality. All Islamic schools of thought and jurisprudence consider gay acts to be illegal. The penalties differ between two schools of thought: The Hanafite school, which is followed in Indonesia, teaches that no physical punishment is warranted. The Hanabalites (who are widely followed in the Arab world) teach that severe punishment is warranted.[28] Homosexuality is considered a bad way of life in Indonesia, akin to prostitution, but gays and lesbians are not bashed. Ammon further expanded in the same essay:

> Being gay is now felt to be a curse by young gays first coming out. As they age, they hide their friendships and underground affairs, going off to meet and cruise anonymously at malls or parks. If they can afford it, many go to the increasing number of bars, clubs and discos on designated nights to socialize with other gay friends in the safety of the dimly lit bar area or the flashing strobes of the dance floor.

Silvan has a number of gay friends and gave her description of the situation in a November 2008 online chat session:

> Gays have their own magazine, their own community at public place or internets. They like to gather together at certain cafes in mall, and wear specific thing to let other know that they're gay. Like a ring in pinky finger. Gays here are not as open like in US, they don't get as much freedom like it would be there.

Silvan further explained that relatively few gay men read BL: "Two of my gay friends like to read yaoi manga. Not many gays here know what that phrase meant since yaoi distributions are limited, except if you're a manga and anime lovers of course."

When asked if gay men browsed the BL *dōjinshi* tables at anime conventions, Silvan typed, "Of course not." She had difficulty comprehending a situation where someone could be openly gay outside of a private setting.

"If they are looking at gay manga everyone will know they are gay. Not just other gays, all the people around them," she typed. I explained to her that it was very common in the U.S. for gay men to browse BL products at anime conventions.

"It's presumed that the people selling at the booth and the other women browsing the booth are tolerant because we all love gay romance stories," I wrote to her.

"If a man goes to a booth of someone selling yaoi dojinshi the girl might think he's a pervert first, who is maybe flirting with her because she drew something dirty," Silvan replied. "If they show they are gay and like the dojinshi the girl will still be embarrassed. It's embarrassing for a man to look at such intimate things. She can be comfortable with other women, but this was not intended for men to see, even if gay. Not unless they are a friend they know from before."

It seems clear that in Indonesia it's a gay man's sex, rather than his sexual orientation, that inhibits him from browsing through BL booths.

Rhea Silvan was brought to the United States as a guest by Anime Central, a convention in Chicago, in May 2009. She had no trouble relating to American fans. There was very little culture shock for her. One notable incident occurred, however, when she sat in on the Yaoi Press industry panel and two cosplayers volunteered to give a passionate male/male kiss in front of the crowd. It was the first time she'd seen two men kiss. "That's something you would never see in Indonesia," she said.

The Internet

The Internet is the most important contributor to BL popularity in Indonesia. Although there is some government censorship, such as blocking all porn sites on the Internet service the government provides free to schools and libraries, access to the Internet remains mostly unrestricted. Most Indonesians on the main island of Java have Internet access, whether in their homes, as with Rhea Silvan, or accessed through Warnet Internet cafes or through a free wireless connection in public places.

Most Indonesian fans discover BL online. The discovery process is not much different there than anywhere else. "First you find some anime or manga you like," Silvan typed during our November 2008 online chat, "then you go online to find more about it. Maybe some pictures for you to print or forums to discuss it. When you search for your anime or manga you start finding sites with yaoi. You get curious about what these sites are about. Then you learn, and usually you get to love yaoi like everyone else. It makes your show like Death Note even more fun. It's something for women that we have all to ourselves to enjoy."

According to Silvan, the Indonesian Yaoi Front is the largest online forum for BL fans in Indonesia. The site links to over 75 member sites, which are usually shrines devoted to a particular BL couple. The site also defines BL, tells members where to find it, and recommends individual titles.

Indonesians also take advantage of several online institutions such as the deviantART gallery site, LiveJournal, or MySpace to share BL content. Silvan told me that downloading anime or manga translated to Indonesian is not too prevalent due to the inexpensive rentals fans can access. Rental kiosks that lend comic books, DVDs, and graphic novels are prevalent throughout Indonesia. "Of course we will download Anime and manga that is not available, like most yaoi," she added during the chat session.

Anime Conventions and Dōjinshi

Of course, fans found ways to converge long before the Internet was prevalent. Comic book and other conventions grew in earnest during the late 1990s in Indonesia. Several throughout the main island of Java celebrate manga and anime.

In our November chat session, Silvan wrote:

> There are many Anime, manga conventions being held in Indonesia. I've been to some of them. The only one that gave deepest impression to me is Animonster Sound 2006,

since that convention has the biggest doujinshis selling booth. Most of the conventions are only about cosplay competitions and some drawing contests, or about Japanese culture, shows like "Taiko."

Silvan added that a close friend of hers reported that Animonster Sound saw between 2,000 and 3,000 attendees.

Many of the conventions have an "artist alley" or "fan market" where amateur artists and *dōjinshika* can sell their creations.

"The comic/doujinshi booths are always dominated with yaoi-related work," Silvan typed. "Some of it has high ratings (adult), some are only shonen ai." An example of amateur Indonesian work can be seen in Figure 2.

Silvan described a scene in which the typical Indonesian rules toward pornography are relaxed: "The convention committee usually never state what the highest rating the artists can make, but they did make sure that a high rating works should be wrapped tightly in plastic cover and had a clear sign of warning on the front cover."

Anime conventions in Indonesia appear to provide an open and free environment for BL fans. "Indonesian yaoi artists get some really good feedbacks from fans when they're selling their works at convention," Silvan wrote. "Most who come are only interested in yaoi related things. Everyone knows that if you want to make some independent printed materials and sell it at convention you better make something with yaoi hints."

Conclusion

Indonesia is a nation desperate to be free of the military oppression it once suffered. However, its population is devout. Its citizens want their beliefs to matter in the political landscape. Right now there is great difficulty trying to finesse a balance between personal freedom and religious belief; if someone is caught with pornography, that person either pays a bribe and goes completely free or is condemned to severe punishment. There is no middle ground. As a result, Indonesia seems to be moving toward ever-more-restrictive pornography laws, as demonstrated by the recent anti-pornography bill that was passed. It looks as though Rhea Silvan will never see her BL work published in her home country. This is a lamentable situation.

I look at the BL situation in Indonesia from several perspectives. First, as a publisher, I wish that Indonesia were more open to erotic works. There is a large demand for BL in Indonesia that can not legitimately be met. I know that if the country were open to such works, there would be a thriving commercial BL market there. Yaoi Press titles would be licensed in the Indonesian language for sale the way they are in German. This would be fantastic for us, since 40 percent of our artists are Indonesian.

Second, as a fan of BL, I think there should be original Indonesian-language BL pouring out of this country. By limiting creators to *dōjinshi* tables at conventions the government is stifling a potential career avenue for hundreds of people. Their BL manga can be transmitted via Internet to U.S. publishers. I know firsthand of the immense talent you can find in Indonesia. This is what many fans want to create and what they want to buy.

Finally, as a friend of Rhea Silvan and W. Tony, I fear they will get caught and penalized for producing erotic work for Yaoi Press. They reassure me that the danger is not significant, but I still worry every time they upload files to our server and each time I mail them contributor copies of their books.

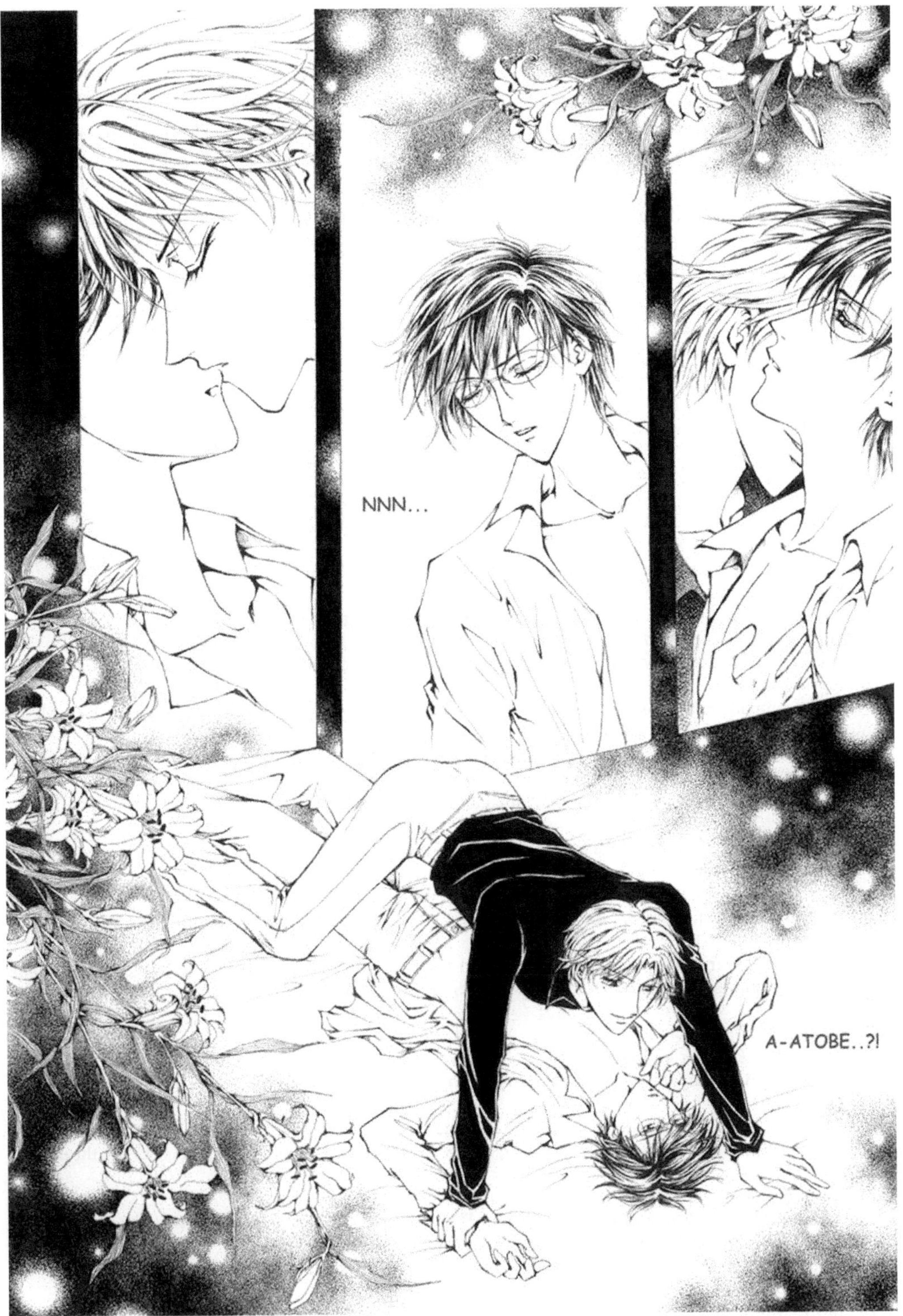

Figure 2. By Good Chaser. *Prince of Tennis* Dōjinshi, Copyright © 2007.

In one respect I find my attitude toward Indonesia to be similar to that of my friends living there. I am in love with this country. I try to focus on the good and ignore the bad. From what I've learned it seems that the more negative aspects usually can be ignored. As for the positive, I find Indonesia to be a nation where the people are kind and welcoming. The BL fans seem to be the same passionate gleeful young people I meet at fan conventions in the U.S.

I still expect BL to be judged in the harshest manner by Indonesian conservatives. I have little doubt that if fans were enjoying BL at the wrong time or in the wrong place there could be devastating consequences. Nevertheless, I hope that someday BL can become a legitimate part of Indonesia culture.

Notes

1. Yamila Abraham, "Re: we are artists for you," email message from author, May 13, 2004.

2. Adetyar Doe, "Re: we are artists for you," email message to author, May 14, 2004.

3. Adetyar Doe, "re: Western Union Sent!," email message to author, July 1, 2004.

4. William H. Frederick and Robert Worden, *Indonesia: A Country Study* (GPO for the Library of Congress. Washington. 1993).

5. "Islam and Homosexuality." Mission Islam, 6 Nov 2007. http://www.missionislam.com/knowledge/homosexualit.

6. Olivia Rondonuwu, "Indonesia's parliament passes anti-smut bill," *International Herald Tribune*, 30 Oct 2008, http://www.iht.com/articles/reuters/2008/10/30/asi.

7. Laine Berman, "LAINE BERMAN sheds a tear for the late great Indonesian comic," *Inside Indonesia*, 1998, http://insideindonesia.org/content/view/761/29/.

8. Andrea Tejokusumo, "'Manga' wields strong influence over local comics," *The Jakarta Post*, 4 Aug 2008, sec. Supplement.

9. Hafiz Ahmad, Beny Maulana, and Alvanov Apalanzani, *Histeria! Komikita.* (Indonesia: Elex Media Komputindo. 2006), 74–75.

10. Jill Forshee, *Culture and Customs of Indonesia (Culture and Customs of Asia)*, (Westport, CT: Greenwood Press, 2006).

11. "Anime News in Indonesia (^ ^)," Anihabara, 6 Aug 2003, http://east.sakura.ne.jp/aniba/aninews/id.htm.

12. Fadli Chan, "The Popularity of Manga Culture," *Dunia Perspektif*, 22 Feb 2009, http://fadlinx.blogspot.com/2009/02/popularity-of-manga-culture.html.

13. Rhea Silvan, "here you go, questionnaire," email message to author, Nov. 6, 2008.

14. Spiegalr. "Banned, Burned, Censored," Listal. 26 Apr 2009. http://www.listal.com/list/banned-burned-censored.

15. Nathaniel Myers, "In Indonesia, Freedom to Differ," *International Herald Tribune*, 26 Mar 2006, http://www.iht.com/articles/2006/03/28/opinion/edm.

16. Ibid., 1.

17. Ibid., 1.

18. Brigitte M. Holzner and Dede Oetomo, "Youth, Sexuality and Sex Education Messages in Indonesia: Issues of Desire and Control," *Reproductive Health Matters* 12, no. 23 (2004): 40–49.

19. Ibid., 44.

20. *Kitab Undang-undang Hukum Perdata* (Indonesia: Indonesian Government, 1945).

21. Guerin, Bill. "No Playmates for Indonesian Playboys," *Asian Times*, 10 Feb 2006, sec. Southeast Asia section.

22. Ibid., 1.

23. Peter Gelling, "Indonesia Passes Broad Anti-Pornography Bill," *International Herald Tribune*, 30 Oct 2008, http://www.iht.com/articles/2008/10/30/asia/indo.php

24. Pam Allen, "Challenging Diversity?: Indonesia's Anti-Pornography Bill," *Asian Studies Review* 31 (June 2007): 101–115.

25. Lily Z. Munir, "Gender equality in a new democracy," *The Jakarta Post*, 29 December 2006, http://www.thejakartapost.com/Outlook/pol03b.asp.

26. Ali Akbar Dareini, "Iran's Vicious Dresstapo Hits Unveiled Gals with Barbaric 'Banishment,'" *New*

York Post (April 25, 2007), http://www.nypost.com/seven/04252007/news/worldnews/ irans_vicious_dress tapo_hits_unveiled_gals_with_barbaric_banishment_worldnews_ali_akbar_dareini__ap_and_post_ wire_services.htm?page=1.

　　27. Richard Ammon, "Gay Indonesia — Jakarta," global gayz, May 2008, http://www.globalgayz.com/coun try/Indonesia/view/IDN/gay-indonesia-jakarta.

　　28. "Islam and Homosexuality," Mission Islam, April 2008, http://www.missionislam.com/knowledge/ homosexuality.htm.

Bibliography

Ahmad, Hafiz, Beny Maulana and Alvanov Apalanzani. *Histeria! Komikita.* Indonesia: Elex Media Komputindo. 2006.

Allen, Pam. "Challenging Diversity?: Indonesia's Anti-Pornography Bill." *Asian Studies Review* 31 (June 2007): 101–115.

Ammon, Richard. "Gay Indonesia — Jakarta." global gayz. May 2008. http://www.globalgayz.com/country/ Indonesia/view/IDN/gay-indonesia-jakarta (accessed Jun 28, 2009).

"*Anime News in Indonesia* (^ ^)." Anihabara. 6 Aug 2003. http://east.sakura.ne.jp/aniba/aninews/id.htm (accessed Feb 17, 2009).

Berman, Laine. "LAINE BERMAN sheds a tear for the late great Indonesian comic." *Inside Indonesia.* 1998. http://insideindonesia.org/content/view/761/29/ (accessed Nov 10, 2008).

Chan, Fadli. "The Popularity of Manga Culture." *Dunia Perspektif.* 22 Feb 2009. http://fadlinx.blogspot. com/2009/02/popularity-of-manga-culture.html (accessed Apr 4, 2009).

Dareini, Ali Akbar, "Iran's Vicious Dresstapo Hits Unveiled Gals with Barbaric 'Banishment.'" *New York Post* (April 25, 2007), http://www.nypost.com/seven/04252007/news/worldnews/ irans_vicious_dresstapo_hits_ unveiled_gals_with_barbaric_banishment_worldnews_ali_akbar_ dareini__ap_and_post_wire_services. htm?page=1 (Accessed November 15, 2008).

Forshee, Jill. *Culture and Customs of Indonesia (Culture and Customs of Asia).* Westport. 2006.

Frederick, William H. and Robert Worden. *Indonesia: A Country Study.* GPO for the Library of Congress. Washington. 1993.

Gelling, Peter. "Indonesia Passes Broad Anti-Pornography Bill." *International Herald Tribune.* 30 Oct 2008. http://www.iht.com/articles/2008/10/30/asia/indo.php (Accessed October 30th, 2008).

Guerin, Bill. "No Playmates for Indonesian Playboys." *Asian Times*, 10 Feb 2006, sec. Southeast Asia section.

Holzner, Brigitte M., and Oetomo, Dede. "Youth, Sexuality and Sex Education Messages in Indonesia: Issues of Desire and Control." *Reproductive Health Matters* 12, no. 23 (2004): 40–49.

"Islam and Homosexuality." Mission Islam. 6 Nov 2007. http://www.missionislam.com/knowledge/homosex uality.htm (accessed Mar 22, 2009).

"Islam and Homosexuality." Mission Islam. April 2008. http://www.missionislam.com/knowledge/homosex uality.htm (accessed April 4, 2009).

Kitab Undang-undang Hukum Perdata. Indonesia: Indonesian Government. 1945.

Myers, Nathaniel. "In Indonesia, Freedom to Differ." *International Herald Tribune.* 26 Mar 2006. http://www. iht.com/articles/2006/03/28/opinion/edm (accessed Nov 14, 2008).

Rondonuwu, Olivia. "*Indonesia's parliament passes anti-smut bill.*" *International Herald Tribune.* 30 Oct 2008. http://www.iht.com/articles/reuters/2008/10/30/asi (accessed Nov 6, 2008).

Spiegalr. "Banned, Burned, Censored." Listal. 26 Apr 2009. http://www.listal.com/list/banned-burned-censored (accessed Feb 14, 2009).

Tejokusumo, Andrea. "'Manga' wields strong influence over local comics." *The Jakarta Post*, 4 Aug 2008, sec. Supplement.

Munir, Lily Z. "Gender equality in a new democracy," *The Jakarta Post.* 29 December 2006. http://www.the jakartapost.com/Outlook/pol03b.asp (Accessed November 12, 2008).

Part Two

Genre and Readership

Better Than Romance?

Japanese BL Manga and the Subgenre of Male/Male Romantic Fiction

DRU PAGLIASSOTTI

The romantic storyline within boys' love manga is important to its readers. In my 2005 survey of such readers,[1] the largest group of respondents reported that the single most important element of BL manga was "slowly but consistently developing love between the couple," and that they read it because "I think it's sweet to see same-sex couples in love." Around a third of the survey's respondents agreed with the statement "I wish I had a romance like the ones in boy's love manga."

Indeed, in their qualitative comments, several respondents situated BL manga directly within the romance genre. For example, their qualitative comments included,

> I see BL manga as an offshoot of shoujo manga and romance novels (both of which I like). Chick lit. And it's been disrespected by most academics just like they disrespect Romance novels (annoyed "feminist" tangent: no one, however, ever disrespects organized sports as "repetitive opiate of the masses" or starts pathologizing its fans or whatever).

> Like women before us that got a thrill out of reading paperback romances, a good story can leave your worries behind, if only for a while. For the most part, it's just the gender that's changed. Also, it can be a lot wilder than those old Harlequin novels, and it allows us to confront some alternative/off the wall activities that might be hard to bear in real life. Sometimes it's a thrill, sometimes it's hilarious. In the end, I love men, and don't mind seeing them love each other sometimes.

Yet, at the same time, other BL manga readers expressed their dissatisfaction with heterosexual popular romance novels and argued that BL manga were, in some way, "better."

A number of the arguments presented in favor of BL manga are similar to those that have already been presented for slash; that is, survey respondents say that they enjoy BL's graphic depictions of sexual activities, androgynous protagonists, shifting point of view/multiple identifications, and egalitarian love relationships.[2] However, BL manga are not identical to either slash or the mainstream Western romance; their roots in Japanese culture and their graphic-novel format differentiate them in several noteworthy ways.

This chapter seeks to firmly situate Japanese BL manga[3] within the romance genre by comparing them with studies of the Western mainstream romance, i.e., studies of commercially published romance novels that feature a heterosexual couple and are marketed to a predominately female demographic. It will also address some of the differences between BL manga, mainstream Western romances, and slash by describing thematic, cultural, and format variations. The chapter will, finally, argue that male/male romance, as a broad category, should be considered a discrete subgenre of the popular romance including not only BL works but also slash and Western mainstream novels that have hitherto avoided categorization and analysis, as well as "gay" romances written by women.

Shared Interests

The fact that female-authored fiction about male/male love is romantic has been mentioned numerous times in discussions of slash fiction but seldom addressed directly or analyzed in depth. Catherine Salmon and Donald Symons observe, "in a rush to show that slash, and by extension its fans, are 'different,' academic theorists have seriously underestimated the similarities between slash and mainstream romances."[4] The use of "similarities" is an understatement — slash is, essentially, a subgenre of the Western popular romance. Slash and BL manga are not identical, however, and together they work to extend and broaden the romantic formula.

In the West, BL manga is sometimes subdivided by readers into two categories: the term *yaoi* is often used to refer to harder, more sexually explicit boy's love stories, and *shōnen-ai* for softer, less explicit stories. Ninety-three percent of the BL manga survey respondents reported reading both yaoi and *shōnen-ai*. BL manga readers also enjoy reading other genres: seventy-two percent of the respondents reported reading same-sex romances, sixty-eight percent reported reading slash, and fifty-five percent reported reading heterosexual romances; in other words, a majority of BL manga readers enjoy other forms of romantic fiction, as well.

In addition, fifty-nine percent of the BL manga survey respondents reported reading same-sex erotica, while thirty-two percent reported reading heterosexual erotica. The statistics on reading pornography will be addressed later. Fewer respondents reported reading other types of homoerotic or purely erotic manga; twenty-four percent reported reading *shōjo-ai*, and fourteen percent reported reading *yuri*, the female/female equivalents of *shōnen-ai* and yaoi, respectively.

Many BL manga readers enjoy romantic and erotic works of various types, there is considerable crossover in the readership of such genres, and the sex of the protagonists doesn't seem to make a great deal of difference, although, not surprisingly, there's an overall preference among BL manga readers for works about same-sex couples.

Types of Romance

The defining characteristic of the romance, John Cawelti argues, is "love triumphant and permanent, overcoming all obstacles and difficulties."[5] The romantic formula can be sorted into six overlapping types, according to Kay Mussell: the series romance, the erotic romance, the gothic romance, the romantic suspense, the romantic biography, and the historical romance.[6] BL manga fall into many, if not all, of these categories.

Series romances focus "on the relationship between two lovers with virtually all suspense deriving from that one aspect of the story,"[7] the complications being primarily internal, rather than external, to the characters. This category embraces the manner of publication as much as the plot of the novels itself; classic Harlequin romances are considered the quintessential series romances, and series romances became popular in Japan in the early 1980s.[8] An example of BL manga that may fit this category is *Only the Ring Fin-*

ger Knows (*Sono yubi dake ga shitteiru*)—a manga and series of novels by Kannagi Satoru and Odagiri Hotaru.[9] This series is longer than the stand-alone novels more typical of the Western series romance, but the problems facing high school students Wataru Fujii and Yuichi Kazuki are primarily interpersonal and linked to their own behavior or reactions, such as lies, gossip, and jealousy, rather than caused by external events.

Erotic romances put sexuality at the center of the story and "cover a wide range of situations linked by a permissive attitude toward premarital sex and by a willingness to examine subjects previously excluded from romances, such as rape and infidelity,"[10] although their heroines are not promiscuous as a rule. Readers unfamiliar with the romantic genre seem unaware of how many romances include sexual content, although Mairead Owen notes that romances "are the most available sources of eroticism for women,"[11] and this erotic content is a significant factor in their popularity, as Carol Thurston shows in *The Romance Revolution.*[12]

A significant amount of "hard" BL manga falls into the erotic romance category, such as, for example, *My Paranoid Next Door Neighbor* (*Tonari no heya no paranoia*) by Minami Kazuka,[13] in which the romantic relationship that develops between Hokuto and Yukito is endangered by schoolmates who seek to smear Hokuto's character and make Yukito break up with him; sex between the two main characters occurs in several graphically illustrated scenes and plays a significant and recurring role in the manga as the characters' relationship develops.

Although mainstream romance novels seldom fall into the "porn without plot" or "plot? what plot?" category—commercial novels that emphasize sex over story are likely to be categorized as "erotica" or "adult fiction" rather than romance—BL manga are more likely to fit this description. For example, *Level-C* (*Keiraku no houteishiki level-C*) by Futaba Aoi and Mitsuba Kurenai[14] has relatively little plot; the male fashion model Mizuki is seduced by a stranger, Kazuomi, to draw him into a commercial campaign, and the bulk of the first volume, which was initially released as a *dōjinshi*, or self-published work, is dedicated to scenes of sex between them. Should it, therefore, be considered an "erotic romance," or PWP fiction? Publishers in the U.S. haven't tried to differentiate between the two, although English-language scanlation circles often use labels such as PWP to give prospective readers an idea of what to expect from a work.

Gothic romances are set "in an enclosed domestic setting, frequently an old mansion with an extended family in residence. The source of danger lies within a small group of tightly linked characters."[15] In these stories, heroines are typically wives who find themselves in suspicious marriages, governesses, or adopted orphans.

Gothic romances seem to be relatively unusual in BL manga. Two of the earliest works of BL manga contain gothic elements but don't entirely satisfy expectations for a popular romance. For example, the *shōjo* called *Heart of Thomas* (*Tōma no shinzō*) by Hagio Moto is set in a German boarding school, and the story includes spurned love, suicide, illegitimate children, sexual abuse, and other secrets existing between and among the school's residents. The characters, however, end the story romantically unreconciled. Another early BL *shōjo, Song of Wind and Trees* (*Kaze to ki no uta*) by Takemiya Keiko may fit the bill better; it also contains a boarding-school-based gothic setting, and two of the characters end up together, although its violent, tragic ending may leave Western romance readers unsatisfied.[16]

Few of the Japanese BL manga licensed in the U.S. fit Mussell's definition of the gothic romance. A number involve individuals living with an eccentric patron in a manor-like setting, such as pianist Kenzo Shinozuka living with patron Lorenzo Carlucci in Ogasawara Uki's *Virtuoso di Amore* (*Netsujou no virtuoso bangai soushuuhen*), or portrait artist Lou, who discovers that his brooding patron Sein is a vampire in *Vampire's Portrait Vol. 1* (*Kyuuketsuki no shouzou*) by Kusumoto Hiroki, but neither of these stories includes an extended family whose secrets and irregularities threaten the protagonist's life or freedom. Other manor-based stories, such as that of the "maid" Midori Ichii who takes his grandmother's place in Shimada Hisami's *Maid in Heaven (Meido in heaven)*, are comedies rather than dramas. The long BL manga series *Love Mode* by Shimizu Yuki, which is primarily set within the gay host club Blue Boy and revolves around the hosts' relationships and the Aoe family's tensions, possesses some gothic elements, but its ensemble cast and open setting are poor fits for the rest of the gothic formula.[17]

Romantic suspense novels combine romance with an adventure in which "the heroine acts decisively to solve a mystery, a present crime or a past puzzle. She may have help from other characters—most notably the hero—but her own actions are integral to the solution."[18]

BL manga include a number of romantic suspense stories, ranging from fantasy (e.g., *Black Knight [Kuro no kishi]* by Tsurugi Kai) to science fiction (*Steal Moon* by Makoto Tateno) to police drama (*FAKE* by Matoh Sanami) and so forth.[19] They differ from Mussell's definition of romantic suspense in several ways, however.

First, it can be difficult to tell which of the male characters is the "heroine" of a BL manga, because both characters may participate equally in the story and be equally integral to the solution of the mystery. BL manga are often narrated from the *uke*'s (the usually less-experienced male's) point of view, but this rule is by no means strict, and chapters may shift from one character's POV to another's over the course of an extended series.

Second, and of more interest, Mussell argues that "the performance of the heroine in solving the mystery is a 'fantasy of competence,' a proof, however oblique, that the conventional values of women's lives ... do not preclude action and adventure."[20] In BL, where both romantic protagonists are male, the ideological goal of redeeming women's values and activities becomes irrelevant. True, the *uke* is often characterized as "feminine"— smaller, weaker, less confident, and more emotional than his partner — but this is not always the case (e.g., the *uke* Yagihashi Koju is the taller character in Misasagi Fuhri's *Idol Pleasures*[21] [*Hazamaniaru sorane*]), and ultimately the *uke* still enjoys the freedoms and privileges of being male in a patriarchal society. By contrast, in BL manga, female characters are often demonized, rather than valorized, by both the *mangaka* and the readers, as M. M. Blair describes.[22] This problematizes any assertion one might want to make that BL manga, as texts, affirm women's lives and competencies.

Romantic biographies "fictionalize the stories of actual women in history,"[23] a popular form of Western mainstream romance. However, fictionalizing the lives of historical male figures isn't as common in BL manga, at least as licensed and translated into English. One example is *Ludwig II* by Higuri You,[24] a manga about King Ludwig II of Bavaria that proposes a romance between him and his stable boy.

Historical romances, romances set in the past, are far more common in BL manga; for example, Yoshinaga Fumi's *Gerard & Jacques* (*Gerard to jacques*) set on the cusp of the French Revolution; Ogasawara Uki's *Black Sun* (*Black sun: Dorei ou*), set in the Middle East during the Crusades; Minami Megumu's short stories in *Pleasure Dome* (*Kanrakukyuu*), which are set in a variety of historical periods and places; and Kodaka Kazuma's *Midaresomenishi: A Legend of Samurai Love* (*Midare somenishi*), to name a few.[25] The central difference between historical romances and romantic biographies is the former's use of fictional characters rather than fictionalized versions of real people.

Elements of Romance

Given the close fit of BL manga into standard categories of Western romance novels, it should come as no surprise to find that their stories are, also, structured like popular romances. The fact that both characters are male leads to minor differences in how plot elements are developed, but the overall pattern remains much the same.

Pamela Regis identified eight essential elements of the Western romance novel:

1. *Society Defined*: Scenes that describe the social context within which the story will take place.
2. *The Meeting*: Scenes that describe the meeting between the romantic protagonists, occurring in the beginning of the novel or described in flashback.
3. *The Barrier*: Scenes that present external or internal reasons why the romantic protagonists cannot become betrothed (in contemporary romantic novels, this can be understood as committed to a monogamous relationship with each other).
4. *The Attraction*: Scenes that develop the reasons why the romantic protagonists should marry.
5. *The Declaration*: A scene or scenes in which one of the romantic protagonists declares love for the other.
6. *Point of Ritual Death*: A moment in which the union between the romantic protagonists seems impossible; the point at which the happy ending is in jeopardy.
7. *The Recognition*: A scene or scenes in which the barriers are removed, usually through the recognition of new information.
8. *The Betrothal*: A scene or scenes in which one of the romantic protagonists asks the other to marry; in contemporary romance novels, a marriage proposal may be replaced by a verbal assumption that the romantic protagonists will end up together.[26]

Most popular BL manga contain these essential elements, although some exceptions and curtailments exist. For example, BL manga may start with an already-established couple facing a barrier to their relationship, and the story goal is to overcome *The Barrier* rather than to reach *The Betrothal*; by contrast, starting with an already-established pair of protagonists is unusual in Western romance novels. In other BL manga, especially shorter works, the story may end with *The Declaration*, either admitted to oneself or confessed to the other. And, finally, some BL manga end at the *Point of Ritual Death*, with the rejection, betrayal, or physical demise of a protagonist.

The *Society Defined* in BL manga is typically Japanese and contemporary, often a boy's school or workplace. The panels and dialog often convey the location and time period in details of dress (e.g., Japanese school uniforms, *yukatas*, kimonos), signage (often left untranslated), honorifics (*-san*, *-kun*), food (*uden, yakitori,* sake), and actions (e.g., practicing martial arts, praying at a temple) and so forth. However, like mainstream romances, BL manga may also be set in different historical periods, different countries, and in entirely fantastic or extraterrestrial locales.

One "society" peculiar to BL manga depicts men possessing the ears and tails of animals but otherwise, usually, dressing and acting like humans. In this "society," the romance occurs with or between such *kemonomimi*: for example, with the transforming dog in Takashima Kazusa's *Man's Best Friend* (*Inu mo arukeba*); with the reincarnated dog of Kirishima Tamaki's *Ruff Love* (*Shiba to issho*); and between the human/animal hybrids in Amagi Reno's *Part-Time Pets* (*Kemomimi shouji*). These are not quite paranormal romances, which might feature romances with shapeshifting spirits, vampires, and the like; *kemonomimi* romances have no mainstream Western equivalent.[27]

The Meeting may be described over the course of the narrative or, quite commonly, especially in BL manga that revolve around an already-established couple, in a flashback. *The Attraction* is often the realization by the viewpoint character that he is becoming emotionally involved with another man — or is the subject of another man's attraction — which often leads directly to confused protests of "but, we're both male!"

The *Barrier*, according to Regis, is central to the romance novel and "establishes for the reader the reasons that this heroine and hero cannot marry."[28] In BL, which often acknowledges social prohibitions against same-sex marriage, the barrier may be characterized instead as establishing the reasons why the two characters cannot settle down into a long-term, mutually committed relationship. Barriers may be internal or external to the protagonist.

In BL manga, a common internal barrier is the protagonist's denial of his attraction to another man, often because he rejects the possibility of a gay identity. This recurring motif has led critics to question whether BL manga can be considered ideologically queer or gay-affirmative.[29] As a literary device, however, the denial of attraction serves to make the couple's eventual acceptance of their mutual but societally marginalized love that much more romantic, as described by Regis:

> Removal of the barrier usually involves the heroine's freedom from societal, civic, or even religious strictures that prevented the union between her and the hero. This release is an important source of the happiness in the romance novel's happy ending. The barrier's fall is a liberation for the heroine. It is a moment of rejoicing for the reader, whose response to the heroine's freedom is joy.[30]

Other BL barriers may include doubts that one protagonist shares the other's romantic feelings, various types of rivalry, the existence of a previous romantic relationship, the necessity of keeping the relationship secret in a society prejudiced against gay couples, or one character's rape of another. External barriers often include finding time for the relationship amid conflicting school, club, family, business, or even criminal obligations.

Cawelti notes that many romances include adventure, since "dangers function as a means of challenging and then cementing the love relationship."[31] Similarly, many BL manga are simultaneously mystery, fantasy, horror, or science fiction adventures, in which case external barriers may include crimes to be solved, killers/monsters/aliens to be defeated, curses to be overcome, and the like.

Finally, Mussell asserts that the core challenge of the romance is the "domestic test," which can be viewed as a sort of meta-barrier:

> only women who pass a domestic test by conforming to a set of expectations in values and activities may earn the reward of being chosen by Mr. Right. [...] Its several aspects conform to the three traditional and interrelated roles of female socialization: wife, mother, and homemaker. Heroines must pass the test in all three areas, but different formulas treat the patterns in characteristic ways or emphasize one area over others.[32]

The hero's acknowledgement of the heroine's success in these three areas signifies that the heroine is fully mature and adult, and thus worthy of the hero's love.

Although BL features two men, in many cases they, too, must pass the domestic test. That is, over the course of the story, one or both BL characters must prove capable of committing to a long-term, monogamous relationship (a "wife" role); of nurturing and comforting each other and/or children, pets, or subordinates (a "mother" role); and of maintaining a household either through their physical work or financial support (a "homemaker" role). Note that the importance of the latter depends on the characters' ages; although BL scenarios that reveal a character's competence at cooking, cleaning, or maintaining an apartment or house are common when the characters are living alone, high-school-age characters are less likely to demonstrate such competencies if they are still living with their families.

After the barrier has been breached, a declaration of love is made. *The Declaration* may, in some BL manga, simply be the internal admission by the protagonist that he loves another man; more often it's a verbal confession of love and/or the character's willing participation in kissing or sex—*willing* is important, because nonconsensual sex is a much more common plot element in BL manga than in popular romance novels.

The *Point of Ritual Death* puts the happy ending in peril; it is often an emotionally charged argument between the two protagonists based on some sort of misunderstanding or conflict of obligations, although in BL manga an arranged marriage to a woman, kidnapping, curses, and actual death may also serve as ritual deaths. Some BL manga will, in fact, end at this point, meshing romance with tragedy. When such a sad ending occurs, however, it usually fits Cawelti's observation that the death of a protagonist in romance is presented "in such a way as to suggest that the love relation has been of lasting and permanent impact."[33] More commonly, however, even death may be overcome as the beloved transforms into a ghost, vampire, or other supernatural creature or is reborn into another body; such plot developments propel the story into the category of paranormal romance.

The Recognition resolves the misunderstanding or conflict or otherwise overcomes the problem of ritual death, leading to *The Betrothal*, which, as mentioned, in BL implies the establishment of a monogamous, mutually committed long-term relationship—in other words, a happy ending.

Happy endings are important in the West; in 1984, Janice Radway found that the most important ingredient in a romance was a happy ending, with the second "a slowly but consistently developing love between hero and heroine" and "some detail about the heroine and the hero after they have finally gotten together."[34] Even today, the national organization Romance Writers of America defines the romance genre as possessing two basic elements: "a central love story and an emotionally-satisfying and optimistic ending"[35]; in other words, the Western preference for romances that have a happy ending hasn't faded over the last two decades.

However, respondents to the BL manga survey did *not* choose a happy ending as the most important element of a BL romance. Instead, the largest group, forty-two percent, chose "slowly but consistently developing love between the couple" as the single most essential element—this was the second choice of Radway's surveyed readers. The second largest group of BL readers (not counting those who chose "other"), making up fifteen percent of the survey's respondents, chose "scenes about the couple after they have finally gotten together" as the second most important feature of BL manga. The third most important feature, chosen by eleven percent of the respondents, was "explicit sexual illustrations." Compare that to Radway's survey, in which "lots of scenes with explicit sexual description" wasn't chosen by *any* of her romance survey respondents. On the other hand, Radway's finding was contradicted by Thurston's surveys of romance readers, which were carried out at about the same time, in 1982 and 1985, in which "detailed sexual description" and love scenes made the top five "most-liked story and character attributes"[36] in romances. Clearly, BL manga readers are less united in their opinion of what is "most important" in BL than are romance readers, although the love story remains central.

But as far as happy endings go, "happy ending" was the least popular choice among the surveyed BL manga readers, considered "most important" by only six percent of the respondents. This suggests that BL manga readers, unlike readers of Western mainstream romances, are far more open to the possibility of romantic fiction that contains sadness, tragedy, and violence.

Sadness, Tragedy, and Violence

In the context of her 1980–81 survey of romance readers, Radway argues that "in those romances where the potential consequences of male-female relations are too convincingly imagined or permitted to control the tenor of the book by obscuring the developing love story, the art form's role as *safe* display is violated."[37] Romances are deliberately idealized fantasies, functioning as a comforting haven for readers who want to escape the problems of their real lives. As Carol Ricker-Wilson notes, "once readers venture out of the formulaic romance genre, fiction is a wild card and identification with female protagonists an emotional risk"[38]; that is, women in other genres may be stereotyped or victimized in ways offensive or disturbing to a female reader. Given the comforting function of the romantic genre, it's not surprising that it usually shuns tragedy and violence. And, in fact, Radway's readers identified rape as the most objectionable element in a romance, with a sad ending the runner-up.

BL manga readers, however, did not agree.

Sad endings are not unknown in romance; for example, Cawelti noted that classic Western romances such as *Romeo and Juliet* or *Tristan and Isolde* end in death, although, as mentioned earlier, such sad endings are not necessarily unhappy endings; that is, the existence of a true and enduring love between the characters is never cast in doubt.[39] However, sad endings are no longer expected or desired by contemporary Western romance readers.

Japanese romance readers, on the other hand, do not seem to have rejected sad endings as thoroughly; Janet S. Shibamoto Smith notes that Japanese romance novels from the 1970s to 2000 can be categorized as "(1) hyperserious novels, ending in *hiren* (blighted love) and (2) novels lighter in overall tone with a *happii-endo* (happy ending)."[40] This seems to fit the Japanese sensibility of *mono no aware*, which can be oversimplified as an aesthetic appreciation for sadness and melancholy.

> [A]s sensitivity to beauty increases and the aesthetic experience becomes richer, a kind of phenomenological reflection upon the fragility of beauty and its mutability spontaneously takes place, fusing with the essential intuition of beauty itself. A special aesthetic feeling of sadness or melancholy will come to form a kind of nimbus to all beauty.[41]

Although discussions of *mono no aware* tend to occur in the context of poetry and serious literature, popular Japanese manga and anime, whether romantic or not, often include melancholy imagery and tragic elements to a much greater extent than is found in popular Western comic books or animations; for example, manga and anime often feature lost loved ones, terminal illnesses, and even the ultimate death of the protagonist. Thus it follows that BL manga may not end happily, either. In fact, some of the earliest BL–themed manga included tragedy or sad endings, such as Hagio's *Heart of Thomas*, which begins with a suicide, or Takemiya's *Song of Wind and Trees*, which ends with a violent death.[42]

One reason why the BL manga survey respondents might not have prioritized a happy ending could be that they were already familiar with the potential for sadness and tragedy found in other forms of manga and anime, and therefore had learned to accept the same potential in BL. It's worth noting, however, that the vast majority of the BL manga that have been licensed, translated, and published in the U.S. feature upbeat endings.[43] One of the handful of exceptions is Kodaka's BL manga *Midaresomenishi*, licensed and published by Be Beautiful. With a plot that includes kidnapping, gang rape, pedophilia, incest, murder, and suicide, and an ending in which the angst-filled main character Shirou continues to flee his pursuing rapist-turned-lover Sougetsu, the story most certainly doesn't fit the usual Western formula for a popular romance. The serialized BL novel *Ai no kusabi: The Space Between* (*Ai no kusabi*) by Yoshihara Rieko, licensed and published by Juné, also features scenes of sexual slavery and violence and ends with a protagonist's death.[44] These are unusual cases, however.

Scanlation groups have been more willing than commercial publishers to offer BL with sad endings, perhaps because they aren't concerned with making money and thus don't feel as much pressure to appeal to a mass audience. These groups have, for example, scanlated such manga as Yuki Kaori's *Boys Next Door* (*Shōnen zanzou*), which features a serial killer who kills his male-prostitute lover and later commits suicide, and Kunieda Saika's "The Sleeping Man" (from the volume *Natsujikan*), in which a ghost returns long enough to confess his hitherto unacknowledged love for a friend.[45]

In addition to being more likely to include sad endings, BL manga are also more likely than mainstream Western romances to include scenes of sexual violence.

This isn't to imply that mainstream romances have never included sexual assault; the popularity of erotic romances grew in the 1970s with the rise of the "bodice-ripper," which featured heroines forced into sex by impassioned heroes. As bodice-rippers became more common in romance publishing, the likelihood of nonconsensual sex forming part of a romance novel's storyline increased. But as Linda J. Lee points out, bodice-rippers were usually historical romances, and "[t]he distance created by the remote historical setting allowed women to 'enjoy' the rape fantasy from a safe distance without ever confusing the eroticized fantasy rape with a brutal, dangerous, real-life rape." In bodice-rippers, she notes, rape functioned as a literary device that allowed the author to involve a "good" heroine in a premarital sexual encounter. However, Lee adds, by the 1980s, in response to feminism and the sexual revolution, "the rape fantasy was rejected"; it is seldom found in mainstream Western romance novels today.[46]

In BL manga, by contrast, nonconsensual sex scenes ("non-con") are relatively common, and many readers enjoy them. As was suggested for sad endings, some of the respondents' acceptance of non-con could be due to their familiarity with the conventions of *hentai*, sexually explicit heterosexual manga and anime, much of which contains images of bondage and rape.[47] In the BL manga reader survey, of the 391 respondents to answer the question, fifty percent thought that rape, explicit sex, sad endings, physical torture, ordinariness, bed-hopping, cruel heroes, and weak heroes were all acceptable in BL manga. Of the remainder, twelve percent said that rape should never be included in BL, eight percent said physical torture, five percent said bed-hopping, and two percent said a weak hero. Fourteen percent of respondents wrote in answers that included objections to pedophilia, bestiality, and *seme/uke* (aggressor/recipient) stereotypes, none of which are likely to be found in mainstream Western romance novels.

Non-con scenes in BL manga may involve sex predicated by one character's use, intentionally or not, of alcohol or drugs; sex demanded as the result of a bet or other negotiation between the characters; the forcing of unwanted sexual acts on one character by another in the course of an ongoing sexual relationship; and other forms of sexual assault. In such scenes, the attacker typically accompanies his actions with comments about the victim's erect nipples and penis and/or his trembling sensitivity to being touched. Although such dialog is also typical in consensual sex scenes, in the context of non-con, it serves to suggest that although the victim may verbally protest, he secretly or unconsciously consents to the act — his body's reaction signifies his consent. This implication is strengthened when the victim inevitably falls in love with his attacker. Non-con storylines between the romantic protagonists may, therefore, be considered extreme extensions of the hurt/comfort theme common in slash; sexual assault serves as an emotional barrier or point of ritual death and, at the same time, an opportunity for the coercer to comfort and declare his love to the coerced.

Non-con may also occur between one of the protagonists and a secondary character. In these cases, the scenes may look the same, but the rape's function within the story differs; the assault serves as a plot barrier that provides a rescue, revenge, and/or nurturing opportunity for the other romantic lead.

Rape may also serve several other plot functions within a BL romance. It may, much as it did in bodice-rippers, provide an excuse for a "good" (and, like as not, supposedly heterosexual) man to engage in a sexual encounter with another man. It may serve as a narrative means by which the victim becomes ascendant over the rapist, whose resort to sexual violence indicates his inability to control his desire.[48] It may act as a "redemptive rape," in which an unlikable character, after being raped or threatened with rape, is transformed into a sympathetic character.[49] It may add to BL's pornographic titillation, which will be discussed at greater length later, by underlining the protagonist's helpless immersion in physical pleasure.[50] It may offer readers an excuse to enjoy rape fantasies without guilt, since text and drawings permit more emotional distance than photos or video of real people.[51] Finally, Kazuko Suzuki argues that women write rape scenes into BL manga as a form of resisting the social stigmatization of a rape victim by portraying "male protagonists, loved by the very partners who rape them, as imbued with innocence,"[52] in which case it may serve to alleviate a BL–reading rape victim's sense of guilt or shame.

Japanese Romances

Analyzing Japanese BL manga within the framework of Western mainstream romances raises questions of cultural comparison; however, Western literature has had a strong presence in Japan since the nineteenth century, when it was imported during the Meiji era in the hope of speeding Japan's entrance into modernity.[53] According to Chieko Irie Mulhern, contemporary popular romantic fiction in Japan was originally translated from Western sources; Harlequin romances entered Japan in 1979, and by 1985 "nearly two thousand Western romances had been translated into Japanese."[54] Mulhern finds that Japanese-written popular romances in the late eighties generally followed Western categories and formulae. The same can be said of Japanese romances in the 1990s, according to Shibamoto Smith.[55] Thus, it seems reasonable to compare BL manga to Western romances, as BL's *mangaka* were likely influenced by decades of storylines drawn from Western or Western-influenced romantic novels. Nevertheless, a few differences between Japanese and Western popular romances have been described.

For example, Mulhern notes that although Western romances often isolate the heroine, which increases her vulnerability, Japanese romances are more likely to provide the heroine with female friends and family members who provide support, although, being "either married, in love with someone, or else related by blood to the hero,"[56] these support characters avoid posing a romantic threat to the budding relationship. The same is true in BL manga. Although the families of BL's protagonists tend to be invisible, the protagonists often have male friends— e.g., schoolmates or coworkers— who may serve the same plot purpose as a heroine's family and friends. Moreover, it's not unusual, in BL manga, for the protagonist's male friends to discover and support — or at least choose not to interfere with — the character's relationship with another man; because these friends are usually heterosexual or in a same-sex relationship of their own, they similarly offer no threat to the budding romance.

Mulhern also notes that a Japanese romantic heroine does not believe "that her relationship with a man is the sole source of her status, desirability, affluence, or right to respect — a cultural assumption that is taken for granted and only questioned after a traumatic event by most Western romance heroines."[57] This observation takes an interestingly different shape in BL. Although BL's protagonists also do not usually believe that their relationship with another man is the source of their status and desirability, in stories in which protagonists do not self-identify as bisexual or gay, they *may* worry about their attraction to another man defining them as gay, which could indeed affect their status, desirability, affluence, and right to respect. In BL manga, the "trauma" that leads the reluctant protagonist to question his internalized heterosexism is likely to be either a non-con sexual encounter or an abrupt awareness of his own physical and emotional reaction to another man's presence.

Mulhern noted that few heroines in Japanese-written popular romances are found in "a predominantly male domain such as law, finance, medicine, or higher education."[58] By contrast, these are all very common settings for BL manga, probably because in Japan they *are* predominantly male domains and therefore natural settings for a BL story. When a BL character engages in a more stereotypically "feminine" career, such as a chef, hair stylist, or fashion model, he is somewhat more likely to be the *uke* in the relationship, although a character's career is a less important signifier of *seme/uke* status than his physical build and personality.

Finally, Mulhern notes that heroines in Japanese popular romances often "manage to faint from anemia, low blood pressure, cold, fatigue, shock, fear, and hunger, only to be nursed tenderly by a contrite or protective hero"; moreover, they "are extremely susceptible to accidents and violent crimes."[59] This is also common in BL manga, with the *uke* usually suffering some sort of ailment or wound that allows the *seme* to feed and/or take care of him, although the reverse isn't uncommon, either. Such hurt/comfort themes allow a male character to demonstrate the tenderness and protectiveness that both romance-novel and BL readers say they find desirable in the romantic hero, as will be discussed further below.

Reader Preferences

Radway asked why women choose to read mainstream romantic fiction; the majority of her respondents said "for simple relaxation" and "because reading is just for me; it is my time," leading her to conclude that the genre is valued because "the experience itself is *different* from ordinary existence"[60]; that is, reading romances offers women relaxing, personal time and an escape from the day-to-day demands of her life.

The BL manga survey listed similar choices to Radway's, as well as others, such as "I think reading boy's love manga supports gay rights" and "I like the idea of soulmate love beyond sex or gender." Respondents could choose more than one reason why they read BL.

The most popular reason BL manga readers chose for enjoying BL was "I think it's sexy to see same-sex couples making love" (eighty-one percent of respondents), with "I like looking at pictures of pretty boys" (seventy-nine percent), "I think it's sweet to see same-sex couples in love" (seventy-six percent), and "I like the idea of soulmate love beyond sex or gender" (seventy-two percent) as close runners-up. Reading BL for relaxation was chosen by forty-eight percent of the respondents.

Many feminist researchers have asked why women would want to read romance novels, which they characterize as unrealistic and patriarchal, and a number of BL researchers (and bemused bystanders) have asked why women would want to read BL manga, which they criticize along similar lines. In fact, they find BL manga even more puzzling than mainstream romances; after all, while it might be understandable that women would enjoy identifying with the heroine of a heterosexual romance, what is the point of their identifying with the hero of a homosexual romance?[61]

A number of explanations have been ventured. Several suggest that BL's pretty boys signify girls. For example, Matsui Midori suggests that they are "the girls' displaced selves [...] they signified the possession of the phallus as opposed to the feminine 'lack.'"[62] Similarly, Sharon Kinsella suggested that the characters are essentially genderless, though female readers will often identify with "the slightly more effeminate male of a couple."[63] Another explanation is that setting a romance between two boys allows women in patriarchal societies to more easily imagine a relationship based on gender equality. For example, Suzuki concluded that "male homosexual love stories, which are read by many girls and young women in developed countries, grow out of their despair of ever achieving equal relationships with men in a sexist society and their quest for ideal human relationships."[64] Along these lines, manga artists cited by Mizoguchi Akiko comment that girls are expected to identify with the androgynous characters, who seek an ideal, completely reciprocal relationship.[65]

What the question ignores is that even women who prefer mainstream, heterosexual romances enjoy reading about the relationship from the hero's point of view and appreciate its inclusion in romance fiction.[66] For example, Thurston's 1985 survey of romance readers showed that over seventy percent wanted the hero's point of view included in the novel; it was the number-one most-liked story attribute. Romance writer Laura Kinsale argued in her 1992 essay that women enjoy identifying with the romantic hero as much, if not more, than the heroine: "If one can bring oneself to admit that a female reader might find it more difficult to *be* this fictitious heroine than to *be* this fictitious man — not because she is a pitiful, victimized woman but because within the reader there are masculine elements that can and need to be realized — then reading a romance is far from internally alienating." In other words, romance readers enjoy sharing the viewpoint of a character who is falling in love; whether that character is male or female is relatively unimportant. Salmon and Symons supported this assertion in 2001 with their finding that seventy-eight percent of a group of female readers who enjoyed mainstream romances and had never read a male/male romance before said that they enjoyed the m/m romance novel *The Catch Trap* at least as much as they enjoyed heterosexual romance.[67]

BL offers a few differences from mainstream romances, however. Salmon & Symons found that slash readers appreciate slash's shifting point of view/multiple identifications, androgynous protagonists, egalitarian love relationships, and graphic depictions of sexual activities. This list is essentially identical to the answers provided by BL manga survey respondents to a question asking why they enjoy reading yaoi and *shōnen-ai*.

Shifting point of view/multiple identifications

Some BL manga readers said they enjoyed the freedom BL offers them to identify with either the *seme* or *uke*, or to avoid the emotional turmoil that may associated with identifying with a female character. The freedom to choose a character with whom to identify is, very likely, another reason why non-con sex scenes are considered more acceptable in BL manga than in heterosexual romances; the female reader doesn't feel compelled to identify with the victim by virtue of her gender. For example, survey respondents wrote,

> I think it is easier to relate to a character. In hetero manga I automatically relate to the female because I am a woman. In yaoi or boys love I can relate to either character more easily.

> I can relate to either character in BL. No role is assigned; many people see a *seme* and a *uke* and believe they represent the male and the female. This may be true in our placement of gender roles and behavior, but they are still both men, so I can chose to relate the *seme* or the *uke*, or both.

> When I read a BL manga or watch an anime, somehow, I feel I am free to enjoy it without being forced to accept a role. It gives me a strange sense of freedom and almost luxury — I feel that this is something that has been made specifically for me as a woman, but it does not come with any demands or restrictions on me as a woman.

> I associate sexual relationships with power relations/issues of domination strongly and since women are conventionally the suppressed party, reading BL manga takes these issues away and allows me to relate (ironically) to the characters from a comfortable distance (because of the gender "barrier"/difference).

> The usual problems between m/f relationships don't really apply in m/m situations. For example, a male partner cannot get pregnant.

Androgynous protagonists

Some BL manga readers objected to what they saw as stereotypes of women in heterosexual romances, particularly in manga and anime, and said they enjoyed BL because it avoided such stereotypes. For example, their comments included,

> Girls in manga are often annoying or overbearing, especially in romance manga where it's often lots of guys falling for one girl (like Miaka in Fushigi Yuugi). So, get rid of the girls and focus on the boys. and you'll have double my attention [period after *boys* in original].

> It isn't that I'm turned off by heterosexual relationships; rather, I am often turned off by anime/manga leading females, who are often somewhat naive, airheaded, or otherwise unappealing. Two males together increases the chance that I will find both halves of a relationship attractive, physically and otherwise.

Yet the depictions of men in BL often emphasize their "feminine" side. Fifty-three percent of the survey's respondents agreed that "I like reading about men dealing with emotions and situations that women usually deal with." Some added,

> In the sort of BL I'm most fond of, the men don't act like women but often they don't really act like "men" either, not in the usual sense of observing all the societal expectations/hang ups. (Or, if they're not hang-up-free, they get over it in humorous or interesting ways.) Rather they seem to occupy a middle ground where they can simply behave like "people." Like a nice, liminal fantasy world.

> Male/male relationships seem to have an element of tension in them. It's easier to imagine sparks flying between two males—whether it involves fighting, strong attraction, or rough sex—than between two females, or a male and a female. In real life I prefer women over men, but because of this tension, I tend to favor BL works over straight or lesbian ones.

> Because it allows access into a space that I know in reality I can never breach— male+male emotional interaction even if it is an idealised fantasy.

Egalitarian love relationships

Many of the BL readers who responded to the survey cited a delight in gender-free romantic roles as a reason to like BL. Seventy-two percent agreed "I like the idea of soulmate love beyond sex and gender." Representative remarks in the qualitative section included,

> As a feminist, I find that boy's love manga is more likely to contain relationships that seem free from constraints of sexual roles...

> I guess it's mostly just the romantic notion that two *people* can be in love, regardless of sex/gender ... the connection between two personalities, even, not necesarily [sic] souls ... though that's quite lovely in itself....

> After studying the social aspects of the genre, what I like best about it is that on it's most basic level, it's an opportunity for Japanese woman to see a story in which the individuals involved in these relationships are equals and have the romance of a straight relationship, and yet have the freedom to move through society that the male body gives them.

However, BL manga does not always escape the ideology of gendered relations because it often depicts characters in a *seme/uke* relationship, in which the *uke* bears many stereotypically feminine signifiers. To be sure, both men in the typical boy's love text tend to be "feminized" in the sense that both are depicted as slender and beautiful, usually with relatively long hair and delicate features, and they often engage in impassioned emotional discourse. The *uke*, however, usually bears other "feminine" signifiers, such as being more often the recipient of sexual overtures and possessive gazes and of being more emotional and uncertain than the *seme*:

> The sexual role of the uke is accompanied by a series of social roles that are typically those of a stereotypically traditional woman: the uke is feminine in his reluctance and timidity, and in being protected and defended (or abused) by his partner in his life every day. The uke weeps, is fragile, is sweet, would like to remain embraced by his companion all night, making himself available but not insisting if the seme ignores his offer.[68]

Western readers evince mixed reactions to the Japanese *seme/uke* convention. Asked whether they identified more with the *uke* or *seme*, the respondents to the BL manga readers survey were almost evenly split between "*uke*," "*seme*," and "neither" (thirty-nine percent, twenty-seven percent, and thirty-four percent, respectively). In the qualitative responses, a few respondents volunteered the *seme/uke* categorizations as a reason for liking BL manga:

> i like to see the dominate [*sic*] male character taking the shy or weak smaller male. sometimes i would like to be that male that gets dominated.

> On the uke seme question I identify with the seme which is the top/aggressor.

> As a lesbian with many gay male friends, I find stuff like "seme/uke" and such utterly silly — but it's a fun silly.

> It is also a game to determine who would be seme and who would be uke.

Other respondents didn't like the *seme/uke* convention:

> the ultra weak crying uke and the super dominant seme make me puke....

> I really wish that there wasn't always a seme and an uke in BL manga.

> I usually want to read stories about masculine men bonding and depending on eachother [*sic*] in life and death situations, rather then constantly seeing the uke saved by the seme.

> I hate the "Seme" and "Uke" stereotypes. It's there in yaoi, and you can't get away from it, but real life doesn't always put an uke and a seme together. Nor do I ever really find any uke or seme types ... bottoms and tops, maybe, but rarely a "male" and "female" role.

Radway asked her romance readers to choose the traits they thought were most important in the hero and heroine; her lists of traits were combined in the BL manga survey and asked about both the *seme* and *uke*.

Radway's readers found intelligence, tenderness, and a sense of humor important traits for a hero[69]; BL manga readers chose intelligence, protectiveness, and beauty/handsomeness as the top three most important traits in a *seme* (eighty-one percent chose intelligence, seventy-two percent chose protectiveness, and seventy-one percent chose handsomeness).

Radway's readers chose intelligence, a sense of humor, and independence as the top three traits in a heroine[70]; BL manga readers chose intelligence and beauty/handsomeness as the top two traits in a *uke*, after which fifty-seven percent of the respondents chose "sense of humor" and fifty-two percent chose "shyness." All other traits for the *uke* were chosen by less than half of the respondents.

The least popular trait chosen by the surveyed BL manga readers for the *seme* was "virginity" (five percent) and, for the *uke*, "lots of sexual experience" (seven percent). This is in keeping with the *seme/uke* convention and also reflects the heterosexual romance's hero/heroine convention, in which the hero is usually more sexually experienced than the heroine.

Although write-in choices were generally in accord with stereotypes for the *seme* (e.g., *bad boy, dominance, confidence*), the write-in responses for the *uke* included a few strong rejections of the *uke* stereotype, including the *uke*'s perceived "femininity," e.g., readers wrote "*uke = the bottom, NOT more feminine*" and said desirable *uke* traits were "*not the stereotypical 'weepy uke' type*"; "*acknowledgement that he isn't a girl with a penis*"; "*not being a uke? I really dislike ukes generally*"; and "*not being a 5 year-old girl always helps.*" This rejection of the *uke*'s tendency to be assigned stereotypically feminine qualities seems to fit in with Western BL manga readers' response that they appreciate the subgenre's freedom from gender stereotypes.

Graphic depictions of sexual activities

As Thurston pointed out, and Salmon and Symons corroborated, sexually explicit scenes are popular among many female romance readers.[71] Erotic romance novels rely heavily on euphemisms rather than explicit anatomical references and make the heroine an active and eager participant in, rather than a passive recipient of, sex. They build up the sexual tension between the two characters over time and emphasize foreplay and the characters' emotional responses to arousal. Slash does the same, although Salmon and Symons add that "the average slash story is no doubt more sexually graphic than the average romance novel."[72] They note, however, that graphic sex isn't necessary in slash and that the focus of the story is on the characters' emotional rather than physical reactions to the relationship.

This is, as far as it goes, also true of BL manga — not all BL manga include sex, and even when they do, the characters' emotional reactions are important. However, BL manga notably differs from the Western romance novel and slash story in its dependence upon imagery to carry its narrative. Although romance novels usually come with colorful covers and slash may take the form of an illustration, in neither is the artwork an essential part of the narrative. In this aspect, then, sexually explicit BL manga may more closely resemble Western pornography[73] than it does Western romance or erotica.

Some, although not a majority, of the surveyed BL manga readers reported enjoying pornography. Of the 391 who responded to the question, thirty-five percent reported reading same-sex pornography and fifteen percent reported reading heterosexual pornography. Twenty-one percent reported reading *hentai*, which is hard-core pornographic manga typically depicting heterosexual encounters. Unfortunately, no question was asked in the survey about *bara*, the gay male subset of *hentai*. Nevertheless, it is clear that a significant number of BL manga readers enjoy other forms of sexually explicit work, as well.

Pornography varies in its level of explicit imagery, and so does BL. For many years, Japanese indecency laws caused manga and anime producers to avoid the graphic depiction of sexual organs and pubic hair, creating a form of visual euphemism akin to that used by Western mainstream romances. Sharon Kinsella describes how Japanese artists worked around the indecency laws:

> Stylistic devises such as drawing objects, such as snakes or fruit, which symbolize or vaguely resemble sexual parts, drawing sexual parts as shadows or silhouettes, or simply portraying sex scenes through contorted facial expressions, perspiration, nose bleeds, and suggestive bulges and creases in character's [*sic*] clothing, had rendered the previous definition of "indecency" relatively ineffectual.[74]

Accordingly, many Japanese BL manga contain scenes in which hands grip blank spaces that spurt liquids or one character penetrates another with emptiness, bringing a whole new meaning to the concept of the absent phallus. However, as interpretation of indecency laws grew more lenient, BL manga became more graphic, and it's no longer difficult to find BL manga that clearly depict erect, veined penises and/or pubic hair.

What this shift in style suggests is that the use of visual euphemism isn't as necessary in BL manga as the use of verbal euphemism is in mainstream romance novels. It's not the image of a penis that dismays romance readers, but the clinical nature of the word "penis." Drawing an erect penis allows the author to sidestep the challenge of choosing a word to describe it that won't break the mood of the narrative.

In fact, its explicit sexual imagery is an important part of BL manga's popularity. As mentioned earlier, the top two reasons surveyed BL readers said they read BL were "I think it's sexy to see same-sex couples making love" and "I like looking at pictures of pretty boys." Longer comments included,

> I like BL manga because it gives women the rare opportunity to see men presented as the primary object of sexual interest. Unlike many BL fans I also enjoy real life depictions of sex between men and gay porn. The one aspect of BL manga that does not always appeal to me is the overblown romanticism.

> BL is a great way to be entertained by sexually exciting material without having to deal with the porn that's made for boys. I love seeing beautiful boys get it on. Non-con is GREAT. Where else can you read or see non-con and have it be ok?

> I think that the boy's love phenomenon is how women today are taking their libidos into their own hands withour [*sic*] feeling like outcasts or social misfits. It's very nice to know that you aren't weird because you like to look at naked men and touch yourself.

> It's for women. We don't have much out there for us that allows us to be in charge of our sexuality. I've seen the studies that "prove" women are not visually excited by graphic sexual images, but those are images made by men for men. They concentrate on the pretty woman and the man half the time is not even attractive. What woman wants to see that? Women don't want to watch women having sex.

Does this mean that BL manga function as "women's pornography"? Salmon and Symons argue that one of the differences between pornography, typically geared toward men, and slash, typically geared toward women, is the function that sex plays within the plot:

> The essence of male-oriented porn is not really the graphic illustration of sex (there is, after all, soft-core porn), but, rather, the depiction of sex as an end in itself. No form of women's erotica depicts sex that way, but in the mainstream romance novel sexual attraction and, usually, sexual behavior are integral to establishing the bond between hero and heroine. In slash, however, the bond of friendship is firmly in place long before sex rears its head.[75]

The preexistence of a friendship — or some sort of relationship, since slashed characters may be rivals or enemies— between the characters before their sexual attraction makes sense in slash because it is fan fiction and usually set during some logical interstice within the course of the canonical narrative. This same sort of prior relationship between characters exists in yaoi *dōjinshi*, which are akin to slash in being based on a preexisting text. In both cases, sex serves to deepen or problematize a relationship that already exists between the characters.

However, when BL works are original, as in the case of commercially published BL manga, there's no need to assume that the characters like or even know each other before sex is initiated. Indeed, as noted earlier, relationships in BL manga may start with stranger rape, such as between men who meet at a club or party, or between students or salarymen who have barely exchanged two words before their sexual encounter. In addition to coerced sex, consensual bondage and S&M situations are also more common in BL manga than in mainstream heterosexual romances.

Steven Marcus's characterization of the Victorian "pornotopia" points out other qualitative differences between pornographic and erotic or romantic writing. Pornotopia, he argues, exists in "no place"; the locale, when named at all, is irrelevant to the plot. Similarly, it exists in "no time"; the significant time elements in the story are only how long a sex act or series of sex acts last. Characterization is unimportant; characters exist only to aid in the description of sexual positions and combinations. Plot is more or less nonexistent, the narrative consisting of a series of physical climaxes but with no story climax or overarching goal for the characters to attain. Marcus writes,

> All men in it are always and infinitely potent; all women fecundate with lust and flow
> inexhaustibly with sap or juice or both. Everyone is always ready for anything, and
> everyone is infinitely generous with his substance. It is always summertime in
> pornotopia, and it is a summertime of the emotions as well—no one is ever jealous,
> possessive, or really angry.[76]

Sexually explicit BL manga possess some of these attributes, and some works possess more than others. For example, locale and time period are often of little importance within the stories—the story could as easily take place in a high school, an office, a shop, a criminal organization, or a host club; the details don't matter. The time is often a generic "the present," and when it isn't, as in the case of historical BL manga, the real events of that historical period seldom make any difference to the story-line. In some of the least original BL manga, characters slip into undifferentiated stereotypes: the *seme*, the *uke*; the salaryman, the student, the teacher, the doctor, the host. In such cookie-cutter, PWP BL manga, the goal of the story is simply to bring the characters together for athletic, dripping sex.

It seems, then, that there may be little difference between some forms of sexually explicit BL manga and pornography, and that BL manga may lend itself more to depictions of a context-free pornotopia than slash. Slash, by definition, cannot be context-free; it is based on already-existing characters and refers to a rich storyworld and character history. Even when slash stories are little more than descriptions of sexual encounters, those encounters take place within a larger story context that is familiar to the fans who read it. Original BL manga, on the other hand, require no such referents.

Despite this, the majority of sexually explicit BL manga use sex in the same way as slash or heterosexual romance; sex emphasizes the characters' deepening relationship and mutual pleasure and—sometimes—creates plot barriers for the characters to overcome. Moreover, in contrast to Marcus' pornotopia, BL manga's protagonists may suffer impotence or not be in the mood; they are, as often as not, likely to grow jealous, possessive, or angry; they seek relational quality rather than quantity (at least, eventually); and quite often they have other goals and ambitions that they seek to realize while they are working through their romantic challenges. BL manga readers may enjoy the sex, but they also enjoy well-plotted, emotionally deep stories. Representative comments about this included,

> Well, if it's nicely drawn, and the story is good, I'll like it, but I'm not one for PWP
> (porn without plot) so ... it's gotta have a reason. I'm not really one for rape/pain with-
> out a reason ... but I'll keep reading after it if the story is good enough.
>
> Porn sans plot is boring. I don't care how pretty the art is—if the story is uttery [*sic*]
> lame, uninteresting, or absent, forget it.
>
> There are many misconceptions about what boy's love manga is. What is it to me? It can
> be sexually explicit, it can be story-driven, it can be completely eye candy, it can be a
> really great story. Personally, I won't read a poorly written story, even if the artwork is
> nice.

Marcus's characterization of pornotopia was drawn from studying Victorian male-oriented pornography. Ann Snitow argues by contrast that what is "pornographic" in female-oriented romance novels is the heroine's helplessness in the face of a sexually charged atmosphere: "In pornography all things tend in one direction, a total immersion in one's own sense experience..." which, because immersion requires the subordination of thought to sensation, emphasizes "the universal infant desire for complete, immediate gratification, to rule the world out of the very core of passive helplessness."[77] Pornography for women, Snitow argues, wraps sex in the emotionalism of romance. If one prefers Snitow's definition over Marcus's, there can be no doubt that many BL manga are, indeed, "pornography for women."

Women's space

Romance novels and BL manga have both been characterized as creating a female-centered space that resists patriarchal pressures or demands. For example, Radway described how her sample population of romance readers "see the act of reading as combative and compensatory,"[78] as providing a space in which they can resist cultural demands placed on them because of their gender and minister to personal needs usually unfulfilled by their family and society. Some BL manga readers feel the same way. For example, survey respondents wrote,

> One thing that isn't exactly "why," but that I like about BL manga/fandom/anime ... it's a chick thing. Yes, technically one could say it's about gay men, but BL manga is usually as much about gay realism as much as the "lesbian" porn guys watch. Online and with friends and at cons, it's really a female space (like romance novels). Though the occasional guy is more than welcome to join us, they're going to be in the minority ... and that's kinda nice. It's by women for women.

> The main reason I love boys' love manga is because I know it was made by a woman for me, another woman. It's a way to celebrate female sexual desires out of the confines of heterosexual relationship definitions. It's a very empowering genre.

> I think Boys' Love is extremely important as a means of purely female sexual expression. I think Boys' Love fandom is a very important look at how women enjoy talking about sexuality and sexual topics with other women in a group setting. It is not like straight porn — men sitting alone watching movies/viewing magazines. Boys' Love is a very community driven form of sexual expression, empowering and envigorating [*sic*] for women.

However, as noted earlier, it's difficult to argue that BL manga, as texts, are female-affirmative when, first, women are largely absent from the stories and, second, when they appear, it's usually in an antagonistic role. BL manga may open a space for women's creativity and sexual pleasure, but they seem to do so at the price of devaluing or erasing women as positive presences within the narrative.

Male/Male Romance

For the most part, Japanese boys' love manga follow the pattern of the popular romance in typology and plot formula, with minor variations attributable to their featuring two male protagonists and originating in a culture with slightly different expectations for a romance novel. However, surveyed readers of boys' love manga do not share all the same values and expectations as surveyed readers of popular romances— BL readers are more likely to accept tragedy and sexual violence within a narrative and are more likely to characterize boys' love as avoiding the stereotyping and gender inequality that they perceive in heterosexual romances. In addition, BL manga's reliance on illustrations and occasional lack of significant plot give it some commonalities with pornography that are not usually found in text-based romantic novels and slash.

BL manga and slash, although usually analyzed as separate entities, can be said to both belong to a larger subgenre of *male/male romance*, which might be defined as *any narra-*

tive that contains as a central plot element the romantic relationship between two or more male characters and is marketed primarily to a female audience.[79]

Identifying m/m romances as a discrete subgenre of romantic fiction permits comparisons between works that have enjoyed a great deal of scholarly analysis, such as slash and BL, and works that share similar characteristics but have, for the most part, been ignored by scholars, such as *The Catch Trap* by Marion Zimmer Bradley, *The Last Herald-Mage* series by Mercedes Lackey, *Swordspoint* by Ellen Kushner, and the numerous m/m romance novels written by women such as Lynn Lorenz, Lee Rowan, Erastes, and many others that were not specifically intended for a gay male audience.[80]

"Marketed primarily to a female audience" was chosen as a defining characteristic instead of "written by a woman" because men can write BL, just as men can write mainstream romance novels (and, alternatively, just as women can write gay male romance novels). What is essential to these genres is not the gender of the author but the conventions of content and form that are called upon within the text to position its reader within a particular engendered space. The implied reader of the mainstream romance is female; and so is the implied reader of BL, even though about ten percent of BL manga and popular romance readers are male.[81] By contrast, the implied reader of the gay male romance is male, although one can assume that a number of women read gay male romances, as well.

Addressing male/male romance as a specific subgenre of popular romance also permits further analysis and refinement of the definition. For example, should books like Anne Rice's Vampire Chronicles novels, the Nightrunner series by Lynn Flewelling, and various novels by Storm Constantine, Sarah Monette, Ginn Hale and similar writers be considered m/m romances, or is their romantic element too peripheral to their central plot to warrant such categorization? To what extent do gay romances problematize the above definition of the male/male romance — do they, in fact, position their implied reader differently from the male/male romance? How? In image-oriented male/male romances, such as manga and film, what does the presumption of a female audience suggest with regard to theories of cinematic spectatorship? To pornographic consumption? Are the women who primarily create and consume male/male romances exploiting or abetting the struggle for gay rights? To what extent is the male/male romance a queer subgenre? The growing popularity of the male/male romance, in the form of slash, boys' love, and original fiction, requires further consideration and analysis.

Notes

1. I put an English-language survey of BL (referred to in the survey as yaoi and *shōnen-ai*) manga readers online from June 28 to November 21, 2005, that attracted a total of 478 respondents, the majority from English-speaking countries. Some of the results from this survey have been previously published in Dru Pagliassotti, "Reading Boys' Love in the West," *Participations* 5, no. 2 (2008), http://www.participations.org/Volume%205/Issue%202/5_02_pagliassotti.htm (accessed July 6, 2009).

2. I have appropriated the phrasing presented in Catherine Salmon & Donald Symons, *Warrior Lovers: Erotic Fiction, Evolution and Female Sexuality* (New Haven: Yale University Press, 2003), 83–86, for ease of comparison.

3. I'm limiting myself to commercially produced BL manga from Japan, which means largely excluding boys' love anime, novels, games, movies, *dōjinshi*, and fan fiction, and boys' love texts created outside of Japan. However, in many cases, readers may safely extrapolate my generalizations to those texts, as well. Within BL manga, I have chosen not to address *shota*, which features love with or between boys under the age of consent; I'm comparatively unfamiliar with it, and it is so likely to be problematic for Western readers that it would require a separate analysis of its own. Finally, a number of my arguments will specifically

relate to BL as a female-authored text read primarily by women; I acknowledge and respect the fact that an increasing number of men are producing and reading BL, and in such cases, I understand that some of my observations may not apply.

4. Salmon & Symons, *Warrior Lovers*, 82.

5. John G. Cawelti, *Adventure, Mystery, and Romance: Formula Stories as Art and Popular Culture* (Chicago: The University of Chicago Press, 1976), 41–42.

6. Kay Mussell, *Fantasy and Reconciliation: Contemporary Formulas of Women's Romance Fiction* (Westport, CT: Greenwood Press, 1984).

7. Ibid, 37.

8. Mulhern, Chieko Irie, "Japanese Harlequin Romances as Transcultural Woman's Fiction," *The Journal of Asian Studies* 48, no. 1 (1989): 50–70.

9. Kannagi Satoru & Odagiri Hotaru, *Only the Ring Finger Knows* (Carson, CA: Digital Manga Publishing, 2004).

10. Mussell, *Fantasy*, 42.

11. Mairead Owen, "Re-Inventing Romance: Reading Popular Romantic Fiction," *Women's Studies International Forum* 20, no. 4 (1997): 544.

12. Carol Thurston, *The Romance Revolution: Erotic Novels for Women and the Quest for a New Sexual Identity* (Urbana: University of Illinois Press, 1987).

13. Minami Kazuka, *My Paranoid Next Door Neighbor* (Gardena, CA: 801 Media, 2007).

14. Futaba Aoi & Mitsuba Kurenai, *Level-C*, Vol. 1. (New York: Kitty Press, 2005).

15. Mussell, *Fantasy*, 43.

16. Hagio Moto, *Tôma no shinzô* (The Heart of Thomas) (Tokyo: Shōgakukan, 1974). Takemiya Keiko, *Kaze to Ki no Uta* (Song of Wind and Trees). 10 vols. (Tokyo: Shōgakukan, 1976–84).

17. Ogasawara Uki, *Virtuoso di Amore* (n.p.: DramaQueen, 2006); Kusumoto Hiroki, *Vampire's Portrait*. Vol. 1 (Gardena, CA: Juné, 2008); Shimada Hisami, *Maid in Heaven* (Torrance, CA: Deux Press, 2008); Shimizu Yuki, *Love Mode*. 11 Vols. (Los Angeles, CA: BLU, 2005–2008). On the other hand, Yamila Abraham's original, English-language BL manga *Dark Prince* seems to fit the gothic-romance pattern relatively well, describing a royal family full of dark secrets and incestuous relationships that threaten the young peasant boy Aeon who is brought into the palace: Yamila Abraham, *Dark Prince*. 3 Vols. (Las Vegas, NV: Yaoi Press, 2007–2008).

18. Mussell, *Fantasy*, 48.

19. Tsurugi Kai, *Black Knight*. 4 Vols. (Los Angeles, CA: BLU, 2006–2009); Tateno Makoto, *Steal Moon*. Vols. 1–2. (Gardena, CA: Juné, 2008–2009); Matoh Sanami, *Fake*. 7 Vols. (Los Angeles, CA: TOKYOPOP, 2003–2004).

20. Mussell, *Fantasy*, 49.

21. Misasagi Fuhri, *Idol Pleasures* (Torrance, CA: Deux Press, 2009).

22. M. Blair, "She Should Just Die in a Ditch," Chapter 7 in this volume. This problem will be addressed again later in her chapter.

23. Mussell, *Fantasy*, 49.

24. Higuri You, *Ludwig II*. Vol. 1. (Gardena, CA: Juné, 2009).

25. Yoshinaga Fumi, *Gerard & Jacques*. 2 Vols. (Los Angeles, CA: BLU, 2006); Ogasawara Uki, *Black Sun* (Gardena, CA: 801 Media, 2008); Minami Megumu, *Pleasure Dome* (New York: Kitty Press, 2007); Kodaka Kazuma, *Midaresomenishi: A Legend of Samurai Love* (New York: Be Beautiful, 2006).

26. Pamela Regis, *A Natural History of the Romance Novel* (Philadelphia: University of Pennsylvania Press, 2003): 30–38. The definitions of each element have been modified to avoid giving the romantic protagonists a gender.

27. Takashima Kazusa, *Man's Best Friend: Inu Mo Arukeba* (Los Angeles, CA: BLU, 2006); Kirishima Tamaki, *Ruff Love* (Torrance, CA: Deux Press, 2008); Amagi Reno, *Part-Time Pets* (Torrance, CA: Deux Press, 2009). *Kemonomimi* are very popular in manga and anime besides BL; they probably migrated into BL as a result of that pre-existing popularity. The closest Western equivalent to *kemonomimi* is the "furry," or anthropomorphic animal, but furries are drawn as humanoid animals—for example, the anthropomorphic-fox Robin Hood in the 1973 animated Disney movie — rather than as regular humans sporting ears and a tail (and/or, more rarely, paws). Moreover, furries do not enjoy the popularity in Western romance novels that *kemonomimi* enjoy in BL manga; they are still primarily found in children's comics and small-press publications.

28. Regis, *Natural History*, 32.

29. For more on this, see Neal Akatsuka's "Uttering the Absurd, Revaluing the Abject," Chapter 9 in this volume.

30. Regis, *Natural History*, 33.

31. Cawelti, *Adventure*, 41.

32. Mussell, *Fantasy*, 89.

33. Cawelti, *Adventure*, 42.

34. Janice A. Radway, *Reading the Romance: Women, Patriarchy, and Popular Literature* (Chapel Hill: The University of North Carolina Press, 1984): 66.

35. Romance Writers of America, "The Romance Genre Overview," http://www.rwanational.org/cs/the_ romance_genre (accessed July 16, 2009).

36. Thurston, *Romance Revolution*, 129.

37. Radway, *Reading the Romance*, 72, italics in original.

38. Carol Ricker-Wilson, "Busting Textual Bodices: Gender, Reading, and the Popular Romance," *The English Journal* 88, no. 3 (1999): 58.

39. Cawelti, *Adventure*, 42.

40. Janet S. Shibamoto Smith, "Changing Lovestyles: Fictional Representations of Contemporary Japanese Men in Love," *positions* 16, no. 2 (2008): 362.

41. Francis Mathy, "Mono no Aware," *Occasional Papers: Center for Japanese Studies* 11 (1969): 147–148.

42. Hagio Moto, *Tôma no shinzô*; Takemiya, *Kaze to Ki no Uta*. The 1988 movie *Grave of the Fireflies* by Isao Takahata may be a familiar example of tragic anime for U.S. readers.

43. When the survey from which this data was drawn was given in 2005, most respondents reported obtaining most of their BL online, which may have familiarized them with titles that have tragic endings. It would be interesting to see whether English-reading BL fans who primarily depend on licensed and translated works give more priority to happy endings, or whether as presumptive anime/manga fans they are also satisfied with sad endings—a comparison with slash readers would also be useful.

44. Kodaka, *Midaresomenishi*; Yoshihara Rieko, *Ai No Kusabi: The Space Between*. 6 Vols. (Gardena, CA: Juné, 2007–2009).

45. Yuki Kaori, *Boys Next Door*. Scanlated by Sakura Crisis. http://sakuracrisis.ukepile.com/projects/ complete/boys-next-door/ (Accessed July 1, 2009); Kunieda Saika, *The Sleeping Man*. Scanlated by Presence Dear. http://presencedear.com/2008/12/31/the-sleeping-man/ (Accessed July 1, 2009). For more discussion of BL manga themes Western publishers choose to bring into the U.S. or to avoid, see Dru Pagliassotti, "GloB-Lisation and Hybridisation: Publishers' Strategies for Bringing Boys' Love to the United States," *Intersections: Gender and Sexuality in Asia and the Pacific* 20 (April 2009), http://intersections.anu.edu.au/issue20/paglias sotti.htm (accessed July 6, 2009).

46. Linda J. Lee, "Guilty Pleasures: Reading Romance Novels as Reworked Fairy Tales," *Marvels & Tales: Journal of Fairy-Tale Studies* 22, no. 1 (2008): 55; Ibid.

47. Joel Powell Dahlquist & Lee Garth Vigilant, "Way Better Than Real: Manga Sex to Tentacle Hentai," in *net.seXXX*, ed. Dennis D. Waskul (New York: Peter Lang Publishing, 2004), 91–103.

48. See discussion of this interpretation of rape in a heterosexual context in Stephanie Wardrop, "The Heroine is Being Beaten: Freud, Sadomasochism, and Reading the Romance," *Style* 29 (Fall 1995): 459–473.

49. See Mary Buhl Dutta, "Taming the Victim: Rape in Soap Opera," *Journal of Popular Film and Television* 27, no. 1 (1999): 34–39.

50. Ann Snitow, "Mass Market Romance: Pornography for Women is Different," in *Woman and Romance: A Reader*, ed. Susan Ostrav Weisser (New York: New York University Press, 2001): 316. First published 1979 in *Radical History Review*, 20, 141–161.

51. Dahlquist & Vigilant, "Way Better Than Real," 100.

52. Suzuki, Kazuko, "Pornography or Therapy? Japanese Girls Creating the Yaoi Phenomenon," in *Millennium Girls: Today's Girls Around the World*, ed. Sherrie A. Inness (Lanham. MD: Rowman & Littlefield, 1998): 258.

53. Graham Law & Norimasa Morita, "Japan and the Internationalization of the Serial Fiction Market," *Book History* 6 (2003): 121.

54. Mulhern, "Japanese Harlequin Romances," 51.

55. Shibamoto Smith, "Changing Lovestyles," 375.

56. Mulhern, "Japanese Harlequin Romances," 60.

57. Ibid, 60. This characterization of the romantic heroine seems dated, however; many heroines in contemporary romances are confident in their abilities, often to the point where one of the central plot barriers to the romance is the heroine's own rejection of marriage — she dreads losing her independence to a man.

58. Ibid.

59. Ibid., 63

60. Radway, *Reading the Romance*, 61, italics in original.

61. Although, for a different perspective on the subject, Stephanie Burley points out that "female homo-erotic desire permeates popular romance." If one accepts this perspective, then perhaps heterosexual female readers feel comfortable with BL because it frees them from the discomfort of their perceived attraction to

the heroine; Stephanie Burley, "What's a Nice Girl Like You Doing in a Book Like This? Homoerotic Reading and Popular Romance," in *Doubled Plots: Romance and History*, ed. Susan Strehle & Mary Paniccia Carden (Jackson, MI: University Press of Mississippi, 2003): 129.

62. Matsui Midori, "Little Girls Were Little Boys: Displaced Femininity in the Representation of Homosexuality in Japanese Girls' Comics," in *Feminism and the Politics of Difference*, ed. Sneja Gunew & Anna Yeatman (Boulder CO: Westview, 1993): 178.

63. Sharon Kinsella, *Adult Manga: Culture and Power in Contemporary Japanese Society* (Honolulu: University of Hawai'i Press, 2000): 117.

64. Suzuki, "Pornography or Therapy?," 244

65. Mizoguchi Akiko, "Male-Male Romance by and for Women in Japan: A History and the Subgenres of Yaoi Fictions," *U.S.–Japan Women's Journal* 25 (2003): 53.

66. The surprise evinced by so many writers about a woman identifying with a male character in BL ignores the popularity among women of other books featuring male central characters — male protagonists are still the majority in genres such as mysteries, thrillers, fantasy, and science fiction, all of which have a large share of female readers.
The interaction a reader has with a fictional character can be complex and multifaceted. Cohen usefully differentiates between identifying with a character; engaging in parasocial interaction with a character; liking or feeling similarity with or affinity for a character; and imitating a character. Identification, he says, "is an imaginative process through which an audience member assumes the identity, goals, and perspective of a character" (261) while engaged with the text; the identification ends "when the audience member is made aware of him- or herself" (252) again. Further, he identifies a number of factors that may affect reader identification with a character — for example, the technology of the text, the level of its narrativity, the duration of familiarity with the characters, the perceived realism of the characters, and similarity between character and reader, "based on a multitude of factors other than demographic similarity of age, gender, or race" (259). Clearly, assuming that female readers can't or wouldn't want to identify with male characters — and male readers with female characters — requires taking a very limited view of the reader's power to imagine and the text's power to evoke. Jonathan Cohen, "Defining Identification: A Theoretical Look at the Identification of Audiences with Media Characters," *Mass Communication & Society* 4, no. 3 (2001): 245–264.

67. Thurston, *Romance Revolution*, 128; Laura Kinsale, "The Androgynous Reader: Point of View in the Romance," in *Dangerous Men & Adventurous Women*, ed. Jayne Ann Krentz (Philadelphia: University of Pennsylvania Press, 1992): 38–39; Salmon & Symons, *Warrior Lovers*, 79. Salmon and Symons found that women who enjoy BL tend to be younger, less homophobic, and considered "tomboys" in their youth, and tend to enjoy buddy, action, science-fiction and horror movies (79–80). See also the report of this research in *The Journal of Sex Research*: Catherine Salmon & Don Symons, "Slash Fiction and Human Mating Psychology," *The Journal of Sex Research* 41, no. 1 (February 2004): 94–100.

68. Veruska Sabucco, *Shonen Ai: Il nuovo immaginario erotico femminile tra Oriente e Occidente* (Roma: Castelvecchi, 2000), 47. Passage translated from Italian by author.

69. Radway, *Reading the Romance*, 82–83

70. Ibid., 77.

71. Thurston, *Romance Revolution;* Salmon & Symons, *Warrior Lovers.*

72. Salmon & Symons, *Warrior Lovers*, 83.

73. Pornography is used here as a general rather than a legal term, suggesting the use of sexually explicit material primarily with the intent of stimulating sexual arousal rather than cultivating aesthetic appreciation. For articles that specifically address BL manga and laws regulating pornography, see Mark McLelland, "The World of Yaoi: The Internet, Censorship and the Global 'Boy's Love' Fandom," *The Australian Feminist Law Journal* 23 (2005): 61–77; and Aleardo Zanghellini, "Underage Sex and Romance in Japanese Homoerotic Manga and Anime," *Social Legal Studies* 18 (2009): 159–177.

74. Kinsella, *Adult Manga*, 141.

75. Salmon & Symons, *Warrior Lovers*, 84.

76. Steven Marcus, *The Other Victorians: A Study of Sexuality and Pornography in Mid-Nineteenth-Century England* (New York: Basic Books, 1974), 273.

77. Snitow, "Mass Market Romance," 316.

78. Radway, *Reading the Romance*, 211.

79. The author has previously explored some of the assertions in this section on her blog, see Dru Pagliassotti, "Boys' Love vs. Yaoi: An Essay on Terminology," http://ashenwings.com/marks/2008/07/17/boys-love-vs-yaoi-an-essay-on-terminology/ and "A Note on Boys' Love & 'Straight' Readership," http://ashenwings.com/marks/2008/07/18/a-note-on-boys-love-straight-readership/. The subgenre's name and definition has changed somewhat in this chapter, however, the former in response to Mark McHarry's comments about character age in BL and the latter as a result of problems operationalizing "created with the intention of appealing to a female

audience" versus "marketed primarily to a female audience"; the latter implies the former but is objectively measurable.

80. For example, Lynn Lorenz wrote in an email to the author on July 16, 2009, that three of her publishers have confirmed, based on sales data, that the people purchasing her male/male romance novels are primarily women.

81. See Pagliassotti, "Reading Boys' Love in the West"; Romance Writers of America, "Romance Literature Statistics: Readership Statistics," http://www.rwanational.org/cs/readership_stats (accessed July 16, 2009). As an aside, only about half of the surveyed BL manga readers, male or female, identified as heterosexual; reader sexuality wasn't reported in the RWA statistics.

Bibliography

Abraham, Yamila. *Dark Prince.* 3 Vols. Las Vegas, NV: Yaoi Press, 2007–2008.

Amagi, Reno. *Part-Time Pets.* Torrance, CA: Deux Press, 2009.

Burley, Stephanie. "What's a Nice Girl Like You Doing in a Book Like This? Homoerotic Reading and Popular Romance." In *Doubled Plots: Romance and History*, edited by Susan Strehle & Mary Paniccia Carden, 127–146. Jackson, MI: University Press of Mississippi, 2003.

Cawelti, John G. *Adventure, Mystery, and Romance: Formula Stories as Art and Popular Culture.* Chicago: The University of Chicago Press, 1976.

Cohen, Jonathan. "Defining Identification: A Theoretical Look at the Identification of Audiences with Media Characters." *Mass Communication & Society* 4, no. 3 (2001): 245–264.

Dahlquist, Joel Powell, and Lee Garth Vigilant. "Way Better Than Real: Manga Sex to Tentacle Hentai." In *net.seXXX*, edited by Dennis D. Waskul, 91–103. New York: Peter Lang Publishing, 2004.

Dutta, Mary Buhl. "Taming the Victim: Rape in Soap Opera." *Journal of Popular Film and Television* 27, no. 1 (1999): 34–39.

Futaba, Aoi, and Kurenai Mitsuba. *Level-C*, Vol. 1. New York: Kitty Press, 2005.

Hagio Moto, *Tôma no shinzô* (The Heart of Thomas). Tokyo: Shōgakukan, 1974.

Higuri, You. *Ludwig II.* Vol. 1. Gardena, CA: Juné, 2009.

Kannagi, Satoru, and Hotaru Odagiri. *Only the Ring Finger Knows.* Carson, CA: Digital Manga Publishing, 2004.

Kinsale, Laura. "The Androgynous Reader: Point of View in the Romance." In *Dangerous Men & Adventurous Women*, edited by Jayne Ann Krentz, 31–44. Philadelphia: University of Pennsylvania Press, 1992.

Kinsella, Sharon. *Adult Manga: Culture and Power in Contemporary Japanese Society.* Honolulu: University of Hawai'i Press, 2000.

Kirishima, Tamaki. *Ruff Love.* Torrance, CA: Deux Press, 2008.

Kodaka, Kazuma. *Midaresomenishi: A Legend of Samurai Love.* New York: Be Beautiful, 2006.

Kunieda, Saika. *The Sleeping Man.* Presence Dear. http://presencedear.com/2008/12/31/the-sleeping-man/ (accessed July 1, 2009).

Kusumoto, Hiroki. *Vampire's Portrait.* Vol. 1. Gardena, CA: Juné, 2008.

Law, Graham, and Morita Norimasa. "Japan and the Internationalization of the Serial Fiction Market." *Book History* 6 (2003): 109–125.

Lee, Linda J. "Guilty Pleasures: Reading Romance Novels as Reworked Fairy Tales." *Marvels & Tales: Journal of Fairy-Tale Studies* 22, no. 1 (2008): 52–66.

Marcus, Steven. *The Other Victorians: A Study of Sexuality and Pornography in Mid-Nineteenth-Century England.* New York: Basic Books, Inc., Publishers, 1974.

Mathy, Francis. "Mono no Aware." *Occasional Papers: Center for Japanese Studies* 11 (1969): 139–153.

Matoh, Sanami. *Fake.* 7 Vols. Los Angeles, CA: TOKYOPOP, 2003–2004.

Matsui, Midori. "Little Girls Were Little Boys: Displaced Femininity in the Representation of Homosexuality in Japanese Girls' Comics." In *Feminism and the Politics of Difference*, edited by Sneja Gunew & Anna Yeatman, 177–196. Boulder CO: Westview, 1993.

McLelland, Mark. "The World of Yaoi: The Internet, Censorship and the Global 'Boy's Love' Fandom." *The Australian Feminist Law Journal* 23 (2005): 61–77

Minami, Kazuka. *My Paranoid Next Door Neighbor.* Gardena, CA: 801 Media, 2007.

Minami, Megumu. *Pleasure Dome.* New York: Kitty Press, 2007.

Misasagi, Fuhri. *Idol Pleasures.* Torrance, CA: Deux Press, 2009.

Mizoguchi, Akiko. "Male-Male Romance by and for Women in Japan: A History and the Subgenres of Yaoi Fictions." *U.S.–Japan Women's Journal* 25 (2003): 49–75.

Mussell, Kay. *Fantasy and Reconciliation: Contemporary Formulas of Women's Romance Fiction.* Westport, CT: Greenwood Press, 1984.

Ogasawara, Uki. *Black Sun.* Gardena, CA: 801 Media, 2008.

_____. *Virtuoso di Amore.* n.p.: DramaQueen, 2006.

Owen, Mairead. "Re-Inventing Romance: Reading Popular Romantic Fiction." *Women's Studies International Forum* 20, no. 4 (1997): 537–546.

Pagliassotti, Dru. "Boys' Love vs. Yaoi: An Essay on Terminology." http://ashenwings.com/marks/2008/07/17/boys-love-vs-yaoi-an-essay-on-terminology/ (accessed July 6, 2009).

_____. "GloBLisation and Hybridisation: Publishers' Strategies for Bringing Boys' Love to the United States." *Intersections: Gender and Sexuality in Asia and the Pacific* 20 (April 2009), http://intersections.anu.edu.au/issue20/pagliassotti.htm (accessed July 6, 2009).

_____. "A Note on Boys' Love & 'Straight' Readership," http://ashenwings.com/marks/2008/07/18/a-note-on-boys-love-straight-readership/ (accessed July 6, 2009).

_____. "Reading Boys' Love in the West." *Participations* 5, no. 2 (2008), http://www.participations.org/Volume%205/Issue%202/5_02_pagliassotti.htm (accessed July 6, 2009).

Radway, Janice A. *Reading the Romance: Women, Patriarchy, and Popular Literature.* Chapel Hill: The University of North Carolina Press, 1984.

Regis, Pamela. *A Natural History of the Romance Novel.* Philadelphia: University of Pennsylvania Press, 2003.

Ricker-Wilson, Carol. "Busting Textual Bodices: Gender, Reading, and the Popular Romance." *The English Journal* 88, no. 3 (1999): 57–64.

Romance Writers of America. "The Romance Genre Overview." http://www.rwanational.org/cs/the_romance_genre (accessed July 16, 2009).

_____. "Romance Literature Statistics: Readership Statistics." http://www.rwanational.org/cs/readership_stats (accessed July 16, 2009).

Sabucco, Veruska. *Shonen Ai: Il nuovo immaginario erotico femminile tra Oriente e Occidente.* Roma: Castelvecchi, 2000.

Salmon, Catherine, and Don Symons. "Slash Fiction and Human Mating Psychology." *The Journal of Sex Research* 41, no. 1 (February 2004): 94–100.

_____. *Warrior Lovers: Erotic Fiction, Evolution and Female Sexuality.* New Haven: Yale University Press. 2003.

Shibamoto Smith, Janet S. "Changing Lovestyles: Fictional Representations of Contemporary Japanese Men in Love." *positions* 16, no. 2 (2008): 359–387.

Shimada, Hisami. *Maid in Heaven.* Torrance, CA: Deux Press, 2008.

Shimizu, Yuki. *Love Mode.* 11 Vols. Los Angeles, CA: BLU, 2005–2008.

Snitow, Ann. "Mass Market Romance: Pornography for Women is Different." In *Woman and Romance: A Reader,* edited by Susan Ostrav Weisser, 307–322. New York: New York University Press, 2001.

Suzuki, Kazuko. "Pornography or Therapy? Japanese Girls Creating the Yaoi Phenomenon." In *Millennium Girls: Today's Girls Around the World,* edited by Sherrie A. Inness, 243–267. Lanham, MD: Rowman & Littlefield, 1998.

Takashima, Kazusa. *Man's Best Friend: Inu Mo Arukeba.* Los Angeles, CA: BLU, 2006.

Takemiya Keiko, *Kaze to Ki no Uta* (Song of Wind and Trees). 10 vols. Tokyo: Shōgakukan, 1976–84.

Tateno, Makoto. *Steal Moon.* Vols. 1–2. Gardena, CA: Juné, 2008–2009.

Thurston, Carol. *The Romance Revolution: Erotic Novels for Women and the Quest for a New Sexual Identity.* Urbana: University of Illinois Press, 1987.

Tsurugi, Kai. *Black Knight.* 4 Vols. Los Angeles, CA: BLU, 2006–2009.

Wardrop, Stephanie. "The Heroine is Being Beaten: Freud, Sadomasochism, and Reading the Romance." *Style* 29 (Fall 1995): 459–473.

Yoshihara, Rieko. *Ai No Kusabi: The Space Between.* 6 Vols. Gardena, CA: Juné, 2007–2009.

Yoshinaga, Fumi. *Gerard & Jacques.* 2 Vols. Los Angeles, CA: BLU, 2006.

Yuki, Kaori. *Boys Next Door.* Sakura Crisis. http://sakuracrisis.ukepile.com/projects/complete/boys-next-door/ (accessed July 1, 2009)

Zanghellini, Aleardo. "Underage Sex and Romance in Japanese Homoerotic Manga and Anime." *Social Legal Studies* 18 (2009): 159–177.

5

Yaoi and Slash Fiction

Women Writing, Reading, and Getting Off?

Mark John Isola

Since the 1970s, the male body has proved to be a productive site in the imagination of American and Japanese females for what has been varyingly theorized as the projection of their sexual fantasies and/or social anxieties, resulting in the visual and verbal narratives of yaoi and slash fiction.[1] In spite of their different national origins, both narrative forms developed concurrently in the 1970s, and each is constructed from a female author or artist's placement of the male body against a hyper-emotionalized and/or hyper-sexualized homoerotic narrative tableau. Even with the efforts of critics to date, yaoi and slash have not yet received sufficient critical scrutiny, particularly as they challenge the established theory of the gaze — from Laura Mulvey's male gaze to Cornel West's normative gaze — now that the circumstances of gazing are being varyingly deployed from non-male, non–Caucasian, and non–Eurocentric perspectives. Between the idea of the homosexual and the ideality of homosexuality, this chapter strives to complicate the critical reception of yaoi and slash narratives, particularly as they pose a challenge for contemporary theory regarding the narrative production and consumption of (homo)sexual narratives.[2]

A Transpositional Genre?

John Storey's rehearsal of the theoretical developments in the understanding of popular culture permits yaoi and slash to be interpreted as pop culture narratives that simultaneously represent a struggle between complicity and resistance to cultural hegemony.[3] These narratives encompass a wide variety of cultural media and authorial perspectives, and they predate the emergence of the Internet, but the medium they have most proliferated in is new media, which can be understood as the emergence of visual and verbal digital narratives, especially as this material is delivered through the television and computer screen. Despite their different national origins, yaoi and slash share a contemporaneous origin, and this paper will conclude with a theory for this seeming coincidence. Nonetheless, despite their different cultural origins, yaoi and slash share many similarities: both are genres primarily produced by women, consumed primarily by women, but are about male homoerotic romance and sex. This similarity has been noted by critics, and Matthew Thorn goes as far as to assert the two are almost identical genres.[4] The impulse to discuss yaoi and slash as the same genre raises the question of how to compare and contrast different narrative forms. For example, how can the sequential art of some forms of yaoi be compared to the prose of slash fiction? And, how can narrative material posted on a Web forum by a seventeen-year-old American female teenage author be compared to the work of a *man-*

84

gaka, who works as a professional artist with editors and assistants? There is also the obvious complication of how narratives that originate from the cultural and linguistic contexts of Japan and Japanese can be compared with narratives that originate in America and in English. Notwithstanding these differences, yaoi and slash share similar narrative considerations of authorship, narratee, and homoerotic subject matter, and this triangulated concurrence recommends a genre consideration, particularly as such functions as a criterion for broad based categorization. This approach feels critically viable, if only to reveal a trend in the production and consumption of popular culture, and there is a certain logic in this, if one acknowledges pop culture's ever-globalizing nature.

There is already an established critical tradition that has managed to traverse the pitfalls that arise for anyone attempting such a worldwide critical purview, and Thorn has gestured toward a way to negotiate these problems. Despite the embedded nature of his ethnographic interviews with Japanese adolescent manga readers, which hinged on the reader's personal history and cultural location, Thorn suggests such idiosyncrasies ultimately contribute to a transnational understanding by informing what consumers "do as participants in popular culture."[5] Thorn embraces the idea of a global media community by suggesting that pop culture material creates a set of shared idioms that transcend regional differences, and regarding yaoi, he asserts, the genre "binds girls and young women who will never meet into a media community."[6] Given the ability of new media to reach a much wider audience than traditional print media, Thorn's assertion, coupled with Stanley Fish's formation of an interpretive community, provides a rationale for reading similarities despite differences.[7]

As pop culture narratives that are widely read on the Internet, yaoi and slash form and frame a multimedia media community that transcends linguistic, national, and cultural borders, and this communitarian impulse suggests the viability of a transcultural critical consideration. For as Dru Pagliassotti's recent findings in her survey of Western yaoi readers demonstrates, there are differences in the ways of reading and interpreting yaoi, but there are also similarities in the production and consumption of these narratives that suggest a shared act of imagining, if not a shared anxiety, which will be explored more in this discussion's conclusion.[8]

Thorn has previously commented on yaoi's communitarian impulse, and Mark McHarry provocatively extends this understanding when he asserts, "Yaoi is remarkable. That fiction in different media in cultures as diverse as Japan and the United States, Latin America, and Europe resonates similarly in so many people may reflect something deep in our imaginations."[9] The psychic resonance McHarry detects may find its roots in the material and the geopolitical, for the American importation of Japanese manga was—at least in part—birthed from the American cultural exportation that began with Commodore Perry's 1853 opening of Japan to Western trade and the post–World War II exportation of American films and comics. This later development would have its most notable impact on the work of Japanese manga artist Tezuka Osamu, who took these influences, made them his own, and exported them back to America in the form of *Astro Boy* and other anime. These titles initiated America to the restyled sequential art of manga, and this influence continues today, mostly notably through the works of Hayao Miyazaki from *Nausicaa of the Valley of the Wind* to *Howl's Moving Castle.* The psychic resonance McHarry detects may find its origin in this material and geopolitical history, which morphed an American pop culture export into an exotic import, and as the art form is imported back into the States, Americans may well detect something resonant in Japanese manga.

Perhaps McHarry's observation of yaoi's psychic resonance is helpfully illuminated by Scott McCloud's contention that the cartoon, which he considers as a simplified iconic image, holds the power to involve the viewer as much or more than the photorealistic image through what he terms the process of amplification through simplification.[10] McCloud asserts the cartoon strips an image down to its iconic form. During this process, McCloud contends there is an amplification of the image's essence, which allows for a universal relation to the image itself. In this way, McCloud posits the image's content exceeds the structure of the pared down form, and he asserts the cartoon functions as an iconic image that allows for self-projection. Accordingly, the visual becomes a vessel for inhabitation, which allows the viewer to morph from observer to participant, a process McCloud calls "viewer-identification."[11]

In thinking about the male body as it is rendered in the similarly pared-down narratives of yaoi and slash, the process of amplification through simplification may permit the female viewer and reader to have a greater degree of androgynous access to the otherwise sexed or gendered image. If so, McCloud's formation goes a long way toward explaining why young girls and women in America, Japan, and beyond find the male body, as it is constructed in the verbal and visual narratives of slash and yaoi, so engaging, for in existential reality, this is not a body to which female artists, authors, or readers have psychological or physiological access. McCloud's theory of the iconic image might additionally aid in interpreting these narratives as they appropriate the male body by evacuating its potential attendant subjectivity for the purposes of the aesthetic expression and/or erotic exploration of a female desire. Such a critical consideration resembles a semiotic practice as this approach endeavors to interpret signs— in their verbal and visual form — whether they are applied to the three-dimensional world of wrestling as in Roland Barthes's *Mythologies* or the virtual world of the Internet, where a majority of yaoi and slash narratives appear. As McHarry suggests, there is an acceptance of yaoi in the West despite the differences between the cultures of America and Japan, and this similar reception may find its basis in the genre's psychic resonance.

From the rationale of a worldwide media community to the contextual considerations of history and economics to the potential for a shared psychic resonance, there is an ample rationale for the consideration of yaoi and slash as variant threads of the same genre. This understanding holds the potential to tease out the critical imperative behind reading the persistent homoerotic presence of the male body in the female imagination as it has increasingly appeared since the late twentieth century, particularly as this narrative impulse has resonated in different media, languages, nation states, and cultures, and the transpositional nature of the genre is perhaps no more apparent than in the breadth of its critical reception.

The Yaoi Ronsō *and Beyond*

The critical reception of yaoi and slash has alternated between considering the narratives as acts of appropriation or as locations of hegemonic resistance. This binary consideration was established during a series of exchanges called the yaoi *ronsō* that took place in the Japanese feminist magazine *Choisir* from 1992 to 1997. The foundational concerns of this discussion have circulated throughout the critical response in America, Japan, and beyond. Scholars Wim Lunsing and McHarry have ably rehearsed the debate's parameters, and the intention here is to provide a brief overview of the discussion to establish its continuity in subsequent critical reception, which has likewise alternated between interpreting the genre as an act of appropriation or agency.[12] This approach feels warranted as the continuity of this variance suggests a need for the re-conceptualization of the narrative production and consumption of gender, sex, and sexuality, particularly when its reception feels contested.

At the beginning of the debate, gay activist and drag queen Satō Masaki expressed the opinion that yaoi was an act of appropriation, and this consideration forms a foundational concern. For Masaki, the problem is that yaoi lacks the authority and authenticity of lived experience; therefore, it risks a socio-political nihilism for the sake of aesthetic expression. Masaki takes particular issue with yaoi's potential to influence the lived experience of the gay individual: "The more confused images of gay men circulate among the general public the harder it is for gay men to reconcile these images with their own lives and the more extreme their oppression becomes."[13] Indeed, there is some evidence of this, for Yajima Masami records the story of a young same-sex attracted Japanese male who claimed yaoi led him to believe "homosexuals must be cute and pretty."[14] From anecdotes such as this, scholar of Japanese media and sexuality Mark McLelland concludes, "The highly idealized 'homosexual' characters and fanciful plots in women's comics therefore do little to foster a sense of recognition or identity in gay male readers."[15] McLelland notes yaoi's particular negative impact on the young man: "As he was neither cute nor beautiful, he worried 'what will become of me?'"[16] The feelings the young man internalized from yaoi exemplify Masaki's concern, and this concern has not been confined to Japan.

With a provocative rhetoric drawn from the history of American racial cooptation, Simon Sheppard characterized yaoi as "a minstrel show" that "puts gay male sex out there for straight people."[17] With Sheppard's quote, a critique similar to Masaki's appears in America as early as 2002, when McHarry recorded this comment at Yaoi-Con, which has served as an annual convention for yaoi producers and fans since 2001. This critical echo suggests a similar constellation of subcultural concern between Japan and America, regarding women writing and consuming a same-sex male desire. McHarry confirms the presence of further cross-cultural similarities in the reception of yaoi when he rehearses how an anonymous yaoi artist "told [him] that some gay-identified men have complained to her that males portrayed in yaoi are not representative of them or of gay males in general, and that they felt uneasy at being objectified by women."[18] This criticism has not been confined to the reception of yaoi, and Thorn detects a similar critique of slash in the West: "In the current environment of open lobbying for homosexual rights, some fans seem to feel the need to justify slash to the gay community, or even to reform slash in such a way as to make it more palatable or 'politically correct.'"[19] Thorn claims no awareness of this politicized concern over yaoi in Japan, yet as the *ronsō* suggests, these concerns may well have predated their appearance in Western criticism.

Masaki's critique set the tone and trajectory for much of the criticism that followed in Japan, America, and beyond, for his concerns additionally presaged Sueen Noh's findings in "Reading Yaoi Comics: An Analysis of Korean Girls' Fandom."[20] In establishing a context for her 1998 research, Noh uses criticisms drawn from Korean comic and gay magazines that echo Masaki's concerns. These criticisms also reach beyond the identitarian concerns of the same-sex attracted male, for Lunsing records lesbian critic Akiko Mizoguchi's agreement with Masaki's contention that yaoi contains the taint of homophobia.[21] From Asia to North America and from yaoi to slash, the female deployment of a same-sex male sexual desire can be observed as having produced a negative critical response that shares the same critical content, if not the same linguistic or political context.

The fulcrum behind Masaki's concern becomes clear when he compares the female yaoi reader to the stereotyped image of the porn consumer: "When you're spying on gay sex, girls, take a look at yourself in the mirror. Just look at the expression on your faces! (You look just like those dirty old men salivating over images of lesbian sex.)"[22] Masaki's criticism should be understood as more resonant than simply idiosyncratic or merely identitarian, for some yaoi producers admit no greater authorial intent than the expression and exploration of a female sexuality through the deployment of a same-sex male sexuality. In his summary of the yaoi *ronsō*, Lunsing records Takemiya Keiko, who claims her popular yaoi title *Kaze to ki no uta* (Song of Wind and Trees; 1976) "was not about gay men but that she used boys' love to liberate girls' sexuality."[23] Beyond the deployment of a same-sex male desire as an appropriative narrative device, Lunsing provides further evidence of a problematic impulse in yaoi when he records Takamatsu Hisako's admission: "She [Hisako] agreed, however, that as a reader of yaoi, she was similar to dirty old men looking at pornography featuring women."[24] On the level of production and consumption, a concern over appropriation hovers over the reception of yaoi and slash, and Keith Vincent helpfully summarizes the imperative behind this concern as it emanated from Masaki's initial criticisms: "yaoi and its readers were violently co-opting the reality of gay men and transferring it into their own masturbatory fantasy."[25]

Through the ethnographic interviews she conducted with Korean female manga fans, Noh finds evidence of what Masaki and others detect — a scopophilic and voyeuristic pleasure behind female yaoi consumption. Lunsing parses Masaki's prior criticism of this tendency as an anxiety over women watching same-sex male desire and argues "gay" manga should receive the same critical scrutiny from Masaki. However, Lunsing misses the central impulse behind Masaki's anxiety, which is predicated upon a fear that yaoi provides a narrative fulcrum from which the non-gay reader will perpetuate a skewed version of gayness and gay people, thereby making gay lived experience more difficult. Masaki's concern is about subjectivity, not sex. Masaki's apprehension has been sustained by McLelland, who asserts "Yet, despite the rather 'fantastic' representation of homosexuality-inclined beautiful youths ... these representations do seem to have affected the way some Japanese women regard actual gay men."[26] This contention contradicts the fantasy/reality binary thought to permeate Japanese manga reading practices, and McLelland corroborates his assertion by rehearsing the stereotypes circulating through mainstream and women's media outlets during the Japanese "gay boom" of the 1990s, where same-sex attracted males were routinely characterized as essentially and effeminately different, where the tabloids promulgated the "best partner" stereotype, and when there was an alleged rise of the "friendship marriage."[27]

Noh's interviews provide further evidence that suggests the outcome Masaki fears by identifying the yaoi narrative as it prefigures and configures the reader's attempts to reproduce self and world as a "yaoi text or context." Noh concludes her research with a pregnant finding: "Consequently, the most significant reason that female fans' readings of yaoi are worthy of note is that yaoi transforms the women's ways of understanding the texts as well as the world."[28] Noh's causal conclusion appears to underscore Masaki's anxiety as he worried over yaoi negatively impacting the already confused understanding of homosexuality. This concern ripples throughout the reception of yaoi and slash as these genres are repeatedly tasked for the deployment of a narrative subjectivity their authors do not occupy, particularly as such has been considered a problematic appropriative act of a gay subjectivity.

The yaoi *ronsō* also initiated the interpretation of yaoi as an act of agency on the part of its producers and consumers, and this antithetical consideration has formed the second foundational concern that continues through the genre's critical reception. Takamatsu Hisako responded to Masaki's criticism by arguing yaoi was liberating for women because unlike heterosexual stories, where women are routinely the object of the male gaze, yaoi constructs an egalitarian model for gazing.[29] Noh's findings suggest readers outside of Japan feel similarly, and Noh goes as far as to summarily state yaoi is "illuminated by a female gaze."[30] Western critics have similarly argued that yaoi functions as an act of agency over sex/gender hegemony by constructing liberatory spaces within which females can negotiate the male gaze. Tina Anderson echoes Takamatsu's opinion when she asserts, "Yaoi allows for that kind of enjoyment—for visual recreation without the self-examination. That's what's so beautiful about it. Women don't have to think about being the ones used and abused and played with."[31] Antonia Levi has described this function when she interprets yaoi's use of same-sex male desire as a narrative device through which Japanese girls and women can negotiate gender inequality to access a more egalitarian vision of romance.[32] Levi's point is bolstered by Japanese yaoi reader Yanagita Akiko, when the latter asserts her interest in yaoi has nothing to do with gay men and everything to do with her dissatisfaction with heterosexual narratives that tended to disadvantage the female.[33] This impulse has been theorized as a resistance to patriarchy, and feminist scholar Ueno Chizuko claims yaoi functions as a buffer that empowers young females to negotiate sex from a distance.[34] Fujimoto Yukari argues likewise when she contends yaoi allows the female viewer to move from the perspective of the violated to the perspective of the voyeur and violator, and Takemiya Keiko claims yaoi is a "first step towards true feminism."[35]

In addition to its feminist impulses, Lunsing has noted the empowering potential of yaoi for Japanese members of the GLBT spectrum. In stark contrast to Masaki's criticisms, Lunsing reports some gay men view yaoi positively: "gay informants could relate their situation and feelings to the manga."[36] James Welker makes the same assertion for some lesbian readers: "Members of the Japanese lesbian community have, however, pointed to boys' love and other gender-bending manga as strong influences on them in their formative years."[37] Welker supports his claim by referencing Oe Chizuka, who "explains that she turned to these manga given the lack of representations of female-female desire that she really identified with."[38] This perspective has not been contained to GLBT readers in Japan. McHarry records the efforts of American gay men as producers and readers of yaoi, and McHarry's observation has been substantiated by Pagliassotti's survey of boys' love readers in the West, which indicates thirty-two percent of the English-language survey respondents and twenty-six percent of the Italian-language respondents identified as gay, lesbian, or bisexual.[39] Similar to the critical continuity that interprets yaoi and slash as an act of appropriation, there is a wide range of representational positions behind the inverse critical continuity that interprets the genre as an act of agency.

During the ongoing yaoi *ronsō*, Tanigawa Tamae countered Masaki's assertion that yaoi fans were like "dirty old men" by redirecting the consideration of oppression to the female reader.[40] Tamae argued Masaki was himself an agent of oppression via his position as a male, and that by virtue of their sex/gender position, female yaoi producers and consumers are more disadvantaged than gay men. Having summarized Tamae's argument, Lunsing concurs, "Their [female yaoi readers] inability to enjoy existing depictions of heterosexual activity combined with unease about female-female sexuality suggests, indeed, that female yaoi fans had the larger problem when it came to dealing with their own sexuality."[41] This valuation has underpinned the interpretation of yaoi as female agency over gay appropriation, and this tendency has permeated the critical reception.

Several critics have used this imperative to interpret the *male cum androgynous* yaoi body as a lesbian persona. Welker references Ueno Chizuko to support this interpretation: "Chizuko has argued that manga artists borrowed a boy's body to draw girl characters and that the beautiful boy is thus the graphic embodiment of the girl's 'idealized self-image.'"[42] Publisher Sagawa Toshihiko concurs: "On the surface, these characters are gay males, but in reality ... they're like young women wearing cartoon character costumes."[43] This critical trend is perhaps best summarized by Patrick Drazen, who comments on Sandra Buckley's understanding of yaoi as "not the transformation or naturalization of difference but the valorization of the imagined potentialities of alternative differentiations."[44] This potential has been expanded upon by other critics, and Welker reads yaoi's gender ambiguity as it allows for the female reader to re-envision the story and opens the text to lesbian reinterpretations.[45] Lunsing aptly sums up this perspective when he asserts: "The implication that gay sex is objectified for the purpose of the sexual liberation of women surely is a queer use of male homosexuality *par excellence*."[46] These considerations recast the appropriating gaze of the "dirty old men" by framing the female gaze of yaoi and slash as an act of agency.

Between charges of gay appropriation to celebrations of queer agency, the concerns of the yaoi *ronsō* continue from first to latest in the critical reception of yaoi and slash. This bifurcated critical continuity evidences something of an interpretive homogeneity that belies the criticisms of differing political, linguistic, cultural, and national contexts, and these critical concurrences may benefit from a global consideration of sexual politics.

Dennis Altman has expressed this desire for a transnational consideration of sexuality: "The more I see, the more skeptical I am of sharp divides between Western and non–Western experiences of sexuality, and the surer I become that we cannot discuss sex/gender structures independent of larger sociopolitical ones."[47] In *The Globalization of Sexuality*, Jon Binnie cautions that any such approach must be wary of replicating metropolitan biases, be suspicious of evolutionary narratives of sexuality and nomenclature, and be mindful of the potential for exporting structures like homophobia.[48] Binnie's final consideration is particularly apt in the study of comparative (homo)sexualities between America and Japan, especially given the former's influence on the latter's sex/gender structures, secondary to the post–World War II MacArthur era writing of the extant Japanese Constitution.

This point of context provides a foundation upon which the critic can interpret correlation without a necessarily reductive veil of cultural or critical presumption, thereby avoiding the cognitive dissonance that results from maintaining the impermeable divide Altman is leery of when interpreting experiences of (homo)sexuality. However, as Pagliassotti's work suggests, a wholly permeable membrane also risks a reductive interpretation, which some critics have detected in the effort to think about the transnational nature of (homo)sexual politics. Pagliassotti's findings gesture toward an important variance between the East and the West regarding the potential for a politicized reading of yaoi, and from this, she concludes: "Further work in this area could be of great utility in describing how literary products may be received and interpreted differently by different cultures around the world."[49]

Binnie similarly identifies this need when he tempers Altman's meta-critical impulse by pointing out the coexisting need for the consideration of local political concerns. Binnie makes this point while commenting on Altman's theory of the global gay as it "tends to present it as a form of 'false consciousness,'" thereby denying the potential for agency in the appropriation of pre-extant gay rights symbols as they are reformulated for the purposes of self-determination and/or resistance in other spaces and territories.[50] Binnie's recalibration may also permit the inclusion of an individual variance, which allows for idiosyncrasy during the production and consumption of a borrowed or shared idiom. In this way, the critic engaging in a comparative reading may consider individual as well as cultural context. This theoretical recalibration more fully actualizes the imperative behind Altman's ultimate desire for understanding "sexuality as involving the complex and varied ways in which biological possibilities are shaped by social, economic, political, and cultural structures."[51] In this way, the critic engaging in a comparative reading may consider individual as well as cultural context. Such a critical move is akin to Thorn's ethnographic interviews of female Japanese readers, which initially led him to conceptualize yaoi's communitarian impulse while interrogating individual interpretive variance.

The inclusion of the local allows for an emendation to Pagliassotti's already productive call for more research into yaoi reading practices, particularly as such permits the possibility of similarity as well as difference, for, as the rehearsal of yaoi and slash's critical reception suggests, perceptions of appropriation and agency can be a matter of micropolitics, which are variable — but not wholly independent of — the larger socio-political sphere Altman gestures toward. Herein may lie something of a productive thread by which to trace the possibility of a global consciousness, but this effort will require a critical approach that moves beyond the bifurcated considerations of the yaoi *ronsō*, which tends to reduce the consideration of the production and consumption of (homo)sexual narratives to a subjective either/or consideration.

Toward a Consideration of Dialectical Productivity

Eve Kosofsky Sedgwick has famously argued for how the homo/hetero binary has structured, if not underpinned, the understanding of modern (homo)sexuality in the West, and her schematic formation offers a helpful way of approaching the concerns of the yaoi debate. Although it may be considered problematic to apply Sedgwick's theories to regions outside the West, it is also problematic not to mention this foundational cognizance, for such an omission would structure the epistemology of (homo)sexuality according to an East/West binary — as if patriarchy and its attendant heteronormativity were only Occidental phenomena and theoretical preoccupations. As the critical work of Japanese theorist Fushimi Noriaki has demonstrated, heteronormativity — what Noriaki terms heterosexualism — does not solely function within the lived experience or critical purview of the West, and the primacy of the homo/hetero binary is pervasive in other modern cultures. Katsuhiko Suganuma succinctly summarizes Noriaki's belief that every individual is subjected to the ideology of hetero-sexualism through the sex/gender regulating discourses of what Noriaki identifies as the hetero-system: "Noriaki argues that no one, neither as a member of a sexual minority nor the majority, lives outside the milieu of the 'hetero-system' as long as they are a member of a society."[52] This assertion frames a first premise for a transnational consideration of sexuality, for if the cultures in question are both patriarchal in nature, it is logical to assume the presence of a hetero-system, for if patriarchy is the ideology, then the mediation of sex, gender, and sexuality are its constitutive discourses. Even if this system were contoured differently, its ultimate goal of patriarchal sexual subjection would be similar.

Noriaki's insights are largely contemporaneous with Sedgwick's, and according to current understanding, his first critical writings were produced around the same time as Sedgwick's *Epistemology of the Closet*, which was published in 1990. As Suganuma summarizes, this critical co-occurrence has prompted Japanese scholars Sunagawa Hideki and Noguchi Katsuzō to posit the idea of a "theoretical synchronicity" between Noriaki's work and the proliferation of queer theory in the West, and their theory of synchronicity raises interesting questions about the coterminous nature of experience with hetero-systems.[53] The presence of Noriaki's work suggests that the application of theory drawn from Sedgwick does not imprint or displace as much as it reflects coextensive critical resistance to systems of oppression. Contrary to casting the application of Sedgwick's ideas as a foisting of Western theory onto non–Western regions, Noriaki's understanding of the hetero-system suggests the aptness of this approach, for the critical use of Sedgwick in light of Noriaki's work may reveal a global cultural intractability, which allows for a productive interpretation of the dichotomous critical reception of yaoi and slash. A productive interpretation of the yaoi debate may find its origins in the emergence of theories like Noriaki and Sedgwick's, particularly as these critical efforts have attempted to theorize the structures of the hetero-system.

Sedgwick proffered her minoritizing and universalizing views as an attempt to describe how, since the late nineteenth century, theories of sexuality have rested upon the understanding of sexuality according to the homo/hetero binary. Sedgwick asserts:

> The first is the contradiction between seeing homo/heterosexual definition on the one hand as an issue of active importance primarily for a small, distinct, relatively fixed homosexual minority (what I refer to as a minoritizing view), and seeing it on the other hand as an issue of continuing, determinative importance in the lives of people across the spectrum of sexualities (what I refer to as a universalizing view).[54]

Having established a foundational theory, Sedgwick follows her definitional move with a statement of intent that foregrounds the ever-present problematic nature of the structures she attempts to define:

> The purpose of this book is not to adjudicate between the two poles of either of these contradictions, for if its argument is right, no epistemological grounding now exists from which to do so. Instead, I am trying to make the strongest possible introductory case for a hypothesis about the centrality of this nominally marginal, conceptually intractable set of definitional issues to the important knowledges and understandings of twentieth-century Western culture as a whole.[55]

Sedgwick acknowledges the lack of an epistemological grounding from which to bring a conclusive understanding, much less an end to the very structures she attempts to delineate, and she admits her deployment of a definition is itself rived with and delimited by the very minoritizing and universalizing impulses she attempts to interpret, thereby perpetuating the structure she seeks to define. Sedgwick's difficulty mirrors the larger post-structural paralysis of attempting to assume an outside perspective from which to speak of culture. Here lies the admitted limit of Sedgwick's efforts in this direction, for her definition is prefigured by the system it seeks to define, thereby circumscribing critical insight by negating the ability to determine without suppositional influence. Sedgwick negotiates this critical morass by foregrounding the need for understanding the centrality of the definition itself, and she posits a binary impulse in the epistemology of homo(sexuality), yet if the fulcrum of the hetero-system is itself a binary structuring, Sedgwick is aware she risks perpetuating the hetero-system as much as she may be able to define it by redeploying its basic either/or structural impulse.

Something of this tendency appears in the criticism of yaoi and slash, as this critical reception has largely been structured along binary terms: appropriation/agency, negative/positive, harmful/salubrious, disempowering/empowering. This trending mirrors the recently entrenched binary considerations of gay studies/queer theory, where the first tends toward fixity and the latter fluidity. This particular way of thinking about (homo)sexuality emerged as a central concern in contemporary theory during the 1990s when emergent theories, like Sedgwick's, ruptured the structures of thinking through the representational aspects of the homo/hetero binary in favor of deconstructing them. This was itself a movement from fixity to fluidity, for if the former is a fetish for fixity, the latter exhibits a fetish for fluidity. However, the first was never as fixed as was thought, and the second is not as flexible as was hoped, and in the contested space between them, the influence of the hetero-system may well appear in the either/or alignment of the discussion, and its pertinaciousness may also be detected in the critical reception of yaoi and slash. This binary consideration reduces the production and consumption of yaoi and slash narratives to a negative or positive evaluation (depending upon position) without grappling with the presence of both. A recalibration to Sedgwick's original theoretical framing may produce something of a methodological approach to resist the already constituted either/or nature of the hetero-system by considering the regulating force of the binary itself.

Instead of alternating between the two poles of a binary, Sedgwick's formation of the centrality of minoritizing and universalizing tendencies may benefit from a dialectical consideration that figures the ratio of each with and without the presence of one being predicated upon the enforced absence, if not abjection, of the other. Sedgwick's minoritizing and universalizing impulses may well perform a discursive function in Noriaki's hetero-system for the purpose of enforcing the larger ideological hegemony of hetero-sexualism. For, when it comes to cultural acts or artifacts already riven with a homo/hetero binary that marks the decentered minority sexual subjectivity, thereby unmarking a centered majority sexual subjectivity that is determined and constructed from the marked, it is not a matter of seeing either this or that but rather seeing the presence of both as constitutive elements of cultural hegemony, as objects and interpretations are already interpolated in understanding. This calls for a critical consideration secondary to the intractability of what Fushimi calls the hetero-system (Sedgwick similarly allows for the ubiquity of such in any male-dominated society). An awareness of this omnipresent structuring, what Anthony Giddens would acknowledge as part of his theory of structuration, holds the potential to parse critical resistance from complicity with a predetermined outcome. The already-constituted nature of the binary may be productively negotiated by the application of a dialectical consideration of minoritizing and universalizing impulses where productivity is considered as the third term.

The lexical ambiguity of the word productivity holds the potential for a rigorous methodological approach for parsing the ratio of minoritizing and universalizing impulses in a cultural act or artifact and likewise holds the potential for a critical and political utility by revealing the hetero-system's pre-figuration and continuation of hetero-sexualism. In other words, the polysemy of productivity provides a multifaceted list of critical considerations that may serve as a method for tracing and/or excavating the discursive apparatus that predetermines the representation of (homo)sexuality. This utility for critically engaging with minoritizing and universalizing impulses is suggested by the simultaneous connotations of the word productivity as a word that conveys:

- the quality of being productive, as such foregrounds the imperative of interpreting how and for whom the binary is productive or fails to be in any given deployment;
- the linguistic sense of generative currency or its lack in a native speaker's deployment of a linguistic structure, as this understanding requires an etymological and ethnographic understanding of the binary for the purposes of providing what New Historicist Stephen Greenblatt might term a thick contextualization;
- the medical sense of the productivity of a cough, as such allows for the understanding of the binary's force of abjection (this is a particularly provocative consideration given Kristevan theory and the fact that the content of a cough is itself a product of the expectorating body);
- the biological sense of the rate of bio-material consumable for fuel produced by an organism, as such holds the potential to gauge the agency and/or appropriation which feeds on the application of the binary;
- the economic sense of the ratio of quantity and quality of units produced to the labor spent per unit, for this allows for the binary's valuation and distinction of the literary versus the popular.

These considerations begin to delineate the critical potential of tasking the minoritizing and universalizing impulses as a dialectic, and it spares Sedgwick's formation the criticism of reductive exclusivity to which it has been prone, for it subjects the entirety of the hetero-system's pre-figuration of hetero-sexualism into question even as this system may itself silence options that cannot be neatly binarized in favor of those that can. On a local concern to this discussion, a consideration of dialectical productivity provides a starting point for grappling with the seemingly simple to understand binary considerations of yaoi and slash's critical reception, since it destabilizes them among similar and dissimilar subject positions, ranging from the individual, the economic, the political, the cultural, and beyond.

Further consideration of a dialectical approach may prove fruitful in providing a comprehensive understanding of how and why the critical reception of yaoi and slash tends to alternate between charges of agency and appropriation, and such an understanding may well reveal the political utility and/or limits of the genre. Moreover, it may bring a deeper degree of understanding to the ethical considerations surrounding appropriative/authorial use and the consumption/production of a textual sexual subjectivity not occupied by an artist, author, or reader, for as previously stated, no matter how androgynous the silhouette, the male body of yaoi and slash is not a corporeality the female author or reader has psychological or physiological access to, and this reality calls for an ethical consideration.

Lunsing suggests a desire for ethical self-reflection can be found at the heart of the yaoi *ronsō*: "[Masaki] began the yaoi dispute on the instigation of a female friend, Irokawa Nao, editor of *Choisir*. The women engaging in the discussion wanted to search their souls and Masaki's writings served as a welcome incentive."[56] Indeed, Masaki's original comments incented this self-examination: "When you're spying on gay sex, girls, take a look at yourself in the mirror." The word mirror may hold thick contextual currency as it additionally suggests the female yaoi reader consider the state of the other while reflecting upon self, given the Shintō reverence of mirrors as the image of self rather than the Lacanian notion of fragmentation. Perhaps it is not Western homophobia, as Matthew Thorn suggests, but the imperative for self-examination that also compels slash fans to question the foundation upon which their writing and reading habits rest.[57] A dialectical consideration may help establish an ethical ratio between appropriation and agency in authorship and readership, for if the fluidity of our fancy denies the fixity of the other, then our fluidity becomes fancifully fixated on self, reducing the coital potential of the transpositional pun to merely masturbatory material.

Concluding an Anxious Rationale

Beyond the reception of yaoi and slash as acts of appropriation or agency, their critical reception has largely tended to interpret a playful impulse in the narratives, but there may be a thread of panic here. Thorn observes, "One precondition for slash and yaoi fandom is an awareness of homosexuality, which nonetheless remains largely abstract."[58] Thorn's observation may point to an understanding of the genre as it results from a metanarrative rupture for the postmodern generations of women who, in addition to facing continued sexual oppression coupled with changing gender roles, have had to face the reality of (homo)sexuality, particularly as it creates the possibility for their opposite sex desire accruing to a body that exhibits a same-sex desire. This anxiety is in addition to having to process the homosexual as sexual competition. The male body of the visual and verbal narratives of yaoi and slash may well be the postmodern female doppelganger, and a female anxiety over (homo)sexuality may have incited the concurrent narrative developments of women writing a same-sex male desire in Japan and America. This raises the problem of reading one nation state in the contextual terms of the other, but such a concern precludes the potential for similar points of context. Either way, an emerging gay visibility can be detected in the Japanese and American cultures of the mid-twentieth century.

Although it served more as a fulcrum for subsequent revolutionary political organization than a revolution in and of itself, Stonewall nonetheless marks a movement toward a gay visibility, and there is evidence of a similar increasing gay visibility in Japan. Mark McLelland asserts, "There was no Stonewall Revolution in Japan, no iconic event that represents a turning point (no matter how imaginary) in this journey [of Japan's sexual minorities]."[59] This may well be the case; however, visibility is not predicated upon revolutionary or iconic events, and as Sunagawa Hideki points out, there has been an increasing gay visibility in the publishing markets of Japan, starting with the 1950s magazines such as *Amatoria,* which was contemporaneous with the appearance in America of the 1950s muscle magazines, not to mention Mattachine's *ONE* and the Daughters of Bilitis's *The Ladder,* and leading up to the 1971 appearance of *Barazoku,* which Hideki considers "the first commercial magazine aimed at gay men."[60] Whether these magazines were vitiated by homophobia or not, they evidence the circulation of material that, in addition to other mainstream representations, suggests a proliferating degree of visibility, if not also an increasing awareness, in the cultural currency of Japan and America for a same-sex male sexual desire, and this visibility may well be the fulcrum behind the developments of yaoi and slash. Such an insight holds the potential to morph Dennis Altman's theory of global (homo)sexuality from a theory of global influences to a reading of global impulses, and just as Hideki and Katsuzō detect a theoretical synchronicity between the works of Sedgwick and Noriaki, there may well be a gay synchronicity between the contemporaneous evolutions of yaoi and slash.

Notes

1. The term yaoi vies with the title boys' love for primacy in describing the verbal and visual narratives under discussion, but since this term accompanied my introduction to the genre, I prefer it, particularly as it tends to foreground the hypersexualization of female produced same-sex male textual sexual desire.

2. As this chapter argues, sexual narratives contain an already-constituted absence and presence of the homo/hetero binary. The phrasing *(homo)sexuality* attempts to invoke a sense of this understanding; this parenthetic formation connotes the discursive pressure of the sex/gender system as it simultaneously constructs heterosexuality as the majority sexuality and homosexuality as a minority sexuality under the larger ideological project of heteronormativity.

3. John Storey, *Cultural Studies and the Study of Popular Culture: Theories and Methods* (Athens, GA: University of Georgia Press, 2003), 4.

4. Matthew Thorn, "Girls and Women Getting Out of Hand: The Pleasure and Politics of Japan's Amateur Comics Community," in *Fanning the Flames: Fans and Consumer Culture in Contemporary Japan*, ed. William W. Kelly (Albany, NY: State University of New York Press 2004), 172.

5. Matthew Thorn. *What Japanese Girls Do With Manga, and Why*. Matt-Thorn.com. http://www.matt-thorn.com/shoujo_manga/jaws/index.php.

6. Ibid.

7. Stanley Fish, *Is There a Text in This Class?* (Cambridge, MA: Harvard University Press, 1980), 148.

8. Dru Pagliassotti, "Reading Boys' Love in the West," *Particip@tions* 5, no. 2 (2008), http://www.partici pations.org/Volume%205/Issue%202/5_02_pagliassotti.htm.

9. Mark McHarry, "Yaoi: Redrawing Male Love," *The Guide* (2003): par 7, http://www.guidemag.com/temp/yaoi/a/mcharry_yaoi.html.

10. Scott McCloud, *Understanding Comics: The Invisible Art* (New York: Harper Perennial, 1994), 30.

11. Ibid., 42.

12. Wim Lunsing, "*Yaoi Ronsō*: Discussing Depictions of Male Homosexuality in Japanese Girls' Comics, Gay Comics and Gay Pornography," in *Intersections: Gender, History, and Culture in the Asian Context* 12 (2006): pars 14–25, http://intersections.anu.edu.au/issue12/lunsing.html and Mark McHarry, "Identity Unmoored: Yaoi in the West," in *Queer Popular Culture: Literature, Media, Film, and Television*, ed. Thomas Peele (New York: Palgrave, 2007), 183–95.

13. Satō Masaki, quoted in McHarry, "Identity Unmoored" 2007, 186.

14. Yajima Masami, quoted in Mark McLelland, "Male Homosexuality and Popular Culture in Modern Japan," in *Intersections: Gender, History, and Culture in the Asian Context* 3 (2000): par 18, http://intersec tions.anu.edu.au/issue3/mclelland2.html.

15. McLelland, *Male Homosexuality*, par 18.

16. McLelland, *Male Homosexuality*, par 18.

17. McHarry, "Identity Unmoored," 187.

18. McHarry, "Identity Unmoored," 188.

19. Thorn, "Girls and Women," 173.

20. Sueen Noh, "Reading Yaoi Comics: An Analysis of Korean Girls' Fandom," http://moongsil.com/study/yaoi_eng.pdf.

21. Lunsing, *Yaoi Ronsō*, par 27.

22. Satō Masaki, quoted in McHarry, "Identity Unmoored," 186.

23. Lunsing, *Yaoi Ronsō*, par 6.

24. Lunsing, *Yaoi Ronsō*, par 24.

25. Keith Vincent, quoted in McHarry, "Identity Unmoored," 186.

26. McLelland, *Male Homosexuality*, par 19.

27. Ibid.

28. Noh, *Reading Yaoi*, 13.

29. Lunsing, *Yaoi Ronsō*, par 15.

30. Noh, *Reading Yaoi*, 7.

31. Tina Anderson, interview by Kai-Ming Cha, "I Want My Boys' Love," *Publishers Weekly*, November 28, 2006. http://www.publishersweekly.com/article/CA6395121.html.

32. Antonia Levi, *Samurai from Outer Space: Understanding Japanese Animation* (Chicago: Open Court, 1996), 135.

33. Lunsing, *Yaoi Ronsō*, par 16.

34. Ueno Chizuko, quoted in Thorn, *Girls and Women*, 179.

35. Takemiya Keiko, quoted in Thorn, *Girls and Women*, 179.

36. Lunsing, *Yaoi Ronsō*, par 29.

37. James Welker, "Beautiful, Borrowed, and Bent: 'Boys' Love' as Girls' Love in *Shōjo Manga*," in *Signs: Journal of Women in Culture and Society* 31, no. 3 (2006): 843.

38. Oe Chizuka, quoted in Welker, "Beautiful, Borrowed," 843.

39. Pagliassotti, *Reading Boys,'* table 3.

40. Lunsing, *Yaoi Ronsō*, par 18.

41. Ibid.

42. Welker, "Beautiful, Borrowed," 842.

43. Sagawa Toshihiko, quoted in Frederik Schodt, *Dreamland Japan: Writings on Modern Manga.*

44. Sandra Buckley, quoted in Patrick Drazen, *Anime Explosion! The What? Why? & Wow! of Japanese Animation* (Berkeley, CA: Stone Bridge Press, 2003), 88.

45. Welker, "Beautiful, Borrowed," 866.

46. Lunsing, *Yaoi Ronsō*, 33.

47. Dennis Altman, "Rupture or Continuity? The Internalization of Gay Identities," in *Postcolonial Queer: Theoretical Intersections*, ed. John Hawley (Albany, NY: State University of New York Press, 2001), 36.

48. Jon Binnie, *The Globalization of Sexuality* (London: SAGE Publications, 2004).

49. Pagliassotti, *Reading Boys'*, par 71.

50. Binnie, *Globalization of Sexuality*, 69.

51. Altman, *Rupture*, 22.

52. Katsuhiko Suganuma, "Enduring Voices: Fushimi Noriaki and Kakefuda Hiroko's Continuing Relevance to Japanese Lesbian and Gay Studies and Activism," in *Intersections: Gender, History and Culture in the Asian Context* 14 (2006): par 6, http://intersections.anu.edu.au/issue14/suganuma.htm.

53. Ibid, par 20.

54. Sedgwick, Eve Kosofsky, *Epistemology of the Closet* (Berkeley, CA: University of California Press, 1990), 1.

55. Ibid, 2.

56. Lunsing, *Yaoi Ronsō*, 26.

57. Thorn, *Girls and Women*, 173.

58. Ibid, 180.

59. Mark McLelland, *Queer Japan from the Pacific War to the Internet Age* (Lanham, MD: Rowman & Littlefield Publishers, 2005), 8.

60. Sunagawa Hideki, "Japan's Gay History," *Intersections: Gender, History, and Culture in the Asian Context* 12 (2006): par 5. http://intersections.anu.edu.au/issue12/sunagawa.html.

Bibliography

Altman, Dennis. "Rupture or Continuity? The Internalization of Gay Identities." In *Postcolonial Queer: Theoretical Intersections*, edited by John Hawley, 19–42. Albany, NY: State University of New York Press, 2001.

Anderson, Tina. "I Want My Boys' Love." Interview by Kai-Ming Cha. *Publishers Weekly*, November 28, 2006. http://www.publishersweekly.com/article/CA6395121.html

Binnie, Jon. *The Globalization of Sexuality*. London: SAGE Publications, 2004.

Drazen, Patrick. *Anime Explosion! The What? Why? & Wow! of Japanese Animation*. Berkeley CA: Stone Bridge Press, 2003.

Fish, Stanley. *Is There a Text in This Class? The Authority of Interpretive Communities*. Cambridge, MA: Harvard University Press, 1980.

Giddens, Anthony. *The Constitution of Society: Outline of the Theory of Structuration*. Berkeley, CA: University of California Press, 1986.

Hideki Sunagawa. "Japan's Gay History." *Intersections: Gender, History, and Culture in the Asian Context* 12 (2006). http://intersections.anu.edu.au/issue12/sunagawa.html.

Levi, Antonia. *Samurai from Outer space: Understanding Japanese Animation*. Chicago: Open Court, 1996.

Lunsing, Wim. "*Yaoi Ronsō*: Discussing Depictions of Male Homosexuality in Japanese Girls' Comics, Gay

Comics and Gay Pornography." In *Intersections: Gender and Sexuality in Asia and the Pacific*, 12 (2006). http://intersections.anu.edu.au/issue12/lunsing.html

McCloud, Scott. *Understanding Comics: The Invisible Art*. New York: Harper Perennial, 1994.

McHarry, Mark. "Yaoi: Redrawing Male Love." *The Guide* (2003). http://www.guidemag.com/temp/yaoi/a/mcharry_yaoi.html.

_____. "Identity Unmoored: Yaoi in the West." In *Queer Popular Culture: Literature, Media, Film, and Television*, edited by Thomas Peele, 183–95. New York: Palgrave Macmillan, 2007.

McLelland, Mark. "Male Homosexuality and Popular Culture in Modern Japan." In *Intersections: Gender, History, and Culture in the Asian Context* 3 (2000). http://intersections.anu.edu.au/issue3/mclelland2.html.

_____. *Queer Japan from the Pacific War to the Internet Age*. Lanham, MD: Rowman & Littlefield, 2005.

Noh, Sueen. "Reading YAOI Comics: An Analysis of Korean Girls' Fandom." http://moongsil.com/study/yaoi_eng.pdf.

Pagliassotti, Dru. "Reading Boys' Love in the West." *Particip@tions* 5, no. 2 (2008). http://www.participations.org/Volume%205/Issue%202/5_02_pagliassotti.htm.

Schodt, Frederik. *Dreamland Japan: Writings on Modern Manga*. Berkeley, CA: Stone Bridge Press, 1996.

Storey, John. *Cultural Studies and the Study of Popular Culture: Theories and Methods*. Athens, GA: University of Georgia Press, 2003.

Thorn, Matthew. "What Japanese Girls Do with Manga and Why." Paper presented at the Japan Anthropology Workshop of the University of Melbourne, Australia, July 10, 1997. http://www.matt-thorn.com/shoujo_manga/jaws/index.php.

_____. "Girls and Women Getting Out of Hand: The Pleasure and Politics of Japan's Amateur Comics Community." In *Fanning the Flames: Fans and Consumer Culture in Contemporary Japan*, edited by William W. Kelly, 169–87. Albany, NY: State University of New York Press, 2004. Repr., http://matt-thorn.com/shoujo_manga/outofhand/index.php.

Welker, James. "Beautiful, Borrowed, and Bent: 'Boys' Love' as Girls' Love in *Shōjo Manga*." *Signs: Journal of Women in Culture and Society* 31, no. 3 (2006): 841–870.

6

101 Uses for Boys

Communing with the Reader in Yaoi and Slash

Marni Stanley

Although popular culture genres such as action manga and television scripts have been generated predominantly by male writers, women have found (at least) two avenues through which to assert themselves in the discourses of popular culture — yaoi and slash. Yaoi are graphic works. Slash stories are generally not illustrated, though drawings and creative Photoshopping or carefully chosen stills are not uncommon. Both are genres of popular culture predominantly produced by women that have, as their common subject, males becoming sexually involved with each other. In published yaoi, which originate in Japan but are available in English translation, these males are original characters who are often young (school classmates are popular) but may also be doctors, diplomats, gangsters, lawyers, cruise-ship captains, business men, and so on. In slash, the characters are usually borrowed from another source, especially television, and may be police, lawyers, space travelers, vampires and their slayers, or any number of other occupations. Increasingly, they are new characters, as more "original slash" is being written.

Critical response to these two genres has sometimes been anxious and derisive about what yaoi and slash might signify about female sexuality. Some psychoanalytic theorists, in particular, have read these texts as attempting to compensate for feminine "lack." They see the authors of yaoi and slash as disempowered female writers compensating for their exclusion from the discourse of male homosexuality/homosociality by writing their own texts. Instead of reading these genres as full of transgressive possibility, they see them as evidence of diminished female sexual agency.

Rather than being overzealous in the application of psychoanalytic theory to these two popular genres, it may be useful to take the word of many of their creators and see these texts as more about pleasure and fun than compensation or lack. What if, as Hélène Cixous so wittily suggests in "The Laugh of the Medusa," women are not obsessively focused on the "little pocket signifier"[1] because they lack one but are, rather, more inclined to laugh at the whole phallogocentric dog-and-pony show? There are other ways to participate in culture than those traditionally assigned to women. Reading women as essentially "lacking" certainly limits one's scope. How much more amusing for women to be subversive in the face of limited participation and to find more playful, more transgressive, more satisfying ways of joining the cultural conversation.

If women writing about sex is still transgressive, then women writing about sex using the male body almost exclusively and then inviting other women to enjoy these stories, or even attempt writing them themselves, is doubly transgressive. Yaoi and slash are transgressive precisely because they are joyous and playful and refuse to take themselves, or the many iconic narratives they subvert, seriously, and because they invite their readers to play along.

99

While both yaoi and slash play with culturally dominant narratives of male action, they also play with ideas of romance, relationship, and sex itself. They joyfully transgress expectations of female sexuality by subverting established, even iconic, narratives, such as buddy flicks, space westerns, and boys' school melodramas, into male homosexual stories. These genres open a whole new world of play for their mostly female creators. And it is a world into which these creators invite their readers in order to share the fun. In both genres the creators directly address the reader and invite — even demand — feedback, engaging the reader's active response in a way few texts do.

Psychoanalytic theorists, with their emphasis on the ways these genres make thinking about sex less frightening for women because they compensate for women's disempowerment, offer a substantive challenge to any reading of these genres as predominantly play. Midori Matsui offers a psychoanalytic reading of yaoi in which she argues of the key characters:

> the boys were the little girls' displaced selves ... the fictitious boys were endowed with reason, eloquence and aggressive desire for the other, compensating for the absence of logos and sexuality in the conventional portraits of girls. In short they signified the possession of the phallus as opposed to the feminine "lack."[2]

The problem with this reading of yaoi is that it emphasizes negative, compensatory motivations, leaving women, as so often in non-feminist psychoanalytic theory, making up for a lack of something.

Sharon Kinsella, though she argues yaoi originated as a form of parody of mainstream manga, also critiques the genre in terms of compensation or substitution: "In the context of the obvious range of restrictions on behaviors and development that women experience in contemporary society, young female fans feel more able to imagine and depict idealized strong and free characters if they are male."[3] She argues that female readers can identify with the "slightly more effeminate male of a couple." This reading, however, misses the point: if both characters are male, why should they limit their identification merely to the more effeminate one, especially if female readers are seeking to compensate for feminine "lack"?

Kristy Valenti similarly claims, "women enjoy yaoi because it is a way for them to be entertained by sex in a non-threatening way, without the anxieties and problems associated with being female, such as pregnancy and misogyny."[4] This interpretation of the genre again implies that women are compensating, in this case for fears and anxieties; a reading that leaves little room for pleasure, rather than reassurance, and none at all for play.

The common ground in these arguments is that they all cast in the negative the motivation for women to write about males in love/lust with each other. This approach argues that these works are motivated by "lack" or "restrictions" or "anxiety." Such a negative understanding of the origins of the genre certainly makes it more difficult to see the playfulness and humor of many of these texts or to understand the role humor frequently plays in the author/reader relationship. In terms of their self-representation in addresses to the reader, the writers and artists of yaoi and slash do not appear to be obsessively trying to resolve sexual or gender-based anxieties; these portions of their texts are too playful for that.

Play, the kind of play that mocks dearly held mainstream truths, is a means of claiming ground, of transgressing the rules in ways that are empowering rather than compensatory. Both yaoi and slash tend to locate their stories in male-dominated worlds where women have often been trivialized and rendered incidental or reduced to acted-upon subjects. These authors have responded by interrupting and disrupting these worlds by playing with social and sexual conventions and by inviting the audience to join in the game. In this way, the authors provide points of access for women into these homosocial discourses and into the representations of sex and sexuality that have heretofore been dominated by men as both producers and consumers.

Writing about slash, Susanne Jung argues that "women writing about men having sex is then doubly transgressive in that it not only violates the notion of female sexual ignorance but also has at its centre ... male homosexuality,"[5] a sexuality that Jung notes is historically characterized by secrecy. In fact, both male homosocial and homosexual worlds have historically been kept secret from women. Not secret in the sense that women did not know about them, but secret in the sense that they were often supported by the structures of male-only institutions and spaces to which women did not have access. Women could not physically enter many of these spaces, or they were curtailed within some public portion of them; and, more important, they did not have access to male homosocial/sexual culture. Whether those spaces were schools and universities, clubs or sporting venues, or even workplaces, the exclusion of women was often fiercely defended and surrendered, where it has been surrendered, only after legal challenge. Many of those spaces are the same spaces where yaoi and slash stories are set.

Some yaoi and slash writers add to their transgressions not only by writing about males having sex with each other but by inviting other women to enjoy the thought experiment and even to have a go at imagining it and elaborating on it for themselves. Many yaoi have an afterword in which the author/artist (or both if they are different people) addresses the reader, generally inviting feedback and engaging the reader directly. Usually referred to in the table of contents as "Bonus Pages," these pages, seemingly superfluous to the story, may include sketches, a short bonus story, or even an "interview" with one of the characters.

Cathy Camper has dismissed these bonus pages in strongly gendered terms: "almost all manga include 'girly-girl' notes from the female creators to their fans, apologizing for mistakes and agonizing over deadlines."[6] Although it is true that some bonus pages are primarily thank-you notes to editors and assistants, other authors use the afterword to provide insight into their attitude to their work.

Writers of yaoi invite and even direct readers to read their texts as lessons on how to develop a more nuanced erotic imagination. Yaoi author Ritsu Natsumizu delights in providing mini imagination workshops for her readers in her bonus pages. For example, at the end of *Crushing Love,* she discusses the "episode of the dazzling hardware store" where she noticed "various thickness chains [*sic*] that are sold by the meter. I was wondering where the local semes get these goods, but I'm glad that they're easily obtainable."[7] Then she demonstrates to her readers how almost anything can be used to exercise one's imagination when she takes two different cookies off her snack plate and imagines two men who would have some of the characteristics of these cookies and then promptly puts them in bed together (see Fig. 1). She ends this segment by teasing her readers with "what kind of wonderful imaginations do you have?"[8] She explicitly invites her readers to develop their fantasy worlds, encouraging them to see this as a trainable skill and praising them for their own imaginations.

In the bonus pages for *Love Bus Stop,* Natsumizu starts with a close-up drawing of the hem of a man's suit pant leg breaking over a dress shoe labeled "parts of the suit that are kinda sexy No.1."[9] She goes on to talk about how magazines and catalogues are a great source of material for fantasy and uses the example of a catalogue of expensive home items to

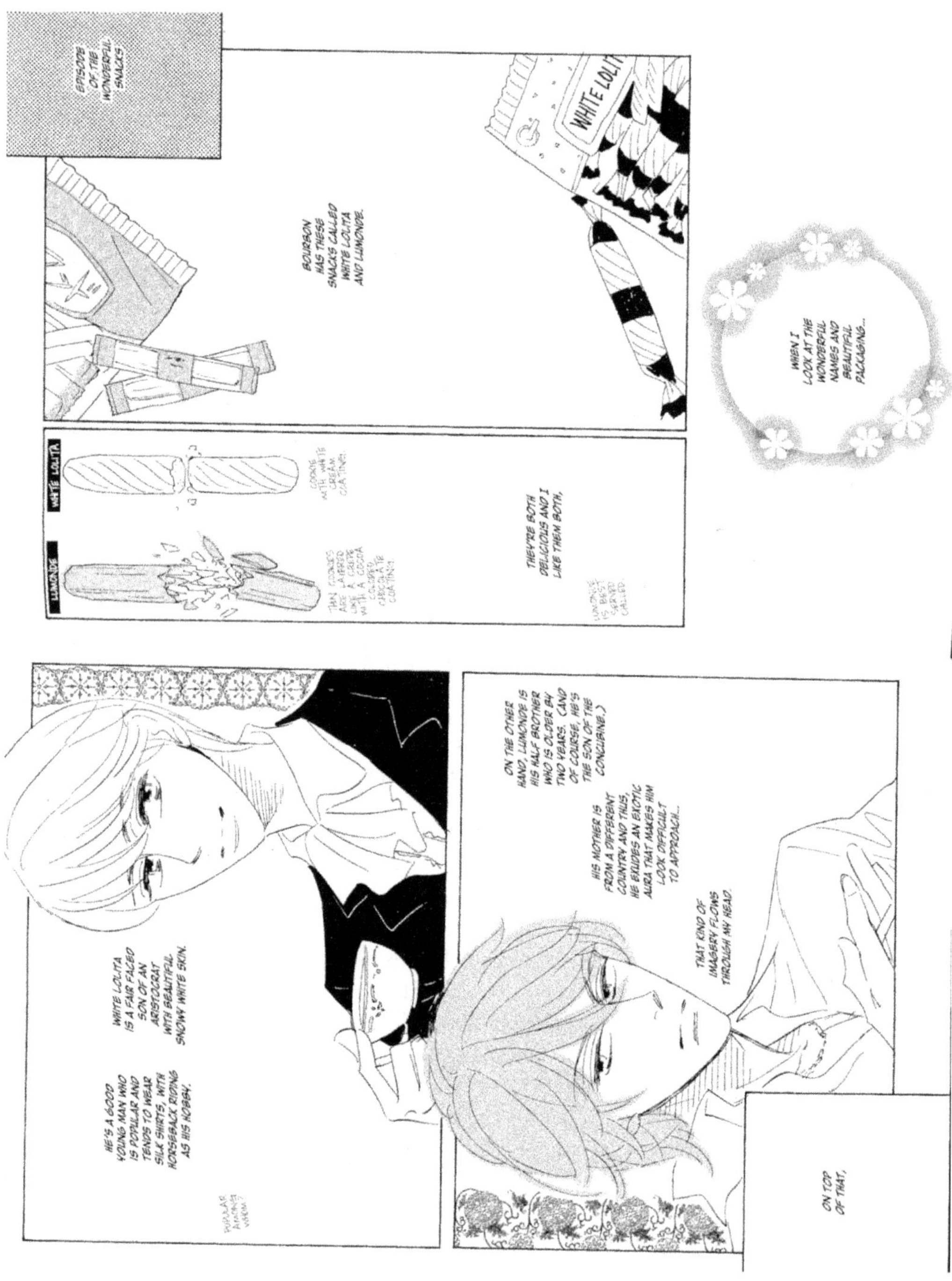

Figure 1. "Episode of the Wonderful Snacks," Ritsu Natsumizu. *Crushing Love.* English translation © 2007 by DIGITAL MANGA, INC, Gardena, CA.

demonstrate. She draws a beautiful and expensive wooden handkerchief case from the catalogue and says, "things like [this] get my heart pumping before the fantasy even starts. Before this, I didn't even know they made handkerchief cases."[10] Then she demonstrates how to use objects from the catalogue as props in a scenario she devises in which a wealthy man seduces a "normal salary man." She ends the exercise saying "How's that? You should try it, everyone."[11] Her explicit invitation to her readers is that they should develop their own fantasy skills through her lesson plan.

Natsumizu takes on the role of the initiate to these pleasures of fantasy, inviting her readers to play in their own imaginations even if they do not write or draw. Nothing in her style suggests or reveals any anxiety or fear or lack. Instead she begins from the position that her readers have "wonderful imaginations" full of potential; her role is to teach by providing her readers with examples of techniques for playing in that unrestricted space. This is the inexhaustible female imaginary of Cixous who, in "The Laugh of the Medusa," tells women "I know why you haven't written" and discusses all the ways writing, like masturbation, makes women feel guilty, even if they only do enough "to take the edge off." Then Cixous goes on to urge, "Write, let no one hold you back, let nothing stop you: not man ... and not *yourself*."[12] Natsumizu may not be a theorist, but she is just as determined to encourage her readers to explore their own potential for fantasy.

Yuzuha Ougi, in the bonus pages of *Brother*, similarly to Natsumizu, gives a lesson on how to set a mood for fantasy:

> In general to talk about how I like to see boy-on-boy kinky scenes depicted. I think it should present a "sexual mood" from beginning to end. Dim the genitals as much as possible, make the sex burst out of the frame, etc. A mood of having sex the whole time. Voices, sweat, facial expressions, everything.[13]

She contrasts her ideal representations of sex with film representations by thinking back to her first experience of seeing a pornographic film: "When I was young I too saw an uncensored erotic video for the first time and I thought it was gross and disgusting and it took a while before I could eat raw fish again. When you watch sex objectively, it's amazing how ridiculous and weird it is."[14] Here we do have some evidence of anxiety, but again, as with Natsumizu, her approach is more educational than compensatory. She goes on to demonstrate how to set a mood by including a sequence of drawings showing one of her two main characters stripping. She talks about why she chooses to draw the specific moments she has selected and what each frame contributes to the creation of a sexy mood. By taking the character out of the story and presenting him in this way in the bonus pages, she is inviting her readers to think about what they find sexy (and not sexy) about the male body.

Other writers use the bonus pages to talk about turn-ons or to play with the idea of objectifying men and turning them into servings for consumption. In the bonus pages for *Loving Gaze*, Akira Kanbe jokes that her problem is controlling the sexual urges of the characters: "As the author it really makes me happy when characters take such a life of their own..., but they become so lively that the sex scenes went on longer than I'd anticipated ... Yikes! I'm so embarrassed..."[15] (her ellipses). Once she's imagined the character, it's not her fault what he gets up to. Since her embarrassment is transparently disingenuous, her afterword functions to celebrate the long sex scenes rather than apologize for them.

Sakufu Ajimine also laments that her characters won't stay in line in her two bonus pages for *Your Honest Deceit*: "I originally intended to pen an adult, elite, gorgeous ... tale, but before I knew it, it devolved into a geezer fetish and windbag lawyer story. (By magic?)"[16]

She accompanies this remark with a simple little sketch of her two protagonists drawn with their bodies in the proportions of young children. She adds that her *seme*, Kitchara-sensei, doesn't seem to do very convincingly lawyerish work and adds "he probably acts the part of the distinguished lawyer to a T somewhere where I can't see him do it. Yuup." As in her previous remark, she jokes that her characters are outside her control; their representation is not her responsibility. On the facing page, the first page of two, she draws Kuze, the *uke*, in what she calls a "'He'd Never Look Like This' picture." Instead of portraying him in his usual business suit, she draws him tanned, dripping wet, and stripping out of a tank top and jeans. The contradiction between the two pages — on the first she asserts her ability to control the characters and on the second she denies it — adds to the sense of playfulness. By emphasizing the ways in which the book seemingly slipped from her control, her false apology instead highlights her role as author/artist and creator of both the characters and the world they inhabit.

Authors can also use the bonus pages to apparently reveal their own turn-ons, such as Kanbe does after *Loving Gaze*: "A scene of Kunieda lightly sweeping Yoshimuzu off his feet and carrying him — that would have been a little turn on for me personally."[17] Like Natsumizu's fantasy workshops, Kanbe's reference to a nonexistent scene, one she toyed with including but ultimately didn't include, invites the readers to use the work as an inspirational starting point from which to extend the fantasy — she treats the story as open-ended, not complete.

Kiriko Fuwa, in the bonus pages of *Weekend Lovers*, also reveals something of her own personal proclivities: "I am completely in love with that type so I was extremely happy to draw it. The combination of glasses, coolness, beauty, and an older uke ... I can take three servings of this."[18] By referencing the fantasy as food, "three servings," Fuwa highlights the idea of these fantasy men as delectable items for consumption. She might also be using the afterword as a kind of "sales pitch" for the fantasy she has put in motion: if the author likes this "type," the reader might too. Thus, these writers use the bonus pages to encourage readers to think about and to play with the idea of fantasy and to be amused by it, definitely not to repress it.

Although the subject matter of both yaoi and slash appears to be male homosexual relationships, these aren't texts that attempt realistic representations of those relationships but rather play with the erotic potential generated by differences in status or power. Mark McLelland argues that yaoi are about "sex which derives its interest from imagining power differentials, not equality."[19] Certainly for many women writers, to talk about the erotics of power in heterosexual relationships raises complex questions about the politics of gender difference and so, by making both members of the couple male, those problems can be erased. Having thus dispensed with gender difference, yaoi authors can, as McLelland suggests, play with the erotics of power by other means, or they may choose to explore other ideas of the erotic altogether.

In the two common situations of office and school romances, for example, power can be created by differences in status, such as those in teacher/student romances such as *Passion* or *Empty Heart*.[20] Both of these works employ a common yaoi plot in which power dynamics are reversed — in this case by making the student the aggressor and the more sexually confident character, and, in the case of *Passion*, the *seme*. Reversing power dynamics is a common plot device. In the four-volume work *Jazz*,[21] a young patient drugs and sexually assaults his doctor, with whom he later develops a relationship. The doctor is the *uke*. By reversing the anticipated power dynamics, these authors remind us that power, especially in sexual relationships, is often more complex than a first glance reveals.

When the story is about two apparent equals, such as two students in the same year, power differentials will be created by differences in wealth, popularity, experience, intelligence, or other markers of success in the school environment. Similarly, power differentials in office romances are often based on rank, but physical size, shyness, business success, and other power dynamics are also used to increase the play of difference. For example, the two interns in "Like a White Phantom"[22] are apparent equals but, whereas Matsuda is confident and happy, Suzaki is shy, sad, hurt by past griefs, and sexually exploited by a senior physician.

In many of these stories, the emotional climax occurs when the dominated character asserts his own desire. In yaoi this does not generally change the *seme/uke* dynamic; it just means that the *uke* finally makes the first move. Valenti describes this as the "cathartic moment, [when] a woman can identify with both the desired and the desiring; this fluidity is usually not afforded to her in more traditional narratives."[23] This climactic moment also signals to the reader that the relationship is truly reciprocal. Since so many yaoi include rape, or, at best, very aggressive seduction, establishing the idea that the relationship is, in fact, mutual, is important. Without a female character to identify with, Valenti argues, women are free to choose to identify with the *uke*, the *seme*, or both. The bonus pages, which so often focus on active reader participation in the play of erotic fantasy, encourage this fluid identification.

Both yaoi and slash participate in the realm of romance and sexual fantasy literature, genres that tend to dispense with theory in favor of praxis by actually engendering feelings of desire, pleasure, arousal and so on in the reader. A critic such as Camper complains that "what's missing from boys' love manga is the heavy baggage of adult sexuality."[24] But, of course, the same can be said for even more traditional written genres of romance and pornography. Fatigue, the stress of work, aging bodies, housework, paying bills, and other facts of adult life that impact adult sexuality are not the natural subjects of any of these genres. In fantasy-based genres, realism is simply not part of the picture.[25] As the slash writer M. Fae Glasgow frankly puts it, "They are also, to get to the core of it for me, stories of sexual and/or emotional satisfaction, attractive fictional men manipulated as much as possible to give as much pleasure as possible."[26] If realism is neither the practice nor the goal of either yaoi or slash, then what is their primary focus?

Slash, like yaoi, is produced and consumed primarily by females, and connections are created through it. The world of slash is very expansive. Thousands of stories are available online originating in many different countries; others are published in zines and books. One can find slash about dozens of TV shows but also about films, books, and historical, real, and original characters.

As with yaoi, slash has many writers who make a point of talking about the importance of the community of producers and consumers of slash and also directly address these audiences. They do this most commonly through brief prefaces to their work in which they may talk about other writers or readers who have provided feedback or encouragement and often invite their own readers to enter these fictional worlds.

Because slash is largely an online phenomenon, the conversations among creators and their audiences create an immediate community of shared interest in this fluid, labile fantasy discourse. The community of slash readers includes both active readers who send feedback and so-called lurkers who read but don't respond. Many slash sites make contacting the author very easy. Some have feedback forms attached to every story. Others allow readers to click on the author's name to send email; feedback is encouraged and lurking is discouraged.

In their prefaces, slash writers often thank other writers or readers for the assistance they provided. For example, in the preface to "Solitary Creatures," Aristide thanks Bone (another slash author):

> This story is dedicated with great love and appreciation to Bone, my own little sunbeam — you are Nell to my Snidely, and I never would have decided to hop into this particular bed if you hadn't pulled back the covers for me...[27] [her ellipsis].

In her author's note for the same story, she calls herself "a new little fish in a big scary pond" but adds, "Happy to be here." By speaking of writing as a bed that Bone has prepared for her, Aristide is playing with the idea that Bone is seducing Aristide into joining her in the "bed" that is slash; the writing itself becomes erotic play. The prolific Alyjude, who has over 130 substantial stories on her Web page for *The Sentinel* fandom, also credits writers and readers with helping her learn to edit her work. In the preface to "Just Another Saturday," she reveals that "this story reposting is a result of several conversations on ... the Sentinel Adult Fiction Discussion List. The wonderful readers and authors inspired me to go back and look at the crap I first produced."[28] The community has clearly been critical, but in ways she has found helpful and productive.

Other writers also focus on the encouragement and support that feedback provides. The writer Bone, whom Aristide thanked, in turn thanks all those who responded to her story "Territorial Imperative." When she adds a second chapter, she says, "I got drunk on feedback and the fingers just started flying."[29] She goes on to write six chapters in all for this one story.

Slash writer Meredith Lynne represents herself as a feedback addict. For her, it's an essential part of the writing experience. As she says in the preface to "Memory Lapse," "Feedback is a wonderful thing. =) If you like this, let me know. Please? You know what an addict I am. I'm pathetic. I write solely for the affirmation of my self-worth as a human being that you all give me through your wonderful letters."[30] She acknowledges the readers who follow her work with that "you know"; they are her reading community and they *know* how much she repeatedly emphasizes the role of feedback in her prefaces.

Of course, slash writers do write for free, so demands for feedback often acknowledge that it is the only payment they get. Evidence that there is a readership out there, that a community of interest has been successfully generated, and that conversation and interplay are now possible are the not-insignificant goals of slash writers.

Slash writers can't receive payment because they generally work with characters that belong to others and, as a consequence, slash stories are also normally preceded by a disclaimer. Some writers use this standardized text to get playful about the idea of ownership, or at least about the idea of playing with others' toys or fictional creations. In the disclaimer for "Paper Cranes," Dierdre writes, "I just want to take them out and play with them for a bit; I promise to return them unharmed, maybe a little bit sweatier than when I found them."[31] They may be someone else's characters, but that won't stop her from giving them a workout.

Similarly, Alyjude, in the disclaimer for "Breathing," takes the same attitude to the characters who, once out in the world, become toys in the toy box: "Officially, these guys belong to Pet Fly et al. I borrow, I play nice, I don't kill 'em or mutilate 'em but I have been known to make 'em have sex. I get nothing for this except fun. Loads of fun. Endless, life-saving fun."[32] She makes clear that for her, slash writing is therapeutic, even life-saving. She is a writer who has a lot of fun writing her prefatory author's notes. As well as playing with the standardized disclaimer, she adds silly lessons for life and generally jokes with the reader. The tone of her addresses to the reader is different from the tone of her stories, in that the content of the stories may be serious.

Many slash writers preface their creations with the standard one-sentence disclaimer and nothing else, but for those who expand, elaborate, and play with it, the disclaimers become an element of narrative technique. They allow the author to break the frame of the story through direct address to the reader and they create an intimacy, a shared attitude, with their community of readers. Francesca, in the preface to "Nature's Blindness," the concluding story in her long Sentinel series, "Nature's Cycles," jokes to her readers: "Warning: gratuitous fetishization of food. Query: if the food scenes are more erotic than the sex scenes, are we approaching realism?"[33] She can assume that most of the readers of this story will have read the thirty stories that precede it in the cycle. Since this story sequence has had a number of supernatural elements (none of which are utilized in this last story), mentioning realism is a joke for those faithful readers who are also presumed to be sophisticated enough to understand the theoretical play. When Aristide prefaces "Fruit of the Vine" with the remarks, "this story was kind of an experiment for me, to see if I could do a few things I haven't tried before. *Sentinel* is just such a ... flexible place, ya know?"[34] (her ellipsis), she is speaking to readers who know her work already. Further, she is speaking to the slash fans for this particular show who will have read enough pieces by different authors to be aware of the different directions in which writers have taken the characters in the flexible world of this particular slash pairing.

Once they go beyond the standardized disclaimer, the authors of these longer prefaces create a direct address to audience, a narrative technique designed to give readers a sense of the author's personality and to foster a relationship with them. Many authors of both slash and yaoi forego the usual authorial distance and instead deliberately court a connection with their readers through their prefaces and afterwords. These brief additions to the main text are often playful and celebratory. The contents are funny and pleasurable, not compensatory. For their female readers, these texts aren't pathetic substitutions for feminine lack; rather, they are disruptive, by their very existence, of dominant narratives of female sexuality and intentionally liberatory of female sexual fantasy.

Slash and yaoi interrupt the dominant narratives of manga, television, and even pornography by giving females a chance to play with boys and the male body in ways that male authors/artists have traditionally assumed to be their right to manipulate and play with the female body. In the worlds of yaoi and slash, it is the male body that is on display. And here it has been rendered poseable, penetrable, and subject to disruptions that serve to queer the dominant narratives in playful and irreverent ways. Playing with boys in ways that the creators of the original television characters never intended (in the case of slash) or that the creators of the original manga genres never foresaw is an essential aspect of the pleasure of these texts. A whole new toy box has been opened by these genres for female artists, writers, and readers.[35]

Notes

1. Hélène Cixous, "The Laugh of the Medusa," in *Feminist Literary Theory and Criticism*, ed. Sandra Gilbert and Susan Gubar (NY: W.W. Norton, 2007), 426.

2. Midori Matsui, "Little Girls Were Little Boys: Displaced Femininity in the Representation of Homosexuality in Japanese Girls' Comics," in *Feminism and the Politics of Difference*, ed. Sneja Gunew and Anna Yeatman (Halifax, NS: Fernwood Publishing, 1993), 178.

3. Sharon Kinsella, "Japanese Subculture in the 1990s: Otaku and the Amateur Manga Movement," *Journal of Japanese Studies* 24, no. 2 (summer, 1998): 302, http://www.jstor.org (accessed September 24, 2008).

4. Kristy Valenti, "'Stop, My Butt Hurts!' The Yaoi Invasion," *The Comics Journal* 269, http://www.tcj.com/269/e_yaoi.html (accessed September 24, 2008).

5. Susanne Jung, "Queering Popular Culture: Female Spectators and the Appeal of Writing Slash Fan Fiction," *Gender Forum: Gender Queeries* 8 (2004), http://www.genderforum.uni-koeln.de/queer/jung.html (accessed August 24, 2008).

6. Cathy Camper, "Yaoi 101: Girls Love 'Boys' Love,'" *Women's Review of Books* 23, no 3 (May June 2006): 26.

7. Ritsu Natsumizu, *Crushing Love* (Gardena, CA: Digital Manga Publishing, 2007), 196–97.

8. Natsumizu, *Crushing Love*, 200.

9. Ritsu Natsumizu, *Love Bus Stop* (Gardena, CA: Digital Manga Publishing, 2007), 171.

10. Natsumizu, *Love Bus Stop*, 174.

11. Natsumizu, *Love Bus Stop*, 175.

12. Cixous, "The Laugh of the Medusa," 415.

13. Yuzuha Ougi, *Brother* (Houston: Drama Queen, 2007), 176.

14. Ougi, *Brother*, 176.

15. Akira Kanbe, *Loving Gaze* (Gardena, CA: Digital Manga Publishing, 2008), 169.

16. Sakufu Ajimine, *Your Honest Deceit* (Houston: Drama Queen, 2007), 195.

17. Kanbe, *Loving Gaze*, 170.

18. Kiriko Fuwa, *Weekend Lovers* (Gardena, CA: 801 Media Inc., 2008), np.

19. Mark McLelland, "The World of Yaoi: The Internet, Censorship and the Global 'Boys' Love' Fandom," Faculty of Arts Papers University of Wollongong (2005), http://ro.uow.edu/artspapers/147 (accessed August 24, 2008).

20. Shinobu Gotoh, *Passion* (New York: Diamond Comic Distributors, 2004); Masara Minase, *Empty Heart* (Houston: Drama Queen, 2006).

21. Tamatsu Takamure, *Jazz* Volume 1 (New York, Diamond Comic Distributors, 2005).

22. Akira Honma, "Like a White Phantom," in *The Judged* (Houston: Drama Queen, 2006).

23. Valenti, "'Stop, My Butt Hurts!,'" 3.

24. Camper, "Yaoi 101," 26.

25. The following readings participate in the discussion of romance and realism: Sally Goade, *Empowerment versus Opression: Twenty First Century Views of Popular Romance Novels* (Newcastle: Cambridge Scholars Publishing, 2007); Tania Modleski, *Loving with a Vengeance: Mass-Produced Fantasies for Women* (New York: Routledge, 1982); Janice Radway, *Reading the Romance: Women, Patriarchy, and Popular Literature* (Chapel Hill: University of North Carolina Press, 1991); Catherine Salmon and Donald Symons, *Warrior Lovers: Erotic Fiction, Evolution and Female Sexuality* (New Haven, CT: Yale University Press, 2003). Salmon and Symons's book deals with slash stories.

26. M. Fae Glasgow, quoted in Shoshonna Green, Cynthia Jenkins, and Henry Jenkins, "Normal Female Interest in Men Bonking," in *Fans, Bloggers and Gamers: Exploring Participatory Culture*, Henry Jenkins (New York: New York University Press, 2006), 83.

27. Aristide, "Solitary Creatures," *852 Prospect*, http://www.852prospect.org/archive/archive/firsts/solitarycreatures.html (accessed March 26, 2008).

28. Alyjude, "Just Another Saturday," *852 Prospect*, http://www.852prospect.org/archive/archive/1-2000-humor/justanother.html (accessed March 26, 2008).

29. Bone, "Territorial Imperative 2," Slash Fan Fiction by Bone, http://www.mrks.org/~bone/sentinel/territorial/ti_2.html (accessed April 13, 2008).

30. Meredith Lynne, "Memory Lapse," *852 Prospect*, http://www.852prospect.org/archive/archive/firsts2/memorylapse.html (accessed June 24, 2008).

31. Dierdre, "Paper Cranes," *852 Prospect*, http://www.852prospect.org/archive/archive/drama3/papercranes.html (accessed March 29, 2008).

32. Alyjude, "Breathing," *852 Prospect*, http://www.852prospect.org/archive/archive/1-2000-firsts/breathing.html (accessed October 29, 2008).

33. Francesca, "Nature's Blindness," Francesca's Sentinel Fiction, http://www.trickster.org/francesca/NatBlind.html (accessed May 21, 2008).

34. Aristide, "Fruit of the Vine," http://www.852prospect.org/archive/archive/firsts2/fruitof.html (accessed March 6, 2008).

35. My thanks to Kathryn Barnwell for her skilled and generous beta-ing of this essay.

Bibliography

Ajimine, Sakufu. *Your Honest Deceit.* Houston: Drama Queen, 2007.

Alyjude. "Breathing," *852 Prospect.* http://www.852prospect.org/archive/archive/1-2000-firsts/breathing.html.

_____. "Just Another Saturday," *852 Prospect.* http://www.852prospect.org/archive/archive/1-2000-firsts/breathing.html.

Aristide. "Fruit of the Vine," *852 Prospect.* http://www.852prospect.org/archive/archive/1-2000-firsts2/fruitof.html.

_____. "Solitary Creatures," *852 Prospect.* http://www.852prospect.org/archive/archive/firsts/solitarycreatures.html.

Bone. "Territorial Imperative 2," *Slash Fan fiction by Bone.* http://www.mrks.org/~bone/sentinel/territorial/ti_2.html.

Camper, Cathy. "Yaoi 101: Girls Love 'Boys' Love,'" *Women's Review of Books* 23, no. 3 (May June 2006), 24–26.

Cixous, Hélène. "The Laugh of the Medusa," in *Feminist Literary Theory and Criticism,* edited by Sandra Gilbert and Susan Gubar. New York: W.W. Norton, 2007.

Dierdre. "Paper Cranes," *852 Prospect.* http://www.852prospect.org/archive/archive/drama3/papercranes.html.

Francesca. "Nature's Blindness," *Francesca's Sentinel Fiction.* http://www.trickster.org/francesca/NatBlind.html.

Fuwa, Kiriko. *Weekend Lovers.* Gardena, CA: Digital Manga Publishing, 2008.

Glasgow, M. Fae. Quoted in Shoshonna Green, Cynthia Jenkins, and Henry Jenkins, "Normal Female Interest in Men Bonking," in *Fans, Bloggers and Gamers: Exploring Participatory Culture,* edited by Henry Jenkins. New York: New York University Press, 2006, 83.

Goade, Sally. *Empowerment versus Oppression: Twenty First Century Views of Popular Romance Novels.* Newcastle: Cambridge Scholars Publishing, 2007.

Gotoh, Shinobu. *Passion.* New York: Diamond Comic Distributors, 2004.

Honma, Akira. "Like a White Phantom," in *The Judged.* Houston: Drama Queen, 2006.

Jung, Susanne. "Queering Popular Culture: Female Spectators and the Appeal of Writing Slash Fan Fiction," *Gender Forum: Gender Queeries* 8 (2004). http://www.genderforum.unikoeln.de/queer/jung.html.

Kanbe, Akira. *Loving Gaze.* Gardena, CA: Digital Manga Publishing, 2008.

Kinsella, Sharon. "Japanese Subculture in the 1990s: Otaku and the Amateur Manga Movement," *Journal of Japanese Studies* 24, no. 2 (Summer 1998): 289–316, http://jstor.org.

Matsui, Midori. "Little Girls Were Little Boys: Displaced Femininity in the Representation of Homosexuality in Japanese Girls' Comics," in *Feminism and the Politics of Difference,* edited by Sneja Gunew and Anna Yeatman. Halifax, N.S.: Fernwood Publishing, 1993.

McLelland, Mark. "The World of Yaoi: The Internet, Censorship and the Global 'Boys' Love' Fandom," *Faculty Of Arts Papers University of Wollongong* (2005). http://ro.uow.edu/artspapers/147.

_____. "Why are Japanese Girls' Comics Full of Boys Bonking?" *Intensities: The Journal of Cult Media.* http://www.cult-media.com/issue1/CMRmcle.htm.

Meredith Lynne. "Memory Lapse," *852 Prospect.* http://www.852prospect.org/archive/archive/firsts2/memorylapse.html

Minase, Masara. *Empty Heart.* Houston: Drama Queen, 2006.

Modleski, Tania. *Loving With a Vengeance: Mass-Produced Fantasies for Women.* New York: Routledge, 1982.

Natsumizu, Ritsu. *Crushing Love.* Gardena, CA: Digital Manga Publishing, 2007.

_____. *Love Bus Stop.* Gardena, CA: Digital Manga Publishing, 2007.

Ouigi, Yuzuha. *Brother.* Houston: Drama Queen, 2007.

Radway, Janice. *Reading the Romance: Women, Patriarchy, and Popular Literature.* Chapel Hill: University of North Carolina Press, 1991.

Salmon, Catherine and Donald Symons. *Warrior Lovers: Erotic Fiction, Evolution and Female Sexuality.* New Haven, CT: Yale University Press, 2003.

Takamure, Tamatsu. *Jazz Volume 1.* New York: Diamond Comic Distributors, 2005.

Valenti, Kristy. "'Stop, My Butt Hurts!' The Yaoi Invasion." *The Comics Journal* 269. http://www.tcj.com/269/e_yaoi.html.

7

"She Should Just Die in a Ditch"

Fan Reactions to Female Characters in Boys' Love Manga

M. M. BLAIR

English-language BL readers frequently comment on online postings of BL manga. Most of these are reaction comments, such as "squee" posts, in which the commenters[1] merely express how happy they are about the storyline, art, sex scene, etc. There are, however, some comments that are markedly different in tone. Comments about the female characters in manga are frequently very negative and occasionally virulently, even violently, misogynistic. Even the smallest of female roles can evoke a disgusted reaction from readers, and the comments increase in both number and antipathy when the character in question could have a negative impact on the relationship between the story's main couple. These misogynistic comments are especially disturbing because the BL genre is written by women and targeted to a female audience; although the audience is not entirely composed of women, it is overwhelmingly female. This means that most, if not all, of the commenters who react so negatively to the female characters are themselves female. Why do female readers react so negatively toward their own gender? Are these reactions exclusive to BL works,[2] or is it likely that the readers carry these reactions across genres within manga and even outside manga to mainstream fiction? In this paper, I intend to explore these questions and propose possible answers to them. I will examine the comments to posts on the Yaoi Daily community, and I will also discuss the results of a survey that I conducted of BL readers' reactions to female characters in BL manga.[3]

The online English-language boys' love manga fandom is huge and is highly participatory. Not only are there many scanlation groups, but there are also many communities and forums (many run by scanlation groups) which have large memberships and are, in general, highly active. One of the more active communities is the Yaoi Daily community on LiveJournal.[4] This community is dedicated to the posting of BL manga scans. As their community profile states, "yaoi_daily is an eye candy (image posting) community devoted to the sharing and promotion of yaoi manga, *doujinshi*, and art in a positive environment, free from criticism for your tastes. From BDSM to shōta, we gather here to bask in its glory, praise beautiful art, and/or get hot 'n bothered."[5] Posts to this community must follow explicit rules. The two most important are that all posts must contain images from a BL work and that the work must not be licensed for distribution in the United States.[6] Members of the community are encouraged to comment on individual posts and the community is a very participatory one, although few serious discussions are conducted in the comments, which are in the main limited to emotional reactions to the manga posted. These include both the "squee" comments and the misogynistic comments mentioned above.

110

One of the first things that should be done, in order to understand why these highly negative reactions to female characters in BL occur, is to try to understand why readers choose to follow this genre. Many papers deal, at least in part, with this issue, although most of them do so by theorizing rather than by asking readers for their reasons. Both of these methods are important in order to truly understand the appeal of BL. Some theorists believe that BL is popular because women are unable to achieve an equal relationship with men, due to innate power differentials encoded in Japanese society, and so women turn to stories that feature a relationship between two men in order to visualize and vicariously experience a truly equal relationship.[7] In a slightly different take on the matter, other theories state that the BL genre is attractive because it gives women access to the phallus,[8] or because it helps to fulfill scoptophilic desire which Freud posited as an innate part of female sexuality.[9] Other theories, most often found in discussions of slash fanfiction, suggest that what readers find appealing in these genres is the way that the characters are depicted in manners that are neither wholly masculine nor wholly feminine.[10] For example, while adult men are generally seen as being more restrained about demonstrating their emotions, many of the men found in BL are relatively open about their emotions. Even when they attempt to hide their emotions, they still act in ways that clearly convey the very emotions they are trying to hide. Men in BL could be seen, therefore, as the idealized men that readers wish they could find in real life.[11]

Although there may be some truth in each of these theories, it would be problematic to look exclusively to them for an understanding of BL's appeal. Few of the authors of these theories surveyed the readers of BL. Although readers may not be conscious of all of their reasons for following a genre, it is still necessary to examine the reasons that they give for their enjoyment. This can be a challenging exercise, since readers may not be willing to analyze why they enjoy something for fear of destroying that enjoyment, or because they do not care why they enjoy it.

In the survey, I did not specifically ask readers why they liked the BL genre. However, I did receive answers that can help illuminate some viewpoints on why the genre is attractive. I suspect, however, that there may be almost as many reasons for liking the genre as there are readers of it. Some of the reasons given by the survey respondents included: "I like the dynamic of two men getting together. And, it's just hot." "I like the romance and the sex. It's hotter and more interesting when it's between two men." "I do like the visuals of the bishounen; the erotic allure of two guys getting it on. I also like the deeper romantic points of relationships that get built by the guys." "I prefer to read mangas [*sic*] which have beautiful art and as a heterosexual woman naturally I like men thus TWO beautiful man [*sic*] making out are a real turn-on!" "I would love to see some realistic approach to men's romance, and I am attracted to the angst created from it." "I read yaoi for the titillation." "I like them because I get to oogle [*sic*] hotly drawn men." "What I appreciate about yaoi is the 'forbidden' aspect." One respondent asked, "must there be a reason? Attraction, lust and sexuality is [*sic*] not a rational process and does not require validation.... Anything my mind cooks up about it is just about self-justification."[12] The most often-cited reason here was that "it's hot." For these readers, a relationship between two men is erotic, and so they enjoy BL; for some this factor is enhanced by the "forbidden" aspect, because homosexuality is still seen by many as being not socially acceptable.

I would like to highlight another reason for enjoying BL that a respondent gave because I believe it sheds light on the problem of misogynistic reactions to female BL characters. The respondent said, "Who knows? Titillation? ... Romance without pesky female competition? (We always compare don't we?) Porn that doesn't involve us as women?"[13] While she does reiterate the idea of male homosexual relationships as titillating, far more important, she brings up two ideas that I think are at the core of the negative comments about female characters: the idea that the reader will, perhaps unconsciously, compare herself to and try to compete with a female character, and the attractiveness of a genre that can depict pornographic situations without using a female body.

This first idea of women unconsciously attempting to compete with the female characters in an interesting one; however, I don't think that the problem is only unconscious competition. In some cases, I believe that the reader will identify the female character as a source of competition, regardless of the fact that the two men in the stories are involved with each other. The men are still the object of desire for the readers. This means that characters who threaten the relationship between the men could also be seen as threatening the desire of the reader.

Another aspect to this negative reaction to female characters stems from the lack of nuance in how the characters are portrayed. Often they come off as somewhat flat, rather than being fully developed, three-dimensional characters. This is less of a problem with the male characters, who are often more nuanced. Even when the male characters are not completely three-dimensional, a predominantly female audience may be more inclined to overlook these less-nuanced portrayals of characters with whom they cannot completely relate because of the gender difference. However, when female characters are portrayed as lacking nuance, a female audience will note this immediately. I believe that the female characters are portrayed in this less-nuanced manner because they are often used as antagonists in the plot and are not intended to be liked; what the *mangaka* wish to highlight are their negative aspects.

Some poorly portrayed female characters in BL may be excused by readers thinking that although they wouldn't act that way, they could imagine other people doing so. Other portrayals of female characters may be so extreme, however, that it throws female readers out of their suspension of disbelief and ruins their appreciation of the story.

The second idea that the respondent brought up also deserves a closer look. The respondent's idea that pornography that involves a female body can be problematic for a female reader is complementary to the theories espoused by Aoyama Tomoko, Suzuki Kazuko, and Matsui Midori. Much traditional pornography is seen as degrading for women. In traditional male-oriented pornography, women are most often the object of the gaze, and they do not obtain subjectivity; this is seen as both a symptom of the patriarchic structure of Western civilization and as a way of reinforcing this same system by denying women subjectivity.[14] While in theory pornography and obscenity are easily definable, in practice it is more difficult.[15] This difficulty was famously expressed by Justice Potter Stewart of the U.S. Supreme Court in 1964 when he declared that he didn't know what precise kinds of material would be considered hard-core pornography but that "I know it when I see it."[16] Obscenity and pornography thus depend on the interpretation of the consumer, and what one person defines as obscene another may not. While many BL works are sexually explicit, others are not explicit in the least. Perhaps because of the origins of the term yaoi, most academic work on BL focuses on the more sexually explicit works and frequently describes the genre as a whole as "pornographic."[17] But even though some BL works could be defined as pornography, the genre as a whole is not pornographic.

As Mulvey points out, in narrative cinema the audience receives pleasure voyeuristically, by means of observing the actions of the characters on the screen; narcissistically, through identification with the characters; and fetishistically, through use of close-ups on body parts.[18] Manga, which contains cinematographic elements, such as the editing of narrative time and of space (depth of field, etc.), can also be examined using this theory. BL can be seen as a way of overturning the patriarchal system. It is written by women specifically for a female audience, and rather than focusing on the female body it is focused exclusively on the male body. This allows women not only to gain subjectivity, because they are the targets of this genre, but it removes their objectivity, because they are not focusing their gaze on other female bodies but instead on men's bodies.

One problem with this view is that, as I mentioned earlier, the men are not portrayed in a stereotypically masculine way but are rather feminized. Men in BL are feminized not only in their appearance, being frequently androgynous, but they are also feminized in their emotional reactions, shown as being more open with their emotions than is considered typical. The *uke* in BL is especially feminized and is frequently depicted as emotionally flustered and quick to cry. In fact, as Nagakubo Yōko points out, many BL stories can be read as mimicking heterosexual romance narratives, wherein the heterosexual fantasies of women are, in BL, simply projected onto two male bodies.[19]

Regardless, BL is still a genre targeted toward a female gaze. Despite the fact that the audience has expanded to include male readers as well, the audience is frequently assumed, especially in academic work on BL, to be mainly female and heterosexual, and BL is produced with the desires of this audience in mind.[20] This brings us back to the question of why an audience in which the majority population is female has such negative reactions to portrayals of its own sex.

I argue that the negative reactions of female readers are caused by their desire to focus entirely on the relationship between the male leads and by the most common use to which *mangaka* put their female characters. It is important to note at this point that female characters are by no means ubiquitous in BL; in fact, it is entirely the opposite. Women are almost entirely invisible in BL. When women do appear, they are rarely fully developed characters and sometimes are not even drawn with facial features, as it is often not necessary for the reader to be able to differentiate one from another.[21]

One of the more common uses for female characters is as a barrier to the male characters' developing relationship. A typical character could be a woman with whom the character's family wants him to develop a relationship, either because homosexuality is still not considered socially acceptable and they want the character to be accepted, or because they do not know that he is gay and are pushing him toward a relationship in general. Alternatively, the female character might be interested in one of the characters and pursuing him, aggressively or not. Regardless of the depiction, the female character will be almost universally hated by fans because she is a threat to the main couple's relationship.

In addition to this, however, she is frequently depicted by the mangaka in a very negative way, so there is little about the character that is likable. This depiction is, in the main, not realistic. While the character's reasons for her actions may be based on realistic motives, her actions themselves are often over the top and not at all how most real women would react in the given situation. An example of this is the character Mejiro Kanako in Kano Shiuko's *Otonage*.[22]

Otonage is a one-volume work that focuses on the relationships of a group of four construction workers, with most of the attention given to the relationship between Nakano Shunji and Mejiro Yasushi. Yasushi and the female character, Kanako, share a last name because they are cousins. They used to be in a relationship, but while they could have married, Yasushi didn't want to have children because of his blood relationship with Kanako. At the beginning of *Otonage*, Yasushi reveals that it was his interest in Nakano that prompted him to break up with Kanako. Despite the fact that he had been living with Kanako for two years at that point, Yasushi moves in with Nakano instead. Although Nakano and Yasushi have a sexual relationship, they have difficulty connecting on an emotional level, and there is a fair amount of violence in their relationship. They have many misunderstandings, and Nakano uses another of the construction workers, Kuroda Taiki, to make Yasushi jealous. This misunderstanding is quickly resolved within the first chapter, but before the reader can get complacent, Kanako is introduced in chapter two.

Kanako very deliberately tries to come between Nakano and Yasushi, and she uses several different ways to do this, all of them underhanded and reprehensible. First, she tells Nakano that she wishes to take back Yasushi. Then she attempts to seduce Nakano, implying that the only reason he is with a man is because he has never had a woman before. Kanako also begins to harass Nakano; she constantly shows up wherever he is, at work or even at the grocery store. Then she implies that the reason she dumped Yasushi is because she is pregnant and she didn't want to hear Yasushi tell her that she should get an abortion.[23] This revelation makes Nakano act differently toward Yasushi, and the two of them fight. Shortly after this, Kanako asks Nakano to accompany her to the gynecologist because she is scared of going alone. At the gynecologist's, it is revealed that, despite having many symptoms of pregnancy, Kanako is not, in fact, pregnant. She herself was convinced that she was pregnant, and she is both saddened and relieved to find out that she was wrong. The knowledge that she isn't pregnant enables Kanako to let go of her remaining feelings for Yasushi, and she bows out of the manga with surprising grace.

Although Kanako's motives for acting the way she does are easily understandable and relatively realistic (she is given a sad back story to explain why she is so fixated on Yasushi), her actions are completely unrealistic and come off as quite creepy. Her main purpose for existing is to cause misunderstandings between Yasushi and Nakano and to make the storyline more emotionally weighty.

Reader reactions to Kanako are vitriolic. In fact, the quote used in the title of this paper comes from a reader comment about Kanako made when *Otonage* was being posted on Yaoi Daily. The full comment sparked a short conversation in the comments. This conversation was held shortly after Kanako had been introduced, before she had actually done much that was objectionable, except lifting her shirt to show her breasts to Nakano.

> LBC: Kanako's a major cunt and she should just die in a ditch, slowly and painfully. Now, where did I put my knives and shovel?
>
> QC: No, no, no, don't use knives, because it's going to be messy, with the blood and all that. You should use some rope. Twist it around her neck then pull it slowly, when she's about to faint, release the rope a little so she won't die that fast then do it again and again until she's dead. *digs hole to bury the body*
>
> LBC: Hehehe, you're right. How 'bout slightly strangling her until she faints and then we bury her alive? Nothing's more traumatizing than waking up in a really cramped space, in the dark, and no one to hear you scream. I'm a [*sic*] such a bitter, horrible bitch, but with Kanako, I don't care.[24]

These were by far the most violent of the comments reacting to Kanako, and the level of hate that they evince was far out of proportion with Kanako's actions at the time when the comments were made.

Many of the other comments in this section were some variation of "Boo ... boo ... boobies ... ARGH!"[25] and mentions of how surprised the reader was when Kanako lifted her shirt. It is very interesting to note that although LBC made some very alarming comments about Kanako, later in the comments on the same post she is far more moderate.

> TB: Sometimes I really dislike yaoiland. Real women are not like that. Ugh.... Just so anoying [*sic*] when the mangakas [*sic*] paint women like that.
>
> LBC: I agree with you. I hate disliking some female characters in Yaoiland, but damn, I hate women like Kanako. I hate it when a woman thinks sex between guys is weird or gross, as if she were any hotter, which she ain't not with that personality/behavior.[26]

When responding to a more levelheaded comment, LBC was herself levelheaded. But in her first comment about Kanako, she reacted far more violently than the situation called for, and with a disturbing amount of misogyny toward a character that, as of yet, had done little to merit it. LBC's comment in response to TB implies that she is not misogynistic in general, but her extremely misogynistic reaction earlier was a result of the way Kanako was depicted. This implies that there are other female characters, even in BL, or yaoiland,[27] that LBC does not find objectionable.

In my survey of BL readers, I asked for their general impressions of female characters in BL manga. None of the replies that I received were misogynistic in the least. One of the responses mentioned that the female characters are usually "handled badly as plot devices." Other respondents elaborated on this, saying that the female characters are "there to add an extra dash of trouble or angst, or to provide the reader with a character to hate" or, "just the side character that has the guy realize he is gay" or, "BL obsessed friends, sisters or moms. Every once in a while there is a girlfriend/best friend who bows out gracefully." Other respondents mentioned that female characters can occasionally be helpful friends who encourage the budding relationship between the main characters. A few respondents mentioned that they try to only read manga in which the female characters are handled as well as the male characters. One of those commenters went on to add, "part of me says 'well, it's not about the girls anyway, so who cares?' and the other part says 'Damnit [*sic*], stop portraying my/our sex like that!'"[28] The moderate private reactions in the survey responses I received, contrasted with the vitriolic public reactions, lead me to believe that such misogyny can be attributed to a symptom of the "anonymity of watching," which is the phenomena of "hatred as public performance" noted by anthropologist Michael Wesch in his work on YouTube.[29]

According to Wesch, the anonymity granted by participating in internet forums, where it is possible to invent an entirely new persona simply by changing usernames, frees people to act in ways that they would never act in real life. In addition, part of the point in commenting is to be noticed, to leave the comment that is the one people respond to, and to participate in a community, even if it is in a negative manner. Posting inflammatory comments can in fact aid this goal, because the more outrageous a comment, the more responses it tends to receive. While I am sure that the people who make these sorts of comments do, in fact, dislike the characters they are referring to, I am not sure that they hate them nearly as much as they say they do.[30] These commenters are reacting to the way the mangaka intends the character to be perceived.

A problem with this theory's application to Yaoi Daily is that it is predicated on anonymity. LiveJournal, however, is a blogging website. Comments, unless they are made anonymously, which is not possible in locked communities such as Yaoi Daily, always contain a username that is also a hyperlink back to the commenter's journal. While it is possible to lock entries so that they cannot be seen by the general public, often journals are completely open and contain significant amounts of information about the users' offline lives. In this way, usernames carry with them the users' identity, or as much of it as they have chosen to share in their journals. Also, Yaoi Daily encourages commenting, and those comments further the development of an identity for a specific username. Although offline lives can be hidden or misrepresented by users, they still create an identity for LiveJournal, which to some extent negates the anonymity of creating a username.

Other research done on anonymity and computer-mediated communication (CMC) can also help to interpret the behavior displayed by commenters on Yaoi Daily. Research on flaming in CMC is particularly useful.[31] As Philip Thompsen notes, whether or not a comment is defined as a flame depends on two separate issues. The first is the behavior or wording of the comment (hostile, emotional, etc.). The second issue is on the recipient's interpretation of the comment.[32] Therefore, a comment could be interpreted as a flame when it was not intended as such; or a comment that was intended to be inflammatory could be evaluated as noninflammatory. Thompsen also notes that flaming behavior depends on the norms of the group in which it takes place, with some groups being more open to uninhibited behavior than others.[33] Other research has determined that anonymity can actually help encourage identification with a group and thus the submergence of individual opinions to the norms of the group in which people are participating.[34]

Because Yaoi Daily is intended as a space to show works featuring a male couple and to share appreciation for these works, and not as a space for appreciating female characters, it has become a place where it is acceptable to say anything a commenter wants about the female characters. Because the female characters are frequently intended by the *mangaka* to be disliked, and because the space in which BL is shared was not set up to avoid these sort of comments, it has become acceptable to be openly misogynistic in comments. Rarely will anyone else call another commenter on this behavior. These misogynistic comments can be read as a symptom of the social norm of Yaoi Daily, and not necessarily as reflecting the offline opinions of the commenters themselves. Bashing male characters, however, needs to be done with caution, and it is always a good idea to imply that the criticism is not truly meant. Oftentimes commenters who make negative comments about the male characters will be called out for them.

I would like to return briefly to two of the responses to the survey that I mentioned above; namely, to the ideas that female characters are usually "handled badly as plot devices" and are "there to add an extra dash of trouble or angst, or to provide the reader with a character to hate."[35] These interpretations tie in with some of the ideas mentioned by Tania Modleski about the villainess in soap operas. As Modleski points out, in soap operas the "one character whom we are allowed to hate unreservedly" is the villainess, who is also, according to Modleski, "the negative image of the spectator's ideal self."[36] Kanako is a perfect example of this. While the male characters have their faults, Kanako is the only character the readers are encouraged to dislike.

The soap-opera villainess is able to overthrow the usual passive feminine role and to control, at least for a time, the course of the narrative. One of the ways in which this happens is by means of pregnancy, exactly the means by which Kanako hijacks control of the narrative from Yasushi and Nakano. This causes Nakano to feel a great deal of anxiety. He is confronted with the possibility that Kanako, by means of her pregnancy, could take Yasushi away from him. This also is a reversal of the way in which gender roles are normally portrayed. Here a man, Nakano, is forced into a passive and anxiety-filled role normally inhabited by female characters. The villainess is both cheered for and jeered by the readers. She is supported because she is a female character who obtains subjectivity, generally by means of turning feminine weaknesses into sources of strengths, but on the other hand, she is hated because she achieves power by underhanded means.[37]

The character Koyama Moe in Homerun Ken's *Boku wa kimi no tori ni naritai*[38] (I Want to Become Your Bird) is used in much the same manner as Kanako is in *Otonage*, but the reader reactions were quite different. The manga starts out with the main character Koyama Kei, Moe's younger brother, having sex with his art teacher and thinking that, despite the fact that he is fifteen, he doesn't know what love is. When Kei goes home, he sees his sister grinning at her cell phone and Moe tells him all about her boyfriend, the "super-cute and dreamy" medical student Fujii. The reader soon learns that Kei and Moe's mother died several years ago. Their father remarried, and he is clearly too busy to have much time for his children. Kei spends a lot of his time hanging out with his maternal uncle, Akatsuka Rintarō, a porn novelist. When Kei is at Rintarō's house in the first chapter, he gets a panicked phone call from Moe. Moe has a date with her boyfriend, but she's let her homework pile up and now she can't make it; also, she can't call her boyfriend because the battery on her cell phone is almost dead. Could Kei go and meet Fujii and let him know that Moe will have to reschedule? Kei runs all the way to where Moe and Fujii were supposed to meet and then, handily for the plot, he passes out from the heat into Fujii's arms. Fujii takes care of Kei and the two of them talk and seem to hit it off. By the end of the chapter, it is clear that Kei has a crush on Fujii, and it is also pretty clear to the reader how this story will go.

Indeed, as the story continues to develop and Kei and Fujii grow closer, it becomes clear that cute, flaky Moe and Fujii have very little in common. Moe starts to feel her own relationship with Fujii threatened by how close Fujii and Kei are becoming, and she tries to keep them apart. For his own part, Kei does his best to break things off with Fujii when he sees that it is hurting Moe. After many misunderstandings, the story ends happily. Moe breaks up with Fujii and finds a new boyfriend who is more like her, and Fujii starts going out with Kei. Indeed, by the end of the story, Moe has become one of Fujii and Kei's strongest supporters.

Moe is depicted in a realistic manner. She may be a bit ditzy and selfish, but she still has a good heart and she cares a great deal for Kei. She is just starting university and is rather self-involved. This characterization is more realistic than the characterization of Kanako and was likely done to help engage the reader sympathetically with Moe. While fans at first reacted positively toward Moe, as the story went on, they began to react in a more negative manner, at least until the very end, when her support for Kei and Fujii caused an abrupt reversal of popular opinion. The first fan reactions to Moe were all along the following lines: "Moe's an adorable spaz. ;P,"[39]; "I feel bad for Moe. :(She's—like someone said above—is actually a sweet, cute character. I hope Fujii doesn't fall for her brother instead. XD;;;"[40]; and "Oh so poignant! I like that they didn't make the sister into some evil bitch, that she's a nice person too and they get along well and love eachother [*sic*].. he's [Kei's] just fallen for her boyfriend. Argh that will make the angst 100x's worse!"[41]

As is clearly visible in these comments, at the beginning of the story everyone was rooting for Moe over Kei. The second comment is especially revealing. Despite the fact that from the moment Kei faints into Fujii's arms it is clear the two of them are going to be the main couple of the story, the commenters still wanted Moe to be happy, even if it meant that Kei and Fujii wouldn't get together. As one remarked, "::sigh:: I wish the sister wasn't so adorable. I just know the uke and seme are gonna get together, and she's probably gonna get hurt, and it'd be so much easier to not care about it if she were annoying."[42]

This is part of the reason I believe that the female characters, when they are being used as barriers to the main couple's relationship, are depicted in such a negative way. The *mangaka* will depict them as grasping or unsympathetic because then the readers will not sympathize in the least. In addition, the *mangaka* might wonder why she should spend a lot of time trying to develop a likable character for a role that is going to be disliked anyway. The way Moe is depicted might be even more effective for the story. Because she is liked, the readers are attempting to cheer for both Moe and Kei at the same time, which gives more emotional depth to the story.[43]

As the story progressed, sympathies started to change. As more and more details were revealed about how Kei was ignored by their father, and as Moe continued her ditzy ways, the readers began to empathize more with Kei and to lose patience with Moe. When Kei sees Moe crying in Fujii's arms at a festival because Fujii had been paying more attention to Kei than to her, Kei resolves to back off because he can see that he is hurting his sister's relationship. Later in the story, Kei first refuses to back out of a planned outing with Fujii to allow Fujii and Moe to go on a date, despite the fact that this refusal clearly upsets Moe. Then, at the very last minute, Kei tells Fujii to go and find Moe because Kei knows that Moe has made plans to meet with her ex-boyfriend. One commenter remarked after this that she kind of wished that Fujii and Moe would stay together because they make a good couple; another commenter responded, "Actually, I felt that way until I realized that ... [t]he sister is really self-centered, and not very thoughtful, either ... I mean, just because she couldn't see her boyfriend, she would run off with her Ex? That is what made me turn...."[44]

Even though Moe's actions are still perfectly understandable and normal, this point in the story, when Moe, upset over Kei's refusal to give up on a meeting with Fujii so Moe and Fujii can go on a date together, agrees to meet with her ex-boyfriend, is when most readers started disliking Moe, although there were still some who defended her.

Moe's most selfish act in the manga is to try to keep Fujii from following Kei after Kei has run away from them crying. Although there were still several commenters who remarked that they could understand why she's acting that way and sympathize with her, most of the comments were far more negative. One commenter remarked that if she were Moe, she would step aside so Kei and Fujii could be together,[45] which strikes me as being a somewhat idealistic thought. Shortly after this incident, however, the situation between the three is resolved when Moe realizes that she and Fujii are not actually a good match and breaks up with him, freeing Fujii to be with Kei.

One of the first comments on the post that contained this part of the story was, "Moe's gotten herself onto good terms with me now."[46] All that was necessary for Moe to redeem herself in the eyes of readers was to bow out of the relationship with Fujii. The fact that she immediately turns around and starts championing Fujii's relationship with Kei only made it easier for readers to absolve her of her earlier selfishness.

Moe is a good example of a female character who is effectively used to help the plot along without being made completely unlikable in the process. An interesting thing about her portrayal is that it is clear that Homerun Ken was trying to make her a sympathetic and semi-realistic character.

An interesting question to briefly look at here is why *mangaka* choose so often to use female characters as a rival, instead of male characters which could be — and sometimes are — used just as effectively. It is important to note that when male rivals occur, they are often not as demonized as the female rivals, nor are they as negatively portrayed by the *mangaka*. There are, of course, always exceptions. The male rival who appears in the last chapter of *Otonage* is characterized as just as unlikable as Kanako; perhaps even more dislikable. Kanako is at least given the opportunity to explain her motives, which makes her slightly more sympathetic, whereas the motives given for the male rival's actions only serve to make Nakano more sympathetic.

The main characters in BL are frequently characterized as not-homosexual, even when they are clearly engaged in a homosexual relationship. It is common for characters to deny that they are gay and then proceed, almost immediately, to become involved in a homosexual relationship. Constance Penley, in an article on Kirk/Spock slash, suggested that this device "allows a much greater range of identification and desire for the [readers]: in the fantasy one can *be* Kirk or Spock (a possible phallic identification) and also still *have* (as sexual objects) either or both of them since, as heterosexuals, they are not *unavailable* to women."[47] This could help account for why female love rivals are disliked in BL even more than male love rivals. Not only are the female characters threatening the relationship between the main characters, they also threaten the reader. A female character becomes a rival for the reader in that she threatens the possibility that the reader can have either of the main characters. Because she is female, this love rival could step into the opening left by the characters' absence of an avowed homosexual identity.

The third character I would like to discuss is the character Miyabi in Shimotsuki Kairi's *Madness*.[48] In addition to writing BL works, Shimotsuki also writes *seinen* and *shōnen* manga.[49] As a result, *Madness* has many elements that are more commonly found in *seinen* and *shōnen* manga, both in the basic plot structure and in the number of bloody scenes that occur.

Madness starts out with a brief explanation that, due to a major earthquake in 2700 A.D., the world has fallen into chaos that even three hundred years later has not been resolved. This leads to an interesting technological situation in which computers, guns and swords all exist side by side and cars seem to have disappeared. Because of the chaos, there has also emerged a very violent group of people known as Madness who delight in bloodshed, although with the murder of their leader sometime before the beginning of the story, the group has disappeared.

One of the main characters in the story is Izaya, a priest, who is caring for a man that his father caged and chained in the basement of their church. This man is none other than the supposedly dead leader of Madness, Kyo, who lost his memory at the time that he was supposedly killed. Another ex-member of Madness attacks the church, attempting to steal Kyo's sword. During the fight, Kyo manages to free himself from the basement of the church and kills his former companion. After this fight, both Kyo and Izaya leave the church and its village, Kyo because he is not welcome, now that he, a mass murderer, is free from his prison, and Izaya because he is the only person who can stop Kyo when Kyo is in the grip of bloodlust.

Not long after they leave the village, Kyo and Izaya encounter another ex-member of Madness, Oboro, who joins them. Soon after this, Izaya gets lost in a city and ends up getting conscripted to work in a brothel. He is saved by the brothel's top prostitute, Urara, from being raped. It is little surprise to the reader when, a chapter later, Urara is revealed to be none other than Miyabi, a former member of Madness and the person who supposedly killed Kyo. Miyabi is drawn in a way that is very reminiscent of female characters in *seinen* works; she is very busty and wears clothes that are frequently on the verge of falling off, and several times she is depicted as wearing hardly any clothes at all. But she is also shown as being courageous, generous, and strong, with a formidable temper and strength of character.

It is only after Miyabi is introduced that the plot of *Madness* really gets started. The manga is currently two volumes long and at present is still being serialized in Japan. During the course of the story, Miyabi frequently comes between Kyo and Izaya, not because she is trying to become romantically or sexually involved with either one of them, but because she likes Izaya as a person. Since he is extremely naïve, she wants to protect him from Kyo. Miyabi's interference results in her interrupting Kyo and Izaya just before they have sex, every single time. While this would normally be grounds for every fan of the series to turn against her (and some do), the majority of the fans still adore her, in part because she also protects Izaya from everyone else, but more because her character is frequently described by fans as "kick ass."

When Miyabi is first introduced, as Urara, she saves Izaya from being raped by offering herself as a substitute, an extremely rare example of heterosexual intercourse in a BL work. Reader reactions were, understandably, very sympathetic toward her. The first comment mentioning Miyabi that wasn't commenting on the size of her breasts mentioned how horrible the situation must have been for her, although in the manga Miyabi looks rather bored. The next comments were a short conversation between several commenters remarking on how beautiful Urara/Miyabi is. This sort of reaction to a female character in a BL manga is also extremely rare. At this point in the story, it was not known that Urara and Miyabi were the same person, although it had been implied. Readers were reacting to Urara mainly because she offered herself up to save Izaya and not because she was an ex-member of Madness. More typical were responses like the earlier "boobies ... ARGH!"[50] comment made in response to Kanako's character in *Otonage*. Comments like that were made before Miyabi was even truly introduced, in response to a small drawing of Miyabi that was part of the front matter in the manga. The poster of the *Madness* was quick to reassure those who reacted negatively to this picture that, while there is a woman in *Madness*, they'll like her.

When Miyabi is first introduced, it is just as an image of her in her Madness days, with some discussion between Kyo and Oboro about who she is. Readers' reactions to her were extremely positive. One of the first reactions was about how sexy Miyabi's character was.[51] That was quickly followed by reactions about how nice it was to see a female character who can kick ass.[52] Because strong, sympathetic, and well-thought-out female characters are so rare, they are welcomed immediately whenever it seems like they might appear, and readers often stick by them even if they start to interfere in the main couple's relationship.

The first time Kyo attempts to have sex with Izaya after Miyabi is introduced, Kyo has just re-lost all memories of who he is and so doesn't care that Izaya is insisting that they need to go save Miyabi and Oboro. Kyo is far more interested in getting Izaya's pants off than he is in running to the rescue of people he doesn't remember. Kyo has Izaya's pants half off and both of them are in the bathtub when the hilt of a sword is introduced to the back of his head by Miyabi, who didn't need rescuing after all. Miyabi goes on to pin Kyo down by resting her foot on his head. The first comment to this was "GAH! We finally get some lovin [*sic*] and its [*sic*] interrupted!!! Poor Kyou [*sic*].. but that pic with Miyabi's foot on his head cracks me up.. hahaha."[53] Other commenters reacted similarly. Extrapolating from the earlier reactions to women in BL manga that I cited, it would be reasonable to expect negative reactions to Miyabi here, but every commenter who mentioned her did so not only positively, but on occasion almost fawningly.

The second time that *Madness* was posted to Yaoi Daily, over a year later, the commenters were a little less forgiving at this scene. One remarked, "I'm sorry, but Miyabi-san's becoming a little obnoxious...."[54] One other commenter agreed, but all of the rest reacted positively. Although several commenters complained that Miyabi could have picked a better time to interrupt, they did not react negatively toward her, and another commenter's reaction was "Oh my gawd [*sic*] I love Miyabi. *gush gush* ♥♥♥."[55] Other than the first comment I quoted, the most negative comment about Miyabi was not about her character, but about her miraculous ability to have her shirts ripped almost entirely to shreds and still stay on. Indeed, Miyabi was so popular that when *Madness* was posted for the second time, most of the comments on the first of these re-postings were about how much they loved the manga and several commenters mentioned that they loved Miyabi. When a commenter mentioned that upon seeing breasts s/he looked away really quickly, others were quick to offer reassurance that Miyabi is actually likeable.

In the survey, I asked readers about what they thought of female characters in other manga genres that they read. The responses I received were similar to what would be expected from what I have discussed about reactions to female characters in BL. Female characters who are strong in their own right are liked, while characters who are overly emotional or dramatic or who exist only to fawn on the main characters (when they are male) or on other male characters are disliked. Also, readers react to how the *mangaka* apparently want their characters to be received. They generally like the characters they are seemingly intended to like and dislike those characters whose attributes imply that they are supposed to be disliked.[56] The same preferences emerged when they were questioned about women in fanfiction and in published books.[57]

It is clear, then, that the misogyny and negativity that is found in many female readers' responses to female characters in BL manga does not necessarily arise from any innate dislike of all female characters in manga or because the readers hold misogynistic views in general. Rather, what happens is that characters that are portrayed in a negative way by the *mangaka*, such as Kanako, are hated because they are seemingly designed to be hated. Characters that are portrayed as realistically flawed, such as Moe, have some supporters, but they are also disliked. Characters that are portrayed as strong and likeable, like Miyabi, are almost universally adored by female readers.

Although Yaoi Daily is intended as a space to appreciate relationships between two men, it does not necessarily follow that in order to fulfill this intention it needs to be a place that is open to hostility toward the female characters. However, the social norm for Yaoi Daily has developed so that dislike of female characters and misogynistic comments about these characters are considered acceptable and unworthy of notice by participants. I believe that this is the result of the dearth of strong, positively portrayed female characters in BL. It is also caused by deliberately negative portrayals of female characters by *mangaka*, which lead to the female characters being cast in the position of the character that readers love to hate. It is also a result of the female characters being seen as threatening the fantasies of the reader. Female characters threaten both the relationship between the main characters and, by virtue of their gender, by close off the opportunity for readers to fantasize about a relationship between themselves and either of the main characters.

Notes

1. For the purpose of this chapter, "poster" will refer to the person who makes the original journal entry and "commenter" will refer to the readers who make comments on that post.

2. These reactions are also frequently noted in readers of the slash fanfiction genre, which like BL focuses on male homosexual relationships and is most frequently written by women for women.

3. This survey was titled "Reader survey on Yaoi/BL/Boys' Love/Shounen ai manga." I designed and conducted the survey. The survey was posted online using the Google Docs forms feature and it was promoted on the Yaoi Daily Café community on LiveJournal. It was also promoted by the authors of several manga blogs in an attempt to move beyond the LiveJournal community. The survey was active from 6 P.M. MST on Oct. 10, 2008, until 3 P.M. MST on Oct. 26, 2008. During this period I received a total of eighty-seven responses.

The survey was conducted to allow complete anonymity for the respondents, since reading in this genre is sometimes seen as strange and perhaps deviant by wider society. All of the subjects were self-selected and most were serious, although a few respondents' results were discarded because they were clearly not serious in their answers and were possibly only interested in attempting to skew the results.

To briefly explain the title of the survey, although there is a marked preference for the term *yaoi*, there is no one term that is universally used to describe the BL genre in English-language fandom. In order to avoid skewing the results by using only one of the terms which might have different connotations for the respondents than it does for me, I used all terms in the survey.

In future citations of this survey I shall refer to it as the "reader survey." In order to differentiate between the different respondents, I shall cite the time the survey was taken when I quote a respondent.

4. Yaoi Daily, http://community.livejournal.com/yaoi_daily/; LiveJournal, http://www.livejournal.com. Due to frequent adult content, Yaoi Daily is a "locked" community; posts are viewable only to members of the community. LiveJournal is a hosting website for online journals that has become one of the favored sites for fan journals and fan communities.

5. Yaoi Daily Community Profile, http://community.livejournal.com/yaoi_daily/profile.

6. All commercially published BL works are acceptable, so a post may be from a manga, a *dōjinshi* with a large print run, or a BL computer game. Although the rules simply mention that licensed works are not allowed, the FAQ (http://www.yaoi.ca/yaoidaily/faq/index.html#4b) refers specifically to "North American publishing companies."

7. For examples of this, see Aoyama Tomoko, "Male Homosexuality as Treated by Japanese Women Writers," in *The Japanese Trajectory: Modernization and Beyond*, ed. Gavan McCormack and Yoshio Sugimoto (Cambridge: Cambridge University Press, 1988), 186–204; Suzuki Kazuko, "Pornography or Therapy? Japanese Girls Creating the Yaoi Phenomenon," in *Millennium Girls: Today's Girls Around the World*, ed. Sherrie A. Inness (Lanham, MD: Rowman & Littlefield Publishers, Inc. 1998), 243–267.

8. See Matsui Midori, "Little Girls Were Little Boys: Displaced Femininity in the Representation of Homosexuality in Japanese Girls' Comics," in *Feminism and the Politics of Difference*, ed. Sneja Gunew and Anna Yeatman (Boulder, CO: Westview Press, 1993), 177–196.

9. Kazumi Nagaike, "Perverse Sexualities, Perversive Desires: Representations of Female Fantasies and *Yaoi Manga* as Pornography Directed at Women," *U.S.–Japan Women's Journal, English Supplement*, 25 (2003): 76–103.

10. See Elizabeth Woledge, "From Slash to the Mainstream: Female Writers and Gender Blending Men," *Extrapolation* 46.1 (2005): 50–65.

11. This argument is very similar to what Janice Radway describes as the appeal of the romance novel in chapter four of *Reading the Romance*. Although the comparison may seem to be a stretch, because romances are focused on a heterosexual relationship, many of the tropes found in romance novels are similar to tropes found in BL. Janice A. Radway, *Reading the Romance: Women, Patriarchy, and Popular Literature* (Chapel Hill, NC and London: University of North Carolina Press, 1991).

12. Blair, "Reader Survey," 10/10/08 19:07; 10/10/08 19:30; 10/11/08 00:28; 10/11/08 06:13; 10/11/08 14:43; 10/13/08 13:46; 10/15/08 18:58; 10/18/08 23:39; 10/11/08 00:42.

13. Ibid, 10/14/08, 09:47.

14. Laura Mulvey, "Visual Pleasure and Narrative Cinema," in *Visual and Other Pleasures* (Bloomington & Indianapolis: Indiana University Press, 1989), 19; Nagaike, "Perverse Sexualities," 79; Tania Modleski, *Loving with a Vengeance: Mass-Produced Fantasies for Women*, 2nd ed. (New York & London: Routledge, 2008), 44–45, 47.

15. Pornography is "the explicit description or exhibition of sexual subjects or activity in literature, painting, films, etc., in a manner intended to stimulate erotic rather than aesthetic feelings; printed or visual material containing this." Obscenity is defined as "1. The character or quality of being offensively indecent, lewdness; an instance of this, *esp.* an obscene expression. 2. The character or quality of being horrible, offensive, or morally repugnant, etc. Also (as a count noun): an extremely offensive or objectionable gesture, statement, event, etc." *Oxford English Dictionary*, draft revision 2008, s.v. "Pornography." *Oxford English Dictionary*, draft revision 2004, s.v. "Obscenity."

16. Jacobellis v. Ohio, 378 U.S. 184, 197 (1964).

17. See for example Nagaike, Suzuki, and McLelland, among others. Mark McLelland, "Loincloths, Ladyboys and Lolita's Little Brother: Women's Culture and the Consumption of 'Gay Pornography' in Japan," in

Queer in the 21st Century: The Body—Queer and Politic, ed. J. Keith Atkinson and Justin J. Finnerty (Fortitude Valley, Australia: Gay and Lesbian Welfare Association, Inc., 2001), 97–118; Mark McLelland, "Why are Japanese Girls' Comics Full of Men Bonking?" *Refractory: A Journal of Entertainment Media*, 10 (2006/2007): http://blogs.arts.unimelb.edu.au/refractory/2006/12/04/why-are-japanese-girls%E2%80%99-comics-full-of-boys-bonking1-mark-mclelland/; Mark McLelland and Seunghyun Yoo, "The International Boys' Love Fandom and the Regulation of Virtual Child Pornography: The Implications of Current Legislation," *Sexuality Research & Social Policy: Journal of NSRC* 4:1(2007): 93–104.

18. Mulvey, 16, 18, 21–22.

19. Nagakubo Yōko 永久保陽子, *Yaoi shōsetsuron: Josei no tame no erosu hyōgen* やおい小説論：女性のためのエロス表現 (Tokyo: Senshū Daigaku Shuppankyoku, 2005), 109–114. Nagakubo's work provides a very good analysis of gender in BL.

20. The breakdown in survey respondents both supports and contradicts these ideas about the composition of the BL audience. Out of the eighty-seven responses I received to my survey, eleven of the respondents identified as male, although five of the responses were almost completely blank after the initial demographic questions and a sixth response was obviously facetious. I also had one respondent identify as intersexed and two each identify as transsexual and other. Again, for the question of sexuality, over half of the respondents identified themselves as heterosexual (fifty-two respondents), but there were a broad variety of responses given, including bisexual (twenty-one respondents), gay (two respondents), lesbian (three respondents), and queer (one respondent).

21. This is itself problematic, in that a genre that is targeted toward women tends to avoid depicting them.

22. Kano, *Otonage*, Attractive Fascinante scanlation. http://community.livejournal.com/afascinante/; Kano Shiuko 鹿乃しうこ. *Otonage*大人気. Tokyo: MagazineMagazine, 2007. Because I am looking at the online English-language fandom's reactions to female characters I have limited the works I am looking at to those that are easily available online as scanlations. However I also include for reference the original Japanese publication.

23. The manga is unclear as to whether Kanako or Yasushi ended their relationship.

24. LBC & QC, http://community.livejournal.com/yaoi_daily/4959431.html, 02/13/2008. Usernames link directly to the users' journals, many of which give details about their personal lives, so in order to protect users' identities, I will not mention their user names or link directly to the comments. I have also chosen to do this because there is still some stigma associated with reading BL, and some readers chose to keep their interest in BL a secret.

25. HT, http://community.livejournal.com/yaoi_daily/4959431.html, 02/13/2008 (accessed Nov. 7, 2008).

26. TB & LBC, http://community.livejournal.com/yaoi_daily/4959431.html, 02/12–13/2008 (accessed Nov. 7, 2008).

27. Because BL works are rarely realistic, some fans have begun to use the term "yaoiland" to describe the "reality" in which these stories take place.

28. Blair, "Reader Survey," 10/10/08 18:16; 10/10/08 19:27; 10/10/08 23:39; 10/10/08 20:52; 10/12/08 02:07.

29. Michael Wesch, "An Anthropological Introduction to YouTube" presented at The Library of Congress, June 23, 2008 (http://www.youtube.com/watch?v=TPAO-lZ4_hU), 27:58–29:52 (accessed Oct. 26, 2008).

30. I believe this to be so based not only on the results of my survey, but also on more moderate or approving comments made by some of the seemingly misogynistic commenters.

31. There are many different definitions of "flaming"; a list is given on page 331 of Philip A. Thompsen, "What's Fueling the Flames in Cyberspace? A Social Influence Model," in *Communication and Cyberspace: Social Interaction in an Electronic Environment*, ed. Lance Strate, Ron L. Jacobson, and Stephanie B. Gibson, 2nd ed. (Cresskill, NJ: Hampton Press, Inc., 2003). The definition I am using here was originally espoused by Keith Dorwick in 1993. Dorwick defines flaming as "the spontaneous creation of homophobic, racist and misogynist language during electronic communication" (3). Keith Dorwick, "Beyond Politeness: Flaming and the Realm of the Violent." Paper presented at the annual meeting of the Conference on College Composition and Communication, San Diego, CA, March 31–April 3, 1993.

32. Thompsen, 336.

33. Ibid., 337–38.

34. Susan E. Watt, Marten Lea and Russell Spears, "How Social is Internet Communication? A Reappraisal of Bandwidth and Anonymity Effects," in *Virtual Society? Technology, Cyberbole, Reality*, ed. Steve Woolgar (Oxford & New York: Oxford University Press, 2002), 66–69.

35. Blair, "Reader Survey," 10/10/08 18:16; 10/10/08 19:27.

36. Modleski, 86.

37. Modleski, 89–90.

38. Homerun Ken, *Boku wa kimi no tori ni naritai*, DokiDoki, Nakama and Smexy Bs joint scanlation

http://www.aragami.org/doki.php. Homerun Ken ホームラン・拳. *Boku wa kimi no tori ni naritai* 僕は君の鳥に
なりたい. Tokyo: Kaiōsha, 2005.

39. BG, http://community.livejournal.com/yaoi_daily/2802118.html, 05/23/2006 (accessed Nov. 7, 2008).
";P" is the poster winking and sticking out her tongue.

40. Sh, http://community.livejournal.com/yaoi_daily/2807586.html, 05/24/2006 (accessed Nov. 7, 2008).
"XD;;;" is the poster grinning with her eyes shut. The semicolons represent sweat drops, which in manga are
a symbol of nervousness, worry, or embarrassment.

41. PA, http://community.livejournal.com/yaoi_daily/2807586.html, 05/24/2006 (accessed Nov. 7, 2008).

42. Hd, http://community.livejournal.com/yaoi_daily/2812539.html, 05/25/2006 (accessed Nov. 7, 2008).
Because only one post of a story is allowed in a day and readers are following many stories at once, in comments on Yaoi Daily characters are often referred to by a descriptor other than their name, which the reader
might have forgotten, such as "the seme," "the uke," or "the girl."

43. On a side note, when they appear, Homerun Ken's female characters are always depicted in a sympathetic way; even if they only appear very briefly, they are always likable.

44. QK, http://community.livejournal.com/yaoi_daily/2825001.html, 05/29/2006 (accessed Nov. 7, 2008).

45. An, http://community.livejournal.com/yaoi_daily/2836155.html, 06/01/2006 (accessed Nov. 7, 2008).

46. Me, http://community.livejournal.com/yaoi_daily/2884482.html, 06/12/2006 (accessed Nov. 7, 2008).

47. Constance Penley, "Feminism, Psychoanalysis, and the Study of Popular Culture," in *Cultural Studies*,
ed. Lawrence Grossberg, Cary Nelson and Paula A. Treichler (New York & London: Routledge, 1992) 488.
Italics in the original.

48. Shimotsuki Kairi. *Madness*, Beautiful Soup scanlation http://soup.umi-sora.com/. Shimotsuki Kairi
霜月かいり. *Madness* マッドネス. Tokyo: Gentōsha, 2004.

49. Manga marketed to young men and boys, respectively.

50. HT, http://community.livejournal.com/yaoi_daily/4959431.html, 02/13/2008 (accessed Nov. 7, 2008).

51. http://community.livejournal.com/yaoi_daily/2692618.html, 04/21/2006 (accessed Nov. 7, 2008).

52. http://community.livejournal.com/yaoi_daily/2692618.html, 04/21/2006 (accessed Nov. 7, 2008).

53. PB, http://www.livejournal.com/yaoi_dailiy, 05/09/2006 (accessed Nov. 7, 2008).

54. LBC, http://community.livejournal.com/yaoi_daily/4707980.html, 11/03/2007 (accessed Nov. 7, 2008).

55. Ki, http://community.livejournal.com/yaoi_daily/4707980.html, 11/04/2007 (accessed Nov. 7, 2008).

56. Blair, "Reader Survey."

57. Ibid.

Bibliography

Aoyama, Tomoko. "Male Homosexuality as Treated by Japanese Women Writers." In *The Japanese Trajectory: Modernization and Beyond*, edited by Gavan McCormack and Yoshio Sugimoto, 186–204. Cambridge:
Cambridge University Press, 1988.

Dorwick, Keith. "Beyond Politeness: Flaming and the Realm of the Violent." Paper presented at the annual
meeting of the Conference on College Composition and Communication, San Diego, CA, March 31–April
3, 1993.

Matsui, Midori. "Little Girls Were Little Boys: Displaced Femininity in the Representation of Homosexuality in Japanese Girls' Comics." In *Feminism and the Politics of Difference*, edited by Sneja Gunew and Anna
Yeatman, 177–196. Boulder, CO: Westview Press, 1993.

McLelland, Mark. "Loincloths, Ladyboys and Lolita's Little Brother: Women's Culture and the Consumption
of 'Gay Pornography' in Japan." In *Queer in the 21st Century: The Body — Queer and Politic*, edited by J.
Keith Atkinson and Justin J. Finnerty, 97–118. Fortitude Valley, Australia: Gay and Lesbian Welfare Association, Inc., 2001.

_____. "Why are Japanese Girls' Comics Full of Men Bonking?" *Refractory: A Journal of Entertainment Media*,
10 (2006/2007): http://blogs.arts.unimelb.edu.au/refractory/2006/12/04/why-are-japanese-girls%E2%80%
99-comics-full-of-boys-bonking1-mark-mclelland/

McLelland, Mark, and Seunghyun Yoo. "The International Boys' Love Fandom and the Regulation of Virtual
Child Pornography: The Implications of Current Legislation." *Sexuality Research & Social Policy: Journal
of NSRC* 4:1(2007): 93–104.

Mizoguchi, Akiko. "Male-Male Romance by and for Women in Japan: A History of the Subgenres of *Yaoi*
fictions." *U.S.–Japan Women's Journal, English Supplement*, 25 (2003): 49–75.

Modleski, Tania. *Loving with a Vengeance: Mass-Produced Fantasies for Women*. 2nd ed. New York & London:
Routledge, 2008.

Mulvey, Laura. "Visual Pleasure and Narrative Cinema." In *Visual and Other Pleasures*, edited by Laura Mulvey, 14–26. Bloomington & Indianapolis: Indiana University Press, 1989.

Nagaike, Kazumi. "Perverse Sexualities, Perversive Desires: Representations of Female Fantasies and *Yaoi Manga* as Pornography Directed at Women." *U.S.–Japan Women's Journal, English Supplement* 25 (2003): 76–103.

Nagakubo Yōko 永久保陽子. *Yaoi shōsetsuron: Josei no tame no erosu hyōgen* やおい小説論：女性のためのエロス表現. Tokyo: Senshū Daigaku Shuppankyoku, 2005.

Penley, Constance. "Feminism, Psychoanalysis, and the Study of Popular Culture." In *Cultural Studies*, edited by Lawrence Grossberg, Cary Nelson and Paula A. Treichler. New York & London: Routledge, 1992.

Radway, Janice A. *Reading the Romance: Women, Patriarchy, and Popular Literature.* Chapel Hill, NC and London: University of North Carolina Press, 1991.

Schodt, Frederik L. *Dreamland Japan: Writings on Modern Manga.* Berkeley: Stone Bridge Press, 1996.

Suzuki, Kazuko. "Pornography or Therapy? Japanese Girls Creating the Yaoi Phenomenon." In *Millennium Girls: Today's Girls Around the World*, edited by Sherrie A. Inness, 243–267. Lanham, MD: Rowman & Littlefield Publishers, Inc. 1998.

Thompsen, Philip A. "What's Fueling the Flames in Cyberspace? A Social Influence Model." In *Communication and Cyberspace: Social Interaction in an Electronic Environment*, edited by Lance Strate, Ron L. Jacobson, and Stephanie B. Gibson. 2nd ed. Cresskill, NJ: Hampton Press, Inc., 2003.

Watt, Susan E., Marten Lea, and Russell Spears. "How Social is Internet Communication? A Reappraisal of Bandwidth and Anonymity Effects." In *Virtual Society? Technology, Cyberbole, Reality*, edited by Steve Woolgar. Oxford & New York: Oxford University Press, 2002.

Wesch, Michael. "An Anthropological Introduction to YouTube" presented at The Library of Congress, June 23, 2008. http://www.youtube.com/watch?v=TPAO-lZ4_hU (accessed Oct. 26, 2008).

Woledge, Elizabeth. "From Slash to the Mainstream: Female Writers and Gender Blending Men." In *Extrapolation* 46.1 (2005): 50–65.

8

Rewriting Gender and Sexuality in English-Language Yaoi Fanfiction

Tan Bee Kee

Aguri: The internet?

Kudou: You don't expect all the horny teenaged girls dreaming of mysterious strangers to keep their fantasies to themselves, do you?

Aguri: I have to read about having sex with teenaged girls too?

Kudou: Of course not. They're the ones who'll write about you having sex with Hidaka.[1]

The term "yaoi fanfiction" is used by English-speaking fans to refer to derivative fan stories, written by mostly female fans, centered around male homoeroticism based on original Japanese sources, such as anime (Japanese animation) or manga (Japanese comics) series. Using close textual analysis of the presentation of gender and sexuality in English-language fanfiction written within the anime/manga series *Weiss Kreuz* (wk) fandom on the Internet as case study, I will show how fans write to express their own visions of romance/sexuality and subvert heteronormative media narratives. However, I will also show that yaoi fanfiction is not without its internal contradictions and limitations as a form of resistance against gender norms.

The fanfictions collected for this project between January 2005–March 2005 were based on a survey of fans on WK mailing lists in late 2004 about the writers and fanfics they felt had been important in influencing WK fandom, fan recommendations on fansites, essays on WK on LiveJournal, and works by "Big Name Fans" (fans who are well-known in the fan community for their activities such as writing fanfictions). Other sources included winners of past WK fanfiction contests and over 5000 fanfics at Fanfiction.net, more than 1000 fanfics at Mediaminer.org, and smaller numbers of fics at Adultfanfiction.net and smaller archives. I went through the fanfiction archives by reading story summaries and taking note of interesting topics and recurrent trends, as well as fics that have garnered unusually large numbers of reviews.

I have chosen to focus on Internet fantexts due to their ease of dissemination and accessibility by any fan with an Internet connection. Analyzing fanfiction in the context of fan commentary, blogs and essays helps us to understand the ways fans read the original media texts. According to McKee, "(w)hen we perform textual analysis on a text, we make an educated guess at some of the most likely interpretations that might be made of that text.... We interpret texts ... in order to try and obtain a sense of the ways in which, in particular cultures at particular times, people make sense of the world around them."[2] Since we cannot read the minds of fans directly to see how they interpret media texts, fantexts are what we have to work with. In this study, I will be analyzing fanfictions as artifacts rooted in social reality with political implications.[3]

126

Henry Jenkins points out that in fields such as film criticism, claims about the audience are derived from textual analysis of the source text, personal introspection etc. However, reception studies "seeks empirical evidence, through historical or ethnographic research, that documents the production and circulation of meaning." Since textually ascribed meanings do not get reproduced fairly directly in spectator's heads, "[t]ext, context, and reader all play vital roles in shaping interpretation."[4] Jenkins suggests that "Less predictable readings reveal more clearly the interpretive process at work, suggesting that there is nothing inevitable about our own interpretations."[5] Yaoi fan reinterpretations are precisely examples of unexpected readings that force the reader to view the original media text in totally fresh ways.

I have adapted ethnographic techniques to cyberspace using Hine's notion of virtual ethnography. Traditionally, ethnography consists of "a researcher spending an extended period of time immersed in a field setting, taking account of the relationships, activities and understandings of those in the setting and participating in those processes. The aim is to make explicit the taken-for granted and often tacit ways in which people make sense of their lives."[6] I have done this by immersing myself in the virtual social environments inhabited by fans, analyzing fan essays about their fanfictions, and monitoring fan responses as well as through correspondence with fan writers in order to understand the way they consume media.

The Western analogue to yaoi would be slash, which is based on Western media sources and has similar themes, although it has somewhat different fan conventions and evolved out of a different cultural context. However, since much useful work has been done analyzing slash, I will be referring extensively to slash theorists. Also, since I am examining English-language fanfiction written by non–Japanese fans, many are slash fans as well and have come into yaoi by way of slash, especially Western fans, as shown in Dru Pagliassotti's English-language survey of BL manga readers conducted online from June 28 to November 21, 2005, that attracted a total of 478 respondents, mostly from U.S., Canada, the UK, or Australia.[7]

Weiss Kreuz is about a team called *Weiss* composed of four young men (Fujimiya Aya, Kudō Yōji, Hidaka Ken and Tsukiyono Ōmi). They work at a florist shop as a cover for their real jobs as assassins for a vigilante organization called *Kritiker,* which focuses on eliminating powerful villains beyond the reach of the law. Weiss is opposed by an assassin group called Schwarz from an evil organization called Estet, composed of Brad Crawford, an American who is able to see the future, Farfarello, an insane Irishman who is immune to pain, Schuldig, a German with telepathic powers and Naoe Nagi, an orphaned Japanese boy with telekinetic powers.

In WK, Weiss live together in the same apartment above the flower shop in the anime, and mutual trust/cooperation is essential for them to survive their dangerous missions because they depend on one another for backup. Deena's "Waking onto Lantern's Bright" emphasizes how the bonds between the boys through their profession deepen into romantic love.

> "We live together, work together, kill together. After all this time, I'd like to think I
> know you guys. We're friends, aren't we Kenken?"
>   He grinned at the older boy. "Cleaning blood stains together really has that bonding
> effect."[8]

Although most of the members of Weiss fall in love with women at one point or another in the series, they are ultimately unable to sustain such romances because their work as assassins makes it too dangerous for them to become involved with civilians. This is often a target of fans who playfully exaggerate homosocial bonds. Kuwabara no Miko's tongue-in-cheek "Male Bonding" features a drinking session between Yōji, Ken and Ōmi that becomes a ménage a trois.[9]

WK is known for its poor animation quality as well as its flimsy, sometimes ludicrous plot. However, it has garnered a huge fandom overseas among female fans. On the English Internet, it was one of the biggest early yaoi fandoms, together with *Gundam Wing*.

The Dissatisfactions of Compulsory Heterosexuality

> The sheer prevalence of the heterosexual "norm" in books and films and ... well, almost everywhere ... and the idea that one *should* find it sexy makes it very hard to admit that you find these kinds of things rather boring or a turn-*off*.[10]

Yaoi fans are dissatisfied with mainstream (heterosexual) portrayal of romance and sexuality in the form of TV programs, romance novels, and movies even if they happen to identify as heterosexual, as seen in the above quote from a fan essay. Henry Jenkins points out that traditional romance generally leaves unquestioned its assumptions about gender. "The woman's perception of a 'dark side' to male sexuality is later attributed to misunderstandings and dissolves in the happiness of the couple's commitment. The woman must accept her role as wife without asserting demands for autonomy."[11]

Ann Snitow, in her analysis of mass market romances, delineates their dark aspects. She shows that the heroine is not allowed by social mores to acknowledge sexual desire honestly and has to do "a lot of social lying to save face, pretending to be unaffected by the hero's presence while her body melts or shivers" because she has to save her virginity for marriage.[12] Distance between the sexes is glorified and the sexual inexperience of the heroine adds to the excitement (Snitow, 426).

> ... What is the Harlequin romance formula? ... All tensions and problems arise from the fact that the Harlequin world is inhabited by two species incapable of communicating with each other, male and female. It is pleasing to think that appearances are deceptive, that male coldness, absence, boredom, are not what they seem.... In spite of his coldness or preoccupation, the hero really loves the heroine and wants to marry her [Snitow, 424, 426].

Since the goal of romance novels is marriage, they end once the "most interesting phase in the love/marriage cycle" is over (Snitow, 426). We do not see the couple change diapers or argue over household chores. As romance novels tend to contain soft-core sex scenes, it has also been suggested that they provide respectable "sexual release" for women too prudish for real porn who believe in maintaining their reputations (Snitow, 427). The romance heroine is passively receptive to the male ego and her sexuality is constrained. As Snitow explains, the Harlequin heroine is not "involved in any overt adventure beyond trying to respond appropriately to male energy without losing her virginity. Virginity is a given here; sex means marriage and marriage, promised at the end, means, finally, there can be sex" (Snitow, 425).

Yaoi overcomes these problems. With two male characters, there are no predefined roles to play in romance. Either character is free to initiate a relationship. They are free from the pressure of "saving themselves" for marriage, firstly because they are both male, and secondly, since gay couples are unable to marry in most countries, including Japan, sex is not confined within marriage. In a story in which the *uke* loses his virginity to the *seme*, it is represented as the "ultimate sign of trust and ultimate surrender of self to the partner," as Cicioni shows in her analysis of slash.[13] In heterosexual fiction, such a scenario would be an act of domination that is often portrayed as a "conquest or a devaluation of the woman."[14]

Gayle Rubin (2006) in "Thinking Sex: Notes for a Radical Theory of the Politics of Sexuality" points out that society divides sexual behavior into the good/healthy/natural and the bad/unhealthy/unnatural. Homosexuality falls into the latter camp as opposed to monogamous heterosexual sex within marriage.[15] She also points out in "The Traffic in Women" that "[g]ender is not only an identification with one sex; it also entails that sexual desire be directed toward the other sex."[16] Same-sex desire in yaoi violates this rule.

According to Dennis Altman, "The repression of polymorphous perversity ... is bound up with the development of very clear-cut concepts of masculine and feminine that dominate consciousness and help maintain male supremacy.... Being male and female is, above all, defined in terms of the other: men learn that their masculinity depends on being able to make it with women, women that fulfillment can be only obtained through being bound to a man."[17]

Fans capitalize on homosocial bonds between two males by blurring the barriers between homosociality and homosexuality. In the original texts, characters are often assigned heterosexual love interests, but in yaoi the fan focus is on male characters' relationships with one another, which displace any heterosexual relationships.

According to Jenkins, referencing Eve Kosofsky Sedgewick, "a patriarchal society consistently constructs boundaries between acceptable and unacceptable forms of male friendship; patriarchy is held together ... through homophobia which is part of a system that enforces compulsory heterosexuality as well as restricts the range of behaviors open to men and women. Fictional representations of male friendship often depend for their emotional power upon the suggestion of strong homosocial desire between men, even as they isolate that desire from any explicitly recognizable form of sexuality...."[18] Yaoi breaks through boundaries by foregrounding sexual potential, which is an undercurrent, even when characters are enemies. In "Rules" by Yoippari, Ken's disastrous first meeting with Aya, which ended in a fight, evolves into a dysfunctional sexual relationship.[19] Even though Schwarz and Weiss are enemies, hatred and bloodlust is flipped into love and desire in yaoi.

The average yaoi story arc traces the ripening of friendship crossing over into the line of romantic/sexual involvement, as in "the first time story" (a story which chronicles a couple's first romantic and/or sexual encounter).[20]

In "First Time Stories," a common subgenre in both yaoi and slash, characters must first acknowledge their own desires and come to terms with their prejudices and preconceptions before they can achieve happiness. Jenkins describes the flow of the typical "First Time Story." "The male protagonist dares not act on his erotic fantasies, convinced that the other partner could not possibly share such feelings and that voicing them could damage the men's working relationship" and that the characters' professional status, their own sense of masculinity, and their friendships would be threatened.[21] This fear usually turns out to be unfounded. In Sky Rat's "Better Days," Ken asks Yōji why he did not confess his love earlier.

> "I didn't want to ruin our friendship." For some reason, this excuse seems a lot lamer
> said aloud than it did in my head.
> "Thought you might say that," he looks thoughtful for a second, "you really thought I

placed so little value on our friendship that I would let it be ruined by something like that?!"[22]

In the actual WK series, Yōji constantly emphasizes his heterosexuality with over-the-top statements such as saying that he did not wish to die with a bunch of men during missions. Fans often joke that he is so exaggeratedly straight that he must be hiding something, and he is often portrayed as a promiscuous bisexual in yaoi fanfics. When Ken in Cassandra Nexus's "In the Rain" takes a peek at Yōji's "little black book," he is shocked to discover that the names are all male.[23]

Homophobia, whether internalized or external, is often an obstacle to be overcome in yaoi. In Nekojita's "Cages," Ken (a lapsed Catholic in the series) is sleeping with his best friend Kase but is in denial about his sexuality. "For a moment (Ken) heard Father Timothy's voice, outlining the hell that awaited sodomites, and his former teammates' homophobia ... 'I'm not some limp-wristed fag, and neither is Kase....'"[24] Fans routinely set up characters to show their disdain for such attitudes. In Opus the Penguin's "A Delicate Subject," a homophobic Ken decides to tell a fey Ōmi to mend his ways because the girls who come to the florist shop are convinced they are all gay.[25] Ōmi suggests that Ken must be unconsciously in love with him to be obsessed with his appearance and behavior. Ken panics and tries to reassure himself of his macho-ness by burying himself in motorcycle magazines, soccer and pornography. Unfortunately for Ken, the fanfic points out in a tongue-in-cheek fashion that the most homophobic men are often the most repressed. Ken's actions backfire when he is inadvertently aroused while watching a men's wrestling tournament.

Often, yaoi and slash fanfics feature plot devices such as undercover missions in which "the characters are asked to shed their normal identities, to assume a mask which not only justifies but actively requires otherwise prohibited forms of intimacy."[26] For example, in Deena's "Something New," Aya and Ken are forced to pose as a couple in order to track down targets on a gay honeymoon cruise, which inadvertently leads to their discovering their desire for each other.[27]

Many fanfic writers use camp humor as a tool to mock gender stereotypes. In Kim's "A Quiet Evening," Farfarello, originally a psychotic murderer, is turned into a sex-obsessed queen in neon pink vinyl pants.[28] Aya, a cool, brooding character, turns out to be a secret fan of Harlequin romances in Fancy's "Hair."[29]

Queer Readings

When writing yaoi fanfiction, yaoi fans adopt a variety of queer reading strategies that differ from fan to fan. People who are against yaoi commonly charge that yaoi fans have made straight characters gay. Certainly, some yaoi fans are obsessed with proving their favorite character is queer by combing the series for "evidence," though most fan "proof" is more or less tongue-in-cheek. Thus, they may either be convinced that the character is really queer or are aware their readings are considered "deviant" but insist on reading the character as queer anyway.

Fans are proud of their active engagement with media texts. Indeed, some of them seem to have read academic discourses on fandom and have appropriated such theories to justify fanfiction. According to Pagliassotti's survey of fans over age 18, 78 percent of respondents reported some level of college education and possess academic cultural capital.[30] The hands-on attitude of yaoi fans may be exemplified by this fan essay quote which seems to be echoing Jenkins:

> But what if you want to *read* the canon characters doing m/m (homoerotic) sex and romance? Simple. In three words: *write it yourself.* If you want to see a certain kind of story and it's not available, don't waste time complaining that it's not available — go make it available. Life is much more satisfying when you cease to be a passive consumer and become an active producer.[31]

Yaoi fans also industriously raid mainstream popular narratives such as fairy tales, movies, and conventional romance novels. For Brett Farmer, referring to Roland Barthes, "the primary aim of any popular myth is the naturalization of ideological meaning and the ratification of the social status quo."[32] Yaoi fans have come up with retellings to suit their own purposes. Sometimes the appropriation can be as simple as changing the sex of the heroine to male. In Swythangel's "Heaven In Your Arms," Ken is a fallen angel who melts Crawford's heart, a plot borrowed from a romance novel.[33] Some reworkings are more sophisticated, such as Lynn Metallium's "The Three Little Bishounen," a naughty retelling of "The Three Little Pigs" in which Ken, Ōmi and Aya are in danger of being "eaten" by the Big Bad Playboy Yōji because of their own sexual desires.[34]

As Ika Willis states, writing slash (and yaoi, in this case) can be experienced as "*both* a hedonistic, erotic practice which could even be opposed to a thoughtful or critical relation to a text, *and*, on the other hand, a deliberate, politically loaded, practice of recontextualization that reorients a text in order to demonstrate that it bears the trace of a desiring structure not wholly congruent with the most literal (which is to say, the most ideologically obedient) reading."[35]

Kustriz states that slash fiction texts and the practices of reading, writing, and rewriting slash may be seen as a practice from which a metatext emerges. "(T)he metatext, is a story that tells us how to live, and it is a story that breaks strongly from normative traditions."[36]

According to Sarah Gwenllian Jones, academic interpretations of slash and other queer readings have traditionally suggested that texts (i.e. canon) are inherently or originally heterosexual; thus slash (and yaoi) readings are resistant, "deviant" readings.[37] Jones herself sees slash as an "actualization" of a "latent" property of the text itself, meaning that queerness is already situated in the text itself (Jones, 82). Willis however, suggests seeing fan readings as reorientation: "fan fiction is produced out of the interaction between canon as made legible by dominant cultural knowledges and formulas for reading, and canon as reoriented by the demands and desires brought to it by the subjectivity of the fan/reader and her knowledge of the world."[38]

WK is basically an action/adventure series driven by missions and assassination targets with a great deal of violence and little romance, but so important is *eros* in yaoi that even the fanfics that revolve around missions are focused on romance and relationships.

To Willis, "(w)riting fan fiction is not simply adding the final piece of a jigsaw completing a text with a known unknown, whose correct shape and dimensions can be deduced: rather, writing fan fiction first of all *makes* gaps in a text that the cultural code attempts to render continuous, and then, rather than filling them in, *supplements* these gaps with intertexts which are not docile..." (Willis, 158).

A good example of this insubordination is "fanon" (a pun on canon, which are the actual details/events that happened in the original source material) which Busse and Hellekson define as "the events created by the fan community in a particular fandom and repeated pervasively throughout the fantext."[39] One of the reasons I have chosen WK is that it is known to have unusually strong fanon for a fandom. Fans often declare that they prefer fanon to what actually happens in canon and fanworks to the actual series, which is lackluster by comparison.

Kat Avila (2005) remarks that watching anime *Fullmetal Alchemist* was never quite the same after seeing a *dōjinshi* of a character giving his brother a blow job.[40] The very existence of a queer fan reading opens the eyes of fans to radical possibilities in life that they would not have imagined before.

Gaytopia

Some fans enjoy yaoi for political reasons because yaoi etches out a space where homosexuality is accepted and happy endings abound, unlike mainstream media representations of gays and lesbians which often portray them as dysfunctional, riddled with AIDS, or suicidal. As a lesbian fan explains, "I'm gay. I like yaoi because it presents what looks like heaven to a gay person. Same sex and no second thoughts about it."[41]

Sometimes, this leads to a queer utopia in which everyone experiences same-sex desires. For example, in Kuwabara no Miko and Talya Firedancer's "A Fine Day for a Group Outing," all the members of Weiss accidentally come out to one another as interested in men.[42]

As Laila explains in her fan essay "The Discreet Charm of Slash," non-fans tend to assume that characters are straight unless proven otherwise.[43] Alexander Doty (1993) points out gays and lesbians do occasionally get married, have children, and have sex with the opposite sex.[44] Many yaoi fans feel that sexual self-identity may change over a lifetime.

> It's perfectly possible for someone who has always self-identified as straight to fall in love with someone of the same gender, and vice versa for those who have self-identify [*sic*] as gay.... That few of them act on it might easily have more to do with societal pressure than it does with their own desires.[45]

Sometimes, a character is so skilled a lover that his partner is seduced to the "homosexual side of the Force" as a fan jokes. In Deena's "Raspberry and Lime Shampoo," Yōji successfully "converts" Ken with his bedroom skills.[46]

The message of yaoi fanfics is that love should transcend social conventions. In Deena's "Waking Onto Lantern's Bright," Yōji persuades Ken to confess his love to Aya because "(l)ove doesn't come around so often that you have the chance to worry about something as trivial as gender."[47]

Characters themselves may reject self-definitions. In Martyl's "Black Gold," Yōji refuses to label himself when Ōmi asks him to clarify his sexual orientation.

> "You know, Omittchi," I say slowly. "I asked myself that once a long time ago. And for a while I really couldn't come up with an answer. But then it came to me. I'm just slutty. Where's my parade?!" I cry throwing up my hands. "Slut pride!"[48]

Yaoi fans often see their own sexuality as queer or otherwise fluid. As yaoi fan Pureyaoi explains, "In the world of yaoi I see more and more female writers who call themselves gay, or bi, or simply refuse to define their sexuality using one of three pre-defined terms (straight, gay, bisexual)" (release the krakon! LiveJournal Blog, comment posted December 7, 2004).

Problematizing Societal Gender Norms

Yaoi features the *seme/uke* concept, which comes from the Japanese. The *seme* (*semeru* means "to attack" in Japanese) is the character in a yaoi pairing who penetrates the other in homosexual anal sex whereas the *uke* (*ukeru* means to receive and has a connotation of passivity) is the receptive partner. *Seme* and *uke* roles in a pairing are usually fixed. Besides being sexual roles, the terms "*seme*" and "*uke*" often reflect corresponding gendered attributes. *Uke* are usually shorter (the "height rule"), prettier and more vulnerable than *seme*; in other words, presenting physical and emotional attributes socially constructed as feminine or female. In yaoi, a pairing written as "Aya x Ken" with an "x" separating the names means that the first name or "Aya" is the *seme* whereas "Ken," or the second name, is the *uke*.

Fans often have strong preferences for certain characters to be *uke* and certain characters to be *seme,* but this is not necessarily absolute and "reversibles" (characters who switch between *uke* and *seme*) are quite common. Fans are well aware of the performative nature of *seme/uke.*This is often shown through humorous parodies in which characters fight over who should be *seme.* In this excerpt from a *Weiss Kreuz* fic called "UkeSeme Dynamics" by Celestel, Ken informs a bemused Aya that he fits the stereotypical profile of *uke* better than Ken does:

> "....Uh.... oh yeah! And I'm the brash, spontaneous one! Like the kind that will sneak up on your type at random times and toss him over the nearest horizontal surface to have my wicked way with...."
> Aya's eyebrows darted up. "My *type*?"
> Ken scowled. "Stop picking at details."
> "I'm particularly interested in these details. What do you mean 'my type,' huh?"
> Ken stammered and turned pink around the ears again. "Y-you know! The pretty, quiet ones. The ones that write poetry and read angsty dramas and foreign books and go to art museums and use fabric softener."[49]

In yaoi, dominance is predicated on character and not assigned by sex. Instead, power is negotiated between two masculine characters.[50] Yaoi deconstructs the idea that sexual attraction must be based on essentialist notions of sexual difference.

Inscribing Feminine Desires

Yaoi rewrites the discourses of sexuality according to feminine tastes. Fans often joke that the yaoi lover never skips foreplay or falls asleep immediately after sex but is always attentive to his partner's pleasure and comfort. The whole body becomes an erogenous zone, and intimacy is shared not only through genital sex, as seen in this passage from Martyl's "The Saga Begins":

> We lie together for the rest of the early morning. We hold each other, whispering softly, touching gently, kissing now and then. It's nice. So nice to just share time like this. I doze, my head resting in the crook of his neck. It fits there so well.[51]

Society conventionally defines only vaginal intercourse as "real," natural, and acceptable sex, but yaoi extends intimacy to cuddling, kissing, and oral/anal sex. Some may argue that the anus in yaoi is actually a coded vagina, but of course anal sex is not confined to homosexuals.

Yaoi fanfics are often known for having unrealistic and formulaic representations of gay sex such as the standard "insert one finger, insert two or three, follow with anal penetration" because it is usually written by women who are naturally distanced from male bodies. This has led to some gay male fans "helpfully" offering sex tips to make sex scenes more realistic. However, such attempts are beside the point, because the sex is not meant to be realistic gay sex but idealized fantasies of what women would like lovemaking to be like. As Jeanne points out in "The Top Ten Things I Love About Yaoi," *semes* may take the "male" role, but they still are not men having sex because:

> ... they don't come, or if they do seem to come they're still hard afterwards and able to turn the *uke* over to do it in a new position. They behave like us (women), and they behave the way I bet a lot of straight women wish their guys could. Which makes the *seme* both a woman *and* a female fantasy of maleness at the same time. Neat trick, huh?[52]

Yaoi fanfiction can get very graphic. However, like slash, which Jung (2004) describes as "romantic pornography," sex scenes usually fulfill narrative functions; they further the plot or are used as a tool for characterization and embedded in characters' pasts, presents, and futures as provided by canon.[53] This is in contrast to the denial of the emotional consequences of sex in most porn because in slash (and by extension yaoi) sex always has direct and dramatic emotional ramifications.[54]

There is a genre of fanfiction called PWP (plot? What plot?) consisting of fanfics with very little plot and consisting mainly of explicit sex scenes. Unlike other fanfics, PWPs are obviously written to titillate and appear at surface level to be no different from regular pornography. However as Teep, a fan, explains, yaoi PWPs are different from regular pornography because female readers need to get to know and have some sort of emotional investment in the characters before they can enjoy the story. The normal work of exposition and characterization is already done by the original text (e.g. the anime) so it becomes possible to skip to the yummy parts, i.e. the sex scenes.[55] In contrast, according to Catherine Driscoll, "Not only is characterization not the point of most pornography, it is even an obstacle to the efficiency of pornography."[56]

Furthermore as Alan Soble shows, in conventional pornography women are subjected to physical, psychological and linguistic violence, denial of female pleasure, and being reduced to crude body parts such as "cunt." Women in conventional pornography have no intrinsic value except as receptacles of lust to provide sex on demand.[57] *Ukes* in yaoi sex scenes are seldom dehumanized in such a fashion. The feminist anti-pornography movement claims that pornography encourages rape/violence against women, and many women have ambivalent feelings about conventional pornography.

Andrea Wood, in describing Japanese yaoi/BL, also points out that the *uke* is not "*visually* infused with negative or disempowering connotations ... his partner is more focused on *giving* him pleasure than on simply taking it for himself.... Therefore, in opposition to a one-sided visualization of pleasure that emphasizes the importance of the penetrating partner's orgasm, a mainstay of heterosexual pornography, yaoi manga are more interested in illustrating both partner's erotic fulfillment and gratification."[58]

For Driscoll, we learn from and negotiate with porn what appears sexy as we learn from and negotiate with romance what it is to appear "in love."[59] Yaoi fans have roundly rejected the social scripts of conventional pornography as models by writing their own stories.

Romantic Ideals

In contrast to heterosexual relationships where women often marry for financial security, social respectability, and other reasons such as family pressure, yaoi fans protest against reality by idealizing homosexual relationships. Suzuki, in discussing Japanese fandom, describes homosexual love celebrated by fans as "love free from calculation, capable of withstanding societal pressure, and achieved only after great sacrifice."[60]

Sometimes the fanfics resemble the traditional form of the gay coming-out story where it takes courage and soul-searching for the protagonist to face up to his desires. In Link621's "But, I'm an Assassin," Ōmi comes to realize that he is gay when he connects the dots.

> Omi swallowed hard, thinking back on the events of the recent past. Watching Nagi go longingly. Kissing Ouka with no passion. Feeling his body run rampant on him as the great Hidaka Ken made a beautiful save that exposed his perfect stomach in the process. Not to mention, meeting Ken, just to nearly throw up he was so paralyzed with awe. He was undeniably attracted to men.[61]

Although yaoi is not meant to be realistic, issues of discrimination and gay rights are sometimes addressed. In Atsureki's "Please, Give Me Another Chance," Ken, who coached soccer part-time, lost many of his charges when the children's parents found out he was dating another man.[62] Love faces family opposition in Swythangel's "Phenomenal Noumenal" when Aya's sister is unable to accept that he is gay, forcing Aya to choose between family and his lover.

> Why was it that she could take others being gay but not her own brother?
> If she was truthful with her brother, she knew that the answer was quite simple. She still thought that gays were not normal. No matter how liberal she acted, she was still just a little bit conservative in her views. It was all very well for others like her friends to be gay but to have a member of her family *be* gay?[63]

In Shoori's "Eight Years in the Making," Aya apologizes to Ken for not being able to marry him and give him the security, benefits, and recognition granted automatically to heterosexual couples.

> "I'm sorry that you can't ... have ... all that," He continued staring at the carpet, his light mood rapidly darkening as he pondered all the things he could never give Ken. A wedding. A traditional home. A family. All the things that Ken wanted, that he could never have if he stayed with him....[64]

However, if a character is willing to put himself on the line for love despite all obstacles, risking the loss of trust and loss of his self-image, this courage usually leads to "perfect physical and psychic fulfillment" in slash (or in yaoi, as in this case).[65]

The raison d'être of yaoi is the romantic cliché which one fan, Leather Daddy, describes wryly as "soul-bonding through anal sex," proffering the typical story arc of a yaoi story:

> <u>Seme's name</u> and <u>uke's name</u> are alone at last, after <u>name of a major canonical conflict or war or event</u>. They can finally consummate their love. But wait! <u>Uke's name</u> is reluctant to do the nasty! Why? <u>Uke</u> is a virgin, and is afraid that <u>Seme</u> won't love him anyways. <u>Seme</u> reassures the uke, and they have wild monkey sex in <u>name of position</u> with a little bit of <u>name of kink</u>. But afterwards, <u>Seme</u> notices something strange! He feels warm inside, as if he's found something he's never known he was missing, like the lost half of his soul. "It's a soul bond!" he realizes. Then they mind-speak, exchanging schmoopy sentiments. But then <u>Uke</u> realizes something. "Oh no! <u>Name of major religous, political, social group, or just friends and family</u> will never approve, because I'm <u>too young / too old / your worst enemy / a completely different species</u>! We must

hide our relationship from the others!" <u>Seme</u> says that no matter what, he'll always love <u>Uke</u>. And then they have sex again. The End.[66]

Soul-bonding occurs in this scene from Martyl's "The Saga Begins" in which Ken makes love with Aya for the first time.

> The pleasure is wonderful all on its own, but that isn't what brings me to tears, it isn't what brings Aya to tears, or causes me to cry out his name and whisper that I love him. It's the joy. The sheer joy of being so close, of making love. It is everything I've been feeling inside shared with the one I love. This is what brings me to tears.[67]

In the same story, Yōji finds out that Aya and Ken are secretly sleeping together and jumps to the conclusion that they are simply using each other for sexual relief. Ken is horrified to hear their relationship described so crudely.

> "Ok, Ken," I say, "if you're not fuck buddies, just what exactly are you? Don't tell me that you're...." ...
> "We are together. We have feelings for each other," Aya says calmly. Ken kisses his shoulder softly and hides his face again. I feel my mouth go dry....
> I sit back and look Ken and Aya over. I can see it now. The bonds. The caring.

Woledge actually coins the word "intimatopia" to describe the primacy of intimacy in slash.[68] Intimacy, not sex, is the foundation of yaoi/slash. The story climaxes when the yaoi couple realizes that they are made for one another.

Not only is sex a spiritual, significant, mutually affirmative act, yaoi fanfics tends to emphasize commitment and staying faithful to one's partner, unlike gay cruising culture, reflecting the preferences of their female writers and readers. For example in Martyl's "The Saga Begins," Yōji hints that he would like to join Aya and Ken in the bedroom, only to be turned down flat.[69] Even though yaoi threesomes operate on the principle that if two boys are hot together, three would be better, anonymous sex and promiscuity are usually not valorized unless it is a fanfic specifically written to amuse, such as the stories from Talya Firedancer's infamous "Subway Trilogy" which has Yōji having sex with strangers on the subway and culminates in an frenetic orgy involving all of Weiss.[70]

Kinship, Family and Gay Marriage

Fans often create yaoi fanfics featuring unconventional family structures to argue for a wider definition of family and kinship beyond the heterosexual nuclear family idealized in industrialized societies. In "Uncle Youji's Book of Love" by Durendal and the Beef Chick, Schuldig and Brad Crawford are a couple and the members of Schwarz form a close, if wacky family.

> NAGI (introducing his lover Omi): This <points to Brad> is my ... father. Yes, that's right, father. Brad. And this <points to Schu> is my, er, other parent, Schuldig.
> SCHULDIG: Oh please, Nagi-baby, call me mom.[71]

Yaoi lovers often show their commitment to their relationships by making some sort of symbolic gesture such as wearing matching rings or getting married.

In "The New World Order" series by Aoe and Shoori, Aya and Ken are unable to marry legally but make a monogamous commitment to one another, adopt Aya's nephew as their son, and grow old together.[72] The boy is raised happily within a vast communal network of "aunts" and "uncles" consisting of the members of Weiss and Schwarz as well as Ken's genetic family. Between saving the world from evil as Weiss, Aya and Ken also share a complete partnership at home, splitting chores and taking care of their son. Since both partners are male, they are not bound by socially predefined scripts for men's and women's work.

Marriage is one of the traditional tools used by society to divide unhealthy households (heterosexual cohabitation, single-parent families, same-sex couples, etc.) from the healthy (heterosexual, nuclear family). Marriage in most societies is seen as the foundation of society and civilization. "State and legal institutions thus do not choose to recognize heterosexual marriage; they must recognize it given its foundational status. Finally, in claiming that their unions are the foundations of civilization, heterosexuals claim to be society's most essential citizens...."[73] The heterosexual married couple has traditionally been the single locus of productive sexuality and one of the usual criticisms leveled at homosexual couples is that their unions are pointless because they cannot produce offspring.[74]

The yaoi family however "proves" that "love makes a family" and affirms that gay couples are able to rear well-adjusted offspring. Same-sex marriage portrayed in yaoi de-centers heterosexuality, showing that it is simply one sexual option amongst many others.[75]

Martyl's "Baby Talk" is set in a future Japan in which gay marriage has already been legalized.[76] Aya and Ken's daughter, Kaori, was the product of Aya's sister's donated egg and Ken's sperm and carried to term in an artificial womb; a move harking towards science-fiction in which new reproductive technologies have often been used to challenge traditional gender roles.

Crimson1's fanfic "Kind des Schicksals" ("Child of Fate" in German) features a scenario in which Shioshiro, the genetic son of Aya and Ken who was conceived through futuristic technology, comes back through time to prevent Ken from being killed in a mission.[77] Shioshiro is portrayed not only as a son anyone may be proud of but heterosexual, pointing out that homosexual unions do not necessarily result in homosexual offspring as conservatives claim. Figure 1 is a fan art created by a fan who loved Crimson1's fanfic "Kind des Schicksals."[78] It features Shioshiro, the genetic son of Aya and Ken, gazing fondly at a childhood family photo with his two fathers.

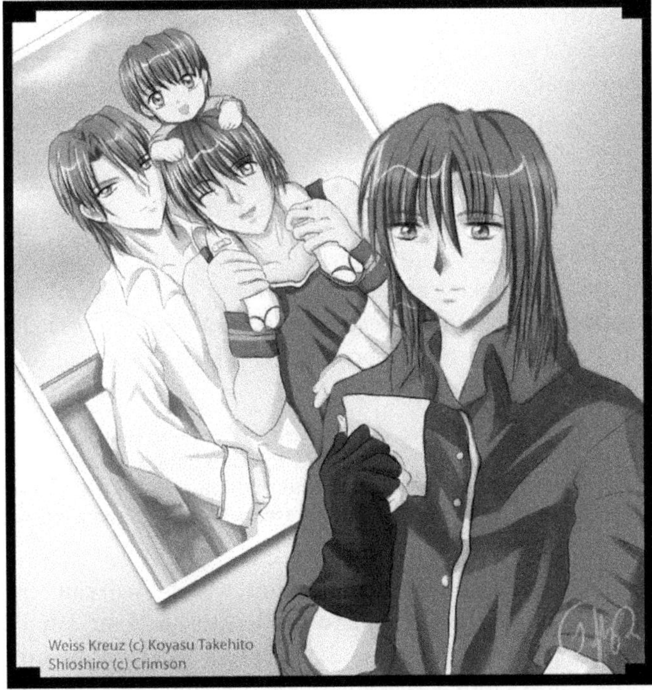

Figure 1. Asaphira, *WK: RanxKen+Shioshiro,* Copyright © 2005.

Nurturance and Eros

Yaoi fanfics do not always have to have explicit sex scenes. WAFF (warm and fuzzy feelings) fanfics are light-hearted, often humorous fanfics which focus on romance and have no sex scenes. They portray the tenderness between partners totally absent from pornography and the mundane domesticity/equality equally absent from romance novels.

Sometimes such stories take place in the context of an established sexual relationship, what Bacon-Smith would describe as an "old married couple" situation in slash.[79] Such stories often revolve around domestic scenes in which a couple cook together, spend time at home, celebrate birthdays or special holidays like Valentine's Day and anniversaries etc. These vignettes of domestic bliss allow us to see the couple's interaction with one another and how they deepen their relationship with the sharing of household chores, eating meals together, and other domestic activities. In slash, these kinds of stories are called "curtain-fics" because they often feature the happy couple shopping for household items.

> "I know that look Ken," he warned. "You want me to do something that you know I
> don't want to do. You want me to go shopping with you."
>   "We're like a married couple!" Ken gushed, batting his eyelashes. "You know me so
> well, darling!"[80]

What Cicioni calls "the eroticization of nurturance" in slash is also an important feature of yaoi. "In a great many stories the discovery of mutual love occurs as one partner recognizes and satisfies a basic need of the other — physical (warmth, food, care during illness) or emotional (reassurance) — and, more or less explicitly, 'mothers' him."[81] Closed but cold environments such as a deserted island, a shack in the wilds, stakeouts and other scenarios provide a chance for one of the partner to provide warmth to the other, with "the warmth moving from the physical dimension to the metaphorical one of closeness and tenderness" (ibid., 163). In Kirachu's fic "Warmth," Ken and Aya share a blanket and become emotionally involved after they were stranded by a car breakdown.

> "Still cold?"
>   "Better."
>   Aya felt a hand groping beneath the folds of the blanket. A hand touched his own.
> The fingers were warm, unlike his own.[82]

Readers can enjoy vicariously the warmth of caring for another and being cared for. Deena's "Raspberry and Lime Shampoo" is set just after Yōji had to kill Neu, a rival assassin who resembled his dead lover Asuka. Ken is worried about Yōji's grief and mental stability and shows his support for Yōji by "mothering him," which eventually leads to the birth of a relationship.

> And then there was Ken's recent maternal shroud.... These days, Ken cooked for him
> and stayed up to wait for him and annoyingly protected him during their missions
> together.... He was very careful with his words around Yohji, no longer blurting any-
> thing and everything out. He treated him like some dainty object that would break at
> any moment.[83]

A whole sub-genre of fanfiction, which I will call "chibification" fanfics, involves adult characters magically transformed into *chibi* or small, child versions of themselves. Swythangel's "Chibification: Raising Ken" is a typical example and features Ken being transformed into a four-year-old after eating some experimental anti-ageing jelly beans in a lab.[84] This fanfic premise allows plenty of cloying, *kawaii* (cute) scenes between child Ken and adult Aya (with whom Ken is secretly in love). Little Ken, unlike his adult self, has no qualms about showing his affection for Aya openly. He is indulged, tenderly bathed, fed and taken care of by Aya, leading to a happy dénouement (and sex) when he is finally transformed back into an adult.

Janice Radway points out that in the family no one supports and nurtures women effectively and emotionally — either women working in the home or women working in the paid labor force.[85] While Radway's study was done during an era when most women were stay-at-home housewives, today's women are in the same position of having to take care of everyone as both "career superwomen" and household managers. This may be a reason why the idea of being cared for is so appealing to writers and readers. Also, drawing on Chodorow's pre–Oedipal model of the mother-daughter relationship, Radway suggests that the romance heroine's desire (and that of the female reader's) for nurturance is the result of a "covert and unconscious wish to regress to the state of infancy in order to experience again, but this time completely and without the slight withholding born of homophobia, that primary love the infant received at the breast and hands of her mother" (Radway, 145). Yaoi vicariously fulfills the fan's sexual and emotional needs.

According to Cicioni, "the central aspect of slash [yaoi, in this case] fantasies is the notion of a same-sex working partnership being extended to the emotional/sexual sphere, with each partner being relied on to always be there and never — unlike the dynamics of the mother/daughter relationship — rejecting the other for someone of the opposite sex."[86] This ideal is seldom fulfilled in reality for women who grow up to transfer their need for love from their mothers to their male partners under compulsory heterosexuality. Yaoi love, however, is reminiscent of the idealized infantile bond because it is unconditional and unrestricted and, best of all, eternal. This love is so strong and unselfish that deathfics which feature the death of a character often have one character making the ultimate sacrifice by dying for his lover. Talya Firedancer's "To Bury the Hurt of Memory" made many fans cry when it was revealed through a surprise ending that Aya had died in order to shield Yōji during a car accident.[87]

Gender Bending

Yaoi characters tend to be androgynous. As Jeanne points out in her fan essay "Why the Guys? Or Navel-Gazing in the Afternoon" referencing feminist critic Joanna Russ on slash, yaoi boys are an amalgam of what *women* consider desirable male and female qualities — male bodies, male status/power, female relating styles, female priorities.[88] However, yaoi fanfics also commonly transgress gender in other ways.

In the series, both Ken and Ōmi have been known to cross-dress to hide their identity on missions. Similarly in fanfics, cross-dressing is a common theme. For example, in Generic Miko's "Unexpected Talents" series, Aya cross-dresses in order to infiltrate a prostitution ring and his unexpected ambiguous beauty arouses Yōji's interest in the process.[89] According to Judith Butler in "Imitation and Gender Insubordination," "gender is a kind of imitation for which there is no original; in fact, it is a kind of imitation that produces the very notion of the original as an effect and consequence of the imitation itself."[90] Yaoi fanfics support the performative nature of gender.

One particularly mind-bending story is "Girl" by Viridian5 and Maya Tawi, in which Aya discovers that he has the ability to alter his sex.[91] During the course of the story, not only does s/he experience what it is like to menstruate and buy women's underwear, Aya's sudden transformation leads to changes in his relationships with his male teammates as well as with Schuldig. Aya gets sexually harassed by male strangers in public, molested on the train, and has sex with a woman in a female body. S/he also has sex with Yōji, not only as a woman and as a man but as an intersex person. Boundaries between straight and gay, male and female are blurred and problematized.

Plots in which characters switch bodies and change sex are also quite common. Sex-change stories often function as a chance for gleeful fanfic writers to inflict biological burdens such as PMS onto bewildered characters.

One sub-genre of yaoi/slash controversial amongst fans is known as mpreg (male pregnancy). The ability to give birth is one of the most important characteristics of being a woman and carries with it an enormous physical, emotional, and financial impact on her life-experience. A pregnant man is vulnerable both physically and emotionally and offers great amusement to fan writers who enjoy this theme. Some have also commented that they enjoyed seeing their favorite male characters in the role of nurturers and "mothers."

Yaoi provides a vehicle for fans to imagine a utopian world unconstrained by biological sex or gender roles as well as a way to critique society's oppression of women. Jung also speculates that slash, and by extension yaoi, may allow readers and writers to put on male drag and explore their own masculinity.[92] In the same vein, the *seme*'s penis has been described as a "latex strap-on" because "it is an fantasy sex toy that is always erect and can accommodate really odd positions."[93]

Power and The Female Gaze

> Bringing You Male Objectification Through Erotica since 1998.— Fan writer Talya Firedancer's LiveJournal Profile.[94]

Laura Mulvey's "Visual Pleasure and Narrative Cinema" (1981) popularized the concept of the "male gaze," in which the male viewer of cinema derives pleasure from looking at passive females.[95] Snitow remarks that women in Harlequin romances are constantly on display. "[A] woman doing what women do all day, is in a constant state of potential sexuality."[96] As a fan astutely notes, women are commonly sexually objectified in popular culture.

> Anyone else noticed how sex scenes in Hollywood movies are normally filmed looking down on the couple — from the typically "male" perspective — rather than upwards? How we're used to seeing actresses stark naked from every conceivable angle and yet a single shot of a penis still provokes embarrassment amongst audiences and *erect* penises are still only ever seen in porn films?[97]

Yaoi turns the tables for female fans who are tired of being sexually objectified and under male sexual scrutiny. In yaoi, males are the objects of desire and there is a degree of pleasurable female voyeurism in watching not only one, but two males having sex. As Fujimoto Yukari states, "women are freed from the position of being unilaterally violated, and gain the perspective of the violator, of the one who watches."[98] Yaoi fans enjoy the subversive thrill of watching males in a vulnerable, submissive position, not only sexually but emotionally. "'A man ain't more vulnerable than when he's got a dick up his ass.' And hey! These guys are vulnerable for *love*! Who could ask for more?"[99]

Nor is voyeurism the only pleasure — the female writer/reader can enjoy identifying herself as either the passive *uke* or active *seme* or both at once. Whereas, as slash fan Heleninhell points out in her essay "I Am Not a Dominatrix: Women and the Active Sexual Role," in conventional sexual fantasy women are either passive or, if they are aggressive, they are usually portrayed as dominatrix because "society posits an active female as a kink."[100] Avila (2005) remarks in her online magazine article "Boy's Love and Yaoi Revisited," "Three years ago, I wrote a brief survey article called Yaoi Comics: Two Guys in Love and the Female Voyeur. At the time, one of my informants told me the title was misleading, and now I understand why—because women aren't on the outside looking in ... they're already inside the men."[101]

The multiple identifications of the fan are facilitated by the fact that fan stories typically depend on more than one point of view and a single event may be repeated two or three times as it is experienced by the different characters present. This allows us special insights into the emotions of the lovers.[102] Cece's "Revealing Myself" is mostly written in the first person from Ken's point of view but shifts to Aya's point of view in the epilogue in which he describes how he feels about Ken's love.[103] This allows the reader to enjoy vicariously the joy of loving and being loved during intimate scenes and to be reassured of the truth of the characters' feelings for each other.

The yaoi fanfic writer frequently decides to put characters into undignified, even degrading situations. Well-known fan writer Chalcedony Cross describes herself proudly as an "unrepentent physical and emotional abuser of imaginary bishounen" on her Live-Journal blog profile.[104]

PWPs often feature outrageous and experimental scenarios such as exhibitionism and use of household objects as sex toys. Writers frequently enjoy challenging one another to write interesting and original sex scenes with unusual premises.

Many fans have said that fanfiction provides a safe way to explore taboo topics. Yaoi fanfics often feature sexual fantasies that push the limits of social acceptability such as tentacle rape, fetishes, incest etc. In Miko no Da's well-known "Sinners and Saints" series, Ōmi enters into a consensual BDSM (bondage domination sadism masochism) lifestyle with Schuldig and Nagi after being rejected by Yōji.[105]

Disturbingly, rape and degradation are sometimes eroticized, as in Generic Miko's "Popcorn" series in which Schuldig sneaks into the Weiss apartment weekly to rape Ken, using his mind-control powers to remain undetected.[106] Cards Slash points out the absurdity of the fannish tendency to wallow in rape in her metafictive fanfic. Here, Ken tries to rebel against the abuse meted out by fanfic writers.

> ... Ken looked at his hands, wondered if it were possible to swallow his own fist so that he could die and never have to come back to this fandom again. But, his mouth wasn't really that big and he didn't think the crazy fangirl—Oh, shit, there were more of them over there next to the Not-Omi. All with freakishly bright eyes (glowing orbs of glow, really) and flowing locks of hair and goth clothes. "Schuldig, can't you save me from these evil fangirls?" Ken mumbled.
>
> "Sorry, after I get done raping you, I have to go let Crawford rape me—and like it without being mind raped. At least you have the advantage of being forced to like it." Sigh.[107]

Yaoi also delves into edgy subject matters such as abusive relationships and abnormal psychology. In Scarlet Fever's twisted "Frail," Ken is tired of his unhappy lifestyle as an assassin and unrequited love for Aya.[108] He engages in a sordid one-night stand with his enemy Schuldig in a sleazy motel and is eventually killed by him. In "Rheotaxis," a well-known fanfic by The RCK, a grown-up Nagi turns Yōji into his sex slave with explicit scenes of non-consensual sex.[109]

Perhaps there is some amount of female sadism in torturing a male character and making them vulnerable, especially stoic, silent characters such as Aya. Yaoi *uke* in fanfics often bear the brunt of stereotypical "negative female characteristics" such as passivity, helplessness, and masochism.[110] Female fans may be displaying their anger at the way women are expected to behave by putting male characters into such roles. In Atsureki's "Love on a Leash," Ken is a mute sex slave who gets raped, beaten, and abused by everyone he meets and passed from owner to owner until he is rescued by Aya.[111] Judging from the more than 600 reviews left on Fanfiction.net for this very popular story, fans seem to feel a mixture of pity, protectiveness, and sadism towards the suffering *uke* whose helplessness strikes them as "cute."

Unsettling Ambivalences

Rape in Yaoi

Male rape permeates yaoi. Women commonly have ambivalent feelings about sexual desire so yaoi rape may be a case of taking responsibility off the *uke*'s hands by having sex forced upon him. Given the contradictory messages from society (women are caught between being "prudes" and "sluts") and risks of sex such as pregnancy and diseases, it is not surprising that this ambivalence and resentment should show up in women's sexual fantasies.

Just because a woman fantasizes about rape, it does not mean that she would enjoy being raped in reality. Rape as sexual fantasy works paradoxically only because the woman who imagines this is actually in control. Linda Williams, author of a study on pornography entitled "Hard Core: Power, Pleasure, and the 'Frenzy of the Visible'" argues in an interview that women are likely to be sensitive to any potential abuse of female anatomy or power, even though that abuse itself can be a turn-on.[112]

Women are free from that baggage when they are looking at male-male fantasy scenarios. Such abuse would be far too real and frightening in a heterosexual context because females do live under the constant threat of male sexual violence and comprise the majority of rape victims.

Furthermore, female victims of rape are commonly regarded as "tainted," while the *uke* who is raped by his lover is portrayed as imbued with innocence. Ladies' comics featuring male-female romances may feature rape but it is not necessarily sublimated into the sphere of "pure love."[113]

In Jacque Koh's fairly typical Yōji x Aya story "Second Chances," Yōji is in love with Aya but unable to express his love.[114] Unfortunately, one night, he rapes Aya when he is drunk, though he regrets his actions when he is sober. Such plots would possibly appear repulsive to the reader if the *uke* were a female character but as Nagaike, writing about Japanese BL explains, rape here does not signify the *seme*'s disruptive sexual/violent desires, but his overwhelming, uncontrollable love for the *uke*.[115]

The debate over whether conventional pornography encourages violence against women and rape has gone on for decades without any resolution because of the difficulty of proving causation. However, it is unlikely for practical reasons that a female will be able to go out and force two males to act out yaoi fantasies for her benefit. Someone who enjoys violent, nonconsensual sex in her fics does not necessarily wish to see it reenacted in real life.

Romantic Rescue

Much personal grief, loneliness, and suffering is already present in WK, for example, during the course of the series Ken becomes homeless, loses his grip on sanity, is jailed, and meets other misfortunes.

Hurt/comfort is a term used to describe a type of story in which one character is hurt physically or emotionally in some way and the other provides love/comfort. Originally a slash term, this is also a common situation in yaoi. In WK yaoi, characters sometimes display self-destructive behavior in reaction to their unhappy pasts or stressful lives; this can range from cutting and attempted suicide to promiscuity. Sometimes a character may be abducted and injured/tortured/raped by an enemy such as Schwarz in the course of a mission or even brutalized by a teammate. In Atsureki's "Surrounded by Darkness" Ken is blinded in the course of duty.[116] Amnesia, comas, even AIDS are common themes.

Fan writers often invent traumatic pasts. Although all of Weiss have tragic backgrounds, fan invention allows writers to explore emotional trauma/psychological damage (e.g., Stockholm syndrome) to a depth not possible in the series as well as from angles not present.

For example, Sidara's "Sünde" ("sin" in German) establishes the fanon that Schuldig is evil because he was sexually abused by his father and was formerly a drug-addicted prostitute.[117] This was parodied in Cards Slash's "Five Ways Ken Hidaka Was Never Raped" in which Schuldig informs Ken, "Crawford rapes me and my daddy probably did and sometimes I was a street whore. I'm a plethora of sad sexual history. My whole evil justification is usually hinged to the fact that I was mistreated as a child."[118]

Such suffering is seldom pointless because it fulfills a narrative function and usually allows another character to realize how much the wounded character meant to him whether it is a past trauma or a recent one. In Martyl's "The Saga Begins," Ken and Aya become lovers after Ken mistakenly thinks Aya was hurt during a mission and realizes his true feelings for Aya.[119] The hurt also allows the other character to comfort and nurse the hurt one.

When rape is perpetuated by someone outside the main couple, it is frequently used as a gambit in hurt/comfort fanfics in which the *seme* teaches the *uke* the joy of sex within a loving relationship, a cliché which some fans describe jokingly as the "Healing Cock."

In Sidara's "Zeit," Ken, who is in love with Aya, is traumatized after being raped by Schuldig.[120] After many obstacles, he is finally able to get over his fear of sex with Aya's help. Cards Slash parodies this recurrent trope in "Five Ways Ken Hidaka Was Never Raped." Schuldig explains why Aya will be upset if Ken gets raped.

> "Because he loves you," Schuldig pointed out. And he promptly set to stripping Ken of the clothes that stood in the way of the highly sexualized rape scene.
> "Aya doesn't love me!"
> There was a knock on the door. Ken opened it and poked his head around the corner to find Aya standing there, all with the bedhair and yawning. A piece of white printer paper in his hand. "Ken Hidaka, I love you with all my heart and soul. Your unending innocence and clumsiness and willingness to get raped to provide me with hurt/comfort scenes makes me love you with all my heart and soul."[121]

The yaoi character is always accepted and reassured by his partner in the end despite losing his virginity, etc., which may reflect the wishes of women for the support of their partners if they themselves were to encounter such a calamity.

The sufferings of characters engaged in commercial sex work, stripping, prostitution, and sexual slavery are also perennial themes in fanfics. There are many fanfics in which

Aya turns to prostitution to pay for his comatose sister's medical bills, only to be saved by a wealthy Yōji in an AU ("alternate universes" are fanfics that feature familiar characters but in totally different settings). In another AU story, Aya purchases and heals Ken, an abused slave. A slash fan explains the eternal appeal of this theme:

> I think the appeal of such stories is that it's the ultimate rescue. From the threat of physical danger that goes along with being a prostitute, from disease, abuse, lovelessness, societal scorn, the very annihilation of the soul. The person is redeemed by love. A lot of romance novels have a rescue theme. I think there's something appealing in that to a lot of women, even if we also know that it's all just one big fantasy, that no man is actually going to come to our rescue and that it would irritate us if he tried....[122]

Of course, the greater the suffering, the grander the final romantic rescue. It is not necessary for a character to be a whore or sex slave. Cinderella stories in which a poor peasant or street waif is rescued by a millionaire or prince are equally popular. Yaoi, especially that written by younger fans, is sometimes unable to transcend such social conditioning about waiting for one's prince to come riding in on a white horse in order to transform one's life.

Gay Politics

> Basically what BL says is, "This isn't about real gay men. I'm just using men in a sexual relationship as a fantasy that has nothing to do with reality."[123]

As some fans have pointed out, many yaoi fans like yaoi fanfiction not specifically because of the homosexuality, but because they "like hot guys" and two or more guys together are better than one.[124] Mark McHarry remarks: "Although most or all of the male characters in a yaoi story prefer sex with males, in almost all of the several hundred yaoi stories I have read, there is little or no sense of a homonormative environment established in opposition to a prevailing heteronormative one, little or no need for same-sex desiring males to form an identity or to, in support of it, allow or prohibit conduct or viewpoints."[125]

While there are many male gay/bisexual fans of yaoi, especially among younger age groups, some gay men are offended at the idea of becoming "sex objects" for female pleasure. According to a fan, Riccichan, young fangirls who have little knowledge of actual gay culture sometimes have trouble differentiating between yaoi as a fandom primarily created by woman and "male homosexuality as it presents itself in our reality," thereby causing unwitting offence by asking ignorant, probing questions when encountering actual gay men (Yaoi LiveJournal Blog Community, comment posted August 5, 2003).

Slash fans have been similarly bedeviled by such a problem. Also, in the politically charged Western context of "open lobbying for homosexual rights, some fans seem to feel the need to justify slash to the gay community, or even to reform slash in such a way as to make it more palatable or 'politically correct.'"[126]

However some fans do enjoy the political loading of the gay identity:

> But I don't read yaoi for (coded) het sex and romance. I read it for *gay* sex and romance.... For me, using the term "gay" has a certain appeal. It's like ... it comes with a tremendous amount of societal baggage ... and if the characters are labelled "gay" it's like they're saying "fuck society, we're going to love who we want to love, and there's not a damn thing you can do about it!" Or something.... It has to do with perceived gender roles, and what's really "normal." Of course, that's just my point of view.[127]

According to Dru Pagliassotti's survey, ninety-six percent of respondents supported same-sex marriage showing that most held progressive attitudes with regards to gay rights.[128] Constance Penley in "Brownian Motion: Women, Tactics, and Technology" feels that fans feel real appreciation for "gay men in their efforts to redefine masculinity, and their feelings of solidarity with them insofar as gay men too inhabit bodies that are still a legal, moral, and religious battleground."[129]

Some Japanese commentators on Japanese yaoi have insisted that to "proscribe [yaoi] as a rejection of womanhood or feminist subjectivity was to militate an equally repressive vision of female sexuality as one that must always culminate in heterosexual sex and sexual fantasies." In other words, they argued that the gay critique of yaoi was itself a form of heterosexism.[130] A gay male yaoi fan also points out that regular porn or *hentai* (a term for Japanese media featuring explicit heterosexual sex) are equally unrealistic, but everyone is aware of and unperturbed by the way they tend to be directed toward men while ignoring women's real experiences (Kei, *ai to yuuki no otogibanashi* Blog, comment posted June 29, 2006).

A female fan, Soul of Tabris, adds that straight men who like "lesbian porn" targeted at men are not interested in lesbian political issues and that they are not interested in watching women who are not conventionally attractive have "lesbian sex" (Yaoi LiveJournal Blog Community, comment posted August 4, 2003). Regardless of whether individual straight men may be interested in lesbian issues, she does underline the fact that female fans in general are held to higher standards of political correctness compared to straight men enjoying "lesbian" pornography catering to heterosexual viewers who are generally understood to be consuming fantasies.

Female Characters

> Pretty Girl With Little Clothing, Quick Wit And Sarcastic Tongue: Hi, I'm here to join Weiss!
> Manx: There's no room for women in this fic.[131]

Yaoi has often been criticized for the "absence" of female characters. There are a number of reasons for this situation. First of all, heterosexual relationships tend to follow socially prescribed gender roles. Radway offers this pessimistic assessment of male-female relations:

> Men tend to relate to women on relatively superficial emotional level just as they define them principally as sexual creatures because their physiological characteristics are the most obvious mark of their difference from men. Given the fact that a woman and any future children she might have are economically dependent on such men, it becomes absolutely essential that she learns to distinguish those who want her sexually from that special individual who is willing to pledge commitment and care in return for her sexual favor.[132]

Given that a woman involved in heterosexual relationships must negotiate this sexual minefield, which has serious implications for her welfare, it is not surprising that yaoi fans should wish to avoid female characters altogether.

The presence of a female character also means that the female reader/writer would inevitably compare herself with the idealized attributes of a fictional girl with a perfect body.[133] Penley comments that it makes sense from a feminist viewpoint that women who write homoerotic romance are alienated from female bodies "that are a legal, moral, and religious battleground, that are the site of contraceptive failure, that are publicly defined as the greatest potential danger to the fetuses they house, that are held to painfully greater standards of physical beauty than those of the other sex."[134]

According to Thorn, some fans actually express wistfully that they wished to be born male so that they can love "a man *as a man*, or, to rephrase it, as an equal, free of predefined gender expectations."[135]

However, there is a darker side to this dislike of female characters. Some fans appear to find female characters a threat because they represent possible love interests for the male characters they fantasize about and get in the way of yaoi pairings they wish to set up.

For example, some WK fans hate Silvia because she not only slept with Crawford and Schuldig (both characters are fan favorites and often paired together) but declared that Schuldig was lousy in bed. Other female characters from WK who frequently become targets for fan hatred include Sally, whose love redeems Farfarello from madness; Sakura, who had an unrequited crush on Aya; and Ōka, Ōmi's cousin who is in love with him.

Some vindictive fans have been known to portray these female characters in a negative light or to kill them off in their fanfictions. As Christine Scodari points out about slash fandom, female competition over men in mainstream culture is so pervasive that even a fictional woman is seen as a threat to a female fan who wishes to fantasize about two fictional men.[136]

Many yaoi fans are rather defensive about this issue. For example, many claim that canon females are disagreeable, weak, or dependent and as such, are unattractive to fans and not worthy of writing about.

> And even as a het (fanfiction focused on heterosexual relationships) fan, there were many female characters I did not like because they seemed to be there simply for the purpose of pairing off with the lead males or because they were helpless or weak or pointless or otherwise counter to my feminist values.... But now that I've become a yaoi fan I must suddenly love them or feel guilty? ... These people ignore the huge number of male characters not liked by the yaoi fandom when they do this [Ari, Yaoi LiveJournal Blog Community, entry posted August 4, 2003].

One might argue that *yuri* (the lesbian equivalent of yaoi) could possibly be more subversive than yaoi with its privileging of self-sufficient female-female romantic/sexual bonds that challenge the patriarchy. However, *yuri* is not very popular among females in Japan and overseas and many *yuri* fans appear to be heterosexual males.

While some of this may be accounted for by the possible homophobia of straight females who are not interested in lesbian relationships, the fact that female bodies suffer from the societal and physical burdens detailed in this article also makes *yuri* unattractive. Moreover, *yuri* produced by male fans may overemphasize physical attributes of characters such as breast size and concentrate on explicit sex rather than the development of relationships. The presence of what one fan describes as "creepy *yuri* fanboys" in the fandom may also put off lesbian/bisexual women from exploring this genre because they are already the targets of male fantasy in conventional media and pornography.

Fanfiction As Act of Resistance

> For young women, it's one of the few outlets in which they can have fun with and share their sexuality — and go as far as they can with their (written) sexual fantasies — in an environment that is safe and supportive.... They are holding conventions, participating in online clubs and forums, and running websites ... the bulk of the writers are young women in their late teens and twenties ... females in their dating years who will be deciding the course of our sexual mores in the near future ... and for the truly creative ones, the future content of our media.[137]

According to an informal poll in an online yaoi forum about whether they would give up yaoi if their lovers objected, most female fans replied that they would never do it just to please their partners. One well-known yaoi writer named Wiggle, who received a message describing her as a "sick balls sucking bitch," reacted by defiantly writing a kinky fic involving erotic use of pubic shaving.[138]

Transgression is part of the pleasure of being a yaoi fan. One often hears of young fans that boldly type their x-rated fics on school computers in full public view. They often persevere even when parents delete their fanfics from the family computer and restrict their computer use. Fans often swap tips on how to hide their yaoi from parents and other authority figures. One particularly memorable online forum signature I spotted around Christmas 2007 featured a stern Santa informing the fan that she would get no presents because she had been naughty. Santa had checked her computer and it was full of yaoi!

For female fans, yaoi fanfiction offers them a creative outlet to engage with love/sexual issues and hone their writing skills. Some even go on to publish original homoerotic stories. They learn from one another how to critically reorient media texts for their own benefit and generate fantexts that are even more complex, satisfying and richer than the original sources.

Yaoi is an active expression of female sexuality and is generally described by fans using positive rhetoric of liberty and pleasure. As a fan admits in "Drawn to it," she reads yaoi "to get turned on."[139] A typical fan view of yaoi is expressed by a fan interviewed in "Drawn Together." "It's becoming a rallying cry at anime conventions— all the girls scream, 'Yaoi! Yaoi!'" she says, using feminist imagery. "It's like burning your bra. It's declaring your sexuality."[140] Many yaoi writers proudly declare their political stances by displaying banners supporting freedom of speech, gay rights, or similar sentiments on their websites. Not all yaoi fans see their writings as political acts but, following the old feminist slogan "The personal is political," every yaoi fan who types her fanfic in privacy is engaged in a quiet revolution of her own.

However, in its glorification of male homosexuality and male bodies, yaoi does run the risk of demonizing female characters and marginalizing women and female bodies. It is limited in its imaginative failure to present alternative sexual/romantic models for women to follow. Yaoi fanfiction can also be regressive or constrained within gender hegemony, especially texts produced by younger, less sophisticated writers.

Moreover, we should not forget that fans do not directly control commercial media production and often possess little socio-economic clout due to age, sex etc. Penley uses de Certeau's notion of "Brownian motion" to show how the actions of slash (and yaoi) fans can be seen as guerilla resistance involving hit-and-run acts of apparent randomness due to their relative powerlessness against the establishment.[141]

Conclusion

Yaoi highlights the gap between reality and women's unsatisfied yearnings. In her study of romance readers, Radway shows that romances create an ideal world that references the inadequacies of heterosexual relationships in reality as well as provides escapism in the temporary, free realm of the imaginary, defusing any reader incentive to transform their situation.[142]

While there is indeed an escapist strain in yaoi, I would argue that yaoi is far more radical than romance novels or mainstream media. Yaoi fans have shown their disaffection with mainstream gender ideology and wrested the production of meanings from commercial concerns. In fanfiction, there is no demarcation among producer/consumer, writer/reader and there is constant dialogue among fans.

Yaoi fandom is a feminine, queer-friendly community on the net where female fans can support and network with one another to circumvent censorship and defy moral gatekeepers such as Internet service providers, family, friends, employers, and even the law. Despite its shortcomings, yaoi fanfiction functions as an alternative discourse in opposition to social discourses that seek to restrain and channel female sexuality into patriarchal institutions.

Notes

1. Lady Bast, "The Interview," GlowingCross.net, http://glowingcross.net/The_Interview_fic.html (accessed March 1, 2005). This fanfic is a metafictive parody in which new character Aguri Kyo is interviewed by *Kritiker* before joining Weiss. He is warned by the existing members that joining Weiss would entail becoming the target of yaoi fanfics.

2. Alan McKee, *Textual Analysis: A Beginner's Guide* (London: Sage Publications, 2003), 1.

3. Ibid., 74.

4. Henry Jenkins, "Reception Theory and Audience Research: The Mystery of the Vampire's Kiss," Professional Homepage, http://web.mit.edu/cms/People/henry3/vampkiss.html (accessed February 6, 2008).

5. Ibid.

6. Christine Hine, *Virtual Ethnography* (London: Sage Publications, 2000), 4–5.

7. Dru Pagliassotti, "Reading Boys' Love in the West," *Particip@tions* 5:2, November (2008), http://www.participations.org/Volume%205/Issue%202/5_02_pagliassotti.htm.

8. Deena, "Waking Onto Lantern's Bright," Boys Next Door, http://www.discarnate.com/boysnextdoor/fiction/weiss/WakingOnto.html (accessed February 14, 2005).

9. Kuwabara no Miko, "Male Bonding," Boys Next Door, http://www.discarnate.com/boysnextdoor/fiction/weiss/WeissBonding.html (accessed February 10, 2005).

10. Laila, "The Discreet Charm of Slash Fiction," Plastic Venus, http://quietladybirman.livejournal.com/34858.html#cutid1 (accessed June 9, 2006).

11. Henry Jenkins, *Textual Poachers* (New York: Routledge, 1992), 219.

12. Ann Barr Snitow, "Mass Market Romance: Pornography for Women is Different," in *Gender, Race, and Class in Media: A Text-reader,* ed. Gail Dines and Jean M. Humez (Thousand Oaks, CA: Sage Publications, 2003), 125.

13. Mirna Cicioni, "Male Pair-bonds and Female Desire in Fan Slash Writing," in *Theorizing Fandom: Fans, Subculture, and Identity,* ed. Cheryl Harris and Alison Alexander (Cresskill, NJ: Hampton Press, 1998), 168.

14. Anne Kustritz, "Slashing the Romance Narrative," *The Journal of American Culture* 26.3 (2003): 377.

15. Gayle Rubin, "Thinking Sex: Notes for a Radical Theory of the Politics of Sexuality," in *Theorizing Feminisms: A Reader,* ed. Elizabeth Hackett and Sally Haslanger (Oxford: Oxford University Press, 2006).

16. Gayle Rubin, "The Traffic in Women: Notes on the 'Political Economy' of Sex," in *The Second Wave: A Reader in Feminist Theory,* ed. Linda Nicholson (New York: Routledge, 1996), 180.

17. Dennis Altman, *Homosexual: Oppression and Liberation* (New York: New York University Press, 1993), 78–79, 90, 92.

18. Henry Jenkins, *Textual Poachers* (New York: Routledge, 1992), 202–203.

19. Yoippari, "Rules," Boys Next Door, http://www.discarnate.com/boysnextdoor/fiction/Rules.html (accessed September 26, 2004).

20. The Fanfiction Glossary, http://www.subreality.com/glossary.htm (accessed August 7, 2007).

21. Henry Jenkins, *Textual Poachers* (New York: Routledge, 1992), 210.

22. Sky Rat, "Better Days," MediaMiner.org, http://www.mediaminer.org/fanfic/view_st.php/38361 (accessed March 1, 2005).

23. Cassandra Nexus, "In the Rain," Kuwabara no Miko's Weiss Kreuz Yaoi Fanfiction Page, http://www.kuwamiko.com/WeissRain.html (accessed February 14, 2005).

24. Nekojita, "Cages," Cat's Dream, http://www.catsdreams.com/fanfiction.html (accessed February 25, 2005).

25. Opus the Penguin, "A Delicate Subject," Fanfiction.Net, http://www.fanfiction.net/s/1363851/1/ (accessed March 2, 2005).

26. Henry Jenkins, *Textual Poachers* (New York: Routledge, 1992), 208.

27. Deena, "Something New," Velvet Underwear: A Shrine to Yoji Kudou, http://www.geocities.com/tsukiyoshi/new.html (accessed March 1, 2005).

28. Kim, "A Quiet Evening," Schwarz Contradiction, http://www.geocities.com/schwarz_contradiction/quietevening.html (accessed February 15, 2005).

29. Fancy, "Hair," Fanfiction.Net, http://www.fanfiction.net/s/980249/1/ (accessed March 2, 2005).

30. Dru Pagliassotti, "Reading Boys' Love in the West," *Particip@tions* 5:2, November (2008), http://www.participations.org/Volume%205/Issue%202/5_02_pagliassotti.htm.

31. Jeanne, "The Top Ten Things I Love About Yaoi," *Aestheticism*, October (2001), http://www.aestheticism.com/visitors/editor/index.htm (accessed April 22, 2007).

32. Brett Farmer, *Spectacular Passions: Cinema, Fantasy, Gay Male Spectatorships* (Durham and London: Duke University Press, 2000), 24.

33. Swythangel, "Heaven in Your Arms," XY: Intoxicating Obsession, http://www.lucidinsanity.com/fanfic/wkfics/hiya1.html (accessed March 7, 2005).

34. Lynn Metallium, "The Three Little Bishounen," Fanfiction.Net, http://www.fanfiction.net/s/1534692/1/ (accessed February 14, 2005).

35. Ika Willis, "Keeping Promises to Queer Children: Making Space (for Mary Sue) at Hogwarts," in *Fan Fiction and Fan Communities in the Age of the Internet*, ed. Karen Hellekson & Kristina Busse (Jefferson, NC: McFarland, 2006), 156.

36. Anne Kustritz, "Slashing the Romance Narrative," *The Journal of American Culture* 26.3 (2003): 382.

37. Sarah Gwenllian Jones, "The Sex Lives of Cult Television Characters," *Screen* 43.1 (2002): 81.

38. Ika Willis, "Keeping Promises to Queer Children: Making Space (for Mary Sue) at Hogwarts," in *Fan Fiction and Fan Communities in the Age of the Internet*, ed. Karen Hellekson & Kristina Busse (Jefferson, NC: McFarland, 2006), 153.

39. Karen Hellekson and Kristina Busse, introduction to *Fan Fiction and Fan Communities in the Age of the Internet* (Jefferson, NC: McFarland, 2006), 9.

40. Kat Avila, "Boy's Love and Yaoi Revisited," *Sequential Tart*, Jan (2005), http://www.sequentialtart.com/art_0105_1.shtml (accessed Jan 16, 2005).

41. Jeanne, "The Top Ten Things I Love About Yaoi," *Aestheticism*, October (2001), http://www.aestheticism.com/visitors/editor/index.htm (accessed April 22, 2007).

42. Kuwabara no Miko and Talya Firedancer, "A Fine Day for a Group Outing," Firedancer's Weiß Kreuz Fanfiction Archive, http://www.fyredancer.net/wk/WKgroupouting.html (accessed February 10, 2005).

43. Laila, "The Discreet Charm of Slash Fiction," Plastic Venus, http://quietladybirman.livejournal.com/34858.html#cutid1 (accessed June 9, 2006).

44. Alexander Doty, introduction to *Making Things Perfectly Queer: Interpreting Mass Culture* (Minneapolis: University of Minnesota Press, 1993), xii.

45. Laila, "The Discreet Charm of Slash Fiction," Plastic Venus, http://quietladybirman.livejournal.com/34858.html#cutid1 (accessed June 9, 2006).

46. Deena, "Raspberry and Lime Shampoo," Boys Next Door, http://www.discarnate.com/boysnextdoor/weiss.html (accessed February 15, 2005).

47. Deena, "Waking Onto Lantern's Bright," Boys Next Door, http://www.discarnate.com/boysnextdoor/fiction/weiss/WakingOnto.html (accessed February 14, 2005).

48. Martyl, "Black Gold," Fanfiction.Net, http://www.fanfiction.net/s/756833/1/ (accessed March 7, 2005).

49. Celestel, "UkeSeme Dynamics," Fanfiction.Net, http://www.fanfiction.net/s/1504297/1/ (accessed March 2, 2005).

50. Anne Kustritz, "Slashing the Romance Narrative," *The Journal of American Culture* 26.3 (2003): 377.

51. Martyl, "The Saga Begins," Fanfiction.Net, http://www.fanfiction.net/s/1518599/1/ (accessed March 8, 2005).

52. Jeanne, "The Top Ten Things I Love About Yaoi," *Aestheticism*, October (2001), http://www.aestheticism.com/visitors/editor/index.htm (accessed April 22, 2007).

53. Susanne Jung, "Queering Popular Culture: Female Spectators and the Appeal of Writing Slash Fan Fiction," *Gender Forum Gender Queeries* 8 (2004), http://www.genderforum.uni-koeln.de/queer/jung.html.

54. Anne Kustritz, "Slashing the Romance Narrative," *The Journal of American Culture* 26.3 (2003): 377–378.

55. Teep, "Why Chicks like Fanfic Porn," Home Page, http://www.bedford.net/teep/fanfic.htm (accessed April 23, 2007).

56. Catherine Driscoll, "One True Pairing: The Romance of Pornography and the Pornography of

Romance," in *Fan Fiction and Fan Communities in the Age of the Internet*, ed. Karen Hellekson & Kristina Busse (Jefferson, NC: McFarland, 2006), 91.

57. Alan Soble, *Pornography: Marxism, Feminism, and the Future of Sexuality* (New Haven: Yale UP, 1986), 56–57, 96.

58. Andrea Wood, "'Straight' Women, Queer Texts: Boy-Love Manga And The Rise of A Global Counterpublic," *Women's Studies Quarterly*. 34(1/2) (Spring 2006): 403.

59. Catherine Driscoll, "One True Pairing: The Romance of Pornography and the Pornography of Romance," in *Fan Fiction and Fan Communities in the Age of the Internet*, ed. Karen Hellekson & Kristina Busse (Jefferson, NC: McFarland, 2006), 88.

60. Kazuko Suzuki, "Pornography or Therapy? Japanese Girls Creating the Yaoi Phenomenon," in *Millennium Girls: Today's Girls Around the World*, ed. Sherrie A. Innes (London: Roman & Littlefield, 1999), 257.

61. Link621, "But, I'm An Assassin," Noire Sensus, http://www.noiresensus.com/bookshelf/pair_kenxom ifics.html (accessed March 1, 2005).

62. Atsureki, "Please, Give Me Another Chance," Fanfiction.Net, http://www.fanfiction.net/s/978867/1/ (accessed March 2, 2005).

63. Swythangel, "Phenomenal Noumenal," XY: Intoxicating Obsession, http://www.lucidinsanity.com/fan fic/wkfics/phen1.html (accessed March 7, 2005).

64. Shoori, "Eight Years in the Making," Bleeding Hearts, http://www.trowaluvsduo.net/weissweb/bleed inghearts.htm (accessed March 7, 2005).

65. Camille Bacon-Smith, *Enterprising Women: Television Fandom and the Creation of Popular Myth* (Philadelphia: University of Pennsylvania Press, 1992), 230.

66. Leather Daddy, "Review of 'Lord of the Rings': A Diamond Between Wood and Stone," Slap to the Head Fanfiction Reviews, http://web.pitas.com/ficbitches/woodandstone.html (accessed June 1, 2006).

67. Marty1, "The Saga Begins," Fanfiction.Net, http://www.fanfiction.net/s/1518599/1/ (accessed March 8, 2005).

68. Elizabeth Woledge, "Intimatopia: Genre Intersections Between Slash and the Mainstream," in *Fan Fiction and Fan Communities in the Age of the Internet*, ed. Karen Hellekson & Kristina Busse (Jefferson, NC: McFarland, 2006), 99.

69. Marty1, "The Saga Begins," Fanfiction.Net, http://www.fanfiction.net/s/1518599/1/ (accessed March 8, 2005).

70. Talya Firedancer, "The Subway Trilogy," Firedancer's Weiss Kreuz Fanfiction, http://www.fyredancer. net/wk/index.html (accessed March 7, 2005).

71. Durendal and the Beef Chick, "Uncle Yohji's Book of Love," Velvet Underwear: A Shrine to Yoji Kudou, http://www.geocities.com/Tokyo/Ginza/5170/Weiss/fanfics.html (accessed March 1, 2005).

72. Aoe and Shoori, "New World Order," Bleeding Hearts, http://www.trowaluvsduo.net/weissweb/bleed inghearts.htm (accessed March 7, 2005).

73. Chet Meeks and Arlene Stein, "Refiguring the Family: Towards a Post-Queer Politics of Gay and Lesbian Marriage," in *Intersections Between Feminist and Queer Theory*, ed. Diane Richardson, Janice McLaughlin and Mark E. Casey (Houndsmill, UK: Palgrave Macmillan, 2006), 153.

74. Michel Foucault, *The History of Sexuality*, trans. Robert Hurley (New York: Vintage, 1980), 3.

75. Chet Meeks and Arlene Stein, "Refiguring the Family: Towards a Post-Queer Politics of Gay and Lesbian Marriage," in *Intersections Between Feminist and Queer Theory*, ed. Diane Richardson, Janice McLaughlin and Mark E. Casey (Houndsmill, UK: Palgrave Macmillan, 2006), 138.

76. Marty1, "Baby Talk," Fanfiction.Net, http://www.fanfiction.net/s/610799/1/ (accessed March 8, 2005).

77. Crimson1, "Kind des Schicksals," Fanfiction.Net, http://www.fanfiction.net/s/2065398/1/Kind_des_Schi cksals (accessed March 2, 2005).

78. Figure 1. Asaphira, *WK: RanxKen+Shioshiro*, 2005, http://www.deviantart.com/deviation/19298909/?qo =206&q=weiss+kreuz&qh=boost%3Apopular+age_sigma%3A24h+age_scale%3A5.

79. Camille Bacon-Smith, *Enterprising Women: Television Fandom and the Creation of Popular Myth* (Philadelphia: University of Pennsylvania Press, 1992), 231.

80. Deena, "Christmas Frenzy," Fanfiction.Net, http://www.fanfiction.net/s/149346/1/ (accessed March 2, 2005).

81. Mirna Cicioni, "Male Pair-bonds and Female Desire in Fan Slash Writing," in *Theorizing Fandom: Fans, Subculture, and Identity*, ed. Cheryl Harris and Alison Alexander (Cresskill, NJ: Hampton Press, 1998), 62–63.

82. Kirachu, "Warmth," Fanfiction.Net, http://www.fanfiction.net/s/1334080/1/ (accessed, February 15, 2005).

83. Deena, "Raspberry and Lime Shampoo," Boys Next Door, http://www.discarnate.com/boysnextdoor/ weiss.html (accessed February 15, 2005).

84. Swythangel, "Chibification (Raising Ken)," XY: Intoxicating Obsession, http://www.lucidinsanity.com/ fanfic/wkfics/chibi1.html (accessed March 8, 2005).

85. Janice Radway, *Reading the Romance: Women, Patriarchy, and Popular Literature* (Chapel Hill and London: University of North Carolina Press, 1984), 94.

86. Mirna Cicioni, "Male Pair-bonds and Female Desire in Fan Slash Writing," in *Theorizing Fandom: Fans, Subculture, and Identity*, ed. Cheryl Harris and Alison Alexander (Cresskill, NJ: Hampton Press, 1998), 172.

87. Talya Firedancer, "To Bury the Hurt of Memory," Firedancer's Weiss Kreuz Fanfiction, http://www.fyredancer.net/wk/index.html (accessed March 7, 2005).

88. Jeanne, "Why the Guys? Or Navel-Gazing in the Afternoon," *Aestheticism,* http://www.aestheticism.com/visitors/editor/index.htm (accessed April 22, 2007).

89. Generic Miko, "Unexpected Talents," East of Sanity, http://www.eastofsanity.com/ (accessed February 14, 2005).

90. Judith Butler, "Imitation and Gender Insubordination," in *Inside/Out: Lesbian Theories, Gay Theories,* ed. Diana Fuss (New York: Routledge, 1991), 21.

91. Maya Tawi and Viridian5, "Girl," Zippos and Safety Pins, http://panthea.populli.net/fiction/girl1.htm (accessed March 18, 2005).

92. Susanne Jung, "Queering Popular Culture: Female Spectators and the Appeal of Writing Slash Fan Fiction," *Gender Forum Gender Queeries* 8 (2004), http://www.genderforum.uni-koeln.de/queer/jung.html.

93. Ibid.

94. Talya Firedancer, "Fyredancer's Profile," LiveJournal Blog, http://fyredancer.livejournal.com/profile (accessed October 11, 2007).

95. Laura Mulvey, "Visual Pleasure and Narrative Cinema," *Screen* 16.3 (1975).

96. Ann Barr Snitow, "Mass Market Romance: Pornography for Women is Different," in *Gender, Race, and Class in Media: A Text-reader,* ed. Gail Dines and Jean M Humez (Thousand Oaks, CA: Sage Publications, 2003), 425.

97. Laila, "In Defense of ... Yaoi," Pale Movies Version 8: Afterglow, http://www.palemovies.com/r_ido_03.html (accessed July 31, 2007).

98. Fujimoto Yukari, *Watashi no ibasho wa doko ni aru no? Shôjo manga ga utsusu kokoro no katachi* (Tokyo: Gakuyou Shobo, 1998), quoted in Matt Thorn, "Girls and Women Getting Out of Hand: The Pleasure and Politics of Japan's Amateur Comics Community," in *Fanning the flames: Fans and Consumer Culture in Contemporary Japan,* ed. William W. Kelly (Albany, NY: State University of New York Press, 2004), 169–187.

99. Jeanne, "Why the Guys? Or Navel-Gazing in the Afternoon," *Aestheticism,* http://www.aestheticism.com/visitors/editor/index.htm (accessed April 22, 2007).

100. Heleninhell, "I Am Not a Dominatrix: Women and the Active Sexual Role," Helen gets the job done, http://web.archive.org/web/19991111184526/members.tripod.com/heleninhell/dominatrix.html (accessed April 15, 2007).

101. Kat Avila, "Boy's Love and Yaoi Revisited," *Sequential Tart* (January 2005) http://www.sequentialtart.com/art_0105_1.shtml (accessed Jan 16, 2005).

102. Camille Bacon-Smith, *Enterprising Women: Television Fandom and the Creation of Popular Myth* (Philadelphia: University of Pennsylvania Press, 1992), 65.

103. Cece, "Revealing Myself," Fanfiction.Net, http://www.fanfiction.net/s/908113/1/ (accessed, February 15, 2005).

104. Chalcedony Cross, "Chal's Profile," LiveJournal Blog, http://chal.livejournal.com/profile (accessed January 21, 2005).

105. Miko no Da, "Sinners and Saints," Love is Love, http://www.darkhuntress.com/miko_no_da/MW1/Index3.html (accessed February 28, 2005).

106. Generic Miko, "Popcorn Timeline," East of Sanity, http://www.eastofsanity.com/ (accessed February 14, 2005).

107. Cards Slash, "Five Ways Ken Hidaka Was Never Raped," Unapologetically Given To Wander, http://cards-slash.livejournal.com/136343.html (accessed April 19, 2007).

108. Scarlet Fever, "Frail (You May As Well Be Me)," The Fountain of Decay, http://www.geocities.com/necrolantry/Frail.htm accessed February 14, 2005).

109. The RCK, "Rheotaxis," Consensus Realities, http://www.therck.org/ (accessed March 1, 2004).

110. Jeanne, "Why the Guys? Or Navel-Gazing in the Afternoon," *Aestheticism,* http://www.aestheticism.com/visitors/editor/index.htm (accessed April 22, 2007).

111. Atsureki, "Love on a Leash," Fanfiction.Net, http://www.fanfiction.net/s/966491/1/ (accessed March 1, 2005).

112. Fiona Ng, "Drawn to It," Nerve.com, http://www.nerve.com/dispatches/ng/drawntoit/ (accessed December 4, 2004).

113. Kazumi Nagaike, "Perverse Sexualities, Pervasive Desires: Representations of Female Fantasies and Yaoi Manga as Pornography Directed at Women," *U.S.–Japan Women's Journal* 25 (2003), 94.

114. Jacque Koh, "Second Chances," Firewolf's Den, http://www.firewolfsg.com/ (accessed February 4, 2005).

115. Kazumi Nagaike, "Perverse Sexualities, Pervasive Desires: Representations of Female Fantasies and Yaoi Manga as Pornography Directed at Women," *U.S.–Japan Women's Journal* 25 (2003), 94.

116. Atsureki, "Surrounded by Darkness," Fanfiction.Net, http://www.fanfiction.net/s/1037952/1/ (accessed March 1, 2005).

117. Sidara, "Sünde," Schadenfreude, http://schadenfreude.noctuidae.org/index.php?page=weisskreuz (accessed January 10, 2004).

118. Cards Slash, "Five Ways Ken Hidaka Was Never Raped," Unapologetically Given To Wander, http://cards-slash.livejournal.com/136343.html (accessed April 19, 2007).

119. Martyl, "The Saga Begins," Fanfiction.Net, http://www.fanfiction.net/s/1518599/1/ (accessed March 8, 2005).

120. Sidara, "Zeit," Schadenfreude, http://schadenfreude.noctuidae.org/index.php?page=weisskreuz (accessed January 10, 2004).

121. Cards Slash, "Five Ways Ken Hidaka Was Never Raped," Unapologetically Given To Wander, http://cards-slash.livejournal.com/136343.html (accessed April 19, 2007).

122. Annabelle Leigh, "Why Prostitute Stories?," Fiction By The Sea, http://members.tripod.com/~AnnaBLeigh/prostitute.txt (accessed April 14, 2007).

123. Kat Avila, "Boy's Love and Yaoi Revisited," *Sequential Tart*, Jan (2005), http://www.sequentialtart.com/art_0105_1.shtml (accessed Jan 16, 2005).

124. Die Tod von Euch, "Yaoi Fangirls," Anime Forum.Com, http://www.animeforum.com/archive/index.php/t-17128.html (accessed May 1, 2007).

125. Mark McHarry, "Identity Unmoored: Yaoi in the West," in *Queer Popular Culture: Literature, Media, Film, and Television,* ed. Thomas Peele (New York: Palgrave Macmillan, 2007), 190.

126. Matt Thorn, "Girls and Women Getting Out of Hand: The Pleasure and Politics of Japan's Amateur Comics Community," in *Fanning the flames: Fans and Consumer Culture in Contemporary Japan,* ed. William W. Kelly (Albany, NY: State University of New York Press, 2004), 173.

127. Andrea Doolan, "Yaoi Story," touyaxyukito.com, http://www.touyaxyukito.com/yaoistory.htm (accessed April 22, 2007).

128. Dru Pagliassotti, "Reading Boys' Love in the West," *Particip@tions* 5:2, November (2008), http://www.participations.org/Volume%205/Issue%202/5_02_pagliassotti.htm.

129. Constance Penley, "Brownian Motion: Women, Tactics, and Technology," in *Technoculture,* ed. Constance Penley & Andrew Ross (Minneapolis: University of Minnesota Press, 1991), 156–157.

130. Keith Vincent, "A Japanese Electra and Her Queer Progeny," in *Mechademia 2,* ed. Frenchy Lunning (Minnesota: University of Minnesota Press, 2007), 72.

131. Rinny133, "The ULTIMATE Weiss Fic!" Fanfiction.Net, http://www.fanfiction.net/s/1033858/1/ (accessed February 14, 2005).

132. Janice Radway, *Reading the Romance: Women, Patriarchy, and Popular Literature* (Chapel Hill and London: The University of North Carolina Press, 1984), 14.

133. Kat Avila, "Boy's Love and Yaoi Revisited," *Sequential Tart*, Jan (2005), http://www.sequentialtart.com/art_0105_1.shtml (accessed Jan 16, 2005).

134. Constance Penley, "Brownian Motion: Women, Tactics, and Technology," in *Technoculture,* ed. Constance Penley & Andrew Ross (Minneapolis: University of Minnesota Press, 1991), 154.

135. Matt Thorn, "Girls and Women Getting Out of Hand: The Pleasure and Politics of Japan's Amateur Comics Community," in *Fanning the flames: Fans and Consumer Culture in Contemporary Japan,* ed. William W. Kelly (Albany, NY: State University of New York Press, 2004), 77.

136. Christine Scodari, "Resistance Re-Examined: Gender, Fan Practices, and Science Fiction Television," *Popular Communication* 1.2 (2003): 115.

137. Lady Cyrrh, "Slash ... and Slash Again Original Slash Reviews," The Official Lady Cyrrh Website, http://www.asstr.org/~ladycyrrh/GOODIES/originalslash_index.html (accessed May 9, 2007).

138. Wiggle, "Sphynx," Pure Yaoi, http://www.pureyaoi.org/fiction/index.html (accessed May 9, 2007).

139. Fiona Ng, "Drawn to It," Nerve.com, http://www.nerve.com/dispatches/ng/drawntoit/ (accessed December 4, 2004).

140. Eliza Strickland, "Drawn Together," *San Francisco Weekly.com* (November 1, 2006), http://www.sfweekly.com/2006-11-01/news/drawn-together/full (accessed April 11, 2007).

141. Constance Penley, "Brownian Motion: Women, Tactics, and Technology," in *Technoculture,* ed. Constance Penley & Andrew Ross (Minneapolis: University of Minnesota Press, 1991), 139.

142. Janice Radway, *Reading the Romance: Women, Patriarchy, and Popular Literature* (Chapel Hill and London: The University of North Carolina Press, 1984), 117–118.

Bibliography

Altman, Dennis. *Homosexual: Oppression and Liberation.* New York: New York University Press, 1993.
Aoe and Shoori. "New World Order." Bleeding Hearts. http://www.trowaluvsduo.net/weissweb/bleeding hearts.htm (accessed March 7, 2005).
Atsureki. "Love on a Leash." Fanfiction.Net. http://www.fanfiction.net/s/966491/1/ (accessed March 1, 2005).
_____. "Please, Give Me Another Chance." Fanfiction.Net. http://www.fanfiction.net/s/978867/1/ (accessed March 2, 2005).
_____. "Surrounded by Darkness." Fanfiction.Net. http://www.fanfiction.net/s/1037952/1/ (accessed March 1, 2005).
Avila, Kat. "Boy's Love and Yaoi Revisited." *Sequential Tart* (January 2005), http://www.sequentialtart.com/art_0105_1.shtml.
Bacon-Smith, Camille. *Enterprising Women: Television Fandom and the Creation of Popular Myth.* Philadelphia: University of Pennsylvania Press, 1992.
Bast, Lady. "The Interview." GlowingCross.net. http://glowingcross.net/The_Interview_fic.html (accessed March 1, 2005).
Butler, Judith. "Imitation and Gender Insubordination." In *Inside/Out: Lesbian Theories, Gay Theories,* edited by Diana Fuss, 13–31. New York: Routledge, 1991.
Cece. "Revealing Myself." Fanfiction.Net. http://www.fanfiction.net/s/908113/1/ (accessed February 15, 2005).
Celestel. "UkeSeme Dynamics." Fanfiction.Net. http://www.fanfiction.net/s/1504297/1/ (accessed March 2, 2005).
Cicioni, Mirna. "Male Pair-bonds and Female Desire in Fan Slash Writing." In *Theorizing Fandom: Fans, Subculture, and Identity,* edited by Cheryl Harris and Alison Alexander, 153–177. Cresskill, NJ: Hampton Press, 1998.
Crimson1. "Kind des Schicksals." Fanfiction.Net. http://www.fanfiction.net/s/2065398/1/Kind_des_Schicksals (accessed March 2, 2005).
Cross, Chalcedony. "Chal's Profile." LiveJournal Blog. http://chal.livejournal.com/profile (accessed January 21, 2005).
Cyrrh, Lady. "Slash ... and Slash Again Original Slash Reviews." The Official Lady Cyrrh Website. http://www.asstr.org/~ladycyrrh/GOODIES/originalslash_index.html (accessed May 9, 2007)
Deena. "Christmas Frenzy." Fanfiction.Net. http://www.fanfiction.net/s/149346/1/ (accessed March 2, 2005).
_____. "Raspberry and Lime Shampoo." Boys Next Door. http://www.discarnate.com/boysnextdoor/weiss.html (accessed February 15, 2005).
_____. "Something New." Velvet Underwear: A Shrine to Yoji Kudou. http://www.geocities.com/tsukiyoshi/new.html (accessed March 1, 2005).
_____. "Waking Onto Lantern's Bright." Boys Next Door. http://www.discarnate.com/boysnextdoor/fiction/weiss/WakingOnto.html (accessed February 14, 2005).
Die Tod von Euch. "Yaoi Fangirls." Anime Forum.Com. http://www.animeforum.com/archive/index.php/t-17128.html (accessed May 1, 2007).
Doolan, Andrea. "Yaoi Story." touyaxyukito.com. http://www.touyaxyukito.com/yaoistory.htm (accessed April 22, 2007).
Doty, Alexander. *Making Things Perfectly Queer: Interpreting Mass Culture.* Minneapolis: University of Minnesota Press, 1993.
Driscoll, Catherine. "One True Pairing: The Romance of Pornography and the Pornography of Romance." In *Fan Fiction and Fan Communities in the Age of the Internet,* edited by Karen Hellekson & Kristina Busse, 79–96. Jefferson, NC: McFarland, 2006.
Durendal, and the Beef Chick. "Uncle Yohji's Book of Love." Velvet Underwear: A Shrine to Yoji Kudou. http://www.geocities.com/Tokyo/Ginza/5170/Weiss/fanfics.html (accessed March 1, 2005).
Fancy. "Hair." Fanfiction.Net. http://www.fanfiction.net/s/980249/1/ (accessed March 2, 2005).
Farmer, Brett. *Spectacular Passions: Cinema, Fantasy, Gay Male Spectatorships.* Durham and London: Duke University Press, 2000.
Fever, Scarlet. "Frail (You May As Well Be Me)." The Fountain of Decay. http://www.geocities.com/necrolantry/Frail.htm (accessed February 14, 2005).
Firedancer, Talya. "To Bury the Hurt of Memory." Firedancer's Weiss Kreuz Fanfiction. http://www.fyredancer.net/wk/index.html (accessed March 7, 2005).
_____. "The Subway Trilogy." Firedancer's Weiss Kreuz Fanfiction. http://www.fyredancer.net/wk/index.html (accessed March 7, 2005).
Foucault, Michel. *The History of Sexuality.* Translated by Robert Hurley. New York: Vintage, 1980.
Fujimoto, Yukari. *Watashi no ibasho wa doko ni aru no? Shôjo manga ga utsusu kokoro no katachi.* Tokyo:

Gakuyou Shobo, 1998. Quoted in Matt Thorn, "Girls and Women Getting Out of Hand: The Pleasure and Politics of Japan's Amateur Comics Community." In *Fanning the flames: Fans and Consumer Culture in Contemporary Japan*, edited by William W. Kelly, 169–187. Albany, NY: State University of New York Press, 2004.

Heleninhell. "I Am Not a Dominatrix: Women and the Active Sexual Role." Helen gets the job done. http://web.archive.org/web/19991111184526/members.tripod.com/heleninhell/dominatrix.html (accessed April, 15 2007).

Hellekson, Karen, and Kristina Busse. Introduction to *Fan Fiction and Fan Communities in the Age of the Internet*, ed. Karen Hellekson & Kristina Busse, 5–32. Jefferson, NC: McFarland, 2006.

Hine, Christine. *Virtual Ethnography*. London: SAGE Publications, 2000.

Jeanne. "The Top Ten Things I Love About Yaoi." *Aestheticism* (October, 2001), http://www.aestheticism.com/visitors/editor/index.htm (accessed April 22, 2007).

_____. "Why the Guys? Or Navel-Gazing in the Afternoon." *Aestheticism*. http://www.aestheticism.com/visitors/editor/index.htm (accessed April 22, 2007).

Jenkins, Henry. *Textual Poachers*. New York: Routledge, 1992.

_____. "Reception Theory and Audience Research: The Mystery of the Vampire's Kiss." Professional Homepage. http://web.mit.edu/cms/People/henry3/vampkiss.html (accessed February 6, 2008).

Jones, Sarah Gwenllian. "The Sex Lives of Cult Television Characters." *Screen* 43.1 (2002): 79–90.

Jung, Susanne. "Queering Popular Culture: Female Spectators and the Appeal of Writing Slash Fan Fiction." *Gender Forum Gender Queeries* 8 (2004), http://www.genderforum.uni-koeln.de/queer/jung.html.

Kim. "A Quiet Evening." Schwarz Contradiction. http://www.geocities.com/schwarz_contradiction/quietevening.html (accessed February 15, 2005).

Kirachu. "Warmth." Fanfiction.Net. http://www.fanfiction.net/s/1334080/1/ (accessed, February 15, 2005).

Koh, Jacque. "Second Chances." Firewolf's Den. http://www.firewolfsg.com/ (accessed February 4, 2005).

Koyasu, Takehito. *Weiss Kreuz OAV Vol.1 Verbrechen*. VHS. Directed by Kimura Shinichiro. Tokyo: Marine Entertainment, 1999.

_____. *Weiss Kreuz OAV Vol. 2 Strafe*. VHS. Directed by Kimura Shinichiro. Tokyo: Marine Entertainment, 2000.

Koyasu, Takehito and Animate Film. *Weiss Kreuz Glühen*. DVD. Directed by Matsui Hitoyuki. Tokyo: Marine Entertainment, 2003.

Koyasu, Takehito and Project Weiss. *Weiss Kreuz Kapitel*. DVD. Directed by Egami Kiyoshi & Tanahashi Kazutoku. Tokyo: Marine Entertainment, 1998–1999.

Kustritz, Anne. "Slashing the Romance Narrative." *The Journal of American Culture* 26.3 (2003): 371–384.

Kuwabara no Miko. "Male Bonding." Boys Next Door. http://www.discarnate.com/boysnextdoor/fiction/weiss/WeissBonding.html (accessed February 10, 2005).

Kuwabara no Miko and Talya Firedancer. "A Fine Day for a Group Outing." Firedancer's Weiß Kreuz Fanfiction Archive. http://www.fyredancer.net/wk/WKgroupouting.html (accessed February 10, 2005).

Laila. "The Discreet Charm of Slash Fiction." Plastic Venus. http://quietladybirman.livejournal.com/34858.html#cutid1 (accessed June 9, 2006).

_____. "In Defense of ... Yaoi." Pale Movies Version 8: Afterglow. http://www.palemovies.com/r_ido_03.html (accessed July 31, 2007).

Leather Daddy. "Review of 'Lord of the Rings': A Diamond Between Wood and Stone." Slap to the Head Fanfiction Reviews. http://web.pitas.com/ficbitches/woodandstone.html (accessed June 1, 2006).

Leigh, Annabelle. "Why Prostitute Stories?" Fiction By The Sea. http://members.tripod.com/~AnnaBLeigh/prostitute.txt (accessed April 14, 2007).

Link621. "But, I'm An Assassin." Noire Sensus. http://www.noiresensus.com/bookshelf/pair_kenxomifics.html (accessed March 1, 2005).

Marty1. "Baby Talk." Fanfiction.Net. http://www.fanfiction.net/s/610799/1/ (accessed March 8, 2005).

_____. "Black Gold." Fanfiction.Net. http://www.fanfiction.net/s/756833/1/ (accessed March 7, 2005).

_____. "The Saga Begins." Fanfiction.Net. http://www.fanfiction.net/s/1518599/1/ (accessed March 8, 2005).

Maya Tawi and Viridian5. "Girl." Zippos and Safety Pins. http://panthea.populli.net/fiction/girl1.htm (accessed March 18, 2005).

McHarry, Mark. "Identity Unmoored: Yaoi in the West." In *Queer Popular Culture: Literature, Media, Film, and Television*, edited by Thomas Peele, 183–196. New York: Palgrave Macmillan, 2007.

McKee, Alan. *Textual Analysis: A Beginner's Guide*. London: Sage Publications, 2003.

Meeks, Chet and Arlene Stein. "Refiguring the Family: Towards a Post-Queer Politics of Gay and Lesbian Marriage." In *Intersections Between Feminist and Queer Theory*, edited by Diane Richardson, Janice McLaughlin and Mark E. Casey, 136–155. Houndsmill: Palgrave Macmillan, 2006.

Metallium, Lynn. "The Three Little Bishounen." Fanfiction.Net. http://www.fanfiction.net/s/1534692/1/ (accessed February 14, 2005).

Miko, Generic. "Popcorn Timeline." East of Sanity. http://www.eastofsanity.com/ (accessed February 14, 2005).

_____. "Unexpected Talents." East of Sanity. http://www.eastofsanity.com/ (accessed February 14, 2005).

Miko no Da. "Sinners and Saints." Love is Love. http://www.darkhuntress.com/miko_no_da/MW1/Index3.html (accessed February 28, 2005).

Mulvey, Laura. "Visual Pleasure and Narrative Cinema." *Screen* 16.3 (1975): 6–18.

Nagaike, Kazumi. "Perverse Sexualities, Pervasive Desires: Representations of Female Fantasies and Yaoi Manga as Pornography Directed at Women." *U.S.–Japan Women's Journal* 25 (2003): 76–103.

Nekojita. "Cages." Cat's Dream. http://www.catsdreams.com/fanfiction.html (accessed February 25, 2005).

Nexus, Cassandra. "In the Rain." Kuwabara no Miko's *Weiss Kreuz* Yaoi Fanfiction Page. http://www.kuwamiko.com/WeissRain.html (accessed February 14, 2005).

Ng, Fiona. "Drawn to It." *Nerve.com* (November 24, 2004), http://www.nerve.com/dispatches/ng/drawntoit/ (accessed December 4, 2004).

Opus the Penguin. "A Delicate Subject." Fanfiction.Net. http://www.fanfiction.net/s/1363851/1/ (accessed March 2, 2005).

Pagliassotti, Dru. "Reading Boys' Love in the West." *Particip@tions* 5:2 (November 2008), http://www.participations.org/Volume%205/Issue%202/5_02_pagliassotti.htm (accessed December 10, 2008).

Penley, Constance. "Brownian Motion: Women, Tactics, and Technology." In *Technoculture*, edited by Constance Penley & Andrew Ross, 163–195. Minneapolis: University of Minnesota Press, 1991.

Radway, Janice. *Reading the Romance: Women, Patriarchy, and Popular Literature.* Chapel Hill and London: The University of North Carolina Press, 1984.

Rat, Sky. "Better Days." MediaMiner.org. http://www.mediaminer.org/fanfic/view_st.php/38361 (accessed March 1, 2005).

The RCK. "Rheotaxis." Consensus Realities. http://www.therck.org/ (accessed March 1, 2004).

Rinny133. "The ULTIMATE Weiss Fic!" Fanfiction.Net. http://www.fanfiction.net/s/1033858/1/ (accessed February 14, 2005).

Rubin, Gayle. "The Traffic in Women: Notes on the 'Political Economy' of Sex." In *The Second Wave: A Reader in Feminist Theory*, edited by Linda Nicholson, 27–62. New York: Routledge, 1996.

_____. "Thinking Sex: Notes for a Radical Theory of the Politics of Sexuality." In *Theorizing Feminisms: A Reader*, edited by Elizabeth Hackett & Sally Haslanger, 527–551. Oxford: Oxford University Press, 2006.

Scodari, Christine. "Resistance Re-Examined: Gender, Fan Practices, and Science Fiction Television." *Popular Communication* 1.2(2003): 111–30.

Shoori. "Eight Years in the Making." Bleeding Hearts. http://www.trowaluvsduo.net/weissweb/bleeding-hearts.htm (accessed March 7, 2005).

Sidara. "Sünde." Schadenfreude. http://schadenfreude.noctuidae.org/index.php?page=weisskreuz (accessed January 10, 2004).

_____. "Zeit." Schadenfreude. http://schadenfreude.noctuidae.org/index.php?page=weisskreuz (accessed January 10, 2004).

Slash, Cards. "Five Ways Ken Hidaka Was Never Raped." Unapologetically Given To Wander. http://cards-slash.livejournal.com/136343.html (accessed April 19, 2007).

Snitow, Ann Barr. "Mass Market Romance: Pornography for Women is Different." In *Gender, Race, and Class in Media: A Text-reader*, edited by Gail Dines & Jean M Humez, 424–433. Thousand Oaks, CA: Sage Publications, 2003.

Soble, Alan. *Pornography: Marxism, Feminism, and the Future of Sexuality.* New Haven: Yale UP,1986.

Strickland, Eliza. "Drawn Together." *San Francisco Weekly.com* (November 1, 2006), http://www.sfweekly.com/2006-11-01/news/drawn-together/full (accessed April 11, 2007).

Suzuki, Kazuko. "Pornography or Therapy? Japanese Girls Creating the Yaoi Phenomenon." In *Millennium Girls: Today's Girls Around the World*, edited by Sherrie A. Innes, 243–68. London: Roman & Littlefield, 1999.

Swythangel. "Chibification (Raising Ken)." XY: Intoxicating Obsession. http://www.lucidinsanity.com/fanfic/wkfics/chibi1.html (accessed March 8, 2005).

_____. "Heaven in Your Arms." XY: Intoxicating Obsession. http://www.lucidinsanity.com/fanfic/wkfics/hiya1.html (accessed March 7, 2005).

_____. "Phenomenal Noumenal." XY: Intoxicating Obsession. http://www.lucidinsanity.com/fanfic/wkfics/phen1.html (accessed March 7, 2005).

Teep. "Why Chicks like Fanfic Porn." Home Page. http://www.bedford.net/teep/fanfic.htm (accessed April 23, 2007).

Thorn, Matt. "Girls and Women Getting Out of Hand: The Pleasure and Politics of Japan's Amateur Comics Community." In *Fanning the Flames: Fans and Consumer Culture in Contemporary Japan*, edited by William W. Kelly, 169–187. Albany, NY: State University of New York Press, 2004.

Tsuchiya, Kyoko. *An Assassin and White Shaman.* (Weiss Kreuz *Manga*) Vols. 1 and 2. Tokyo: Shinshokan, 1998.

Vincent, Keith. "A Japanese Electra and Her Queer Progeny." In *Mechademia 2*, edited by Frenchy Lunning, 64–79. Minnesota: University of Minnesota Press, 2007.

Wiggle. "Sphynx." Pure Yaoi. http://www.pureyaoi.org/fiction/index.html (accessed May 9, 2007).

Willis, Ika. "Keeping Promises to Queer Children: Making Space (for Mary Sue) at Hogwarts." In *Fan Fiction and Fan Communities in the Age of the Internet*, edited by Karen Hellekson & Kristina Busse, 153–170. Jefferson, NC: McFarland, 2006.

Woledge, Elizabeth. "Intimatopia: Genre Intersections Between Slash and the Mainstream." In *Fan Fiction and Fan Communities in the Age of the Internet*, edited by Karen Hellekson & Kristina Busse, 97–114. Jefferson, NC: McFarland, 2006.

Wood, Andrea. "'Straight' Women, Queer Texts: Boy-Love Manga and the Rise of a Global Counterpublic." *Women's Studies Quarterly* 34(1/2) (Spring 2006): 394–414.

Yoippari. "Rules." Boys Next Door. http://www.discarnate.com/boysnextdoor/fiction/Rules.html (accessed September 26, 2004).

PART THREE

*Boys' Love and Perceptions
of the Queer*

Uttering the Absurd, Revaluing the Abject

Femininity and the Disavowal of Homosexuality in Transnational Boys' Love Manga

Neal K. Akatsuka

It's the ultimate expression of love — to wear matching rings with your significant other, showing the world that you are a couple. High school student, Wataru Fujii, also wears one though he is single. When he accidentally switches rings with popular and handsome senior, Yuichi Kazuki, they discover that their rings pair up! Since then, Kazuki, who is known for being kind to all becomes strangely harsh to Wataru. They alternate between hot and cold, as in between clashes they begin to sort their feelings for one another. Are Wataru and Kazuki the worst of enemies or are they actually soulmates?[1]

The above synopsis of *Only the Ring Finger Knows* (*Sono yubi dake ga shitteiru*) enticingly discloses what is in store for readers who dare to venture into the manga's contents — not just any turbulent romance, but a romance between two boys. Far from being an exceptional narrative, *Only the Ring Finger Knows* belongs to a sub-genre of *shōjo* (girls') manga known variously as boys' love (hereafter BL), yaoi, and *shōnen-ai*.[2] The BL sub-genre, as Dru Pagliassotti defines it, is "a narrative about the romantic or erotic relationship between two or more male characters that has been created with the intention of appealing to a female audience."[3] While this may seem a curious phenomenon to some because the target audience is females rather than gay males, BL manga have become transnational cultural commodities.[4] Beginning in the late 1990s with *Kizuna* in 1998 and *FAKE* in 1999,[5] the BL manga market in North America as of 2008 has expanded to about 350 licensed titles translated and re-released into English from Japanese. This is in addition to numerous unofficial fan translations (i.e., "scanlations" — translated scans of Japanese originals) available online that preceded the arrival of official translations into the North American market and continue to be made for manga currently unavailable in English. Although there is no commercial market for scanlations, because they are illegal due to copyright infringement, they have expanded the number of BL texts available to readers who patronize such Web sites.

The successful introduction and sale of BL manga in North America — as well as in other Western countries, such as Spain, Italy, and France[6] — show that the enjoyment of cultural commodities such as BL manga may be less restricted by socialization into a certain culture than by economic or political barriers. Culture does, of course, have an effect on the economy and politics as well as the kinds of BL texts selected for translation by publishers. Furthermore, BL texts are not necessarily easy to obtain online or offline (e.g., due to censorship laws). For example, Pagliassotti found that certain themes, such as *shota* (intergenerational homoerotic/romantic narratives involving young boys), are avoided or adapted by U.S. publishers for the U.S. market due in part to social norms (in this case regarding child pornography).[7] However, I want to point out that BL manga, when accessible, are enjoyed outside of Japan, and thus the enjoyment of their narratives is not necessarily contingent upon a single cultural logic, history of sexuality, or understanding of gender. Contrary to Mark McLelland's argument that BL is possible as a valid fantasy topos for women in Japan because of Japanese society's particular understanding of homosexuality, the appeal of BL may be something more transnational in character, something Iwabuchi Koichi calls "cultural odorlessness."[8] Iwabuchi argues that major audiovisual cultural commodities, such as manga, exported from Japan are culturally odorless in the sense that while these commodities may signify "Japaneseness," this signification is not in itself particularly relevant to its transnational appeal. This odorlessness is enabled in part by the softening or erasure of more explicit visual references to the commodity's country of origin (e.g. racial and bodily images) so that a particular culture is not imprinted onto the commodity.[9] This is part and parcel of globalization, which has blurred and problematized distinct cultural boundaries and proliferated a sense of "familiar difference and bizarre sameness" simultaneously.[10] While readers may interpret and appreciate BL in multiple ways, BL narratives speak in a way that is intelligible and appealing transnationally.

In this chapter I offer an alternative reading of BL that seeks to evaluate the underlying logic of BL narratives and theorize what within these texts appeals to audiences transnationally (with a focus on the Western context). I locate this appeal in BL's potential to create an affirmative feminine space and subjectivity that subverts, although reifies in other ways, the heteronormatively gendered hierarchy of patriarchy. I will argue that such a space is possible through the simultaneity of a homosexual pretext embedded within a heteronormative subtext constructed through the narrative topoi of BL such as the disavowal of homosexuality. Reading BL in this manner allows for an analysis of the transnational appeal of BL that takes into account the paradoxical multiplicity yet commonality of the positions, identities, and motives of its readership.

BL as a Gendered Space for Fe(male)s

Ōgi Fusami argues that readers of *shōjo* manga, "even males, are all engendered — hailed in the Althusserian sense — by the category of *shoujo*. In [BL] representations, which do not show women as central, the *shoujo* type unveils itself as a code and an institution."[11] This institution is based upon "Japanese modern femininity in the Meiji period [1868–1912]: a feminine image based on westernization following Japan's centuries-long isolation and on the virtues of the so-called 'good wife and wise mother.'"[12] The BL text encoded as *shōjo*— a code, an institution, an ideology — always already anticipates its readers are *shōjo* (i.e., adolescent girls), requiring readers, regardless of their actual age or gender identity, to therefore read the text from the perspective of *shōjo*. To a certain extent this code is specific to the Japanese sociohistorical context and subject to hybridization within new contexts. Yet the code and the particular way it positions readers is also relevant in the West. Through a 2005 English-language survey ($N = 478$) and comparison with a separate 2006–7 Italian-language survey ($N = 313$) of readers of BL manga, Pagliassotti found that the majority of respondents began reading BL manga in their teens and early twenties are now between eighteen and thirty-four years old, are female (eighty-nine percent in the English-language survey and eighty-two percent in the Italian-language survey), and identify as heterosexual (forty-seven percent in the English-language survey and sixty-two percent in the Italian-language survey).[13] That the primary readership in the West resembles the reader anticipated by the *shōjo* code of the BL text reveals the extent to which its hail travels transnationally and is answered.

It is important to emphasize though that the reader anticipated is not the only reader who reads BL texts. The surveys reveal that BL manga readers also include males (eleven percent in the English-language survey and thirteen percent in the Italian-language survey), heterosexually identified males (three in the English-language survey), and non-heterosexually identified males and females.[14] Yet contrary to this heterogeneous composition, as Andrea Wood points out, past studies have analyzed BL as almost an exclusively heterosexual female genre.[15] This is exemplified by Suzuki Kazuko's interpretation of BL as an expression of girls' and young women's "despair of ever achieving equal relationships with men in a sexist society and their quest for ideal human relationships."[16] While this may be true to a certain extent, this characterization is ultimately limited in that it rearticulates a heteronormative framework of desire, which suggests women only want to explore relationships vis-à-vis men. Furthermore, as a male presence in readership is rarely acknowledged, this position is inevitably marginalized and subsumed within the presumption of a (solely) female readership.[17] While the way that readers are positioned by the text as *shōjo* is not necessarily altered, the conflation of the position that readers are interpellated into by the hail of the text and the multiple positions readers inhabit prior to the hail of the text is problematic insofar as it does not take into account broader sexual and sexed positions that the appeal of BL reaches.

In order to move beyond this restrictive method of analysis and develop a more nuanced perspective on BL and its textual pleasures, we must view the BL readership as always already fe(male)s. "Fe(male)s" alludes to the engendering consequences of the ideology of the BL text on its audience, which positions both males and females as female, as opposed to a known audience of (heterosexual) females. At the same time, through its focus on (biological) sex as opposed to (social) gender, as well as being unmarked by age and an accompanying social positioning (e.g., woman, girl), the concept can emphasize the (female) person who has not yet come into fully gendered being and the social weight such a being is invested with. That is, readers are positioned with a particular relationship to femininity similar to adolescence—a liminal period of relative agency as they are not yet adult, fully engendered women (whose agency is constituted as a lack in the Lacanian theory of the Symbolic—see below).

It is this audience, hailed fe(male)s, that analyses should speak toward, and the particular feminine perspective required by BL that should be taken into account in analyzing the transnational appeal of BL. Along similar lines, Matthew Thorn argues,

> I think we can appreciate why yaoi and slash-style fan productions find favor among a certain demographic cohort of women in many industrialized nations. I would argue that what these fans share in common is discontent with the standards of femininity to which they are expected to adhere and a social environment and historical moment that does not validate or sympathize with that discontent.[18]

I would expand this position to say that readers cannot be contained by the category of "women," but rather need to encompass fe(male)s, whose discontent extends to the socially degraded valuation of femininity itself. This stance could potentially encompass both queer and heterosexual females and males.[19] Of course, the explicit portrayal of homoeroticism may prevent homophobic readers from delving beyond the texts' surface imagery.[20] Furthermore, as males, regardless of their sexuality, are hailed by *shōjo* manga to read as fe(male)s, they may resist such a hail because of a fear of feminization. Under the gender politics of patriarchy, male feminization usually entails a loss of (claim to) power and agency, suggesting a reason why male readership tends to be relatively low.

Embedding Narratives of BL in Heteronormative Intelligibility

While BL, broadly defined, encompasses erotic or romantic relationships between males, these relationships are narrated in particular ways to the sub-genre that have consequences for how gender and sexuality are constructed. In the third period (1991 to the present) of the general yaoi phenomenon that Mizoguchi Akiko outlines, BL is differentiated broadly in its use of a new body-type aesthetic (more masculine and muscular) and in contemporary settings, compared to previous periods, which utilized a similar narrative premise of romantic or erotic relationships between men.[21] In addition, certain topoi dominantly structure BL narratives: (1) "rape as an expression of love," (2) "one or both of the protagonists maintaining that they are straight even after they are homosexually involved," (3) "the top [*seme*]/bottom [*uke*] roles in sex corresponding to the masculine/feminine appearance of protagonists," (4) "the roles never reversing," and (5) "sex always involving anal intercourse."[22] I would also add the topos of the narrative being from the *uke*'s perspective.[23] While these topoi are not always present in their entirety, nor absolutely followed, they are the topoi that form the assumptions of most BL narratives (or rather, their ideology) and to which many BL manga respond. For example, Fujiyama Hyouta (Fujiyama Hyōta), the author of *Spell*, remarks in her afterword that while she was successful in portraying the narrative from the *seme*'s perspective, she was "dissatisfied" and ended up writing a follow-up short story from the *uke*'s perspective.[24] Here Fujiyama's statement gestures toward her conscious reversal of the perspective topos and her later discomfort with this reversal.

These topoi construct narratives of BL in a particularly heteronormative manner. Even though females are usually marginalized figures of desire in BL texts and thus rendered invisible (in terms of significance to the narrative and its focus on love and desire), rather than homosexuality losing all meaning since the possibility of heterosexuality should also therefore be rendered invisible, sexuality often remains a critical issue for one or more of the protagonists. This, I would contend, is because of the way the topoi structure BL narratives; even if heterosexuality is not explicitly presented within narratives as a possibility, it always already exists as a presumption of reality. This presumption structures the way the protagonists are characterized and interact with each other. For example, the third topos reconstructs a heteronormative gender dyad whereby the *seme* represents masculinity and the *uke* represents femininity, despite the characters both being male. This hierarchical structure is reified through the fifth topos, in which anal sex with its configuration of sex positions corresponds to heteronormative assumptions of engendered power positions (i.e. top as masculine, bottom as feminine).

Due to this, Mizoguchi argues that the topoi are meant to "achieve 'heterosexual romance' narratives for heterosexual female readers."[25] That is, while BL may posit a homosexual pretext of a homoerotic romance between two or more males, this is premised on a heteronormative subtext intended to place the pretext within a realm of intelligibility for presumed heterosexual females. However, I would point out that even though a heteronormative subtext is constructed, this subtext is also revealed as failing to control and fix identity through the pretext of homosexuality. Thus the subtext and pretext do not act in binary opposition to each other, but rather, as Alexander Doty points out, "the queer often operates within the nonqueer, as the nonqueer does within the queer (whether in reception, texts, or producers)."[26] The simultaneous presence of the heteronormative and the homoerotic is revealed by the disavowal of homosexuality (or the second topos). This revelation is crucial for the gendered work of BL in its performativity.[27]

The Performativity of Disavowal and Ignorance

The disavowal of homosexuality — or the maintenance of heterosexuality in Mizoguchi's phrasing — can obviously be a concise utterance, such as in Shiozu Shuri's *Eerie Queerie* (*Gōsuto!*) when Mitsuo exclaims, "We aren't gay!" to a crowd of his classmates.[28] However, the disavowal does not need to be uttered out loud to be performed — indeed, the utterance itself is not necessarily a straightforward, effective mechanism, as Mitsuo's classmates laugh at him and twist his words to support their accusation that he is gay.[29] To better understand the multiple ways in which this topos can be narrated, I would like to explore three examples from three separate BL manga. These examples demonstrate how ignorance, personal reflection, and external circumstances (usually in addition to an utterance) can all be mobilized within stories to distance not only the character(s) from homosexuality, but also the readers who are immersed in the drama of the character(s). This disassociation in turn has consequences for the epistemology of BL and thus how readers come to know (and not know) not only BL, but also the logic(s) of gender and sexuality it poses.

Homosexuality as an unintelligible impossibility — *Only the Ring Finger Knows*

As Wataru reveals to Kazuki that the gift he has just given is not from him, Kazuki slowly corners Wataru against a wall. After teasing Wataru for a little while, Kazuki whispers Wataru's name and slowly leans in as if to kiss him.[30] As Figure 1 shows, the scene is extended through a whole page and focuses on Wataru's somatic reactions (e.g. body feeling warm, blushing) and psychological confusion. Wataru is ultimately portrayed as ignorant of even the possibility of homosexuality, unable to imagine the link between his somatic reactions, the homoeroticism of the situation, and his sexuality. This is further confirmed in a later scene when Wataru thinks, "To be honest, I don't even understand my own feelings yet. I never even imagined that I would fall in love with another man. And there's still a part of me ... that doesn't want to accept it."[31] Homosexuality cannot even be imagined as a possibility and is disavowed.

Love as transcending (homo)sexuality — *Spell*

After finally confessing his love to Kisugi in a bout of jealousy, Natori is guided by Kisugi to loosen his pants. Natori questions his identity and feelings toward Kisugi as his

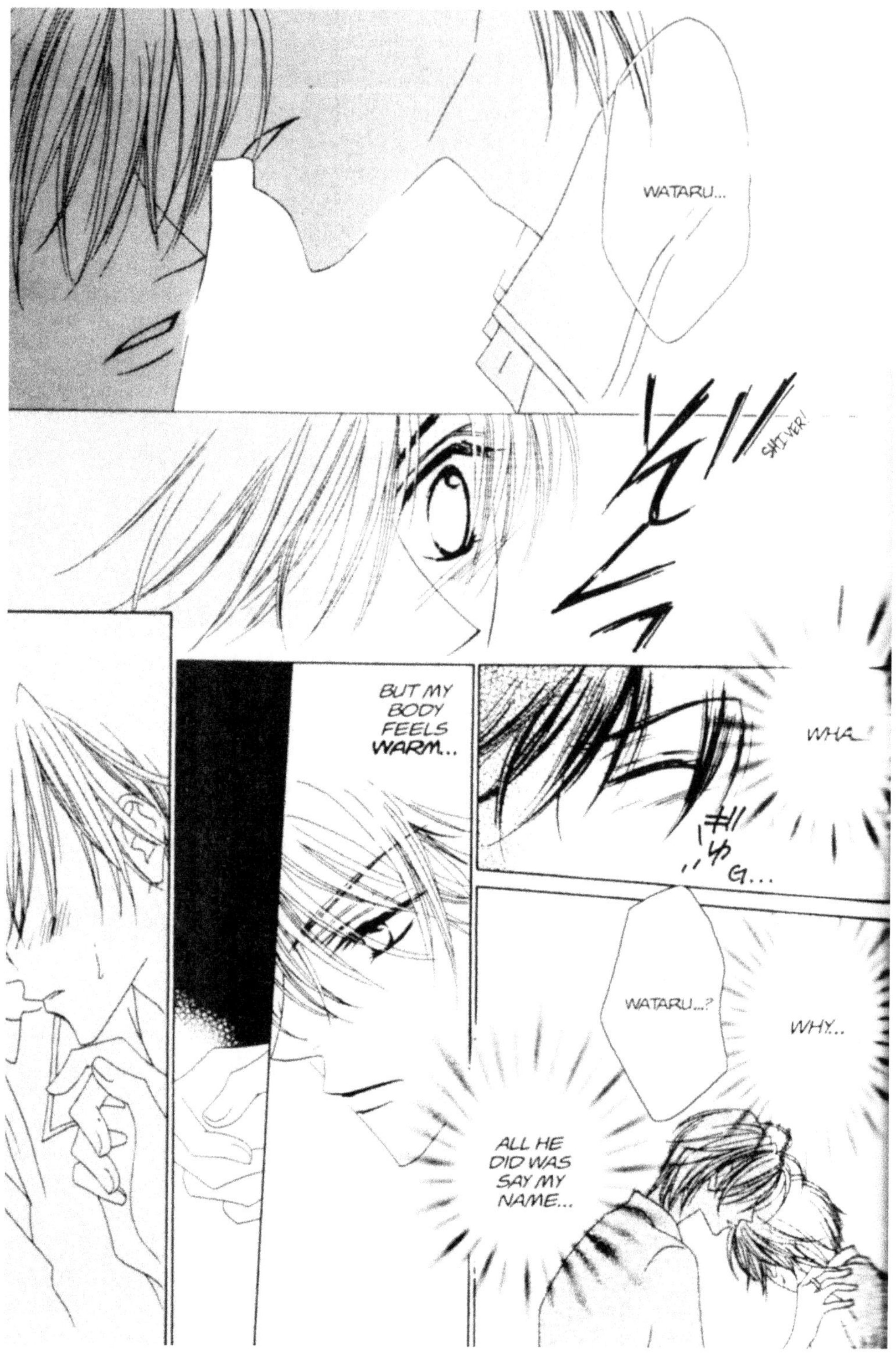

Figure 1. Wataru confused by his somatic reaction to Kazuki's seduction. Credit: Original Japanese version *Only the Ring Finger Knows—Sono Yubi Dake Ga Shitteiru* © 2002 Satoru Kannagi & Hotaru Odagiri. Originally published in Tokyo, Japan in 2002 by Tokuma Shoten Publishing Co., Ltd. English version in U.S.A. and Canada published by Digital Manga, Inc. under license granted by Tokuma Shoten Publishing Co., Ltd. English translation © 2004 by DIGITAL MANGA, INC.

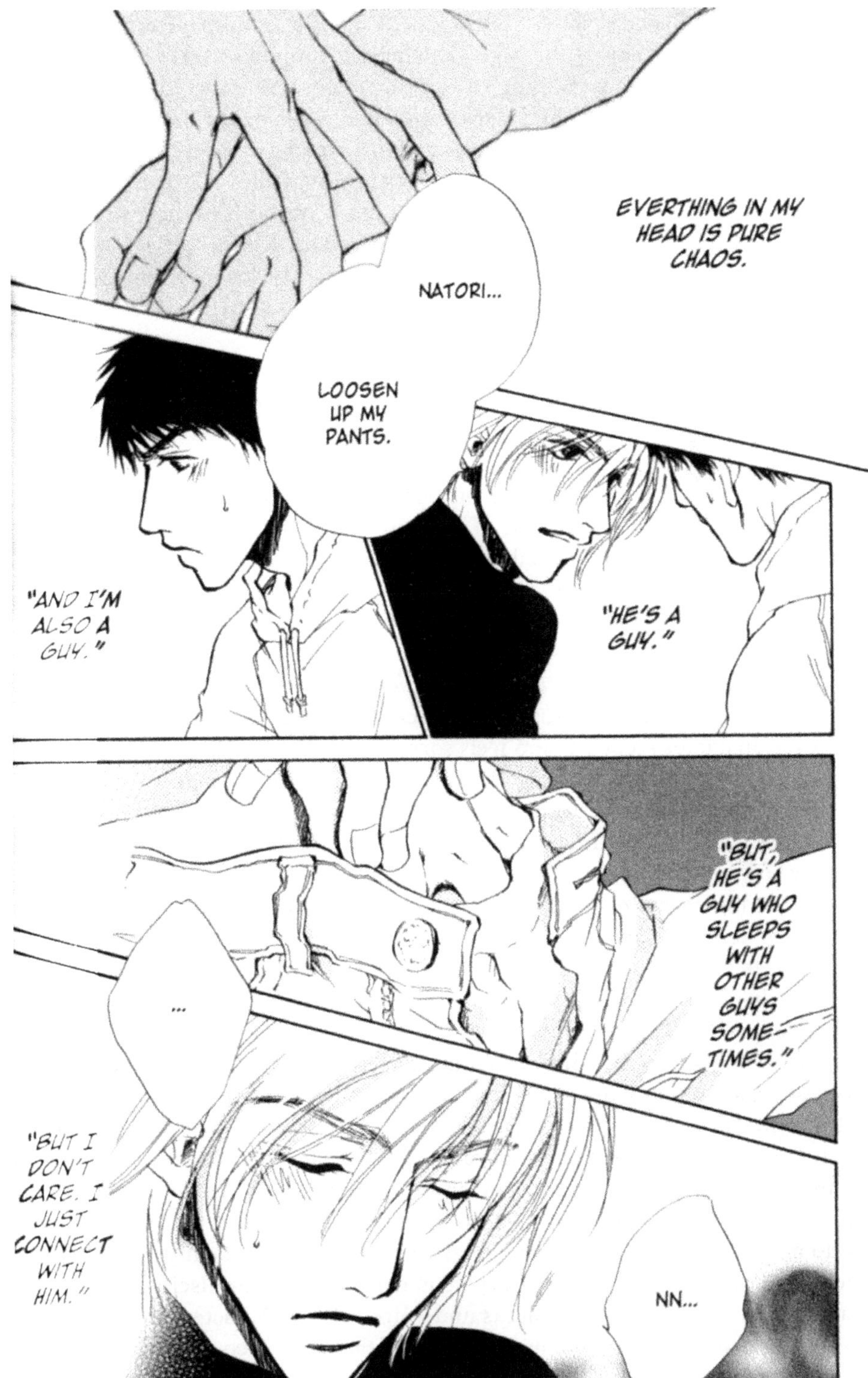

Figure 2. Natori ponders the implications of his actions in terms of his identity. Credit: Original Japanese version *Spell—Superu* © 2003 Hyouta Fujiyama. Originally published in Japan in 2003 by Frontier Works Inc. English translation © 2007 by DIGITAL MANGA, INC.

hand disappears into Kisugi's pants.[32] Like Figure 1, Figure 2 shows how this introspective moment is extended throughout the page, drawing attention to Natori's inner monologue, "He's a guy. And I'm also a guy. But, he's a guy who sleeps with other guys sometimes. But I don't care. I just connect with him." This monologue reveals that Natori has come to the conclusion that although they are both adolescent males and Kisugi sleeps with males (note, this behavior is not labeled homosexual), he loves him regardless. That is, Natori's love is not simply because Kisugi is a male (which would imply Natori is homosexual) or because Kisugi sleeps with males (which would imply Natori wants Kisugi to sleep with him and, again, that Natori is homosexual), but because of an unnamed "connection." In this round-about manner, homosexuality is disavowed through disengagement with sexuality as the character claims his love transcends (homo)sexuality.

Possession and lack of control—
Eerie Queerie! Volume 1

Mitsuo's spirit watches in horror as his body, possessed by the spirit of Kiyomi, suddenly confesses to Hasunuma in front of all their classmates. As everyone else does not know that Mitsuo's body is possessed and it is Kiyomi's spirit revealing her feelings, his classmates marvel at Mitsuo being gay.[33] One classmate even exclaims, "This is the first time I've ever seen a real gay guy." The humor of the scene is obviously based on the classmates' misunderstanding that Mitsuo is in control of himself and thus homosexual. In this case, homosexuality is *meant* to be disavowed, even while it is being parodied, due to Mitsuo's possession by a girl and his subsequent lack of control.

However, in a later scene Mitsuo feels sorry for Kiyomi and allows her to again possess his body so that she can have her first kiss with Hasunuma.[34] In this scene, Mitsuo willingly lets his body be used to kiss another adolescent male, which could be read as homosexual, but at the same time could be read as heterosexual because it is Kiyomi who would *really* be kissing Hasunuma. How can we read this situation? How do we determine the sexuality of the characters? This problematic is at the heart of the disavowal topos— what may seem homosexual can also be read in another way as heterosexual. The disavowal thus functions in two major ways: (1) hermeneutic ambiguation of identity and (2) exposure and parody of the heteronormative equation of identity.

While some scholars have argued that the disavowal (in addition to other BL topoi) is homophobic, I would rather draw attention to its performativity.[35] Eve Kosofsky Sedgwick argues, "Ignorance and opacity collude or compete with knowledge in mobilizing the flows of energy, desire, goods, meanings, persons."[36] Ignorance and knowledge both work to constitute what is to become material reality. In this vein, the disavowal is a performative act that prevents readers from knowing what the identity of the disavower *really* is; from claiming epistemological authority over the characters and the narrative. Because readers do not know for sure, they can fantasize and create their own truth. This ambiguity is facilitated by the absence of a third-person narration, the omniscient authorial voice. The reader is left with only the thoughts and voices of the characters to draw inferences from; even then, only one perspective—usually of the *uke*—is consistently followed. The hermeneutic ambiguity that the disavowal therefore creates enables multiple readings of any text by readers with multiple positions, motives, and desires. For example, while one could interpret the characters in *Spell* as homosexual, one could also believe that Natori, who indirectly disavows homosexuality, is heterosexual yet has sex with Kisugi because their love transcends sexuality and gender, as mentioned above. By not avowing and stead-fastly following a sexual definition of either homosexuality or heterosexuality, the charac-ters do not contradict either reading — their story can thus be read in multiple ways while potentially affirming all readings.

At the same time, the disavowal of homosexuality, premised through the other BL topoi on a homo/heterosexual binary, also renders explicit how the heteronormative equa-tion of intelligible gender identity is "institute[d] and maintain[ed through] relations of coherence and continuity among sex, gender, sexual practice, and desire."[37] Judith Butler argues that heteronormativity requires that identities that do not follow this equation, such as an affirmative (male) femininity, cannot exist.[38] However the disavowal renders this nar-row equation of intelligibility and its notion of fixed identity as absurd through parody. For example, in *Freefall Romance* (*Rakka sokudo*), Renji initially disavows homosexuality as he looks upon his drunken friend, Youichi, thinking, "He has sex appeal, and he's pretty good-looking. If only he was a girl, I would have done her by now. What am I thinking?"[39] He soon conveys his thoughts to Youichi, which results in the Youichi asking, "What [do] you mean erotic? I'm a 25-year-old guy. You don't swing that way, do you?" Renji replies, "No ... I don't, but," and trails off.[40] Renji then caresses Youichi's face slowly, sending Youichi running out the door wondering why Renji, who he knows is heterosexual, would do such a thing.[41] This scene not only reveals the heteronormative equation via Renji's logic of desire that follows from his identity as a male, but also parodies it by demonstrating its limitations. The disavower, Renji, says he is not homosexual because it does not make sense in the heteronormative equation — he is a male, and as a male he is attracted to females. However, if Renji is not homosexual — indeed if he is heterosexual — what does it mean that he desires Youichi, another male?

The queerness of BL is not so much due to the homoerotic images within the manga itself, but rather its problematization of what intelligible gender and sexual identity means. To disavow is to render one's self unstable and contested, fluid yet fixed in pinpoints of intelligibility. While to claim oneself as queer may be to say that one is something — whatever that might be — the disavower in BL claims nothing except to say "I am not homo-sexual, whatever my actions." Narratives of identity and behavior are pitted against each other, resulting in a subjectivity that rather than *is* something, only *could be* something. The heteronormative equation is exposed as not only inadequate, but also unreasonable, untenable, and absurd through the abject, unstable identity of the disavower within the equation's conceptual framework. The arbitrariness of the performance of identity is exposed.

The two functions of the disavowal complement each other in priming the BL narra-tive for what I will argue is the transnational appeal of BL — the revaluation of femininity. Because one cannot know identity with any epistemological certainty due to the ambigu-ous logic that structures how we should know, the instability of the heterosexual matrix is made known and can no longer be taken for uncontestable truth. Simultaneously, the het-eronormative equation that results in a fixed identity is exposed and parodied by the iden-tities that it cannot allow to exist, yet do, in BL. If identity is not fixed and the heterosexual matrix does not have to be taken for granted, then desire does not have to follow from gen-der or sex. That is, one can desire and/or be desired, regardless of gender or sex. Further-more, there is no reason to hold that the value-laden gender hierarchy posed by heteronormativity must be taken as valid. In this context, femininity can be reclaimed by the fe(male) readers of BL manga and revalued.

A Revaluation of Femininity

The significance of this reclamation and revaluation derives from the particular relationship that fe(male) readers are positioned to have with femininity. From the particular perspective of adolescent boys in BL, fe(male)s are presented with the same dilemma that the liminality of adolescence presents to adolescent females—the period will end and they will be transformed into adults.[42] For fe(male)s this entails positioning themselves as not only feminine, but also accepting the second-class accoutrements of femininity in patriarchy. In *Tales of Love*, Julia Kristeva argues that in secular patriarchal cultures women have become conflated with the maternal.[43] The maternal, in turn, is necessary for persons to abject to become subjects. Due to this conflation, women, femininity, and maternity are all abjected, which Kristeva argues accounts for the actual denigration of women and increased antifeminism.[44] This entails women facing the paradox of becoming a social subject through an internal abjection of themselves as women/feminine/maternal. As Butler has famously argued, gender is performative and its performance is imposed on us by heteronormativity.[45] By performing femininity then, fe(male)s construct their subjectivity as the abject gender, or rather, signify their own lack of subjectivity within the Symbolic.[46] To resolve this crisis of being aware yet unable to disavow their own (future) femininity as abject, I argue that fe(male)s can use BL as a space to affirm their (future) femininity as subjectivity. Not coincidentally, the character that performs the disavowal and provides the narrative viewpoint is usually the *uke*, the character constructed through the other BL topoi as the feminine presence.

It is through the *uke* as male femininity that fe(male)s can mitigate their relationship to femininity in light of its abjection. That is, femininity is re-performed and iterated anew under the guise of the abjectness of male femininity—an identity, like affirmative femininity, that is not meant to exist under heteronormative patriarchy. However, in BL the *uke*, unlike women, is both object (feminized by and relative to the *seme*) and subject (as man, or soon-to-be-man, in the Symbolic). He presents that "fragile border (borderline cases) where identities (subject/object, etc.) do not exist or only barely so—double, fuzzy, heterogeneous, animal, metamorphosed, altered, abject."[47] In this position, *uke* as subject can revalue femininity because he is the privileged benefactor of patriarchy as well as deconstruct its abjection by parodying this privilege through *uke* as object. That is, rather than being rendered unintelligible for being feminized, the *uke* as objectified by the *seme* is desired and valued because of his femininity. In effect, the *uke* naturalizes an affirmative femininity as being intelligible and desirable. For example, in *Spell*, Natori, while frustrated that Kisugi already has a boyfriend, exclaims, "if Kisugi wasn't gay or bi ... If he was with a girl, I probably wouldn't have these feelings anyway."[48] Natori (the *seme*) desires Kisugi (the *uke*) because Kisugi is being feminized by another male. If Kisugi were situated as the masculine subject vis-à-vis a woman, Natori would not feel the desire he feels. Natori desires rather than despises Kisugi exactly because he is abject due to his femininity.

This line of thought runs contrary to the heterosexual matrix, which posits male sexual penetration as a loss of masculinity and condemnation to femininity. In BL, anal sex undermines the sense of loss and abjection perpetuated through a heteronormative hierarchy of penetrator-penetrated by validating the beauty and pleasure of being penetrated and feminized. As Nagaike Kazumi observes, "*uke* characters are portrayed as enjoying sex as freely as *seme* characters do."[49] Similarly, Wood argues that while the "*seme-uke* dichotomy tends to reinforce notions of active/passive sex roles, it is important to emphasize that in general these comics do not *visually* infuse the role of *uke* with negative or disempowering connotations."[50] Even when the *uke* is raped by the *seme*, the demeaning and objectifying penetrative act is reconstructed as one of love — an affirmative and erotic sexual act (see the first topos above). This is not to dismiss the real-world horror and consequences of rape, but rather to co-opt and invert the patriarchal force that renders feminization a devaluating and destructive act. Thus, the compulsory nature of performative gender, whereby "acting out of line with heterosexual norms brings with it ostracism, punishment, and violence,"[51] is removed in BL in the *uke*'s affirmation of and through femininity. In this way, femininity is portrayed as constitutive of subjectivity rather than as a lack in the Symbolic.

The utility of the *uke* as male femininity is also supported by the ways in which his utility can fail. If he is perceived as too feminine — too much like a girl — his likeness can be perceived as uncanny and rejected. After all, the *uke* is meant to contain femininity *as a male*. Karen Nakamura and Matsuo Hisako, in their study of female masculinity in Takarazuka theater, argue that "for fantasy to work, it must provide something outside of the normal."[52] Analyzing how fans, in Kaja Silverman's terminology, "suture" themselves, they found that fantasy was disrupted if fans (both males and females) were asked to suture to characters whose performance made too explicit the sex-as-gender equation (e.g., "female-actors-playing-female-roles"). It is the "artifice of female masculinity" that allows men and women to suture themselves most effectively.[53] To construct an affirmative male femininity, not only must the *uke* be feminized, but he must also be maintained as male and thus present the artifice of male femininity.

This requirement in part explains the marginalization of female characters in BL. While McLelland argues "women protagonists are redundant because female subjectivity is already embodied in the 'male' characters,"[54] this may only be part of the picture. I would argue that females are also marginalized because their physical body and interaction with the male protagonists rearticulates too blatantly the problem of sex as gender and masculinity as privileged over femininity. That is, it reasserts the very heteronormative equations that the *uke* is meant to subvert.

By marginalizing females, the *uke* is reconfirmed as male through the physical and performative contrast females provide, while females' problematic presence is not emphasized. For example, in *Only the Ring Finger Knows*, Wataru (the *uke*) remarks that due to a rumor that his sister is dating the popular and beloved Kazuki, he has "become the enemy of the entire school's female population."[55] Ironically, the reader could have assumed that Wataru goes to an all-boy's school; the female population he references only make sporadic, peripheral appearances — often to move along the story between the two male protagonists or, as in this case, to confirm the *uke* as male through differentiation.

However, the importance of the male femininity of the *uke* does not necessarily mean that fe(male)s can only identify with the *uke* to mitigate their relationship to femininity. Shigematsu Setsu, in an insightful analysis of *ero* manga (erotic comics made for men) and their depiction of rape and *rorikon* (literally "Lolita Complex," referring to erotic/romantic narratives about older men and younger girls), discusses the identifications made while reading manga as

> oscillating and fluid, shifting and incomplete, moving among multiple contradictory (psychic) sites that are constituted differently depending on the specific history and experiences of the subject. Some of these possible sites might be expressed as: I desire to be the object of desire/I hate the object of desire/I conquer the object of desire/the object of desire wants me/the object of desire hates me.[56]

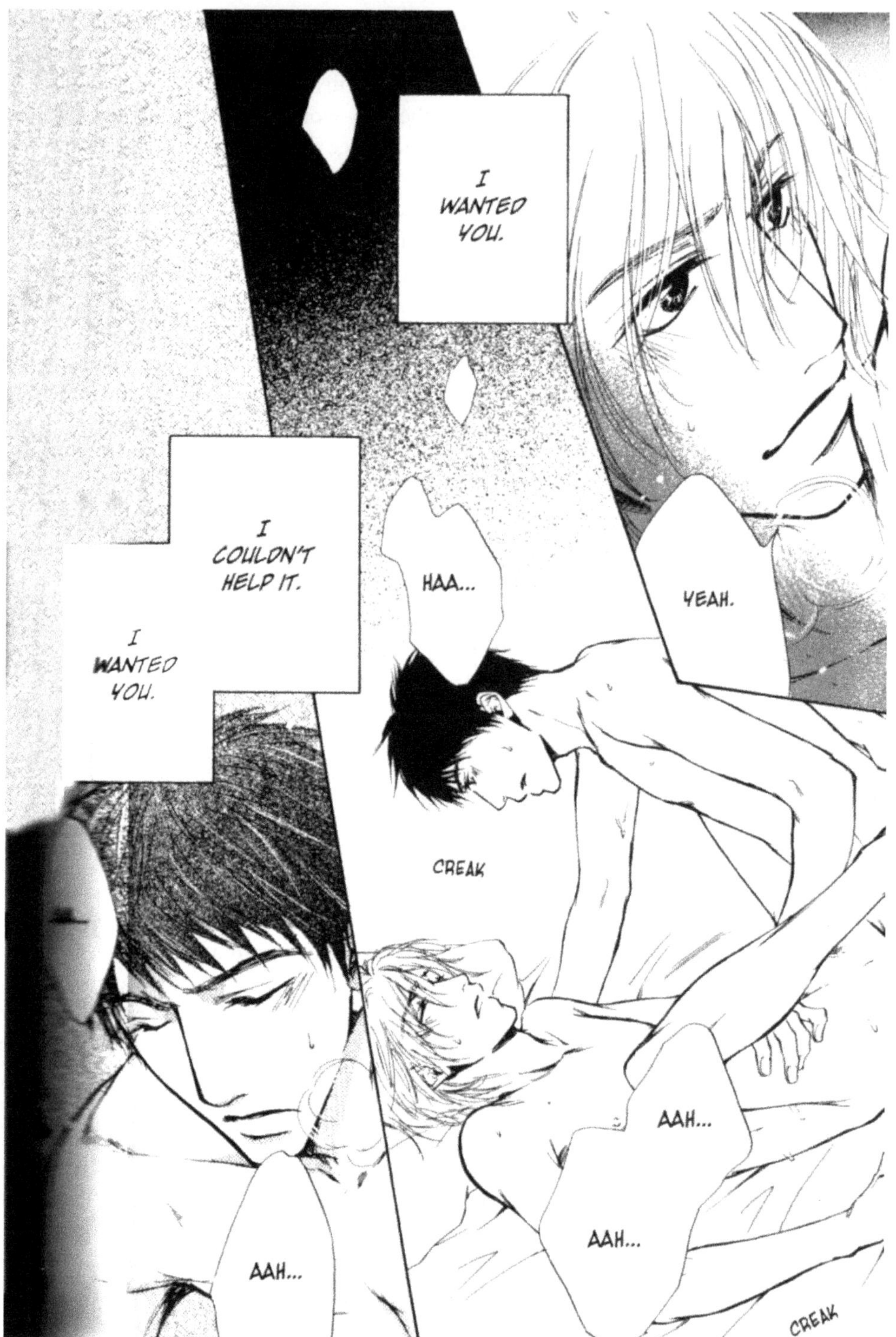

Figure 3. The sex scene between Natori (*seme*) and Kisugi (*uke*) shifts from the perspective of Natori, to a voyeur perspective, to the perspective of Kisugi. Credit: Original Japanese version *Spell—Superu* © 2003 Hyouta Fujiyama. Originally published in Japan in 2003 by Frontier Works Inc. English translation © 2007 by DIGITAL MANGA, INC.

BL does not require readers to identify with either *seme* or *uke*, but rather facilitates shifting through the multiple psychic sites through the layout of the manga.[57] As manga is usually divided into multiple frames, strips, and screens, as opposed to a continuous flow of images as in film, Shigematsu argues that the manga reader's perspective, and therefore identification, is similarly multiple and fractured.[58] That is, different frames position readers to see the narrative from different perspectives, regardless of which character provides the narrative viewpoint.[59] As Figure 3 shows, even as Natori narrates the story through his internal monologue, the page is divided into frames that shift the reader's perspective from that of Natori viewing Kisugi, to a voyeur perspective of both Natori and Kisugi, to that of Kisugi viewing Natori. Within this one scene, the reader is given freedom to identify with the *seme*, the *uke*, neither, or both. The degree to which fe(male) readers will identify with any one perspective, or psychic site, may be influenced more by their own personal history with patriarchy and less with an essentialized position of womanhood.

By traveling through various psychic sites, readers can revisit the gender dyad and its hierarchy of value and mitigate their own ambivalence toward femininity. Unlike Shigematsu, then, I believe that this act of reading — while not necessarily causing the reader to think certain thoughts or identify in any one way — greatly facilitates a catharsis through its multiple psychic stimuli. In *Eerie Queerie,* for example, there is a short story about the spirit of Kiyomi, a girl who hates her mortal life for its lack of subjectivity (e.g., always being unable to express herself, worrying about what others thought of her). By possessing Mitsuo (the *uke*'s) body, she visits several psychic sites, such as becoming the object of desire for Hasunuma (the *seme*), hating Mitsuo for being the object of desire, and being hated by Mitsuo who is the object of desire. In the end, Kiyomi is able to move on, having resolved her ambivalence toward her lack of subjectivity (i.e., femininity) and her past through a catharsis reached through the *uke* as intermediary.

BL and the Politics of Gender and Sexuality

Readers of BL, variously positioned within particular sociohistorical contexts, inevitably have multifaceted and contradictory interpretations of any individual text within the sub-genre. I do not assume that there is one way to read BL or to enjoy its textual pleasures. However, the topoi of BL, particularly the disavowal of homosexuality, structure the BL narrative in ways that distinguish reading BL manga from reading *ero* manga or reading another sub-genre of *shōjo* manga.

Through the particular imaginary of BL, fe(male)s can claim agency and femininity can be resignified through a variation on the discourse of femininity.[60] This is clear when BL manga, which construct an affirmative narrative of femininity, are seen as mass-produced and -consumed texts not only within Japan, but also transnationally. In this way BL manga exemplify "subversive repetition" writ large.[61] By reading BL, then, fe(male)s are embedded within a new discourse of gender and hailed in the new terms posed by the BL feminine.

However, this subversive discourse should not be treated as unproblematic. Although BL narratives enable the construction of an affirmative feminine subjectivity and space, they do so through the co-option of homosexuality removed from context and neutralized within heteronormative parameters. By limiting its engagement with homosexuality through the construction of an indeterminate epistemology, the constructed feminine space marginalizes the real-world limitations, anxieties, and dangers surrounding homosexuality. Whether the character is homosexual is usually not resolved through avowal, and so the text does not fully engage with the consequences if the character actually did avow. This ambiguity is productive for the sake of appealing to a multi-positioned audience as it accommodates a wide range of interpretation, truth production, and engagement. To produce this space, though, social norms — structural clues that would overdetermine the outcome — are evacuated. Thus, BL is not necessarily either pro-gay or homophobic. It is not necessarily anything outside of the interpretation by the reader.

The homosexual never fully materializes in BL even if the text is haunted by its specter. Rather, homosexuality remains more of an aesthetic than a position with personal and social consequences. Therefore, I would argue that the queerness of BL is not queer enough. That is, although BL, similar to queer theory, problematizes and deconstructs the homo/heterosexual binary in favor of more ambiguous sexual and gendered identities by mobilizing contradictory definitions of sexuality (i.e., sexual behavior versus claimed sexual identity), this is a means rather than an end. BL queers identity without the anti-homophobic political agenda that queerness usually entails. This leaves BL as both too queer, as it cannot unproblematically be declared heterosexist or homophobic due to the focus on love through homoeroticism, yet not queer enough, as it cannot unproblematically be declared pro-gay or anti-homophobic due to its treatment of homosexuality as an aesthetic without social consequences. Readers will resolve this paradox and how it relates to them through their own interpretations, but this resolution will not be reached primarily through an anti-homophobic agenda of the text. Of course, we need to also consider the purposes for which ambiguity is mobilized — not for sexual liberation, but for gender revaluation. Either goal is important, but we should be cautious about the achievement of one goal through the other, as this co-option is rarely innocent of the politics of power, particularly when considered within the webs of transnational capitalism. As an aesthetic to be consumed, the homosexual threatens to merely become a commoditized sign with no reference in social reality. As Rosemary Hennessy warns,

> the appropriation of gay cultural codes in the cosmopolitan revamping of gender displays the arbitrariness of bourgeois patriarchy's gender system and helps to reconfigure it in a more postmodern mode where the links between gender and sexuality are looser, where homosexuals are welcome, even constituting the vanguard, and where the appropriation of their parody of authentic sex and gender identities is quite compatible with the aestheticization of everyday life into postmodern lifestyles. In itself, of course, this limited assimilation of gays into mainstream middle-class culture does not disrupt postmodern patriarchy and its intersection with capitalism; indeed it is in some ways quite integral to it.[62]

Like the marketing of lesbian images analyzed by Danae Clark, gays in commodity culture are welcome as "consumer subjects but not as social subjects."[63] I am not saying that writers or readers of BL manga are unaware of, denying, or denigrating the existence of queer individuals in real life. What is troubling to me is not that writers or readers are homophobic, but that they could easily consume BL's queerness without necessarily being anti-homophobic.

Notes

1. Kannagi Satoru and Odagiri Hotaru, *Only the Ring Finger Knows* (Carson, CA: Digital Manga Publishing, 2004), book cover.
2. For my purposes, I will use the term "boys' love" or "BL" to refer to this sub-genre, whereby I rely on

the periodization of the sub-genre mapped by Mizoguchi Akiko. In this way, I focus my analysis on mainstream boys' love manga from 1991 to the present, rather than, for example, *bishōnen* (beautiful boy) manga of the 1970s. This is appropriate because the texts I analyze are licensed English translations available in North America of Japanese originals published after 1991. Mizoguchi Akiko, "Male-Male Romance by and for Women in Japan: A History and the Sub-Genres of *Yaoi* Fictions," *U.S.–Japan Women's Journal* 25 (2003): 49–75. For analyses of the *bishōnen* period of the 1970s, see Aoyama Tomoko, "Male Homosexuality as Treated by Japanese Women Writers," in *The Japanese Trajectory: Modernization and Beyond*, ed. Gavan McCormack and Yoshio Sugimoto (Cambridge: Cambridge University Press, 1988), 186–204; Suzuki Kazuko, "Pornography or Therapy? Japanese Girls Creating the Yaoi Phenomenon," in *Millennium Girls: Today's Girls Around the World*, ed. Sherrie Inness (London: Rowman & Littlefield Publishers, Inc., 1998), 243–267; Ōgi Fusami, "Gender Insubordination in Japanese Comics (*Manga*) for Girls," in *Illustrating Asia: Comics, Humor Magazines, and Picture Books*, ed. John Lent (Honolulu: University of Hawai'i Press, 2001), 171–186; and James Welker, "Beautiful, Borrowed, and Bent: 'Boys' Love' as Girls' Love in *Shôjo Manga*," *Signs* 31, no. 3 (2006): 841–870.

3. Dru Pagliassotti, "Boys' Love vs. Yaoi: An Essay on Terminology," http://ashenwings.com/marks/2008/07/17/boys-love-vs-yaoi-an-essay-on-terminology/.

4. Andrea Wood, "'Straight' Women, Queer Texts: Boy-Love Manga and the Rise of a Global Counterpublic," *Women's Studies Quarterly* 34, no. 1/2 (2006).

5. Veruska Sabucco, "Guided Fan Fiction: Western 'Readings' of Japanese Homosexual-Themed Texts," in *Mobile Cultures: New Media in Queer Asia (Console-ing Passions)*, ed. Chris Berry, Fran Martin, and Audrey Yue (Durham: Duke University Press, 2003).

6. Ibid.

7. Dru Pagliassotti, "GloBLisation and Hybridisation: Publishers' Strategies for Bringing Boys' Love to the United States," *Intersections: Gender and Sexuality in Asia and the Pacific* 21 (2009), http://intersections.anu.edu.au/issue21/pagliassotti.htm.

8. Mark McLelland, "No Climax, No Point, No Meaning? Japanese Women's Boy Love Sites on the Internet," *Journal of Communication Inquiry* 24, no. 3 (2000): 287; and Iwabuchi Koichi, *Recentering Globalization: Popular Culture and Japanese Transnationalism* (Durham, NC: Duke University Press, 2002), 27.

9. Iwabuchi, *Recentering Globalization*, 28.

10. Ibid., 15.

11. Ōgi Fusami, "Gender Insubordination in Japanese Comics (*Manga*) for Girls," in *Illustrating Asia: Comics, Humor Magazines, and Picture Books*, ed. John Lent (Honolulu: University of Hawai'i Press, 2001), 182.

12. Ibid., 171.

13. Dru Pagliassotti, "Reading boys' love in the West," *Participations* 5, no. 2 (2008), http://www.participations.org/Volume%205/Issue%202/5_02_pagliassotti.htm.

14. Ibid. The options for identifying sexuality in the two surveys included "bisexual," "gay," "lesbian," "other," "not interested in sex," "don't know," "prefer not to say," and "queer" (in the Italian-language survey only). By "non-heterosexually identified males and females," I am amalgamating the responses from both males and females to these categories.

15. Wood, "'Straight' Women, Queer Texts," 396. For examples of past studies, see Behr Maiko, "Undefining Gender in Shimizu Reiko's *Kaguyahime*," *U.S.–Japan Women's Journal* 25 (2003): 8–29; Mizoguchi, "Male-Male Romance by and for Women in Japan," 49–75; and Matthew Thorn, "Girls and Women Getting Out of Hand: The Pleasure and Politics of Japan's Amateur Comics Community," in *Fanning the Flames: Fans and Consumer Culture in Contemporary Japan*, ed. William Kelly (New York: State University of New York Press, 2004), 169–187.

16. Suzuki, "Pornography or Therapy," 244.

17. Wim Lunsing, "*Yaoi Ronsō*: Discussing Depictions of Male Homosexuality in Japanese Girls' Comics, Gay Comics and Gay Pornography," *Intersections: Gender, History and Culture in the Asian Context* 12 (January 2006), http://intersections.anu.edu.au/issue12/lunsing.html.

18. Thorn, "Girls and Women Getting Out of Hand," 180.

19. In this paper I use "queer" as an umbrella term for non-heterosexual sexualities. In contrast, when I use "homosexual" or "gay," I refer to a sexuality based on desire between people of the same sex; specifically, desire between two males.

20. Mizoguchi, "Male-Male Romance by and for Women in Japan," 66.

21. Ibid., 56.

22. Ibid.

23. Mizoguchi's analysis in "Male-Male Romance by and for Women in Japan" of topoi is based on her research on BL manga in Japan, which I found to be reproduced in my own research on officially translated BL manga in North America. I would like to emphasize that the texts I analyzed are translated Japanese texts

and therefore the topoi and the particular way they structure BL narratives may be specific to Japanese BL. The topoi, particularly the disavowal of homosexuality, may be less common in Original English Language (OEL)/Western BL.

24. Fujiyama Hyouta, *Spell* (Gardena, CA: Digital Manga Publishing, 2007), 179.

25. Mizoguchi, "Male-Male Romance by and for Women in Japan," 56.

26. Alexander Doty, *Making Things Perfectly Queer: Interpreting Mass Culture* (Minneapolis: University of Minnesota Press, 1993), 3.

27. By "performativity," I am referring to Judith Butler's notion of gender performativity whereby (gender) identity is constructed through discourse and acts rather than being taken for granted as a pre-existing condition. In this way I want to emphasize how the disavowal of homosexuality constructs and mobilizes gender and sexuality within a BL manga in particular ways for the readers of the manga. Gender and sexuality within BL manga, in my view, is thus more fluid, less given, and open for revaluation.

28. Shiozu Shuri, *Eerie Queerie! Volume 1* (Los Angeles: TOKYOPOP Inc, 2004), 52.

29. Ibid.

30. Kannagi and Odagiri, *Only the Ring Finger Knows*, 63.

31. Ibid., 130.

32. Fujiyama, *Spell*, 88.

33. Shiozu, *Eerie Queerie! Volume 1*, 12.

34. Ibid., 37.

35. See Mizoguchi Akiko, "Homophobic Homos, Rapes of Love, and Queer Lesbians: Yaoi as a Conflicting Site of Homo/Hetero-Sexual Female Sexual Fantasy" (paper presented at the Association for Asian Studies Annual Meeting, New York, USA, March 27–30, 2003), http://www.aasianst.org/absts/2003abst/Japan/sessions.htm. Interestingly, Lunsing in *"Yaoi Ronsō"* notes that assuming the disavowal is homophobic is problematic because it is also a topos used in gay texts, such as Japanese gay manga (that is, manga made for gay men by gay men) and gay pornography.

36. Eve Kosofsky Sedgwick, *Epistemology of the Closet* (Berkeley: University of California Press, 2008 [1990]), 4.

37. Judith Butler, *Gender Trouble: Feminism and the Subversion of Identity* (New York: Routledge Classics, 2006 [1990]), 23. Homo/heterosexual binary refers to Rosemary Hennessy's distinction between queer and lesbian/gay, whereby lesbian/gay, as opposed to queer, "assumes a polarized division between hetero- and homo-sexuality and signals discrete and asymmetrically gendered identities." "Queer Visibility in Commodity Culture," *Cultural Critique* 29 (Winter 1994–95): 34. I would argue that BL manga tend to assume and reify such a binarized definition of sexuality through the heteronormative subtext structured by the BL topoi. For example, although bisexuality is a sexual identity sometimes claimed by or for a character, it is not usually represented visually or pursued as a storyline within BL narratives due to the sub-genre's exclusive focus on male-male relationships. In *Spell*, Kisugi is named as a bisexual by one of his friends, but he is only shown with a boyfriend and never portrayed as involved with a female in the text.

38. Butler, *Gender Trouble*, 24.

39. Fujiyama Hyouta, *Freefall Romance* (Gardena, CA: Digital Manga Publishing, 2007), 11–12.

40. Ibid., 17.

41. Ibid., 22.

42. Hiromi Tsuchiya Dollase, "Early Twentieth Century Japanese Girls' Magazine Stories: Examining *Shōjo* Voice in *Hanamonogatari* (Flower Tales)," *Journal of Popular Culture* 36, no. 4 (2003): 737.

43. Julia Kristeva, *Tales of Love*, trans. Leon Roudiez. New York: Columbia University Press, 1987.

44. Ibid., 374.

45. Butler, *Gender Trouble*, 198.

46. Ibid., 38. The Symbolic, as conceptualized by Jacques Lacan, is one of the three structures of the psyche. One enters the Symbolic (and thus interaction with others) through language and the acceptance of the rules and laws of society (i.e., the Name-of-the-Father). How one becomes a subject vis-à-vis others therefore is intimately tied with the rules and laws of (patriarchal) society.

47. Julia Kristeva, *Powers of Horror: An Essay on Abjection*, trans. Leon Roudiez (New York: Columbia University Press, 1982), 207.

48. Fujiyama, *Spell*, 66.

49. Nagaike Kazumi, "Perverse Sexualities, Perversive Desires: Representations of Female Fantasies and *Yaoi Manga* as Pornography Directed at Women," *U.S.–Japan Women's Journal* 25 (2003): 85.

50. Wood, "'Straight' Women, Queer Texts," 403.

51. Judith Butler, "Imitation and Gender Insubordination," in *Queer Cultures*, ed. Deborah Carlin and Jennifer DiGrazia (Upper Saddle River, NJ: Pearson/Prentice Hall, 2003), 363.

52. Karen Nakamura and Matsuo Hisako, "Female Masculinity and Fantasy Spaces: Transcending Gen-

ders in the Takarazuka Theatre and Japanese Popular Culture," in *Men and Masculinities in Contemporary Japan: Dislocating the Salaryman Doxa,* ed. James Roberson and Suzuki Nobue (New York: RoutledgeCurzon, 2003), 66. Takarazuka refers to the popular Japanese all-female theater troupe, Takarazuka Revue.

53. Nakamura and Matsuo, "Female Masculinity and Fantasy Spaces," 68.

54. Mark McLelland, "The Love Between 'Beautiful Boys' in Japanese Women's Comics," *Journal of Gender Studies* 9, no. 1 (2000): 22.

55. Kannagi and Odagiri, *Only the Ring Finger Knows,* 118.

56. Setsu Shigematsu, "Dimensions of Desire: Sex, Fantasy, and Fetish in Japanese Comics," in *Themes and Issues in Asian Cartooning: Cute, Cheap, Mad, and Sexy,* ed. J.A. Lent (Bowling Green, OH: Popular Press, 1999), 136.

57. Ibid., 144.

58. Ibid.

59. Ibid.

60. Butler, *Gender Trouble,* 198.

61. Ibid., 198–199.

62. Hennessy, "Queer Visibility in Commodity Culture," 62–63.

63. Ibid., 32.

Bibliography

Aoyama, Tomoko. "Male Homosexuality as Treated by Japanese Women Writers." In *The Japanese Trajectory: Modernization and Beyond,* edited by Gavan McCormack and Yoshio Sugimoto, 186–204. Cambridge: Cambridge University Press, 1988.

Behr, Maiko. "Undefining Gender in Shimizu Reiko's *Kaguyahime.*" *U.S.–Japan Women's Journal* 25 (2003): 8–29.

Butler, Judith. *Gender Trouble: Feminism and the Subversion of Identity.* New York: Routledge Classics, 2006 [1990].

_____. "Imitation and Gender Insubordination." In *Queer Cultures,* edited by Deborah Carlin and Jennifer DiGrazia, 354–371. Upper Saddle River, NJ: Pearson/Prentice Hall, 2003.

Dollase, Hiromi Tsuchiya. "Early Twentieth Century Japanese Girls' Magazine Stories: Examining *Shōjo* Voice in *Hanamonogatari* (Flower Tales)." *Journal of Popular Culture* 36, no. 4 (2003): 724–755.

Doty, Alexander. *Making Things Perfectly Queer: Interpreting Mass Culture.* Minneapolis: University of Minnesota Press, 1993.

Fujiyama, Hyouta. *Freefall Romance.* Gardena, CA: Digital Manga Publishing, 2007a.

_____. *Spell.* Gardena, CA: Digital Manga Publishing, 2007b.

Hennessy, Rosemary. "Queer Visibility in Commodity Culture." *Cultural Critique* 29 (Winter 1994–95): 31–76.

Iwabuchi, Koichi. *Recentering Globalization: Popular Culture and Japanese Transnationalism.* Durham, NC: Duke University Press, 2002.

Kannagi, Satoru, and Hotaru Odagiri. *Only the Ring Finger Knows.* Carson, CA: Digital Manga Publishing, 2004.

Kristeva, Julia. *Powers of Horror: An Essay on Abjection.* Translated by Leon Roudiez. New York: Columbia University Press, 1982.

_____. *Tales of Love.* Translated by Leon Roudiez. New York: Columbia University Press, 1987.

Lunsing. Wim. "Yaoi Ronsō: Discussing Depictions of Male Homosexuality in Japanese Girls' Comics, Gay Comics and Gay Pornography." *Intersections: Gender, History and Culture in the Asian Context* 12 (January 2006), http://intersections.anu.edu.au/issue12/lunsing.html (accessed Oct. 20, 2008).

McLelland, Mark. "The Love Between 'Beautiful Boys' in Japanese Women's Comics." *Journal of Gender Studies* 9, no. 1 (2000a): 13–25.

_____. "No Climax, No Point, No Meaning? Japanese Women's Boy Love Sites on the Internet." *Journal of Communication Inquiry* 24, no. 3 (2000b): 274–291.

Mizoguchi, Akiko. "Homophobic Homos, Rapes of Love, and Queer Lesbians: Yaoi as a Conflicting Site of Homo/ Hetero-Sexual Female Sexual Fantasy." Paper presented at the Association for Asian Studies Annual Meeting, New York, USA, March 27–30, 2003a, http://www.aasianst.org/absts/2003abst/Japan/sessions.htm (accessed Sept. 13, 2008).

_____. "Male-Male Romance by and for Women in Japan: A History and the Sub-genres of *Yaoi* Fictions." *U.S.–Japan Women's Journal* 25 (2003b): 49–75.

Nagaike, Kazumi. "Perverse Sexualities, Perversive Desires: Representations of Female Fantasies and *Yaoi Manga* as Pornography Directed at Women." *U.S.–Japan Women's Journal* 25 (2003): 76–103.

Nakamura, Karen, and Hisako Matsuo. "Female Masculinity and Fantasy Spaces: Transcending Genders in the Takarazuka Theatre and Japanese Popular Culture." In *Men and Masculinities in Contemporary Japan: Dislocating the Salaryman Doxa,* edited by James Roberson and Nobue Suzuki, 59–76. New York: RoutledgeCurzon, 2003.

Ōgi, Fusami. "Gender Insubordination in Japanese Comics (*Manga*) for Girls." In *Illustrating Asia: Comics, Humor Magazines, and Picture Books,* edited by John Lent, 171–186. Honolulu: University of Hawai'i Press, 2001.

Pagliassotti, Dru. "Boys' Love vs. Yaoi: An Essay on Terminology." http://ashenwings.com/marks/2008/07/17/boys-love-vs-yaoi-an-essay-on-terminology/ (accessed Sept. 13, 2008). 2008a

_____. "Reading boys' love in the West." *Participations* 5, no. 2 (2008b), http://www.participations.org/Volume%205/Issue%202/5_02_pagliassotti.htm (accessed March 8, 2009).

_____. "GloBLisation and Hybridisation: Publishers' Strategies for Bringing Boys' Love to the United States." *Intersections: Gender and Sexuality in Asia and the Pacific* 21 (2009), http://intersections.anu.edu.au/issue21/pagliassotti.htm (accessed Feb. 9, 2009).

Sabucco, Veruska. "Guided Fan Fiction: Western 'Readings' of Japanese Homosexual-Themed Texts." In *Mobile Cultures: New Media in Queer Asia (Console-ing Passions),* edited by Chris Berry, Fran Martin, and Audrey Yue, 70–86. Durham, NC: Duke University Press, 2003.

Sedgwick, Eve Kosofsky. *Epistemology of the Closet.* Berkeley: University of California Press, 2008 [1990].

Shigematsu, Setsu. "Dimensions of Desire: Sex, Fantasy, and Fetish in Japanese Comics." In *Themes and Issues in Asian Cartooning: Cute, Cheap, Mad, and Sexy,* edited by J.A. Lent, 127–164. Bowling Green, OH: Popular Press, 1999.

Shiozu, Shuri. *Eerie Queerie! Volume 1.* Los Angeles: TOKYOPOP Inc, 2004a.

_____. *Eerie Queerie! Volume 3.* Los Angeles: TOKYOPOP Inc, 2004b.

Suzuki, Kazuko. "Pornography or Therapy? Japanese Girls Creating the Yaoi Phenomenon." In *Millennium Girls: Today's Girls Around the World,* edited by Sherrie Inness, 243–267. London: Rowman & Littlefield Publishers, Inc., 1998.

Thorn, Matthew. "Girls and Women Getting Out of Hand: The Pleasure and Politics of Japan's Amateur Comics Community." In *Fanning the Flames: Fans and Consumer Culture in Contemporary Japan,* edited by William Kelly, 169–187. New York: State University of New York Press, 2004.

Welker, James. "Beautiful, Borrowed, and Bent: 'Boys' Love' as Girls' Love in *Shôjo Manga*." *Signs* 31, no. 3 (2006): 841–870.

Wood, Andrea. "'Straight' Women, Queer Texts: Boy-Love Manga and the Rise of a Global Counterpublic." *Women's Studies Quarterly* 34, no. 1/2 (2006): 394–414.

10

Boys in Love in Boys' Love

Discourses West/East and the
Abject in Subject Formation

MARK MCHARRY

A work many consider foundational to boys' love is Takemiya Keiko's multi-volume *Kaze to ki no uta* (Song of Wind and Trees; 1976). It was a best seller on publication and remains in print. Takemiya begins her story in a Catholic boarding school in Provence, southern France, in 1880. The main character is Gilbert Cocteau, a thirteen-year-old student unable to befriend anyone and the target of almost constant ridicule.

Her tale was inspired by a movie made of Roger Peyrefitte's novel *Les Amitiés particulières* (Special Friendships; 1944), to which she and Masuyama Norie invited their flatmate Hagio Moto.[1] Peyrefitte tells of two schoolmates, Georges, age fourteen, and Alexandre, twelve, who fall in love. Their Jesuit school, in the neighboring Languedoc region, undoes their love by coercing Georges, who had initiated the relationship, into renouncing Alexandre. Peyrefitte gradually deepens their awareness, and that of the reader, of the lethality of the forces surrounding them. He convinces the reader to accept Alexandre's decision to use the little power he has, that over his own life, to end it. The genius of Peyrefitte's novel as he builds to this inevitability is to make the reader complicit in the erasure of a young life.[2]

In *Kaze to ki no uta*, Gilbert's anguish shocks from the outset. An alarm clock's ring snaps him awake from an afternoon tryst with an upperclassman. Gilbert rebuffs the boy's attempt at prolonging their encounter, hurrying off only to be intercepted by the school's headmaster, who takes him to his office and has sex with him on the man's desk. Gilbert is there, languidly posing against a window, not yet fully dressed, when a new pupil arrives, his soon-to-be roommate, Serge, also thirteen.

Takemiya depicts Gilbert as able to relate to others only through sex. He either prostitutes himself to or demands sex from students and faculty, or he is coerced into sex, which can involve non-consensual bondage and sadism, or into non-sexual acts that are degrading and/or dangerous—a vulnerability he seems to encourage, insisting early on in the story that resistance is "pathetic," even though he does resist again and again.[3] He rejects or ignores a few people's attempts—notably those of Serge—to become close.

Judith Butler has characterized gender as performative, "produc[ing] on the skin, through the gesture, the move, the gait (that array of corporeal theatrics understood as gender presentation), the illusion of an inner depth" (2004, 134). Takemiya expresses Gilbert's vulnerability in the most direct way possible, on his skin, in images of him naked or in partial states of dress. She does so in words, too, as in a student's observation to Carl, a dormitory master, that "The only way to ... persuade him is through his skin."[4]

To be the object of a forced erotic act as Gilbert so often is traduces the ability to act on desire. His libidinal economy is one of ceaseless negotiation, resistance, and submission,

177

a metaleptic displacement of desire. It is a state sometimes reduced in English-language commentary to "promiscuity," meaning casual or indiscriminate sexual behavior.[5] Yet Gilbert's anguish is far from casual.

"Abject" in popular use means "one cast off ... an outcast; a degraded person,"[6] which Gilbert is. But that is a partial description. In psychoanalytic thought derived from Freud and Lacan and elaborated by Julia Kristeva, Elizabeth Grosz and others, the abject state is implicated in the formation of subject. In Kristevan terms Gilbert's rejection of others is a recognition of "the impossible [that] constitutes [his] very *being*" (Kristeva 1982, 4). It is a state where laughter masks "a hatred that smiles, a passion that uses the body for barter instead of inflaming it" (8, 4). It is a "violence of mourning" brought about by what "disturbs identity, system, order. What does not respect borders, positions, rules" (15, 4). Brought about above all by *jouissance*[7]:

> Jouissance alone causes the abject to exist as such. One does not know it, one does not desire it, one joys in it [*on en jouit*]. Violently and painfully. A passion. And, as in jouissance where the object of desire, known as the object *a* [in Lacan's terminology], bursts with the shattered mirror where the ego gives up its image in order to contemplate itself in the Other, there is nothing either objective or objectal to the abject [9].

Gilbert has suffered a great loss. Takemiya makes its cost clear, for example, as when a younger Gilbert submits to a man's rape of him. Gilbert's strangulated *"oui, oui"* is written in Western characters, clarion amid the Japanese, a signal of the weight of the act (vol. 1, 266).

The most urgent representations of human desire and loss are in terms of sex and death. Takemiya's depiction of Gilbert's so-called promiscuity is a masterful way of showing the extent of his calamity. Emphasizing the undoing of his corporeality via drawings of his body is a perfect visual expression of the undoing of his mental state.

This was a reason that *Kaze* was controversial on its publication. Uli Meyer in this volume quotes Matthew Thorn: "There were nine years between original conception and approval for publication, because [Takemiya] refused to remove or fudge the sexual aspect." Beyond that, the images of Gilbert's erotic actions with other males may be the first such widely circulated in Japan since the sexually explicit prints of the Edo period (1603–1868 CE).

Kaze to ki no uta and other popular *shōjo* manga gave birth to discourses that stand in uneasy contrast to the prevailing discourses in Japan about sex, which were imported from the West during the Meiji period (1868–1912 CE), in the wake of treaties imposed by the United States. These discourses established normative categories of gender that replaced *nanshoku*, and *joshoku* (male love of females) with the dyad of *dōseiai* (same-sex love) and *iseai* (cross-sex love) (Pflugfelder 1999, 251–52).

The modern discourses in Japan and the West classified male-male erotic activity as deviant — and still do if it is age discrepant, is among young adolescents or if one of the partners exhibits insufficiently masculine qualities. They consider sexually explicit illustrations of any kind as potentially harmful, especially if they are of minors. Yet boys' love *mangaka* may employ all of these themes in a widely popular regime of scopic pleasure for female readers.

Contemporary boys' love discourses owe the eroticism of *bishōnen* (beautiful boys), an erotic object of the adult male gaze for more than a millennium, to *nanshoku* (male-male love, most often between an adult and an adolescent). Boys' love sometimes includes another aspect of historical Japanese practice: *kōshoku*, the Edo-period notion of erotic love in a context of playfulness, pleasure, and curiosity.[8] Like *nanshoku*, *kōshoku* was a *dō* (way) and was to be cultivated as an ideal for a *tsūjin* (connoisseur) pursuing it. *Kōshoku* was present in much of Edo period *gesaku* (parodic playful writing). The word was immortalized in the titles of a series of novels by the writer Ihara Saikaku and in the work and life of *ukiyo* (floating world) notables such as Santō Kyōden, Shikitei Sanba, Ōta Nanpo, and Hiraga Gennai.[9]

In Meiji, *kōshoku* became re-defined as "lustful." Takayuki Yokota-Murakami observed that "the new paradigm stigmatized active sexuality. Sexual lust was now to be distinguished from chaste love and, therefore, to be recognized" (1998, 95). Recognized, that is, as a disciplinary category.

Aspects of *kōshoku* as positive are frequently present in contemporary boys' love manga. One example is Minami Kazuka's *Tonari no heya no paranoia* (*My Paranoid Next Door Neighbor*; 2007) (fig. 1). Her story is about a present-day high-school student, Yukito, unhappy that a friend whom he had not seen since the end of middle school was coming to stay at his house. Minami uses their encounters to show Yukito learning that physical pleasure may lead to an emotional bond. This is the reverse of contemporary Western ideology, which holds that physically expressed love should follow emotional love. To accomplish her end Minami must emphasize eroticism: Yukito's body is an erotic object almost every time he's seen.[10] As a reviewer for the trade magazine *Publishers Weekly* commented when the manga was translated into English for sale in the U.S., "every aspect of life in this story is permeated with sex."[11]

That is a problem for boys' love in the West. Laws in the U.S., Canada, and Australia have put those who read boys' love manga at risk of imprisonment.[12] These have taken effect amid "an explosion of cultural concern," as Steven Angelides put it, over child sexual abuse worldwide (quoted in McLelland 2005, 2).

Child sex abuse discourses are a recognition of the continuing exploitation of powerless individuals and a determination to use a supremely powerful means— the state — to protect them. On the other hand, boys' love discourses are independent of the state, being "an exploration of issues of self-identity and sexual expression outside of state-sanctioned monogamous, heterosexual and 'family friendly' bounds," writes Mark McLelland (2005, 27).[13]

Peyrefitte's *Les Amitiés particulières* won the Prix Renaudot and catapulted him to literary fame. He wrote it in what had been "one of the most liberal milieux on earth" for its time (Sheridan 1999, 376). Contributing to this was an age-discrepant homoerotic discourse in French literature in which many writers and artists participated.[14] One of the most influential novelists of the twentieth century was Nobel laureate André Gide. He was, according to biographer Alan Sheridan, the first open homosexual in the West to publish the first serious study of homosexuality, *Corydon* (1924). It is a justification not of malemale eroticism in general but of adult-adolescent relationships, or pederasty, a word then used in France and some other Western cultures as an equivalent for age-discrepant homosexuality.[15] Gide considered it the most important of his books. He also praised Peyrefitte's *Les Amitiés* on its publication.

These individuals were controversial for their lives as well as their works. Gide's accounts of his life, including what he described as his frequent "prowling" [*roder*] for young adolescents, were published after his death.[16] Peyrefitte's came during his lifetime. His *Notre Amour* (Our Love; 1967) describes a life-long relationship he and a twelve-year-old, Alain-Philippe Malagnac d'Argens de Villèle, began in 1964.

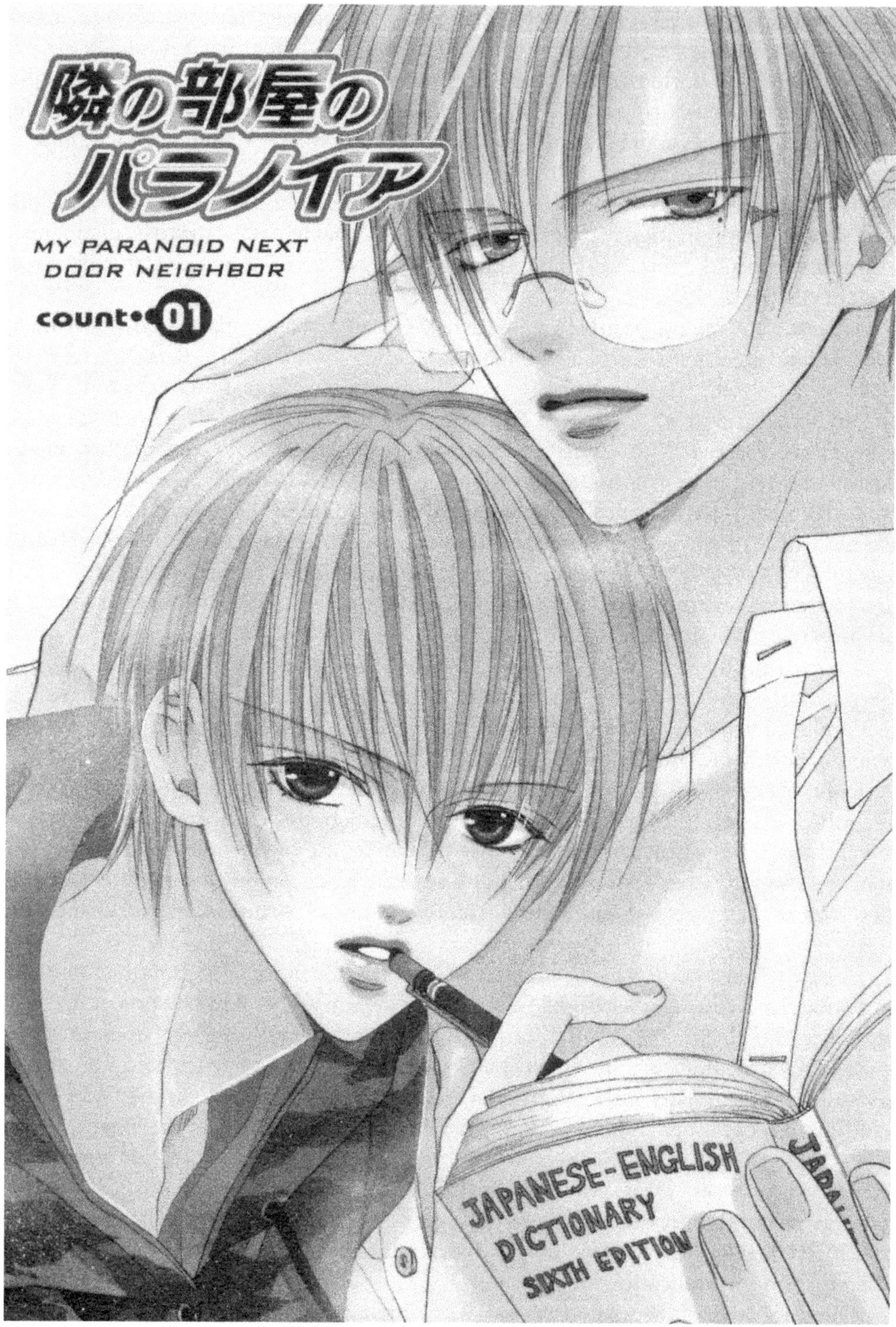

Figure 1. Minami Kazuka, *Tonari no heya no paranoia.* Yukito (left) and his friend Hokuto at the story's start. MY PARANOID NEXT DOOR NEIGHBOR — Tonari No Heya No Paranoia © 2003, 2004 by Kazuka Minami. All rights reserved. Image used under permission granted by Digital Manga, Inc.

These works contributed to this discourse, which has continued, albeit greatly attenuated, into the twenty-first century.[17] It is one of many Western post–Enlightenment discourses about sex identified by Michel Foucault. He characterizes them as multiple, increasing (1978, 30), demanding examination and seeking causation (59), "an entire glittering sexual array" to produce truth at "a nearly fabulous price" (72). They resulted in an explosion in the number of perversions to be controlled as individuals' sexual practices were identified and catalogued as imagined types, one being the homosexual, which has been elaborated to such an extent as to become a "species."[18] Confession became key to transformation of sex into discourse and to unlocking truth (61); it could exonerate, redeem, and purify (62). Truth and sex became institutionalized and separated, no longer linked by transmission from one body to another as they were in Ancient Greece (61) and are in the French age-discrepant and Japanese boys' love discourses.

The French age-discrepant discourse as seen in *Les Amitiés* fits Foucault's model. Peyrefitte describes the school's incessant quest to uncover the "truth" of Alexandre's and Georges's relationship, coercing them into the Catholic sacrament of confession, placing them under almost constant surveillance, examining their letters, threats of ruination via expulsion and exposure, and attempts by one of the priests to seduce the boys for himself. All this so their friendship could be identified as homosexual and the Church's hold over their bodies reified.

In Edo period Japan, *nanshoku* practitioners were not a Foucauldian type to be categorized so as to subject them to the state's regulation of sexual expression but could be any male engaging in a kind of play. The hundreds of thousands of women who bought and sold boys' love *dōjinshi* at Tokyo's Comic Market in 2009 are playing, too; some might call themselves or be called in the mainstream news media "*otaku*" or "*fujoshi*" (rotten women) but they are not a species.

Child abuse, including sexual abuse, is a major plot element in *Kaze to ki no uta* (as well as in Hagio's *Tōma no shinzō*). The way Takemiya approaches this is little like the way in which it is managed by discourses in the West, whereby a story such as *Les Amitiés* would attempt to deny or negate it. In *Kaze* it's as if these discourses do not exist. Gilbert does not confess to anything and he is not (consciously) seeking exoneration or redemption.

Foucault's notion of subjectivity is that it is "an effect of power" (Mills 2004, 30) and is exercised on the body: "power relations can materially penetrate the body in depth, without depending even on the mediation of the subject's own representations" (Foucault 1980, 186), power "wrapp[ing] the sexual body in its embrace" (Foucault 1978, 44).

Far from being embraced by power, in frame after frame we see Gilbert resisting attempts to examine his physical or mental state, running away from (sometimes toward) centers of power (almost always people, not institutions), often outdoors, many times in the woods. Gilbert is penetrated physically by more powerful individuals but his spirit eludes penetration. It is like the wind which accompanies him, that in fact may be him, a free and constantly shifting presence. In Japan wind may be divine[19]; in some ways Gilbert is *kami* as well as human.[20] Serge reminisces about the boy he came to love:

> You were the wind whistling through my branches.
> Can you hear the rustling song of the wind and trees? [Vol. 1, 57].

Unlike Georges and Alexandre, who are victimized, Gilbert's abjectness makes him subversive, a challenge to the male hierarchy of the school as he pulls its members into having sex with him.

In a pivotal scene near the end of the first volume, Gilbert introduces Serge to homoeroticism. At hearing Serge's outraged incredulousness that Gilbert could barter his body, he cringes but says, "Yes. I like it.... Do you know what I mean by that? ... Two men can be joined physically.... That pleasure is impossible to put into words, Serge." Kneeling over him, Gilbert then initiates a kiss, which a stunned Serge reciprocates (Vol. 1, 313).

The point of view here and throughout most of *Kaze* is Gilbert's. In boys' love the point of view is often the person with nominally less power, the younger partner, or *uke*, rather than the older partner,[21] unlike in much of the French age-discrepant male-male erotic discourse.

The boundaries in boys' love, among its characters as well as the frame that surrounds its discursive field, tend to be approached in something other than a straight line of temporal progression. Elizabeth Grosz writes that "The boundary between ... self and other ... must not be defined as a limit to be transgressed so much as a boundary to be traversed" (1995, 131). "Traverse" is a word which admits of an oblique approach, a playing at the limits, and it carries a temporal resonance.

Many *uke* play with the boundaries of conventional masculinity and femininity, rewriting submission as power and power as submission. Boundaries are a product of passage: "[I]t is movement that defines and constitutes boundaries" (Grosz 1995, 131). Movement is also part of "queer," which Eve Kosofsky Sedgwick defined as "a continuing moment, movement, motive — recurring, eddying, *troublant*" (1993, xii). In boys' love, boundary transgression is not necessarily one binary crossing but continued crossings back and forth, or queer divagations along boundaries, between subject and object, and hetero and homo, a consistent undercutting of hetero- and homonormativity.

It is very often the *uke* who initiates passage through or along boundaries, as Gilbert does with his kiss, his stab of shame giving way to affirmation leading to action. The *uke* plays with time as well as with space. In Higuri Yū's widely read manga *Gakuen Heaven* (Academy Heaven; 2006) the boarding school student Keita stops time at a critical moment. Just after admitting to himself his attraction to the upperclassman Niwa, Keita takes hold of Niwa and gazes at him. For the first time in the manga, there is only silence. Before this Higuri drew dialogue, thoughts, and/or sound effects on each of *Gakuen Heaven's* pages. Keita's action halts the rhythm of the sequential images. Time itself seems to stop as we look at him and Niwa looking at one another.

There may be no better way to show the force underlying Keita's and Niwa's emotions than to stop or defeat time. No better way to thrust readers into the depths of the imagined emotions, as if their emotions were the only thing able to be experienced, as if ontological time had collapsed and space expanded to make their bonding the only thing in the universe.

Queer temporal-spatial divagations go against the grain of statist ideologies, which, writes Jonathan Boyarin, employ "a particularly potent manipulation of the dimensionalities space and time." One such is states using history as a way to create rhetorically fixed national identities, excluding some individuals and helping legitimate the state's monopoly on control (Boyarin 1994, 15–16). States do this in part by mapping history onto territory. Accordingly, the *uke*'s movement along and across boundaries and his stopping or slowing time represent a profound expression of power against dominant notions of telos. His actions are in part a refusal of an identitarian process described by Lee Edelman: "Politics is a name for ... desire['s] ... teleological determination (2004, 9). [It] names the struggle to effect a fantasmatic order of reality in which the subject's alienation would vanish into the seamlessness of identity" (8).

One purpose of border crossing by the *uke* may be to acquire subjectivity. Rather than an identity for the ends of the state, the boys in boys' love seek an autonomy in the ability to love whom they wish. The western discourses of age-discrepant relationships, protection of sexually abused children, and some of the functions of power relations on subjectivity described by Foucault seem to be irrelevant to Gilbert and may be so to much of contemporary boys' love in Japan and the West. Takemiya uses the abuse Gilbert suffers more to imperil his subjectivity than to circumscribe his field of action.

In theory elaborated about the body, Elizabeth Grosz writes that the developing subject (ego) must be interlocked with a signifying system (1990, 81); it becomes a subject only when it can signify its corporeality (85). Gilbert is in danger of losing materiality altogether to the abject: "[T]he abject entices and attracts the subject ever closer.... It is an insistence on the subject's necessary relation to death ... being the subject's recognition and refusal of its corporeality" (89).

As *jouissance* is perforce erotic, and the abject dependent on *jouissance* for causation, depictions of the abject state must involve eros. Abjection in subject formation is most clearly a process of childhood. At the psychoanalytic level of Kristeva's thinking, abjection "marks the threshold of the child's acquisition of language," in which the spaces between subject and object "need to be oppositionally coded for the child's ... subjectivity to be definitely tied to the body's form and limits" (Grosz 1990, 86). Sara Beardsworth calls abjection "the most unstable moment in the maturation of the subject." It hinges on "the need of a place for the 'ego' to come into being" (2004, 81).

Childhood and adolescence, where the subject may risk dissolution before it has a chance to gain a purchase on life, show the abject to its greatest effect. In many boys' love stories, including *Kaze*, the *uke* must overcome the abject before he can productively relate to others. *Jouissance* may dissipate identity[22] but the abject can kill. To the extent that boys' love depicts abjection in subject formation it must depict young males erotically.

The discourses described above in contemporary France and Japan arose in part from attempts at managing life in a world hostile to one's erotic desires. Discourses are a means of producing and organizing meaning (Edgar 2008, 96). Power acts on discourse production and subjectivity.

In Japanese boys' love power may not be part of the processes described by Foucault but it does in the end deny Gilbert the subjectivity to be autonomous. In Western nations discursive power could change the meaning of boys' love from "boys in love" to "child pornography."

Whatever commonality there is among contemporary boys' love discourses in the East and West may come in part from the power relations underlying the repression of the autonomy of the child and supporting the maintenance of a unitary sexual identity in children.

Boys' love participants claim power to represent a type of child, the male adolescent, and in so doing create entertainment that obstructs (queers) the ability of the state to organize sexual identities. In Japan as in the West, this effort invests the child's already liminal status with a queer sexual behavior otherwise closed to them because of their role as asexual surety for heterosexual reproduction (Edelman 2004, 11). It inverts the idea of the child from Edelman's characterization of "the telos of the social order ... the one for whom that order is held in perpetual trust" (ibid.) into queer. It inverts the figuring of the queer, which Edelman writes is "the bar to [the] realization of futurity" (4), into actually having a future.

In having the *uke* seize and redeploy telos for his own ends, bonding with another male, boys' love creators are resisting the prescription of fictively coherent sexual identities. This is potentially a model for boys' love consumers, especially same-sex-attracted teen and young adult males.

Stories are a key to understanding ourselves, whether they are used in psychoanalysis, in popular fiction or in other discursive forms. Drawn images, with their immediacy, illusion of completeness, and ambiguity have the power to stimulate the imagination — to imagine new outcomes — in a way that the printed word alone cannot.

I have found no evidence that boys' love works have harmed real children.[23] There is abundant evidence, on the other hand, that Western homophobia harms the lives of real people, including youth considered gay or queer-identified. In the U.S. they commit suicide at far higher rates than their non-gay-identified peers.[24] They are routinely the target of violence, sometimes murderous. Effeminate boys in particular may be left "in the position of the haunting abject," writes Sedgwick, not just of adult predation but of "gay thought itself."[25]

Boys' love manga and anime, in which the adolescent male is predominant, may offer real-life young males a way to safely explore their sexualities, as they do for some females, and to help them form their subjectivities, as indeed some gay male youth report that they do[26] — in sum, to help them *have* a future — if discourses in Japan[27] and the West[28] about boys' love are not foreclosed by Western discourses about child sex abuse.

Notes

1. Thorn, Matthew. 2005. "The Moto Hagio Interview." The movie *Les Amitiés particulières* inspired Hagio to draw *November Gymnasium* (1971) as well as *Tōma no shinzō* (Heart of Thomas; 1974). Takemiya named the school Lacombrade Academy, the name taken from that of Francis Lacombrade, who played Georges in the movie. Gilbert shares the surname of Jean Cocteau, a well known dramatist-ballet librettist-novelist-poet and homosexual who lived from the last decade of the nineteenth century into the 1960s. These are two of several playful anachronistic hommages in her work. Another is a panel showing Academy students drawing the face of Tetsuwan Atomu (Mighty Atom), a popular manga character created in 1951 by Tezuka Osamu (Schodt 1999, 244).

2. In the movie, faster paced, Alexandre's suicide comes rather as a shock.

3. "If you can't win, you should accept that calmly, without resistance. Anything else is just pathetic" (1995, vol. 1, 56). Page numbers refer to the 1995 Hakusensha edition. Translations from the Japanese are adapted from a scanlation by YAOIRULEZ.

4. Vol. 1, 82. Carl repeats this to himself thereafter (ibid., 86, 298). Gilbert himself says, after catching Serge to prevent his falling, "All that ever satisfied me was the hot touch of skin against skin.... Just to be held, to touch someone's skin — that is what I want" (34–35).

5. *Oxford English Dictionary Draft Revision June 2008.* For "promiscuous" as a description of Gilbert, see, e.g., Wikipedia, "Kaze to Ki no Uta," http://en.wikipedia.org/wiki/Kaze_to_Ki_no_Uta (accessed July 11, 2009).

6. *Oxford English Dictionary Second Edition 1989.*

7. Roland Barthes described *jouissance* as "violent pleasure that dissipates cultural identity to the point of discomfort and which unsettles the subject's relationship to language and representation." It is distinct from *plaisir*, "which is linked to cultural enjoyment and comfortably reinforces the identity of the ego..." (Moore 1998, 191 n. 4). Both are descriptions of erotic pleasure.

8. For *kōshoku*'s connotations of playfulness see Yokota-Murakami (1998, 41); for "curiosity" in the use of a related term, *iro-gonomi*, see ibid. (101); for *kōshoku*'s being "pleasure in love" see Sargent (1959, xxv n. 2). Cf. Keene for *kōshoku*'s meaning "to love" (1976, 168).

Unlike *kōshoku*, which denigrated an intense involvement with one's lover as *yabo* (uncool) (Yokota-Murakami, 50), much contemporary boys' love manga seeks to have its characters connect or bond in a state of emotional love, even as it depicts their sexual activity as *asobi* (play), a word still used today for homosexuality, whose connotation of mimetic experimentation undercuts Anglo-European conceptions of homosexuality as a fixed identity.

9. About half of Saikaku's prose works concern love, including three of his best-known novels: *Kōshoku ichidai otoko* (*The Man Who Loved Love*; 1682), *Kōshoku gonin onna* (*Five Women Who Loved Love*; 1686) and *Kōshoku ichidai onna* (*Life of an Amorous Woman*; 1686). He also wrote a best-selling collection of *nanshoku*-themed short stories, *Nanshoku ōkagami: honchō waka fūzoku* (*Great Mirror of Male Love: the Custom of Boy-Love in Our Land*; 1687).

Gennai was Edo Japan's leading promoter of European scientific methodology as a way to strengthen the nation (Screech 1999, 9). He was also an eloquent proponent of *nanshoku*. In a lyrical passage in the novel *Nenashigusa* (*Rootless Grass*; 1763) Gennai uses Heian court poetic diction to describe an encounter between an actor and a samurai (the latter in reality a *kappa*, or water sprite who had taken human form) (Gennai 2002, 473–79). It is an exquisitely tender scene of erotic bonding.

He also wrote more practically: *Mitsu no asa* (*Threefold Dawn*; 1768), the title a pun lampooning the start of the New Year, and *Edo nanshoku saiken* (*Edo* Nanshoku *Up Close*; 1783) are guides to the male brothels of Sakai-chō, an Edo district to which Gennai was a frequent visitor. In *Mitsu no asa* Gennai hypothesized that a decline of *wakashugata* (male adolescent role actors) in the playhouses had lead to a decrease in the demand for *iroko* (lit., love boys, or male prostitutes who worked in and around the theaters), but he was optimistic there would be an imminent resurgence of *nanshoku*. His argument was discussed critically by the scholar Ishizuka Hōkaishi in the 1840s (Pflugfelder 1999, 93), an example of *nanshoku* discourse continuing until less then a dozen years before the U.S. intervention.

10. Yukito and Hokuto are age similar, but as *uke* Yukito looks much younger than Hokuto. Both are taking the entrance examinations to university, which would make them seventeen or eighteen.

11. Fiction Reviews: Week of 8/27/2007. *Publishers Weekly*, http://www.publishersweekly.com/article/CA 6471321.html (accessed July 20, 2009).

12. In the U.S. a federal statute enacted in 2003 prohibits, among other acts, possession of a cartoon if it "depicts a minor engaging in sexually explicit conduct" and is adjudged obscene, as well as any image that "is, or appears to be, of a minor engaging in ... sexual intercourse" and which "lacks serious literary, artistic, political, or scientific value" regardless of whether it is found obscene. In either case the image must have been received via mail or computer or carried across a state border. *U.S. Code* (2003) 18, §§ 1466A.

On May 20, 2009, Glenwood, Iowa resident Christopher Handley pled guilty to two counts in violation of this law, one of possessing obscene visual representations of the sexual abuse of children, the other of mailing obscene matter. For more information about Handley's prosecution, see Matthew Thorn, "Christopher Handley and me (Edited)," matt-thorn.com Generic Blog, May 26, 2009, http://matt-thorn.com/wordpress/?p =318 (accessed July 18, 2009).

In Canada federal law prohibits possession of child pornography, this being defined "as any visual representation showing 'a person ... depicted as being under the age of eighteen years and ... as engaged in explicit sexual activity' (s. 163(1))" (Zanghellini 2009, 166).

In New South Wales, Australia, any depiction of incest or child sexual abuse is prohibited. Publications that "depict in a way that is likely to cause offence to a reasonable adult, a person who is, or appears to be, a child under 18 (whether the person is engaged in sexual activity or not)" and have "depictions of children, actually or apparently under the age of 16, in a sexual context" are also criminalized (ibid., 167).

13. Aleardo Zanghellini lists discursive conventions of boys' love such as the appearance in manga of "*bishounen*, who are required to be *kawaii* (cute) regardless of age [which] often make[s] them look younger than their assigned age" and the *seme-uke* roles arising in part from the tradition of age discrepant male-male erotic relations, which, together with the use of angst as a plot element, "explain ... why BL/*yaoi* work may also feature non-consensual, underage (*shotacon*), and incest themes, and hence why they may well run afoul" of child pornography laws (2009, 172).

14. Lawrence Schehr describes interconnections in the works and lives of well-known French cultural figures from the twentieth century's first four decades: important figures such as Gide, Marcel Proust, Jean Cocteau and Jean Genet, as well as popular writers: "[A]s this generalized discursive field developed ... male-male desire and male-male culture were repeatedly encoded in French literature.... [N]arrative could no longer pretend that it is heterosexual and that homosexuality does not exist" (2004, 5–7). There was also in Paris then a visible male homoerotic culture, including magazines in the 1920s publishing homoerotic fiction as well as bars, saunas and cruising areas (7).

15. Sheridan writes that "for the French reader, this term [*pédéraste*], too, was synonymous with 'homosexual,' being its current, colloquial equivalent. Until fairly recently all homosexuals were referred to as 'pédérastes'—'pédés,' for short, with a touch of contempt" (1999, 378). Gide "was drawn sexually to adolescent boys, that is, boys who were already biologically men" (377). Gide was writing against Magnus Hirschfeld's notion of *sexuelle Zwischenstufen*, an intermediary state of sexuality between male and female (376).

16. Gide described his many erotic encounters, which he called his "*petite aventures*," in, among other places, his *Carnets de Égypte* (written in 1939) and his journals. Sheridan describes one of these when Gide

shared a compartment with two brothers aged fourteen and sixteen on a train to Weimar in 1903. Gide commented: "Moll, K. Ebing and others maintain that homosexuals tend to exaggerate, to invent such stories. Mind you, I can scarcely believe what happened myself" (Sheridan 1999, 201, citing *Journal* I, 2nd Pléiade edition, 1996, 359–60). Richard von Krafft-Ebing and Albert Moll were German psychiatrists in the latter nineteenth and latter nineteenth-early twentieth centuries, respectively.

17. One example is Gide's *Le Ramier*, first published in 2002. It describes his night with a fifteen-year-old in Bagnols-de-Grenade, Ferdinand, whom he nicknamed "le ramier" (woodpigeon) for the way he moaned ("one would say like a dove cooing") as Gide kissed him (Gide 2002, 27–8). In the preface Gide's daughter Catherine characterizes their encounter as positive, writing that the story's "sensation de fraîcheur et de poésie et la nouvelle transmet au lecteur l'émoi de la découverte érotique, la joie de la complicité, la victoire du désir et du plaisir partagés. Je trouve ce petit texte plein de joie de vivre. Toute perversité en est totalement absente" (9–10). (The story's "sensation of freshness, poetry and the new transmits to the reader the excitement of erotic discovery, the joy of complicity, the victory of desire and of shared pleasure. I find this little text full of the joy of life. Perversity is totally absent.") (My translation.)

18. In Foucault's oft-quoted aphorism, "The sodomite had been a temporary aberration; the homosexual was now a species" (1978, 43). He writes that homosexuality was a "medical category" characterized in 1870 by the German sexologist Carl Westphal (ibid.). In fact Westphal coined the term *Konträre Sexualempfindung* ("contrary sexual feeling") (Bullough 1995, 38). The first use of "homosexual" (*Homosexualität*) was two years earlier, by Karl Maria Kertbeny (Kennedy 1997, 30).

19. The *kami kaze* (divine wind) which flow from Mt. Fuji, Japan's symbolic center, have been mythologized in literature, art and popular culture over hundreds of years.

20. *Kami* are spirits of varying powers that may take various forms, including human. They are "like mirrors of human activity and character," in the words of leading *kokugakusha* (native scholar) Kada no Azumamaro (1669–1736 CE), reflecting the concealed aspects of humans as humans represent the revealed aspects of *kami* (Nosco 1990, 84). Azumamaro viewed *kami* as superior but not always transcendent alter egos to humans. This view was common in contemporary Shintō circles (ibid.). Azumamaro noted, "Since men make mistakes, the *kami* also make mistakes. The difference between them is in the correction of these errors. The *kami* recognize their mistakes and correct them, which is one respect in which they are superior to men" (84–85). A later prominent *kokugakusha*, Motoori Norinaga (1730–1801 CE), wrote that *kami* are "first the deities of heaven and earth who appear in the ancient records and the spirits of the shrines where they are worshiped" but they also can be "birds and beasts, trees and plants, seas and mountains, and so forth" (217). They can also be human (218). According to Harry Harootunian's account of Motoori's thinking, "men and *kami* were associated in a continuous series denoting kinship" (Harootunian 1988, 88), "united by their mutual capacity to feel deeply for things (*aware*)" (115). "Virtue requires the *kami* to feel deeply and be moved" (ibid.); *kami* "revealed the idea that humans possess the spark of divinity" (88). For the purposes of this chapter I consider Gilbert's interactions with others solely at the level of human inasmuch as the other characters take him as such.

21. *Kaze* was written before the *seme/uke* topos became popular in Japanese boys' love. In some ways, Gilbert is a prototypical *uke*. In other ways, he is not. Of the two characters who figure as objects of erotic interest for him, Serge is only slightly taller, is the same age, and has no more power to overcome sexual predation against him than does Gilbert. The other, Auguste Beau, is older and much more powerful, but his utter indifference to others is not typical of contemporary *seme*.

22. Leo Bersani describes the dissipative qualities of losing one's identity: "Male homosexuality advertises the risk of the sexual itself as the risk of self-dismissal, of *losing sight* of the self, and in so doing it proposes and dangerously represents *jouissance* as a mode of ascesis" (1987, 222).

23. In its ruling overturning a U.S. law prohibiting "sexually explicit images that appear to depict minors but were produced without using any real children," the U.S. Supreme Court found that the government showed "no more than a remote connection" between these images and any harm to children. *Ashcroft v. the Free Speech Coalition* 535 U.S. 234 (2002).

24. According to findings reported in the *Journal of Adolescence*, about eight percent of youth nationally attempted suicide in 1996 (Morrison and L'Heureux 2001, 39). By comparison, the Massachusetts Department of Education reported that gay, lesbian, bisexual and questioning (GLBQ) youth in Massachusetts were four times more likely to have attempted suicide than their heterosexual-identified peers in 1995. The authors term the similarity of the data gathered by Massachusetts and by state agencies in Vermont and Washington as "striking" (ibid., 40). Three other studies in 1993 and 1994 report anywhere from eighteen and one-half to forty-two percent of GLBQ youth attempted suicide. These teenagers also comprise a disproportionate number of completed youth suicides. A 1989 U.S. Department of Health and Human Services report indicated that gay and lesbian youth may be two to three times more likely to commit suicide than their heterosexual counterparts (ibid.).

25. Sedgwick calls this an "annihilating homophobic, gynephobic, and pedophobic hatred internalized and made central to gay-affirmative analysis" (1991, 21).

In her examination of the "apparently burgeoning epidemic of suicides and suicide attempts by children and adolescents in the United States" (18), she quotes from the American Psychiatric Association's *Diagnostic and Statistical Manual III*, which identifies boys "display[ing] a 'preoccupation with female stereotypical activities as manifested by a preference for either cross-dressing or simulating female attire, or by a compelling desire to participate in the games and pastimes of girls'" as meeting the diagnostic criteria of "Gender Identity Disorder of Childhood" (20). Noting that the monographic literature about this condition since DSM-III's publication "is ... as far as I can tell exclusively about boys" (19), she cites representative examples which characterize male effeminacy as a global character pathology.

Together with a male effeminophobia in the gay movement, which has meant that the movement "has never been quick to attend to issues concerning effeminate boys" (20), she reasons that the "great advance in recent gay and lesbian thought" of "theoriz[ing] gender and sexuality as distinct though intimately entangled. ... may leave the effeminate boy once more in the position of the haunting abject — this time the haunting abject of gay thought itself" (ibid.).

26. Consider a comment in *Publishers Weekly* to a blog entry about yaoi by one of its reporters. The poster, Breaking the ice, says:

> Back to Yaoi. Its not unreal as you kind ladys would believe. I'm a 17 year old male teen and I'm living a yaio dream with my*blush* mate. He and I are really close and both of us are really good artists. We draw and post alot of (you quessed it) yaio. Its not unreal and its not just for girls. thank you (Breaking the ice)

27. Saitō Tamaki briefly discusses half-a-dozen Japanese critical works about boys' love, including Nagakubo Yōko, *Yaoi shōsetsu ron* (A Theory of Yaoi Fiction), Tokyo: Senshū Daigaku Shuppankyoku, 2005; Nakajima Azusa [Kurimoto Kaoru], *Bishōnengaku nyūmon* (A *Bishōnen* Primer), Tokyo: Shinshokan, 1984; Nobi Nobita [Enomoto Nariko], *Otana wa wakatte kurenai: Nobi Nobita hihyō shūsei* (Adults Just Don't Get It: The Criticism of Nobi Nobita), Tokyo: Nihon Hyōronsha, 2003; and Sakakibara Shihomi, *Yaoi genron: yaoi kara mieta mono* (An Illusory Theory of Yaoi: What Yaoi Shows), Tokyo: Natsume Shobō, 1998. Saitō Tamaki, "Otaku Sexuality," in *Robot Ghosts and Wired Dreams*, ed. Christopher Bolton et al. (Minneapolis: University of Minnesota Press, 2007), 247 nn. 4, 5, 6; 248 n. 12.

28. Males comprise approximately fifteen to twenty percent of the attendees at the West's largest boys' love and yaoi fan convention, Yaoi-Con. Many are young and dress themselves as the embodiment of boys' love, the *bishōnen*. Their presence has become the number-one topic on Yaoi-Con's Forums. The dozens to hundreds of visitors each day to the Forums are producing discourses about males participating in yaoi (McHarry 2008).

Males in boys' love and yaoi may be applying in real life something closer to boys' love and yaoi fictional characters' free-floating conceptions of self, a self that refuses identity or fixed position, even as it grounds itself firmly in a male body and affirms the desirability of male-male eroticism (McHarry 2007, 190–191).

Bibliography

Beardsworth, Sara. *Julia Kristeva: Psychoanalysis and Modernity*. Albany, NY: State University of New York Press, 2004.

Bersani, Leo. "Is the Rectum a Grave?" *October* 43 (1987): 197–222.

Boyarin, Jonathan. "Space, Time and the Politics of Memory." In *Remapping Memory: The Politics of Time-Space*, edited by Jonathan Boyarin, 1–37. Minneapolis: University of Minnesota Press, 1994.

Breaking the ice. Message 22, June 8, 2007. Comment to Heidi MacDonald, "Why girls love boys love." *The Beat: The News Blog of Comics Culture. Publishers Weekly*, http://pwbeat.publishersweekly.com/blog/2006/11/03/why-girls-love-boys-love/ (accessed August 4, 2009).

Bullough, Vern L. *Science in the Bedroom: A History of Sex Research*. New York: Basic Books, 1995.

Butler, Judith. "Imitation and Gender Insubordination." In *The Judith Butler Reader*, edited by Sara Salih, 119–37. Malden, MA: Blackwell, 2004.

Edelman, Lee. *No Future: Queer Theory and the Death Drive*. Durham, NC: Duke University Press, 2004.

Edgar, Andrew and Peter Sedgwick, eds. *Cultural Theory: The Key Concepts*. 2nd. ed. London: Routledge, 2008.

Foucault, Michel. *The History of Sexuality, Volume I: An Introduction*. Translated by Robert Hurley. New York: Pantheon Books, 1978.

_____. *Power/Knowledge: Selected Interviews and Other Writings*. Edited by Colin Gordon. New York: Pantheon Books, 1980.

Gennai Hiraga. "Ryōgoku Bridge," *Nenashigusa*. Translated by Chris Drake. In *Early Modern Japanese Literature: An Anthology, 1600–1900*, edited by Haruo Shirane, 473–79. New York: Columbia University Press, 2002.

Gide, André. *Corydon*. Paris: Gallimard, 1924.

_____. *Le Ramier*. Paris: Gallimard, 2002.

Grosz, Elizabeth. "The Body of Signification." In *Abjection, Melancholia and Love: The Work of Julia Kristeva*, edited by John Fletcher and Andrew Benjamin, 80–103. New York: Routledge, 1990.

_____. *Space, Time, and Perversion: Essays on the Politics of Bodies*. New York: Routledge, 1995.

Harootunian, Harry D. *Things Seen and Unseen: Discourse and Ideology in Tokugawa Nativism*. Chicago: University of Chicago Press, 1988.

Higuri Yū. *Gakuen Heaven*. Translated by Christine Schilling. Los Angeles: BLU, 2006.

Ihara Saikaku. *The Great Mirror of Male Love* (*Nanshoku ōkagami*). Translated by Paul Gordon Schalow. Stanford, CA: Stanford University Press, 1990.

_____. *The Japanese Family Storehouse* (*Nippon eitai-gura*). Translated by G.W. Sargent. Cambridge, UK: Cambridge University Press, 1959.

Keene, Donald. *World Within Walls: Japanese Literature of the Pre-Modern Era, 1600–1867*. New York: Holt, Rinehart and Winston, 1976.

Kennedy, Hubert. "Karl Heinrich Ulrichs: First Theorist of Homosexuality." In *Science and Homosexualities*, edited by Vernon Rosario, 26–45. New York: Routledge, 1997.

Kristeva, Julia. *Powers of Horror: An Essay on Abjection*. Translated by Leon S. Roudiez. New York: Columbia University Press, 1982.

McHarry, Mark. "Identity Unmoored: Yaoi in the West." In *Queer Popular Culture: Literature, Media, Film, and Television*, edited by Thomas Peele, 183–95. New York: Palgrave Macmillan, 2007.

_____. "Fan Girls' Beautiful Boys: Western Embodiments of Japanese Yaoi and Boys' Love." Paper presented at the joint conference of the Popular Culture and American Culture Associations, San Francisco, March 20, 2008.

McLelland, Mark. "The World of Yaoi: The Internet, Censorship and the Global 'Boys' Love' Fandom." *Australian Feminist Law Journal* 23 (2005): 61–77. Repr., http://ro.uow.edu.au/cgi/viewcontent.cgi?article=1152&context=artspapers (accessed July 20, 2009).

Mills, Sara. *Discourse*. New York: Routledge, 2004.

Minami Kazuka. *My Paranoid Next Door Neighbor*. Translated by Leona Wong. Gardena, CA: 801 Media, 2007.

Moore, Suzanne. "Getting a Bit of the Other: the Pimps of Postmodernism." In *Male Order: Unwrapping Masculinity*, edited by Rowena Chapman and Jonathan Rutherford, 165–92. London: Lawrence & Wishart, 1988.

Morrison, Linda L. and Jeff L'Heureux. "Suicide and Gay/Lesbian/Bisexual Youth: Implications for Clinicians." *Journal of Adolescence* 24 (2001): 39–49.

Nosco, Peter. *Remembering Paradise: Nativism and Nostalgia in Eighteenth-Century Japan*. Cambridge, MA: Harvard University Press, 1990.

Peyrefitte, Roger. *Les Amitiés particulières*. Paris: Pédro Torres et Éditions T.G., 2005. First published 1944 by Éditions Flammarion.

_____. *Les Amitiés particulières*. DVD. Directed by Jean Delannoy. Paris: TFI Video and René Chateau Video, 2004. The movie was first publicly shown on September 4, 1964 in Paris.

_____. *Notre Amour*. Paris: Éditions Flammarion, 1967.

Pflugfelder, Gregory. *Cartographies of Desire: Male-Male Sexuality in Japanese Discourse, 1600–1950*. Berkeley, CA: University of California Press, 1999.

Saitō Tamaki. "Otaku Sexuality." Introduction by Kotani Mari. Translated by Christopher Bolton. In *Robot Ghosts and Wired Dreams: Japanese Science Fiction From Origins to Anime*, edited by Christopher Bolton, Istvan Csicsery-Ronay Jr., and Takayuki Tatsumi, 222–249. Minneapolis, MN: University of Minnesota Press, 2007.

Schehr, Lawrence. *French Gay Modernism*. Urbana, IL: University of Illinois Press, 2004.

Schodt, Frederik. *Dreamland Japan: Writings on Modern Manga*. Berkeley, CA: Stone Bridge Press, 1999.

Screech, Timon. *Sex and the Floating World: Erotic Images in Japan, 1700–1820*. Honolulu: University of Hawai'i Press, 1999.

Sedgwick, Eve Kosofsky. "How To Bring Your Kids Up Gay." *Social Text* 29 (1991): 18–27.

_____. *Tendencies*. Durham, NC: Duke University Press, 1993.

Sheridan, Alan. *André Gide: A Life in the Present*. Cambridge, MA: Harvard University Press, 1999.

Takemiya Keiko. *Kaze to ki no uta*. Tokyo: Hakusensha, 1995. Ten volumes. First published 1976 by Shōgakukan.

Thorn, Matthew. "Girls and Women Getting Out of Hand: The Pleasure and Politics of Japan's Amateur

Comics Community." In *Fanning the Flames: Fans and Consumer Culture in Contemporary Japan*, edited by William W. Kelly, 169–87. Albany, NY: State University of New York Press, 2004.

_____. "The Moto Hagio Interview." *The Comics Journal* 269, July/August (2005), http://www.matt-thorn.com/shoujo_manga/hagio_interview.php (accessed July 18, 2009).

Yaoi-Con Forums, http://www.yaoicon.com/component/option,com_fireboard/Itemid,258 (accessed August 4, 2009).

Yokota-Murakami, Takayuki. *Don Juan East/West: On the Problematics of Comparative Literature*. Albany, NY: State University of New York Press, 1998.

Zanghellini, Aleardo. "Underage Sex and Romance in Japanese Homoerotic Manga and Anime." *Social Legal Studies* 18 (2009): 159–77.

11

Queering the Quotidian
Yaoi, Narrative Pleasures and Reader Response
Mark Vicars *and* Kim Senior

Introduction

> The reader is at once interpreter and interpretation [and] is always situated inside contexts of discursive practices in which are inscribed values, interests, attitudes and beliefs.... Each and every instance of consciousness or utterance is framed by a specific situation.— Freund 1987, 109

Literacy and sexuality could be said to be on the move: politically, socially, and culturally, and this chapter attempts to articulate an understanding of the socio-cultural conditions in which literacy and sexual identity are practiced. It takes, as focus for critical inquiry, how yaoi is used by "Western" readers (a gay man and a straight woman) to resist and (re)perform heterogendered pedagogies in everyday life. The experiences outlined in this chapter bring together two seemingly disparate lives from working class United Kingdom and middle class Australia. United in the project of (re)imagining and reconstructing identity, yaoi is positioned as a fugitive text where the (hetero)normative is disrupted and where the quotidian codes that govern gender and sexuality are poached for "perverse" purposes and pleasures. In this chapter, we consider how responses to texts unavoidably occur in time and in certain kinds of spaces and are shaped by the normative discourses of practice that sanction how affect, pleasure, power and identities are experienced. Our responses to texts were, to some extent, acts of self creation through which we as readers sought to recover some thematic continuity of self. They offered a way of being in the world where we were able to embrace and acknowledge our queer lives as our own creations. It is, therefore, in our social, cultural and sexual position in relation to texts that we have attempted to re-experience unimagined significances and to re-imagine the effects between "proper" and "improper" ways of being and doing gender and sexuality.

Yaoi manga flirt with and explore the privileges and penalties associated with transgressing "the normal." They can be read as "intersubjective spaces of cultural translation," spaces "where one can find an overlay of codes, a multiplicity of culturally inscribed subject positions, a displacement of normative reference codes, and a polyvalent assemblage of new cultural meanings" (McLaren 1994, 65). In the telling of our stories, we have sought to speak from and work our interpretation of the structural devices of *yamanashi—ochinashi— iminashi* to play with the theoretical positioning of our personal and professional relationships and to speak of and about our deterritorializations of self:

> yamanashi— *like a day dream or the twilight between dream and sleep ... where there is no need to "climax" but it is possible to rest in perpetual abeyance ... to pause, redirect, and relocate our imaginings to another moment....*

ochinashi— *to trouble the routine and the mundane....*

iminashi— *to play with belonging (within the text, to a text and beyond the text) ... these are not texts wishing to lecture, instruct, inform or tell the reader (like so much adolescent and children's lit!) but one in which both the writer and reader come together for no reason other than to play, to subvert, to disrupt....*

Yamanashi—ochinashi—iminashi *speak of and about the possibilities that are afforded by the uncertainties that come from the being doing of liminality in everyday life.*

Yaoi texts for us operated on a personal and social level in the ongoing processes of belonging and becoming, and if as it has been suggested that "a text can only come to life when it is read, and if it is to be examined, it must therefore be studied through the eyes of the reader" (Iser 1971, 2–3).

By focusing in on the blends of the emotional, psychic, and cultural in which subjectivity is formed, we have situated our textual lives as a form of landscape from which to elucidate doubled understandings of our readerly/writerly (Barthes 1974) relationship with manga and the cultural discourses of gender and sexuality. Employing Appadurai's (1996) concept of ethnoscape as that which is "not objectively given relations that look the same from every angle of vision but, rather, that they are deeply perspectival constructs, inflected by the historical, linguistic and political situatedness of different sorts of actors," (33) our practices of reading have produced supplementary texts. If, "the more one interprets the more one finds not the fixed meaning of a text, or of the world, but only other interpretations" (Dreyfus and Rabinow 1982, 107), then our interpretations provide a space for alternative visions of belonging and becoming; for queering quotidian practice and resisting heteronormative, teleological narratives of identity.

Out of the Ordinary (Mark Vicars)

In dreams, finally, individuals even in the most simple societies have found the space to refigure their social lives, live out proscribed emotional states and sensations, and see things that have then spilled over into their sense of ordinary life. All these expressions, further, have been the basis of a complex dialogue between the imagination and ritual. ... the imagination has broken out ... and has now become a part of the quotidian mental work of ordinary people.... It has entered the logic of ordinary life [Appadurai 1996, 5].

Growing up in a small town in the north of England in the 1980s, I have always felt pressured to legitimize and explain what it is that I am and what I do, especially to myself. I didn't do the everyday heterogendered rituals of "fighting, fucking and football" that made visible and reified normalcy (Mac An Ghaill 1994). My boyish comic books *Whizzer and Chips, The Beano* and *Dandy* reinforced gendered expectations and while I enjoyed reading *Desperate Dan,* it was not for the weekly serialized narrative but for the visual beefcake. In *Dennis the Menace,* I identified more with the character of Walter, the soft sissy boy who dislikes rough and tumble, and when I was given imported American comic books for my twelfth birthday, I found the visuals of *Superman, He-Man* and the like incredibly erotic: the bulging biceps, the ripped torsos provided me with my formative erotic experiences. My reading has always been affected by the social and cultural contexts in which I constructed my sexual identity and if, as it has been suggested, the marginalized individual, by necessity, has to create another story that they can read themselves into (Appiah 1994), it has been between the pages of fiction that I have imagined, scripted, and played out my sissy-boy desires.

My nascent understandings of self were formed in the days, months, and years spent genuflecting at the everyday altars of the heteronormative whilst secretly longing for something queer to happen. A lot of what I read I would use as a template on which I constructed and scaffolded my subaltern needs. I would invent sexual scenarios and my "perverse" imaginings repeatedly reconstructed texts in ways that insinuated and inserted a queer presence in the everyday comics and storybooks of my youth. Invariably, my symptomatic readings had a dominant theme that got recycled and was reiterated from one text to another. The first time I saw the film *Seven Brides for Seven Brothers*, I loved the romanticism and I loved the kidnapping idea. I wanted to be one of the kidnapped girls because I knew I would get to be banged senseless in a log cabin by Howard Keel. Martin (1996) speaks of the queer possibilities of identifying in this way and says books "produced the fantasies into which she [Martin] escaped or imagined escaping the painful effects of the rules governing sexuality, gender and maturity" (35). Growing up having to keep my desires silent, texts became the main instruments of my confession. Throughout adolescence, I cast aside my comic books, but as my identifactory indeterminacies grew stronger so did my queer reading praxis. I sought refuge within the fictional worlds of literature and the romantic offerings of cinematic musical theatre. It was into these texts that I uttered performatives of my innermost hopes and desires and staged resistances to the everyday architecture of heterosexuality. Texts became much more than a representation of an imaginative world, and I increasingly read to escape the prevailing normativities that were disciplining my being. Reading became so much more than deciphering tiny bunched-up print; it was a way of realizing my fantasies, of working out the "great unmanageable unknowns by means of small knowns" (Holland 1980, 127). In my readings, I constructed subaltern fantasies of an "other" self and another life. I actively sought out texts in which my particular claims of self were able to be enunciated and validated. Sedgwick (1994) has noted how "for many of us in childhood the ability to attach intently to a few cultural objects, objects of high or popular culture or both, objects whose meaning seemed mysterious, excessive, or oblique in relation to the codes most readily available to us, became a prime resource for survival" (3).

I used all my powers of concentration to visualize, from texts, experiences of which I had no knowledge and was not likely to encounter in my suburban world. My imaginary endeavors, far from being parasitic on the "real world," were, in many ways, linked to my calling forth of utopian constructions of self (Vygotsky 1978, 92). I have come to recognize, in the tellings of myself, a story of continually negotiating separation in the ways that I belong, act, speak, and represent myself as a gay man. Having spent years listening to instructing parental and institutional voices that promulgated hegemonic social and cultural roles having to do with gender and sexuality, I have never been quite sure out of which voice I should speak.

I excel in displacement activities. I can quite happily spend an hour or so in imaginary interior design and will contentedly abandon an afternoon to sift through long abandoned drawers in the hope of finding some interesting letter or artifact. It was in one such recent foray I came across photographs of my secondary school. I involuntary shuddered at the image of the uniformed child and immediately tried to distance myself from this unearthed presence of the past in the present. Attending school, in this case a Church of England High School, educated me to the consequences of showing what the voice inside my head was telling me to do and how to be. I quickly realized I had to monitor what I said; I had to be on guard against the authority of that incessant interior monologue. I became attentive to how I expressed myself. I learnt what was the culturally and socially accepted, what constituted "normal" patterns of behavior. As there was nothing vaguely queer at that time and place in my life, my sexual subjectivity was primarily textual and it was predicated on my "capacity to keep a particular narrative going" (Giddens 1991, 54). I struggled to perform in, and participate with, cultural notions of gendered heterosexuality. However, my imaginary and fugitive readings playfully disrupted the governing heteronormative discourses of everyday life. They became my way of out of a working class straight cultural imaginary and as an act of self creation and survival; I imaginatively evoked worlds of sexual heterodoxies. Drawing from otherwise "straight" texts tacit knowledges and pleasures, I conjured up future queer times and places. Reflecting on photographs taken throughout my schooled adolescence, I detect a characteristic pose captured in the coerced smile, the sideward momentary look, the furtive gaze. Martel (2003) has noted that "It often happens that we do not remember the first time we did something, or even any one particular time, but remember only the repetition, the idea that we did the thing over and over" (8).

I find in numerous other school and family photographs the same representation of a fragmented self. Focusing on these images evokes intense emotion. They take me to an intimate place where it is difficult to diffuse a truth from the clamorous voices of the past. As I begin to reflect on the memory of myself and entering the strange yet familiar world of the past, I am drawn immediately to its capital and I find myself thinking about those occasions when heteronormative values disparaged a Queer identity. I am getting lost in past imaginings and struggle to find the language to share and interpret my world. I selectively revise scenes and reorder fragments in an attempt to make sense of those critical, defining transitional moments that have been located in a multiple embodied life. Turning once again to those moments where I resisted erasure, circumnavigated boundaries, and acted in ways that disrupted the social construction of gender and sexuality, I find that I am able to interrogate and acknowledge how reading *différance*, that is "the hidden way of seeing things" (Derrida, 1982, 22) created possibilities for self definition. My being — my presence — increasingly disrupted the narratives of normalcy. Rutherford (1990) talks of difference, in terms of identity, as a state of being that provides unity and coherence. However, my becoming involved disunity and incoherence. It was in the process of reading *différance*, in the simultaneous negotiation of that which differs from the center and that which is differed by the center, that it became possible to reconsider other ways of being. Experiencing the force with which the center exerts authority and authorizes the marginal made me ever attentive to the tacit knowledges of self that were at play. My sexual desire disrupted the infinite heterogendered narratives of my youth in which I was told what I had-to-be and how I had-to-become. My sexual difference and my reading of *différance* brought into view previously unimaginable horizons of impossible possibilities.

When I was sixteen, I told my father I was Gay. He said, "I know, you had better go and tell your mother." As I entered the bedroom where she lay, her gnarled fingers misshapen through rheumatoid arthritis, she clutched the heated pad she used to alleviate painful joints. Heavy curtains were blocking out the afternoon sun; she had been prescribed new anti-inflammatory drugs that had a side effect of drying up her tear ducts. Twice daily a pipette containing synthetic "natural tears" would lubricate her eye and keep them functioning. "I've something to tell you, I've already told Dad." I inwardly flinched; I had thought "Coming Out" would be a one-off declaration, not a repetitive performance. "I think I might be Gay." Why did I say "think"? There was no doubt, in my body, I knew. "I haven't got a son I've got two daughters...." "What have I done wrong?" "...It is wrong; it's in the Bible.... You'd better leave."

The silence between us irrevocably fractured, she turned her face away from where I stood and started to cry. The tears came quite freely now. I abandoned the melodrama that was being played out behind the net drapes of my parents' house and fled, not quite skirts billowing, to the end of the road to catch a bus to a friend's house. Her parents had been informed of this possible scenario and were willing to let me stay until I had got things sorted out. My plan was to move to London and find the life that I knew was out there waiting for me but would not be found on the streets of this small northern town.

As I was drinking hot sweet tea and retelling the events that led to my outcast state the telephone began to ring. "It's for you, it's your father," my friend's mother called through to the kitchen where I was still in the process of thawing out from the reaction of my parents. *If only I had kept my mouth shut.* Nervously, I took hold of the receiver. "We want you to come back, your mother and I have been talking and we don't want you to leave. I'm coming to pick you up." I stop. I stop and think what kind of future my father had planned for me. He always joked about getting a string of donkeys on the beach as I hadn't proved too bright at school. I forget how many times I had heard "You're not a chip off the old block, that's for sure, why when I was your age I could clear a five bar gate." "Are you a Queen?" I had no idea what he was talking about but could detect from the tone of his voice that whatever it was I had better not be one. As I sat at that Formica-topped kitchen table, the gathering place for every important family event I can ever recall, I tried hard to numb myself to the situation, to the disappointment etched on the faces of my parents. Martel (2003) notes, "Will I be understood when I say that sometimes numbness can hurt? That you don't want to feel because what you feel will be pain, so you try not to feel, and just sit there, immobile, numb, in pain?" (40).

My father stood by the door and waited for me to give him the answer he wanted. "No!" "How do you know that you are...?" He avoided saying it. "Have you had sex with a girl?" "Yes," I lied. "Have you had sex with...." Again, he couldn't bring himself to say it, to name me. "No," I lied.

This was the last time my sexuality was ever mentioned. It was tiptoed around like I had some terminal illness that if named would rear up and consume us all with one fell blow. The lesson I learnt from my initial revelation was one of how language and discourse is always productive: It brings a situation into play, enunciates evaluations of the situations, and extends action into the future. What went and remained unsaid remains far more descriptive and meaningful to my interpretation of that situation. I knew through their silence that my parents were holding out for a reversal, for a change of mind. In giving voice to what lay on the inside I had created myself as I wanted to be seen and heard. In their silence they were unseating that creation and hoping for an erasure of its possible existence.

Throughout this period of my life I was avidly reading the literature that historically chronicled gay experience. I sought out gay fiction in an attempt to gain insight into what had been constructed by others, for me, as a dangerous twilight world. I consumed autobiographies of famous Queers (Wilde, Crisp, Genet, White), thrilling in their daring resistances to orthodox heterosexuality, and found between those pages what my father had known and feared all along. It was to be some years later, when I encountered sadomasochistic (SM) yaoi for the first time, whilst living and working in Tokyo, that I experienced again how fictional life worlds can provide experiences and sensations that are otherwise beyond the everyday reach and embody versions of what we have only imagined ourselves being. It was in texts such as *Sadistic Boy, Hoshi no yakata* and *Amai hari*, SM yaoi manga that depict graphic scenes of sexual dominance, submission and violent sexual practices that I once again experienced "moments of biographical disruption" (Sparkes 1996).

A Strange Landscape (Mark Vicars)

Throughout my time in Japan, I led a double life. Chauncey (1994) has noted how some middle-class gay men utilize a strategy of leading a double life, of passing when needed but participating in the gay subculture when they can. Being an outsider, a *gaijin sensei*, I didn't understand much of what was going on around me. Not speaking the language, I floated around on the surface, guided by my nocturnal wanderings in the gay bars and clubs of Shinjuku ni chōme. I fell into sexual encounters and relationships with Japanese men, who much to my amusement avidly read yaoi that at the time I thought as strange little comic books.

My uncertainties of participating in what I considered at that time and in my naivety to be peculiarly strange Japanese behaviors meant I became an avid reader and doer of all things Japanese. Alongside my translated reading of *The Tale of Genji*, Sei Shōnagon, and the homoerotic novels of Mishima Yukio, I also had to hand yaoi manga that I had begged or borrowed from my lovers. As I sat somewhat nonplussed through hours of kabuki and attended Buddhist temples and retreats, my excursions into manga, were, in comparison, not that discombobulating. As I read I began to make sense of the partial and contradictory nature of the social, cultural and sexual practices of my new Japanese life. SM yaoi as part of that journey afforded a daring resistance to the regimes of the normal (Warner 1999). Contextualizing my reading experiences of SM yaoi in relation to my ongoing understanding of self, they mirrored my confusions of my being out of place.

Re-thinking reading as a literacy performance (Blackburn 2002–2003) through which identities can, over time, become known, displaced and reconfigured I have come to realize how at specific times in my life my interactions with texts were intimately connected to and part of the process of practicing a social and sexual identity. Reading SM yaoi made me rethink how "the body is the *site*, or place where the *'truth'* of identity is revealed" (Fraser 1999, 109) and I will now explore how my embodied responses to SM yaoi manga became performative acts or processes of identification in my ongoing journey of becoming.

Pornography or Pedagogy? (Mark Vicars)

It has been suggested how bodily experiences are "often central in memories of our lives, and thus understanding of who and what we are" (Connell 1995, 53) and it was through SM yaoi texts that I came to experience an uncanny series of splittings and deterritorializations of self. Bataille (1962) suggests that the territory of the erotic experience is that of pressing subjectivity closer to its limits than almost any other experience and it was in the graphic particularities, the contexts, the contingencies of the economies of sadomasochistic desires that I found my thrill. I became hooked on the visual carnivalesque pleasure play of sexual taboo.

SM yaoi manga was an escape from logic of sexual and cultural heteronormativity. SM yaoi manga depicted a world of sexual practices and relations that transgressed normative orders. The theatrics of SM yaoi manga inverted a world of heterosexual relations. They opened up a space, overflowing with pure artifice, puns, and playfulness that distorted, distended, and deformed my everyday experiences of self/other. These texts re-appropriated the quotidian codes that govern gender and sexuality and misused and abused them for "perverse" purposes and pleasures. In the artificial and excessive antics of SM power play, here was something being expressed consciously and intentionally that set out to queer social, cultural and political values and sexual sensibilities.

SM yaoi manga playfully reworked identity in terms of masquerade. Disrupting the normative discourses of heterosexual relations, SM yaoi manga situated sexual Otherness as a ludic construction, one in which the boundaries between what is real and unreal, time-present, past and future, the normative body and gendered identities, are contested and reworked. In my limited reading and understanding of SM yaoi manga, I enjoyed the transient artificial architecture of self. The stylized aesthetic offered alternatives to traditional heteronormative representations of gender, the body and the family and instantly appealed to my different ways of being and knowing. If "the word difference" has become a discursive "motif for that uprooting of certainty [representing] an experience of change, transformation and hybridity" (Rutherford 1990, 10), then encountering SM yaoi manga in my early twenties in Japan induced in me an unsettling of my understandings of who I was as a gay/queer man. I was attracted to the storylines that didn't fit in with dominant cultural sexual sensibilities and pleasures. The confusion of trying to make sense of the visuals that spiraled and sparked off parallel stories was at times overwhelming. There was just too much going on and as I tried to make sense, my challenge, as a reader, was to find meaning outside of the ordinarily available emplotments. SM yaoi manga marked a distinction between the common sense, or traditional, notion of homosocial behaviors, sexualizing them with forbidden corporeal pleasures. SM yaoi manga queered the straight male body by making it an object of conquest and by situating it in narratives of surrender.

Epistemology of the Anus (Mark Vicars)

Thinking from Haraway's (1992) push for articulation rather than representation leads me to suggest how responses to texts are neither objective nor disembodied but are best understood as material in themselves. She notes how representation locks the reader/viewer in the subject/object space whereas articulation can offer the possibility of new discursive configurations of identity to proliferate. In SM yaoi manga a counter narrative is established of what male bodies are and what they can do. The young *uke* by allowing himself to be dominated by the older *seme* and by offering little resistance to penetration situates, centrally within the narratives, the anus as a marker of prohibition and the anus as a site of pleasure. The pleasures of the anus in SM yaoi manga can be read in terms of unbecoming, particularly if we consider the way that male subjectivity within heteronormative discourse is situated within discursive fields and is constituted as a process of constructing an ongoing defense against penetration. Segal (1994) has commented, "If we look at how bodies appear in personal sexual narratives, it is clear that they encode culturally significant, as well as maturationally specific, understandings of physical organs and their functioning" (228–229).

My understandings of the performance of gendered masculinity relied on a cultural code (Barthes 1974) that referred to and sedimented a shared body of knowledge about how the male body in the world works. The male body is supposed to rehearse narratives of hegemonic masculinity. It is through the public performances and rituals of the male body, in the pursuit and display of a hypermasculinity, that meanings around the male body are formed and immersed in a logic of practice. It is in the ritualistic activities of everyday life that the body comes to perform meanings of itself, and Carbado (2005) has remarked:

> gender for men is also socially constructed and agency denying. One must learn to be a man ... because manhood is a socially produced category. Manhood is a performance. A script. It is accomplished and re-enacted in everyday social relationships. Yet, men have not been inclined to examine the sex/gender category we inhabit, reproduce, and legitimize. Nor have men developed a practice of exposing the contingency and false necessity of manhood. There is little effort within male communities to locate or even imagine, the pre-patriarchal man, the man whose personal identity has not been overdetermined by his gender [192].

Masculinity, as an intertextual social process, invariably requires a universal signifier of maleness and anxieties of sexual surrender and conquest by another male that are routinely located in hegemonic understandings of gender and sexuality which focus on the enacted passive role taken within imagined sexual acts. SM yaoi manga queers the knowledges, practices, and identities of the heterosexual cultural code that reinforce the performativity of the impenetrable male body. The *seme/uke* relationships reveal and situate the anus "as the site of persecution of the desire to desire, the place where the self plays out its struggle against dissolution" (Theweleit 1989, 320). The psychic, biological, and cultural expectations of what male bodies are supposed to be and do, normatively invoked by the rigid taxonomies of gender and sexual identities, are played with throughout SM yaoi manga in the *seme/uke* relationship.

In SM yaoi manga the exclusions and prohibitions around the penetration of the male body put into motion other, unnamable pleasures. Penetrative experiences as body reflexive practices are seen to produce vast deterritorializations. The storylines open up the male body and psyche to different meanings of masculinity through which new meanings and subjectivities are generated. The *uke* in being pursued and penetrated by the *seme* relocates the male body outside of hegemonic heterogendered discourses. The male body is an ongoing site of dilemma as the active/passive, masculine/feminine boundaries, heterogendered discursive relationships that bind individual bodies to cultural norms get questioned.

Themes such as incest, rape, older/younger sexual relationships are challenging to read and disrupt the panoptic narratives of categories and pleasures of normalcy sanctioned by the heteronormative cultural code. Foucault (1977) has noted in *Discipline and Punish* that "like surveillance ... normalization becomes one of the greatest instruments of power, the power of normalization imposes homogeneity" (Foucault 1977, 196). SM yaoi manga opens up a space for the reader to critically consider how practices of self, connected to and reified by the conventions of bodily practices, are structured by heteronormative performatives of what male bodies are and what they are allowed to do.

In *Bodies That Matter,* Judith Butler (1993) has asserted how bodies are materialized through the process of performativity and how identity is inherently unstable but it is through the process of reiteration and repetition of the conventions of everyday life that we come to enact our identities and discursively construct ourselves. She has argued in *Excitable Speech* (1997) how the "improper" use of the performative by those who are not permitted to have a voice can be employed to deconstruct "prevailing forms of authority and the exclusions by which they proceed" (Butler 1997, 158). Diving into the textual worlds of SM yaoi manga, I became entrapped in a network of relations, of differences, displacements, traces, and deferrals. The storylines produced feelings of indeterminacy, fragmentation, discomfort, and a sense of excitement. I felt I had entered a twilight world which inverted and spun queer fantasies from everyday heterosexual situations. With each the turn of the page I emerged into a new landscape of potentialities that troubled routine understandings of what males are and what they do. SM yaoi manga authorized a position from which I began to enunciate alternate sites of subject and identity formation and through which I played with the fantasy of belonging to another world, of the corporeal pleasure of being the object of desire and of relinquishing control. My pleasures within these texts were fuelled by the Dionysian qualities of disruption, immediacy, and excess, and I felt increasingly at home in traversing social, sexual, and textual orthodoxies.

Troubling Texts (Mike Vicars)

> ... constructions of selves might be seen as a matter of using texts strategically to desta-
> bilize the identities that sought to constrain ... and name and suggests that ... the "idea
> of readers constructing their own senses of self, their own uses of text, and their own
> identities from those uses is an enactment of *subjectivity*" [Hagood, 2004, 158, emphasis
> original].

Inhabiting imaginary spaces to reconcile the ruptures in an emerging concept of selfhood, I have come to realize how my involvement with SM yaoi texts facilitated imaginal dialogues that became an essential part of my ongoing narrative construction of self. Reflecting on my connections to these texts, I have come to understand how in many ways they afforded resistances to the rituals of everyday life and became part of the active process of taking up certain subject positions in an ongoing process of becoming.

My encounters with SM yaoi manga were brief but potent. In the five years I spent living and working in Japan, I became a regular consumer of manga. I hesitate to call myself a reader as I did not understand the language or how to read them properly. I experienced them improperly and they connect me to a time in my life that was all about impropriety. They evoke memories and emotions of a time and place and if "emotions are ... but processes that are best understood with reference to the cultural scenarios and associations they evoke" (Rosaldo 1984, 141–142) then SM yaoi articulated all that which was queer to my Western eyes. They were odd, singular, quaint, sick, ill. That which deviates from the expected or normal; strange: unconventional, eccentric: that of a questionable nature or character; suspicious; fake; counterfeit. Oblique, off-center; that which deviates from the customary; bizarre, cranky, curious, eccentric, erratic, freakish, odd, outlandish, peculiar, quirky, strange, unnatural, unusual, weird. Causing puzzlement; perplexing: curious, shady, suspect and suspicious. However, I became hooked on the thrill of finding in these texts unthinkable pleasures that confronted the highly conventional stories of sex and gender. SM yaoi had a seductive and compelling appeal that helped me to temporarily step outside my own world and consider alternative possibilities and other realities. SM yaoi are palimpsest texts that turn inside-out "normal" expressions of feeling within a homosocial context. Making visible what is felt on the inside they present a challenge to normative identity categories and render them unstable in the process and these peculiar texts provided me with plateaus from which I begin to construct new understandings of self.

In the next story, another interpretation and understanding of yaoi manga is voiced, one that speaks about dissonant understandings of self drawn from experiences of growing up in middle-class Australia and of having to live up to and play out performances of heterosexual femininity.

Dreaming Beside a Path Well Worn (Kim Senior)

> we should find countless intermediaries between reality and symbols if we gave things all the movements they suggest. George Sand, dreaming beside a path of yellow sand, saw life flowing by. "What is more beautiful than a road?" she wrote. "It is the symbol and the image of an active, varied life." [...] Each one of us, then, should speak of his roads, his cross-roads, his roadside benches; each one of us should make a surveyor's map of his lost fields and meadows [Bachelard 1994, 11].

My stories, the stories I chose to tell as a reader, took some time to come to this page. Reading has, and remains, an integral part of my pragmatic life (I read as part of my life as an academic, it consumes my conversations with friends and students alike and is a requisite for sleep); the "what" of reading has worn deep ruts into my every day. The "why" is a far less familiar track. Family anecdotes about my obsession with reading are deeply rooted in childhood reminiscences: "Kim always had her nose in a book." And I have guilty memories of pretending to be completely oblivious to my surroundings curled up in a corner with a book: "She gets so engrossed," I hear my mother proudly telling another, "she's our bookworm!"

Reading was a form of entertainment and escape. In the mid–1970s (when I was twelve years old) my father was posted to Belgrade, Yugoslavia. My mother, father, and two younger sisters and I took our first overseas trip — our first trip on a plane — to relocate for two years. Many children of the expatriate community attended boarding schools and so ours was a small circle at the tiny American/international school. For those of us who did not speak the local language there was no television, no radio. It was long before VCRs and the Internet. The European winters seemed long, dark, cold, and confining (being snowed in for days at a time was novel but quickly lost its novelty). Reading not only whiled away many long hours but provided space. In Australia my sisters and I were used to expanse, but in this politically and linguistically alien environment we were kept very close. We were kept close to our home and kept close to each other. I read as a way out: a way to escape the anxious gaze of my parents.

I read anything. Exhausting the school's library, I devoured a classmate's comic book collection (*Whizzer and Chips*, *The Beano*, and *Buster*). There is something ironic about identifying with characters (predominately male) obsessed with soccer, fish-and-chips and "rotters" — idiosyncratically "British" fare. Some classmates and I also read record albums; while listening to records we dissected the lyrics and sleeve art of Cat Stevens and the Beatles.

We returned to Australia when I was fourteen and, perhaps because of the contrast with the previous cold and controlled twenty-four months, I remember the few weeks we spent on holiday at Bondi Beach, Sydney with idyllic clarity. Bryan Ferry songs filled the air; the broad cloudless sky hugged the horizon; the surf was blue, glassy and seemed to be over-populated by sandy salt encrusted young men on surfboards. This was the Australia later (in)famously portrayed in *Puberty Blues* (Lette and Carey 1979). It remains quintessential Australia in the collective imagination and in my adolescent memory.

From the Benches (Kim Senior)

My home town, suburban Canberra, hundreds of kilometers from the coast was, however, bereft of sand and surfies. Kathy Lette and Gabriel Carey may have folded gritty towels, fetched Chiko rolls and sat for mindless hours on the beach while the boys surfed; we inland sisters, by contrast, were expected to stand for frigid hours on the sidelines of rugby league fields while the boys played. "We" belonged even when we didn't. A nerdy girl, one who was *not chosen* (in the language of the time, "going with" a guy) or waiting on the sporting sidelines *to be chosen,* found our way to the school library — in company, but not always in companionship, with "the Greek" chicks and the geeks. The library was a refuge; a comfortable place to do your homework and a quietly supervised space away from the hierarchical struggles being played outside.

Australia was, and is, a country obsessed by sport and sporting prowess; male sport and male sporting prowess. Even nerdy boys (*Dr. Who* fanatics and science geeks) could redeem themselves in the summer months by playing cricket, but the world in Anglo-Australian Canberra belonged to the rugby league players and their groupies. A third group, the sons of first-generation southern European migrants, either embraced the sports field in defense of their place in the food chain or alternatively proved their place off the field. "Aussie" girls were fair game in this particular sport; playing around with their "own" girls was only sanctioned by marriage. So, what were a teenage "Anglo-Australian" girl's options? In the words of Kathy Lette, it was to be a "sperm spittoon" (2003), to aspire to be a sperm spittoon, or to be a surrogate sperm spittoon. This nerdy girl refused to play. Stuck in the relative safety of the library I read. This time I read to escape the contemptuous gaze of my peers.

Reading this time offered a two-fold escape from confinement; it afforded academic success (dateless weekends and countless hours in the library had an unexpected pay-off) and an introduction into a whole new understanding of gender and gendered identity. It was in the library of my senior secondary school that I stumbled upon Germaine Greer, Dorothy Parker, Simone de Beauvoir, Virginia Woolf, *Ms.* magazine, Marilyn French and Jane Austen. In class, turgid Patrick White and Joseph Conrad reigned, but I snuck back to the ribald, defiant, witty and "shameless" group on the library shelves. I read them quietly (and sometimes secretly, in the case of Greer's *Female Eunuch* and de Beavoir's *Second Sex*), but in the lines and in the passages of these texts I got to play. In these texts I got to play rough. I began to understand the anger I felt at being prescribed roles, behaviors, or a way of being that was not of my own making or choosing.

To a Crossroad (Kim Senior)

A student exchange scholarship before going to university was my first opportunity to travel to Japan. I lived and attended high school in a small coastal town in Kyūshū; population around 40,000 Japanese people, one American Lutheran missionary, and one reclusive Italian Catholic priest. A little older than most exchange students at eighteen years of age meant that the strict protocols of Japanese high school life (uniform dress code, curfew and venue restrictions, i.e., coffee shops, which were strictly out of bounds) and my limited language competence once more found me in a confining social context. At school I threw myself into the study of calligraphy (attending *shodō* classes), Japanese language (private tutoring from the English-language staff) and Japanese history (I became enamored by the Heian period and the works of Murasaki Shikibu and Sei Shōnagon). After school, while other students attended sports, cultural clubs or *juku* (cram school), my host grandmother and I found a companionable silence in front of TV *jidaigeki* (period dramas) and when my ten-year-old host brother came home, his preference for *Doraemon, Dr. Slump* and *Lupin.*

Limited luggage space meant that I could only bring a couple of favorites for company on the twelve-month exchange: *Emma* and *Pride and Prejudice.* The school's English-language book collection despairingly consisted of an encyclopedia set from the early 1960s and some highly abridged versions of Shakespeare for the purpose of teaching English. Having exhausted all sources at hand, I had to start looking elsewhere for reading matter. I felt I had outgrown my juvenile delight in comic book reading and the afternoon television of my host brother only seemed to confirm a distain for his predilections for boy's-own-life adventure and themes (i.e., a fascination with bodily functions). However, whiling away time in bookshops and in front of the television made me realize there was something more to manga and anime than the comic books of my earlier experience. I began paying more attention to what my classmates and host brothers and sisters were reading. My first purchase was volumes 4 to 6 (dealing with Heian Japan) of the *Nihon no rekishi* (Japanese History) series. These volumes were written for middle primary school students and made use of *furigana* for more complex *kanji* and names of historical figures. I would look up names in my Japanese history dictionary and piece together the narrative across my English reference books, the Japanese History textbook we used in class and my manga. Later I borrowed my host sister's copies of *Urusei yatsura, Inuyasha* and *Ranma 1/2* and happily I struggled *kanji* by *kanji*, phrase by phrase, line by line, dictionary in hand.

The Symbol and the Image of Active, Varied Reading (Kim Senior)

At first I painstakingly fixed upon the meaning of the words in the manga, but this eventually proved fruitless and unsatisfying. The "plain form" of Japanese verbs was new to me and many words did not appear in the Japanese-English dictionary. I gave up trying to translate the text to understand; instead I read the page. I pulled my disciplined "Western" eyes away from script to explore (the) script. I flicked across the frames. Moved back. I noticed the shift in the "aspect-to-aspect transitions" (McCloud 1993, 79). I placed myself within the pages to assemble a moment or an interval in the narrative. I read the page in much the same way I watched a scene in the afternoon *jidaigeki* (archaic language and references left my ears to lift the occasional familiar word, to listen for tone and silence, and my eyes to watch for formulaic "stances," looks and gazes to make my way into the "story"). Reading in the past had been the instrument of escapism and an opening to a subaltern feminist discourse; now read*ing* became an act of alterity.

Thwarted by attempts at straight translation I began pulling my eyes away from a familiar decoding practice into a plural envisioning of a text. LaMarre (2000) suggests that the use of poetic techniques such as *kumiawasemoji* (an assemblage of *kanji* to form another word) and *mitate* (a visual pun using *kanji*) in Japanese symbolizes the rebus quality involved in "reading" or "writing" the language. He particularly notes how these techniques function not as "subordinate to the linguistic message or to grammatical signification.... In other words, secondary revision never subsumes or exhausts the rebus but runs parallel to it" (19). These insubordinate (re)visions are less familiar and perhaps more disconcerting to those readers of alphabetic traditions. "Western" readers are familiar with puns and wordplay, especially in the writing of post-structural and postmodern pundits; however, it takes on a whole new level in Japanese. From Buddhist texts (notably *zenga*) to the elaborate use of homonyms in *tanka* poetry, wordplay in Japanese is an honored tradition that has found multiplicitous use in manga. Sergei Eisenstein suggested that the manner in which Japanese characters were assembled was a form of montage and indicative of the "inherently 'cinematic' nature of Japanese culture" (Schodt, 1983, 25). Interestingly, one of the most influential and internationally renowned manga artists of the twentieth century, Tezuka Osamu (1928–1989), described his manga not as drawings but in terms of script: "I don't consider them pictures—I think of them as a type of hieroglyphics.... In reality I'm not drawing. I'm writing a story with a unique type of symbol" (Schodt 1983, 25).

Words (*kanji*) that are more than words (*moji*). Words that are symbols (*kumiawase-moji*) and sometimes symbolic of not-this-word (*mitate*). Symbols that are pictures and pictures that are symbols.

The Symbol and the Image of Not-the-Sperm-Spittoon (Kim Senior)

Takahashi Rumiko's playfulness with adolescent sexual appetites in *Urusei yatsura* made an interesting counterpoint to my own observations of Japanese high school culture. On the one hand relationships between young people in Australia seemed far more "grown up" and open than what I noticed of my Japanese peers. There was little, if absolutely no, physical contact between the sexes that I could see in Japan; although hand holding and tactility amongst young women was a noticeable exception. It confused me. The manga I read explored the intricacies and social sensibilities of lust and desire, but I saw and heard nothing of the "normal" behaviors I associated with such excitation (girls watching "their guy" play or practice sport, kissing publicly—and passionately!—when there was no teacher or adult of consequence about or the constant stream of sexual innuendo). Instead I linked arms with my female classmates in the corridors and between classes; on occasion my best friend and I even held hands as we talked over lunch. All behaviors that would roundly, and without exception, brand me as a "leso" in an Australian context; after all any young woman who was not, or did not aspire to be, a sperm spittoon had to be a lesbian.

Gender shifting in *Ranma 1/2* was another conundrum. In a culture where gender roles were symbolically (pink school slippers for the girls and blue for the boys) and explicitly ("boys don't do household chores") maintained, this story explored the comical adventures of a gender bending martial artist for a teenage audience. While I considered 1980s Australia far more liberal—it was a favorite conversation shocker for my host family to get me to explain to their dinner guests that my father did the vacuum cleaning and other household duties in Australia *willingly*—I had to reconsider this position.

Had I ever read about such topics as an adolescent? Had I heard discussion about such a topic without derisive tones or moral outrage? If I was honest with myself, I was left little doubt that in "liberated" Australia, gender ambiguity was perhaps an even greater transgression. Manga, embroiled in an intricate and centrifugal interplay between and at the boundaries of culture, identity, text, image, reality, and imagination, queered the way I read the narratives of sexual normativity and construction of Other in my everyday life in Japan and Australia. I began to appreciate the possibility of seeing words and images not as binaries and not one subjugated by other, but rather as a complex carnival (Bakhtin 1984); the possibility to imagine and inhabit a space beyond essentialist renderings.

I read manga only intermittently after the student exchange. They were impossible to buy in Canberra. But an opportunity to travel to Japan on a twelve-month university scholarship not only allowed me to catch up with my Japanese host family and make new friends, but pick up the threads of favorite manga series. Japanese university life was a far cry from my sequestered year in Kyūshū, and an active social life left little time or interest in adventuring beyond familiar mangaka. I packed a few favorite volumes to return home for graduation knowing that I would have to rely on visiting friends or a second-hand network to keep reading manga. Back in Australia there was seen to be some idiosyncratic value in reading comics in another language, but they were still comics. A twenty-something young Australian woman desperate to be taken seriously did not read comics. I shelved them alongside my other adolescent fads and student phases and got on with beginning a career and getting married. For a long period reading comics was an extravagant, hedonistic pastime lost to the necessity of growing up — performing teacher, wife and mother.

Countless Intermediaries Between Reality and Symbols: Getting Fucked and Fucking Over (Kim Senior)

When do we draw?

When we were little. Before the violent divorce between Good and Evil. All was mingled then, and no mistakes. Only desire, trial, and error. Trial, that is to say, error. Error: progression.

As soon as we draw (as soon as, following the pen, we advance into the unknown, hearts beating, made with desire) ... [Cixous 2005, 26].

In my forties I returned to post-graduate study. The "book club" from senior secondary school (Austen, Greer, and Murasaki and others) played a central role in theorizing my research; and not with a little initial bemusement, manga returned to my life (Senior, 2008). During the two decades between undergraduate and post-graduate study I continued to read *about* manga: I was particularly drawn to its potential as a strategy to teach Japanese language and delighted in publications such as *Mangajin* and *Do-It-Yourself Japanese Through Comics* (Nagatomo and Steinberg, 1995). Occasionally acquaintances or students asked me to translate or give the gist of a narrative as professionally translated manga imported from the United States were limited and prohibitively priced. Reading comics and manga for pleasure was limited to reading them with my son; he is of the *Pokémon* and *Dragon Ball* TV generation. I tried to transfer his TV interests to *Tintin* or "real" books based on *Pokémon* characters. Borders bookshop came to our city and with it a graphic novel section. Suddenly *Dragon Ball* led to *Dragon Ball Z*, led to *Naruto*, led to *One Piece*. There was no stopping him and I remembered how much I enjoyed reading manga. I marveled over the variety of titles and even noted the Korean or other international authors on offer as we sought out the next volume my son was after. I picked up a few titles that caught my eye, returning them to the shelves like a curious bystander before anyone would suspect my real interest. My days of reading manga for pleasure were a thing of the past. So I thought.

As part of a recent research project at a school, I found myself in conversation with a small group of avid manga readers. I brought along well thumbed but long shelved copies of *Urusei yatsura* and *Ranma ½* and they introduced me to the world of *dōjinshi*. They introduced me to the prolific CLAMP and the manga *Gravitation*. Now as a researcher I could legitimately rummage along the graphic novel shelves and sit for hours reading adolescent literature. But unlike the boys-own-adventures of my son's taste, I found these new writing/drawing/readings far more engrossing. They made conscious anger and discontentment that had been mostly lost and forgotten on the well-worn road of a grown-up woman's life.

I was aroused by the ambiguous and extravagant texts. The narratological structure of *Gravitation* resonated *jouissance* (Barthes, 1975): that dissolution of reader as subject and writer/drawer as object. The unexplained and unquestioned presence of homosexual or transgender relationships in CLAMP's *Tokyo Babylon* spoke to playfulness and possibility. The transgressive act of these women authoring, creating and appropriating space in the male dominated manga industry took me back to the cold Canberra rugby fields and the nerdy girl hiding in the library. The graphic sexual images in yaoi shock the nerdy girl, but they fascinate the straight woman. How had performing wife, mother and researcher taken me back to that library? When had manga reading for my pleasure been taken from me? When, and why, had I *allowed* it to be taken from me? When did getting fucked become getting fucked over?

At the end of *Puberty Blues* (Lette and Carey 1979) Kathy and Gabriel stalk down the beach with their own surf board leaving the beach to their own gritty towels and the derisive gazes and jeers of their peers. They leave "getting fucked over" behind as they create their own way. The pleasure I get from yaoi manga is no well-behaved pleasure. It is the

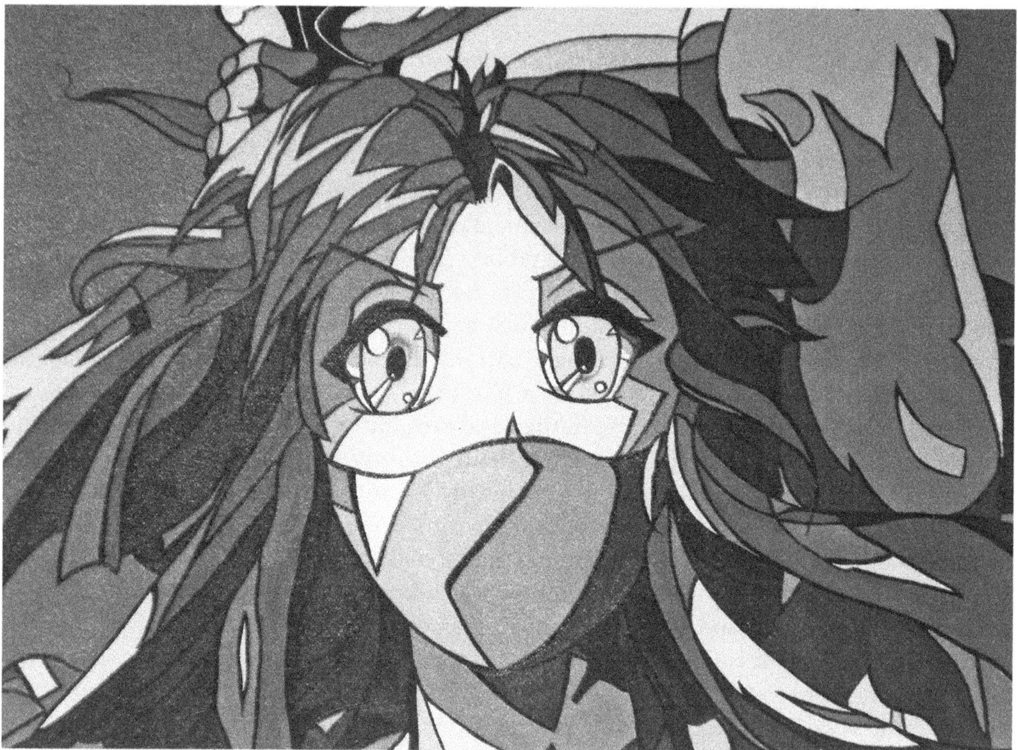

Figure 1: "silent" by Bianca Hill, © 2007 (acrylics on canvas, original 150 cm × 50 cm).

painful ache, the bittersweet stinging discomfort of confronting the nerdy girl still hiding in the library. The "book club" was a wonderful beginning to unravel the hetero- masculinized world of 1970s and 1980s Australia, but it is the graphic pages of yaoi that smash that world and dare me to (re)imagine my becoming woman.

I get to fuck the passive *uke*. I fuck over the complicit bystander. With/in these graphic texts I get to confront the female teenage peers of the past who collaborated in the sperm-spittoon game. I get to fuck over the complicit bystanders: the teachers that failed to present any other alternative ways of being in or outside the classroom that challenged the status quo. And I get to fuck over the silent bystander within me; the one that allows the normalizing games and performances of sexuality and gender to go on uninterrupted, circulating and accepted. The bystander that falls all too easily into the seductive straightforwardness of doing a life laid out rather than creating a life of our own. "Silent" (Fig. 1) was my seventeen-year-old niece's response to reading some of my earlier writing. I look at the way she draws and narrates her-becoming (see Fig. 2) and wonder how I may create and (re)envision an insubordinate queer self?

Revisiting the Past in the Present: A Methodological Approach (Kim Senior)

> Identity, as a socially constructed phenomenon, may change over time. In other words, one may, on occasion redocument one's own identity. This redocumentation typically involves recasting one's identity around a new set of relevancies (e.g., linguistic descriptions such as "gay" rather than "straight," "adult" rather than "adolescent") which in turn involves a recasting of one's entire biography as "leading up to one's present identity" [Weinberg 1979, 147–148].

Giroux (1987) has noted how a person's "stories, memories, narratives and readings of the world are inextricably related to wider social and cultural formations and categories" (177) and throughout adolescence the divisions we experienced were generated from being between or on the wrong side of the boundaries of inside/outside, hetero/homo, self/other. Struggling with our queer interiority, feeling unconnected and set apart became our "mode of response to the very forms of power that each day reproduced it" (Barker 1989, 88). Our stories, whilst telling of central moments and critical incidents, also articulate something of the process of how life stories are able to offer a more ambiguous, complex and chaotic view of reality (Hatch & Wisniewski 1995). Resisting hegemonic modes of knowing and telling we have written fragments of discourse intended to evoke in the minds of the reader how we used texts to scaffold our emergent fantasies of possibilities for becoming. Each memory that has been triggered in the writing of our stories, its interpretation and analysis, has been reworked to uncover the layers of understanding. A "layered account is that which decenters the authority of science by including narrative reflections, fantasies, and emotions along with statistics and abstract theory" (Ronai 1995, 397) and we have drawn on our multiple and overlapping histories to tell of how our performances of non-normative identities textualized our everyday lives and inculcated our fugitive reading practices. Our encounters with texts can be thought of as offering a history of our interactions with ourselves and others in the world; and how they became our way of negotiating identifications and of interpreting and reincorporating the self as "Other." Rosenblatt (1978) has suggested how "a person becomes a reader by virtue of her/ his activity in relationship to a text" (Rosenblatt 1978, 18). Throughout our stories, we have accounted for how, as

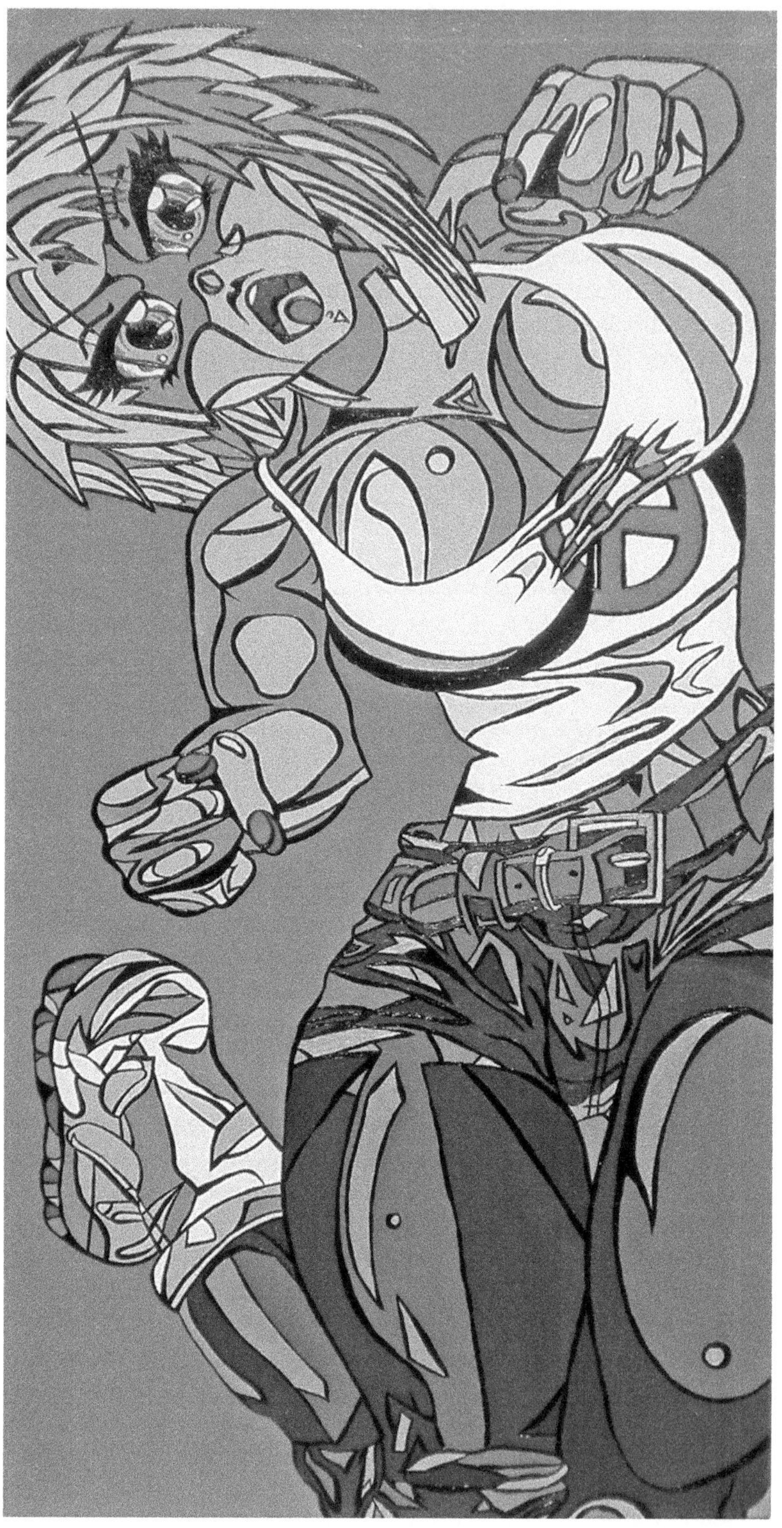

Figure 2: "self portrait" by Bianca Hill, © 2008 (acrylics on canvas, original 65 cm × 35 cm).

particular and collective subjects, we came to read ourselves into texts and how our writerly responses made the unavailable available, the absent present, and the silenced voiced. Said (1991) has noted how culture exerts pressures and how it creates the environment and the community that allow people to feel they belong. However, having an experience of not belonging was for us "the splinter in [our] eye [and it was] the best magnifying-glass" (Adorno 1978, 50) through which we began to dissect how and why our identities were questionable. Yaoi texts increasingly offered us a way to resist the normative culture that had always been present (Said 1991).

With/in the Space of Différance (Kim Senior)

Everyone, at some time in their life, must choose whether to stay with a ready-made world that may be safe but which is also limiting or to push forward, often past the frontiers of common sense, into a personal place, unknown and untried (Winterson 1991, xiv).

Within the field of literacy there has been a significant ongoing debate as to how identities can be constituted through literacy practices; how subjects position themselves in relation to texts in order to mount a challenge to dominant discourses and how literacy becomes a practice for negotiating the structures of power and domination (Willis 1995; Street 1994). In this chapter, our narratives have endeavored to trace, how, as subjects, we re-imagined ourselves through our textual practices. Working from an understanding of identity as a "performative struggle over the meanings of experience" (Langellier 2001, 3), we have written about how yaoi manga are texts where "identity finds a way to re-create itself" (Holland 1980, 126).

Yaoi queers the (re)citation of heteronormative identities scripted by the "heterosexual matrix" (Butler 1990) in the staged hybrid performances of gender ambiguities and sexual indeterminacies. They displace the power of a bipolar identification, to disassemble "unity and coherence" and to "decentre centers and disrupt hierarchies" (Kamberelis 2004, 167). In yaoi manga, the mocking of the authority of the prohibitions of everyday life exceed capacity for interpretation. They are marginal expressions that disrupt the heteronormative ways of being and knowing. If, as it has been suggested, that "margins are places, where the marginal can find a space in which they can articulate themselves and be heard" (Hetherington 1998, 72), then thinking about how yaoi manga centralize "the explorations and productions of desires ... [that are] ... in excess of the socially possible or acceptable" (Light 1984, 7), they can be read as transgressive interpellations into and of the quotidian that re-make the disciplined spaces of everyday life "smooth" and "habitable" (de Certeau, 1984).

As the discourses and practices of hegemonic gender and sexuality took hold in our lives, we discovered, without instruction, a new way of reading that involved so much more than religiously following the text in front of us, that provided an escape from the impossibility of living inside infinite heterosexual narratives. Yaoi manga offered us opportunities to playfully reconstruct subjectivity, and as writerly interventions in and against the ideology of normative gender and sexuality, they provided indeterminate, intertextual opportunities for self-rearticulation. Conceived by the authors and "given up" to a mutually, yet not concordant discursive project of identity play, yaoi texts intervene their way between an imposed "literality." They are supported by *dōjinshi* networks (such as Comic Market in Tokyo, cosplay and manga swap meets in Australia) that are dispersed, diasporic and international. They are not just the province of *otaku* but as our stories demonstrate they find their nomadic traces in the lives of two seemingly unconnected people born into a generation that would appear to be disconnected from the phenomena. They became for us transitory, evanescent spaces between reality and imaginary; critical spaces from which to challenge the legitimacy of the heteronormative symbolic and social capital and to renegotiate the difficulties, pains, pleasures and needs of our lives.

Bibliography

Adorno, Theodor. *Minima Moralia: Reflections on a Damaged Life.* Translated by Edmund F. Jephcot. London: Verso, 1978.

Appadurai, Arjun. *Modernity at Large: Cultural Dimensions of Globalization.* London: University of Minnesota Press, 1996.

Appiah, Kwame. "Identity, Authenticity, Survival: Multicultural Societies and Social Reproduction." In *Multiculturalism,* edited by Amy Gutman. Princeton, NJ: Princeton University Press, 1994.

Atkinson, Elizabeth. "The Postmodern Prism: Fracturing Certainty in Educational Research." In *Educational Research in Practice: Making Sense of Methodology,* edited by Joanna Swann and John Pratt, 35–50. London: Continuum, 2003.

Bachelard, Gaston. *The Poetics of Space.* Translated by Maria Jolas. Boston: Beacon Press, 1994.

Bakhtin, Mikhail. *Rabelais and His World.* Translated by Hélène Iswolsky. Bloomington, IN: Indiana University Press, 1984.

Barker, Martin. *Comics: Ideology, Power and the Critics.* Manchester, UK: Manchester University Press, 1989.

Barrett, Michèle. Introduction to *Virginia Woolf: Women and Writing,* 1–39. London: Women's Press, 1979.

Barthes, Roland. *S/Z.* Translated by Richard Miller. New York: Hill and Wang, 1974.

_____. *The Pleasure of the Text.* Translated by Richard Miller. New York: Hill and Wang, 1975.

_____. *Empire of Signs.* Translated by Richard Howard. New York: Hill and Wang, 1982.

Bataille, Georges. *Eroticism: Death and Sexuality.* Translated by Mary Dalwood. San Francisco: City Light Books, 1962.

Blackburn, Mollie. "Disrupting the (Hetero)normative: Exploring Literacy Performances and Identity Work with Queer Youth." *Journal of Adolescent & Adult Literacy* 4 (2002–2003): 312–24.

Butler, Judith. *Gender Trouble: Feminism and the Subversion of Identity.* London: Routledge, 1990.

_____. *Bodies That Matter: On the Discursive Limits of "Sex."* London: Routledge, 1993.

_____. *Excitable Speech: A Politics of the Performative.* London: Routledge, 1997.

Carbado, Devon. "Privilege." In *Black Queer Studies: A Critical Anthology,* edited by E. Patrick Johnson and Mae Henderson, 190–212. Durham, NC: Duke University Press, 2005.

Chauncey, George. *Gay New York: Gender, Urban Culture, and the Makings of the Gay Male World.* New York: Basic Books, 1994.

Cixous, Hélène. *Stigmata: Escaping Texts.* Abingdon, UK: Routledge, 2005.

Connell, Robert. *Masculinities.* St. Leonards, N.S.W., Australia: Allen & Unwin, 1995.

de Certeau, Michel. *The Practice of Everyday Life.* Translated by Steven Rendell. London: University of California Press, 1984.

Derrida, Jacques. *Margins of Philosophy.* Translated by Alan Bass. Chicago: University of Chicago Press, 1982.

Dreyfus, Hubert and Paul Rabinow. *Michel Foucault: Beyond Structuralism and Hermeneutics.* Chicago: University of Chicago Press, 1982.

Ellsworth, Elizabeth. *Teaching Positions: Difference, Pedagogy, and the Power of Address.* New York: Teachers College Press, 1997.

Foucault, Michel. *Discipline and Punish.* Translated by Alan Sheridan. New York: Vintage, 1977.

Fraser, Mariam. "Classing Queer: Politics in Competition." *Theory Culture & Society* 16 (1999): 107–31.

Freund, Elizabeth. *The Return of the Reader: Reader-Response Criticism.* London: Routledge, 1987.

Gee, James. *What Video Games Have to Teach Us About Learning and Literacy.* London: Palgrave Macmillan, 2003.

Giddens, Anthony. *Modernity and Self-Identity: Self and Society in the Late Modern Age.* Stanford, CA: Stanford University Press, 1991.

Giroux, Henry. "Critical Literacy and Student Experience: Donald Graves' Approach to Literacy." *Language Arts* 64 (1987): 175–81.

Hagood, Margaret. "A Rhizomatic Cartography of Adolescents, Popular Culture, and Constructions of Self." In *Spatializing Literacy Research and Practice,* edited by Kevin Leander and Margaret Sheehy. New York: Peter Lang, 2004.

Haraway, Donna. "The Promises of Monsters: A Regenerative Politics for Inappropriate/d Others." In *Cultural Studies*, edited by Lawrence Grossberg, Cary Nelson and Paula Treichler, 295–337. London: Routledge, 1992.

Hatch, J. Amos and Richard Wisniewski. *Life History and Narrative*. London: Routledge/Falmer, 1995.

Hetherington, Kevin. *Expressions of Identity: Space, Performance, Politics*. London: Sage, 1998.

Holland, Norman. "Unity, Identity, Text, Self." In *Reader Response Criticism: From Formalism to Post-Structuralism*, edited by Jane Tompkins, 118–33. Baltimore, MD: Johns Hopkins University Press, 1980.

Irigaray, Luce. *Je, Tu, Nous: Toward a Culture of Difference*. New York: Routledge Classics, 1990.

Iser, Wolfgang. "Indeterminacy and the Reader's Response in Prose Fiction." In *Aspects of Narrative: Selected Papers from the English Institute*, edited by Joseph Hillis Miller. New York: Columbia University Press, 1971.

Kamberelis, George. "The Rhizome and the Pack: Liminal Literacy Formations with Political Teeth." In *Spatializing Literacy Research and Practice*, edited by Kevin Leander and Margaret Sheehy, 161–97. New York: Peter Lang, 2004.

LaMarre, Thomas. *Uncovering Heian Japan: An Archaeology of Sensation and Inscription*. Durham, NC: Duke University Press, 2000.

Langellier, Kristin. "'You're Marked': Breast Cancer, Tattoo and the Narrative Performance of Identity." In *Narrative and Identity: Studies in Autobiography, Self and Culture*, edited by Jens Brockmeier and Donal Carbaugh, 145–84. Amsterdam and Philadelphia: John Benjamins, 2001.

Langer, Judith. *Envisioning Literature: Literary Understanding and Literature Instruction*. Newark, DE: International Reading Association and Teachers College Press, 1995.

Leck, Glorianne. "Queer Relations With Educational Research." In *Power and Method: Political Activism and Educational Research*, edited by Andrew Gitlin, 77–96. New York and London: Routledge, 1994.

Lette, Kathy. "George Negus Tonight." By George Negus. ABC Australia, 6:30 P.M., February 10, 2003 http://www.abc.net.au/dimensions/dimensions_in_time/Transcripts/s780748.htm (accessed August 12, 2008).

Lette, Kathy and Gabrielle Carey. *Puberty Blues*. Melbourne: McPhee Gribble, 1979.

Light, Alison. "'Returning to Manderley': Romance Fiction, Female Sexuality and Class." *Feminist Review* 16 (1984): 7–25.

Mac an Ghaill, Máirtín. *The Making of Men: Masculinities, Sexualities and Schooling*. Buckingham, UK: Open University Press, 1994.

Martel, Yann. *Self*. London: Faber & Faber, 2003.

Martin, Biddy. *Femininity Played Straight: The Significance of Being Lesbian*. New York: Routledge, 1996.

McCloud, Scott. *Understanding Comics: The Invisible Art*. New York: Harper Perennial, 1993.

McLaren, Peter. "White Terror and Oppositional Agency: Towards a Critical Multiculturalism." In *Multiculturalism: A Critical Reader*, edited by David Theo Goldberg. Cambridge, MA: Basil Blackwell, 1994.

Nagatomo, Kazuhiko and Miho Steinberg. *Do-It-Yourself Japanese Through Comics*. Tokyo: Kōdansha, 1995.

Napier, Susan. *Anime from Akira to Howl's Moving Castle: Experiencing Contemporary Japanese Animation*. New York: Palgrave Macmillan, 2005.

Ronai, Carol. "Multiple Reflections of Child Sex Abuse: An Argument for a Layered Account." *Journal of Contemporary Ethnography* 4 (1995): 395–426.

Rosaldo, Michelle. "Toward an Anthropology of Self and Feeling." In *Culture Theory: Essays on Mind, Self, and Emotion*, edited by Richard Shweder and Robert Levine, 137–57. Cambridge, UK: Cambridge University Press, 1984.

Rosenblatt, Louise. *The Reader, The Text, The Poem: The Transactional Theory of the Literary Work*. Carbondale, IL: Illinois University Press, 1978.

Ross, Kristin. "Watching the Detectives." In *Postmodernism and the Re-Reading of Modernity*, edited by Francis Barker, Peter Hulme and Margaret Iversen, 46–65. Manchester, UK: Manchester University Press, 1992.

Rutherford, Jonathan. *Identity: Community, Culture, Difference*. London: Lawrence & Wishart, 1990.

Said, Edward. *The World, The Text and the Critic*. New York: Vintage, 1991.

Schodt, Frederik. *Manga! Manga! The World of Japanese Comics*. Tokyo: Kōdansha International, 1983.

Sedgwick, Eve Kosofsky. *Tendencies*. London: Routledge, 1994.

Segal, Lynne. *Straight Sex: The Politics of Pleasure*. London Virago, 1994.

Senior, Kim. "Letters as an Imaged-Based Methodology in Educational Research." In *Researching Education Visually-Digitally-Spatially*, edited by Julianne Moss, 183–208. Rotterdam: Sense Publications, 2008.

Shiach, Morag. *Hélène Cixous: A Politics of Writing*. London: Routledge, 1991.

Sparkes, Andrew. "The Fatal Flaw: A Narrative of the Fragile Body-Self." *Qualitative Inquiry* 4 (1996): 463–494.

Street, Brian. "Cross-Cultural Perspectives on Literacy." In *Language and Literacy in Social Practice*, edited by Janet Maybin. Philadelphia: Multilingual Matters, 1994.

Theweleit, Klaus. *Male Fantasies Vol. 2*. Oxford: Polity Press, 1989.

Turner, Victor. *The Ritual Process: Structure and Anti-Structure*. Ithaca, NY: Cornell University Press, 1977.

Vygotsky, Lev. *Mind and Society.* Cambridge, MA: Harvard University Press, 1978.
Warner, Michael. *The Trouble with Normal: Sex, Politics, and the Ethics of Queer Life.* New York: The Free Press, 1999.
Weinberg, Thomas. "On 'Doing' and 'Being' Gay: Sexual Behavior and Homosexual Male Self-Identity." *Journal of Homosexuality* 4 (1979): 143–168.
Willis, Ingram. "Reading the World of School Literacy: Contextualizing the Experience of a Young African American Male." *Harvard Educational Review* 65 (1995): 30–49.
Winterson, Jeanette. *Oranges Are Not the Only Fruit.* London: Vantage, 1991.

12

Gay or Gei?

Reading "Realness" in Japanese Yaoi Manga

ALEXIS HALL

Among the shelves of Japanese manga that can be found in any popular bookstore in the United States, one is likely to find an increasing number of yaoi manga. What does the emerging popularity of yaoi tell us about the relationships between culture, sexuality and media across national borders? How do culturally specific conceptions of sexuality affect readings of Japanese yaoi manga? To answer these questions, this essay brings together cultural studies scholarship on audiences and cross-cultural communication with queer theory on the globalization of sexuality. I investigate American fan responses to yaoi manga and argue that American consumers of yaoi bring culturally specific assumptions of sexual identity to the text, which thereby influence their judgments regarding its quality, specifically that surrounding the idea of "realness."

Yaoi is a sub-genre of Japanese manga almost exclusively aimed at and created by women that features male/male romantic or sexual relationships. Japanese manga, which is similar to comics or graphic novels, makes up a huge portion of Japan's publishing industry and is one of its largest exports. Thus, one of the fascinating aspects of yaoi is its emergence as a global commodity. The movement of yaoi manga from Japan to the United States complicates the process of how it is understood and raises a number of interesting questions regarding the global circulation of commodities, meaning-making across cultures, and constructions of sexuality.

The way American audiences discuss yaoi manga reflects both their assumptions as an expression of Western mores and the expectations and value they place on the text as a Japanese product.[1] Cross-cultural communication theories suggest that ethnocentrism, stereotypes, cognitive biases, and social identity mediate the ways in which audiences interact with cultural material.[2] Consequently, cultural background and influences affect audiences' worldviews and the ways they process information. These influences cause certain elements that are assumed by Western society to be taken for granted, even in situations in which they may not apply. Thus, even without deliberate adaptation or prior Japanese cultural knowledge, fans interpret and analyze yaoi texts by their own culturally influenced standards.

The concept of ethnocentrism seems to be especially helpful connecting these theories of cross-cultural communication with other theories regarding globalization and particularly the globalization of sexuality. Because yaoi deals with same-sex sexual content, I focus on the assumptions that Western audiences bring to yaoi manga texts regarding sexuality, most clearly displayed by audience constructions of gay identity. These readings often enact an understanding of sexuality that privileges a specific Western construction that is set up as "right" and universal, despite different global and social contexts.

Work done by Veruska Sabucco similarly addresses how understandings of global sex-

211

uality apply to yaoi manga by focusing on the meaning-making process. In the chapter "Guided Fan Fiction: Western 'Readings' of Japanese Homosexual-themed Texts," Sabucco explores the ways in which Western audiences "creatively read" Japanese yaoi and boys' love manga. Most notably, she relates this to the "queer" content of yaoi manga by arguing that "Japanese 'queer' culture represented by *shōnen-ai* and yaoi is not the same queer culture created by their Western fans; it is a partially different culture, born from the process of 'interpretation, appropriation and reconstruction' that those manga and anime undergo."[3] Because Western readers may associate the representation of male/male sexuality with a certain ideology of gay identity and because this ideology is thought to be ubiquitous globally, these ideologies are applied to yaoi texts and mediate the meanings and impressions that readers gain from these texts.

Methodology

In October 2006, I attended Yaoi-Con in California where I sat in on panels and interviewed American yaoi fans. I spoke to a total of twenty-one participants in fifteen short sessions. Respondents were from different backgrounds but were predominantly women (two were men) and ranged in ages from eighteen to fifty.[4]

The interviews elicited diverse responses, many of which highlight the relatively unexplored territory of American yaoi fans. By addressing topics unique to American fans, these responses diverge from previous work on yaoi manga in Japan. These responses highlight the variances in meaning-making across cultures and the assumptions American yaoi fans enact through their readings of yaoi texts.

Reading "Realness"

One concept that was raised repeatedly by interviewees is that of "realness." These references relate both to the idea of yaoi as an "unreal" or fantastical genre, something akin to a romance novel, and the distinction between representations of sexuality in yaoi manga and the "real" experiences of same-sex-desiring men. These discussions of realness illuminate a number of complex assumptions and ideas that not only expose the ways in which fans relate to yaoi manga texts but also the ways in which they understand sexuality and identity. American yaoi fans judge the "realness" of yaoi manga by relating it to their own conceptions of "gayness." These constructions of "gayness" emphasize scenes of victimization and "coming out" as the two most salient factors of "realness." I argue that this interpretation is based on assumptions that largely ignore the complexity of ways in which sexuality is expressed both in the U.S. and in Japan. An understanding of same-sex sexuality that takes into account the culturally specific aspects of sexuality in Japan brings into question the assumptions on which these constructions of realness are based.

Many of those who address realness set up a dichotomy between "realness" and yaoi manga. One female respondent, who refers to herself as 9th Circle of Hell, makes a point of highlighting the distinction between yaoi and reality:

> I think it's very important to recognize that it is a work of fiction. And particularly yaoi is a work in fiction. I mean, women writing about gay male sex. They haven't had it. So, in a sense you're not ... it's not a realistic depiction. Plus, it's like romance novels aren't a

> realistic depiction of het[erosexual] sex. So, keeping that in mind, I think something I have heard gay men say is that they love a lot of yaoi because it romanticizes it. It's not just what you get in real gay fiction that's like mechanic: You do this, I do this, and then we fuck. This actually has a story and it's romantic. And so in a way it's almost kind of like, you know, you think of it as sort of a romance novel. It's a work of fiction, it's romanticized, it's a fantasy, so you don't look for reality. You don't look for an instruction manual. You don't think this is the way things really are. Because in a lot of yaoi, for one thing, it doesn't mean anything that you're gay. Everyone accepts it. Or you're not gay, even though you have sex with a lot of men, you're not really gay. So you know. It's a story; it's a work of fiction. You have to just keep that in mind.

This response begins to raise a number of themes regarding the ways realness is valued and evaluated: experience, romanticism, and gay men as "legitimate" judges of realness in yaoi.

This interviewee is quick to distinguish that yaoi is fiction. This is likely because within manga and anime fandom, those who view textual material as representative of "Real Japan" are viewed negatively. While I would argue that the division into "good fans" and "bad fans" is arbitrary and inaccurate for many reasons, including that there is a great wealth of cultural information to be gained from manga and anime, 9th Circle of Hell's ability to distinguish between "reality" and fiction seems to give her a sort of superiority over these other fans.

Once she acknowledges it as fiction, however, 9th Circle of Hell explains how yaoi can be freely enjoyed for its fictitiousness. It's noteworthy that she mentions romance novels, as these are one of the main texts which are enjoyed despite or because of their deviation from "reality."

In contrast, she refers to gay men's fiction, fiction primarily by and for gay men, as "real." By this, she suggests that gay men are more legitimate judges of yaoi's realness because they have "experience," while the female writers and consumers of yaoi "haven't had it," so their representations and understandings are not as relevant. This distinction hints at the ways in which the realness of yaoi manga is conceived and determined.

She continues by explaining what she likes to see in yaoi manga in terms of reality:

> So I actually like the stories that sort of explore that you know, when a character has to come out to his or her family. Or they acknowledge the fact that they are ... you know, they're pretending to be roommates and not really in a relationship. Or that it's not all smooth sailing and everyone is like "oh, we don't care." That it actually ... they exist in what could be a real society.

Her idea of a "real" society with regard to same-sex sexuality is clearly marked by the situations and conditions that she lists: coming out, acknowledgment of identity, and possible adverse reactions from others. These characteristics, coming out into a gay identity and the resultant anti-gay persecution, largely define what most respondents consider when evaluating the "realness" of yaoi manga. It seems that these aspects are used to judge the "realness" of yaoi manga because they are considered to be some of the most important and salient aspects of "real gay lives." These features can be said to make up a specific ideology of same-sex sexuality that is rooted in Western, largely white and middle class, representations of gayness. This ideology has become the dominant conception of gayness in general discourse. It is this specific representation that is enacted as the "reality" against which yaoi manga is judged.

This can be seen from the responses of other female respondents who also addressed the issue of "reality." In response to my question asking how yaoi presents sexuality, respondents Hemlock and TJ discuss the realness of the yaoi genre in general:

HEMLOCK: Yaoi-land is ... Yaoi-land has a certain set of rules.

TJ: [laughs] I wouldn't say it's entirely realistic.

HEMLOCK: Ever! When's the last time you saw them open up a bottle of lube? Come on!

TJ: That may have something to do with the invisible dicks too.[5]

HEMLOCK: You never see anything! The miraculously wet [unintelligible] it's like it's all easy and perfect. Which is in a way, it's fantasy so it should be kinda easy. I mean there's certainly enough angst to go around anyway. And not everyone likes that, but....

TJ: The whole thing is supposed to be you know, arousing and sensual and exciting. It's not really that sensual to "okay stop a minute. Okay now open the [condom? lube?] You know, it's not.

HEMLOCK: ... AIDS test....

TJ: It's kind of what flows with the whole sensual feeling.

HEMLOCK: And some of them are more realistic than others. Um, some of them actually touch on — especially when they're high school students — they touch on about what their friends are going to think. And usually there's always that slight hesitation like, "it's not natural" but then it's just like swept under the rug kind of. So yeah, Yaoi-land is certainly a place. It's got its own time and rules.

From this exchange, one can see that Hemlock and TJ do not expect yaoi manga to be realistic. They acknowledge that it maintains its own norms and "sets of rules." Hemlock's comment about "Yaoi-land" does not seem to be a negative one. She acknowledges that yaoi manga does not always adhere to standards of "realistic" representations of sexuality. By acknowledging this, she can still enjoy yaoi manga for what it is without needing or desiring it to be "realistic."

At the same time, the set of criteria by which the "realness" of yaoi manga is being judged becomes evident: Do they use lube and condoms? Do they have any worries regarding AIDS? TJ suggests that a story cannot include "real" issues without interrupting the sensual feelings of the story. This statement implies that readers value these "sensual" feelings more than "realism." But as Hemlock observes, there is enough variation among yaoi series to find some that are more "realistic." Based on her response, one can see that she considers yaoi manga that addresses "what [the character's] friends will think" or addresses the naturalness of male/male sexuality to be "realistic." This suggests that to her, "reality" is the world in which homosexuality is non-normative and problematic. Thus, an acknowledgment of the ways in which same-sex sexuality functions vis-à-vis heteronormativity is necessary for a manga to appear "realistic." This is opposed to many yaoi manga in which sexuality is unaddressed and sex is romanticized.

TJ elaborates on this theme as she continues:

> It's nice that you don't see a whole lot of persecution. Or at least I haven't in what I've read. It's not like "Oh my god you're gay!" You don't see the whole persecution thing. It's not entirely realistic I suppose, but — and again, it's idealistic. It's nice.

She suggests that what makes yaoi "not entirely realistic" is that it does not portray persecution of homosexuality. This conversely assumes that a portrayal of persecution would lead yaoi manga to be read as more "realistic." Even so, she insists that she particularly enjoys this aspect of yaoi manga, despite, or indeed because of, its lack of "reality."

In contrast to respondents who focus on how yaoi manga is not realistic, one respondent discusses instances of realism. Respondent Ash comments on a specific yaoi manga-ka, Miyamoto Kano, saying about her works in particular, "It's real! I think it's real." What is it about the works of this author as opposed to others that sets them apart in terms of realness? A close reading of Miyamoto's work may clarify what Ash means by "real."

A few of Miyamoto's works, including *Not/Love*, *Two of Hearts*, and *Say Please*, have been published in English, while many other of her works have been scanlated (scanned, translated, and edited) into English by online scanlating groups and are thus available to English-speaking yaoi audiences who read yaoi online. One of Miyamoto's titles that Ash mentions in particular is *Rules*. *Rules* is the story of high school student Yuki Konoe. Yuki is in love with one of his (ostensibly heterosexual) classmates, Atori. Despite this, he has started having sex with a slightly older bisexual man named Hikaru whom he met in the gay district of town. *Rules* follows Yuki as he explores his feelings for both Atori and Hikaru.

One of the notable aspects of *Rules* is that Yuki mentions that he has known about his sexuality from a very early age. His narration reads:

> From young [*sic*] I have been interested in boys. In the past, the me who didn't know better kept on thinking I am abnormal. Or even felt that a weirdo like me should not even have been born into this world.— And so I've done lots of stupid things. Of course, I'm not stupid enough to end my own life.... But I've never managed to get past this shadow. Only after I've entered high school have I learnt to face myself, and know that in this world there are actually lots of others like me.[6]

Frank statements of an innate sexual preference or identity such as this are somewhat of an exception to the norms of yaoi manga. Characters largely consider their same-sex attraction as an isolated incident and not in terms of any sort of sexual identity it might imply. Thus, it is possible that this reference to innate sexual preference is one of the features that led Ash to view this manga as more "real" than other manga.

Another aspect that may have a part in Ash's reading of *Rules* as a "realistic" manga is that Yuki tells other people about his sexuality. In one scene, Hikaru, whom Yuki has just slept with for the first time the night before, comes to Yuki's school after class to bring him a disc he left at Hikaru's home. Yuki is with his friends at the time, including Atori. Once Hikaru leaves, his friends question him about how he knows the attractive older boy. One friend asks in jest if Hikaru is Yuki's boyfriend. Yuki freezes and abruptly admits that, yes, Hikaru is his boyfriend. Yuki's friends are surprised but nonchalant about the confession. Yuki, however, becomes upset and runs home.

While it is not unheard-of in yaoi manga that others know about a character's sexuality, especially the protagonist's best friend, this scene can be read more as a "coming out" scene, in the Western sense, a factor that multiple respondents mention as a determining factor in the "realness" of a manga. What makes this scene different from other yaoi manga in which characters admit their homosexual activity to friends is that Yuki is not in love with Hikaru (at this point). In many other yaoi manga, homosexuality and same-sex attraction are not necessarily based on any sort of history of same-sex attraction within a character's past. When same-sex attraction does occur within the story, it is often presented not as an endorsement of male-male love in general, but a specific situation in which one male character is in love with someone who also happens to be male. Thus, even when characters confess their same-sex desires to their friends or other characters, it is more of an isolated confession of love as opposed to any sort of "coming out" in the Western sense, in which an individual adopts a gay identity. However, because Yuki is not in love with Hikaru and the narrative previously mentions his attraction to boys since his youth, this can be read as a "coming out" scene. Because "coming out" is a pervasive aspect to gayness in the United States, it is likely that this scene contributes to Ash's reading of this manga as "real" or at least, more "real" than other yaoi manga.

With regard to yaoi manga representations of sexuality in general, Ash continues:

> The guys ... they're always confused. I do think there's a lot like that. Like I thought "Cut" was pretty real, by Toko Kawai. That's one of my favorites. And they [the characters] talk about that too you know. The guy's like "oh, I'm not gay" but you know ... you're in this relationship with your friend and [laughs] I think ... I've heard that's a very Japanese thing, to be like "I'm not gay, I'm just having sex with you" and we do that in America.... That's why we have the answer choice on the CDC [Center for Disease Control] questionnaire "Men who have sex with men" cuz people won't admit that they're gay. And they ran into so much of that. Like "You're not gay?" "Hell no I'll kill you." "Do you have sex with men?" "Yes, three times a week." I mean seriously like that's what we study in school, like how that came to be.[7]

Her response highlights the intersections between the male-male sexuality depicted in yaoi manga and notions of gay identity. Ash seems to indicate that yaoi manga in which characters address the issue of gay identity are realistic. While the standards by which the "realness" of yaoi manga is judged originate from Western, largely American notions of homosexuality, she astutely notes that these standards do not necessarily apply to Japan and sometimes do not even apply within the U.S. She does not insist that only those characters that embrace the "gay" identity present realness because she acknowledges the varied ways in which individuals both in the U.S. and Japan negotiate sexuality and identity. Her mention of "men who have sex with men" as a category addresses the divergent ways sexuality and identity may operate even within the United States. This challenges many of the assumptions regarding the universal nature of sexuality, and brings into question preconceptions regarding the "realness" of yaoi manga.

In regard to how she sees yaoi manga as "real," female respondent Neon claims that "a lot of times the characters in yaoi or manga have to deal with the same issues that real ... uh ... real gay men have to deal with. And the ... like the prejudice and the ... stereotypes." While this opinion differs from most of the other respondents in terms of how "real" yaoi manga is in general, it clearly articulates the value system by which the "realness" of yaoi manga is judged: its relationship to "real gay men."

One of the few gay male respondents similarly evokes "realness" in relation to real gay men. Rhys evaluates yaoi's "realism" based on its relation to his own experiences as a gay man. In response to a question of how he thinks yaoi presents sexuality, he responds:

> I mean it's somewhat accurate. I guess, I mean, some ... some of the guys you know aren't always just like *uke* or *seme* or something like that. Some of them are more [unintelligible] so, when it comes to actually portraying the sexuality itself, it's a fairytale, pretty much. I mean, well ... it's like any kind of romance novel, I guess. Real people don't act like that.

His experiences as a gay man inform his understanding of "gayness." He privileges this experience in his judgments of realness in yaoi manga. This privileging of "real gay male experience" in reference to yaoi was also addressed by 9th Circle of Hell and demonstrates the tendency exhibited by many respondents in which they perceive the "realness" of yaoi in relation to their conceptions of "gayness."

"Realness," "Gayness," and Global Sexuality

Based on these theories and responses, it becomes evident that "realness" is not judged on any number of textual factors including setting or characters, but on how accurately the yaoi manga depiction of same-sex *issues* and *interactions* relates to the reader's conception of "real gay life." This is demonstrated, although not always explicitly, in the ways respondents articulate what does and does not make yaoi manga realistic.

Certainly, this judgment of "realness" or "accuracy" is subjective. This subjectivity is evident through the variation of responses. Gender, sexual orientation, education and any number of factors may influence conceptions of gayness. Neon, for instance, was one of the few respondents to claim that, in general, yaoi manga accurately reflect real gay men's lives. This may be largely in part because Neon, as a woman, may have a very different conception of "real gay men's lives" than a respondent such as Rhys who identifies as a gay man himself.

Similarly, respondents emphasize certain characteristics as belying the "realness" of the yaoi manga text, but some of these characteristics differed. TJ mentions that the lack of prejudice in yaoi is a factor that makes it unrealistic. It is striking that it is negative features such as these that are the factors that determine the realism of a yaoi manga series. While violence and anti-gay discrimination are certainly present in the lives of many gay men, it is troubling that this association goes so far to victimize gayness that any representation that does not fall within the confines of these negative factors are viewed as "unrealistic" or "idealistic" as TJ says. In other words, this response suggests that "real" gayness is reached through experience of victimization.

Due to cultural differences between the Japanese point of origin and the American point of consumption, differences in the conception of gayness, and thus the perception of realness of yaoi manga by the reader, may be affected. Rhys, because of his experiences as a gay man living in the United States, seems to feel himself to be a qualified judge of the "realness" of yaoi manga based on his real life experiences. When asked during an interview with a female friend how yaoi presents sexuality, he responded, "I think that's more of a question for me." This shows that he believes his gay experience gives him authority on the subject over his female counterpart because yaoi deals with same-sex sexuality. This privileging of gay "experience" was also addressed by 9th Circle of Hell, who suggested that yaoi couldn't be real because the female *mangaka* could not experience the gay male sex about which they were writing.

However, it is interesting that Rhys should feel himself to be a better judge of realness by virtue of his gayness than, for instance, Japanese women audiences by virtue of their Japaneseness. Rhys does not have the experiences of Japanese gay man. This suggests that in this context gayness as a factor is privileged and viewed as more important than ethnicity and cultural knowledge. This is likely because American readers find the same-sex sexuality present in yaoi manga is clearly identifiable, whereas the ethnicity of the characters may be ambiguous. The privileging of sexuality over culture also indicates an assumption regarding the universality of gayness in which certain modes of sexuality are viewed as universal without regard to culture specificities.

The idea that there is a universal precedent of gay identity assumes a commonality of identity and expression across the global world that may not necessarily be accurate. This idea of a universal gay identity is enacted in events such as the 1994 NYC gay pride parade which boasted the theme "Stonewall 25: A Global Celebration of Pride." As Martin Manalansan provides as an example, a guide from the activities advertises, "People will celebrate the rebellion that transformed the existing Homophile Movement into our contemporary, global, Lesbian, Gay and Transgender rights Movement."[8] The idea that the very specific site of rebellion at Stonewall transformed into a "global" movement assumes much, notably a U.S.–centric conception of sexual identity and the universality of sexual rights.

Ash addresses these assumptions when she articulates the differences and similarities between same-sex sexuality in the U.S. and Japan. She asserts that the ways in which gayness operates in Japan may be very different from how it operates in the U.S., but in some ways it may be similar. She remarks, "I've heard that's a very Japanese thing, to be like 'I'm not gay, I'm just having sex with you.'" Whether her assertion regarding sexual identity in Japan is accurate or not, this response highlights that a yaoi manga may still be "real" based on its relational representation of "gayness," but this idea of "gayness" may be conceived differently in different cultural settings; in this case, Japan and the United States.

While there are certainly a myriad of ways in which gayness is expressed within a given culture, it is easy to see the differences and culturally specific ways in which gayness is conceived when one looks outside of the West. Compared to the U.S., Japan certainly has a very different history regarding male homosexual practices. Historically, male/male sexual practices have been sanctioned as long as they did not impede the continuation of the family structure, namely marriage and reproduction. Thus, there were three main sites of male homosexual activity: "Homosexual behavior was formally organized in such institutions as samurai mansions, Buddhist monasteries, and male brothels linked to the kabuki theater."[9] All of these sites maintained certain stratified roles, specifically by age and, as mentioned, were tolerated as long as they did not interfere with the duties of marriage and reproduction.

Despite this history, however, contemporary Japan maintains a different attitude towards homosexuality. Scholar Joseph Hawkins suggests that in the Meiji Period (1868–1912 CE) Japan began adopting Western influences, including homophobia. While homosexual behavior had previously been comparatively uncensored, when Japan adopted Western ideologies, particularly psychology, it "led to the classification of some sexual patterns as 'aberrant.'"[10] Since the acceptance of some of these Western ideologies, Japan has arguably become more critical of homosexuality than it was in the past. While there are still comparatively few legal or moral restrictions, individuals who do not observe the social obligations of marriage and reproduction may face criticism within Japanese society.

Perhaps one of the most notable differences between the two countries regarding sexuality is that in Japan there is a somewhat different conception of "gay identity." In the U.S., gay identity is often associated with a political identity of outness and visibility. Because this sort of group identity is less evident in Japan, it is frequently assumed that there is a weak or non-existent gay identity in Japan as opposed to the "progressive" gay identity found in the West, specifically the U.S. However, this assumption ignores many of the historical and cultural specificities concerning homosexuality in Japan. Indeed, because of Japan's history with homosexuality and the absence of Judeo-Christian morals, there have never been the same sorts of legal restrictions against homosexuality in Japan that there have been in the U.S., such as sodomy laws. There was one sodomy law in Japan from 1873–1883 but it was repealed and "only twenty occurrences of sodomy were punished as criminal under the new law, though it is clear from the record that the practice was much more widespread."[11] This stands in stark contrast to the lengthy history of sodomy laws in the West. Likely because there was little legal restriction on male-male sex in Japan, and thus no need to fight against laws such as these. The rights-based gay identity that is so obvious in America was never as strongly developed in Japan.

Mark McLelland, one of the prominent English-language researchers on homosexuality in Japan, suggests that many same-sex oriented individuals in Japan resist the "gay" identity because they don't necessarily view their sexual acts as a determining factor in identity. While in America the idea that "the personal is political" roots many rights discourses around identity politics, in Japan, sexual acts are more often viewed as *asobi* (play) and not an identity-determining factor.[12] Because of the relative lack of legal and moral restrictions, individuals can usually participate in these acts without restriction and thus have not developed the political gay identity often found in the United States which focuses on a legal rights discourse. This is not to say that other forms of discrimination and other expressions of gayness more in line with the American conception of gay identity do not also exist in Japan; they do. A number of public gay figures and activism-based groups do exist. However, they exist alongside these multiple other expressions of same-sex sexuality.

If we consider contemporary yaoi manga without the specific lens of gay identity in the American sense, but with knowledge of how these multiple expressions of same-sex sexuality co-exist in Japanese society, the readings of "realness" based on its representational relation to gayness illuminate nuances in how we discuss sexuality in a global context.

Conclusion: Adventures in Yaoi-land

When yaoi manga is brought into the American context, Western values have a significant influence on readings of yaoi by American fans. By adopting, negotiating, or rejecting American discourses of sexuality and identity, these fans ascribe unique meaning through their readings of yaoi manga. Readers seem to apply popular understandings of sexuality to yaoi manga. American fans apply ideas of a universal gay identity in their readings of yaoi manga while using these conceptions to judge the realness of yaoi manga. Some fans assume that the gay identity found in dominant Western ideology applies globally. In these cases, fans consider yaoi manga to be unrealistic because the male/male sexuality represented in yaoi manga does not display their conception what "real" gayness should look like. For the most part, this conception includes scenes of victimization and "coming out" into a "gay identity." However, other fans negotiate this dominant theory of universal gay identity by acknowledging the variation of same-sex sexualities globally and even within the West. For these readers, the perception of yaoi manga's "realness" may be influenced by knowledge of same-sex sexuality in Japan. In either case however, the fact that yaoi does not represent "real" gay sexuality to American fans does not seem to affect their enjoyment of yaoi manga. In fact, the absence of a U.S.–based male/male sexual identity may in fact be a large part of yaoi's appeal to American audiences.

American audiences often read in a contradictory manner. Their readings are at once ethnocentric in that they privilege familiar ideologies, and simultaneously exotifying in their emphasis on the "otherness" or "Japaneseness" of yaoi manga. This contradiction is part of yaoi's appeal. "Yaoi-land" exists as a space in which dichotomies fail to account for the range and variation of meaning and understanding that occur through reading yaoi manga cross-culturally. It is for this reason that the study of yaoi is beneficial in its openness to possibility and multiplicity.

This essay has only begun to explore the complexities of yaoi. The cross-cultural nature of this work addresses the layers of cultural meaning attached to yaoi manga, and the processes involved in meaning-making across cultural lines. Additionally, my focus on audience responses to yaoi begins to explore what has been relatively unaddressed in previous work on yaoi: fan understandings of yaoi manga in their own words. These fan responses complicate any monolithic understanding of who reads yaoi and how they make meaning of it through their variation and contradictions.

Notes

1. Shinobu Price, "Cartoons from Another Planet: Japanese Animation as Cross-Cultural Communication," *Journal of American and Comparative Cultures* 24 (2001), 153.

2. William B. and Bella Mody Gudykunst, eds., *Handbook of International and Intercultural Communication* (London: Sage Publications, 2002).

3. Veruska Sabucco, "Guided Fan Fiction: Western 'Readings' of Japanese Homosexual-themed Texts," in *Mobile Cultures: New Media in Queer Asia,* ed. Chris Berry, Fran Martin and Audrey Yue (Durham, NC, & London: Duke University Press, 2003), 71.

4. While the demographic information of respondents such as sexual identity was optionally requested, I have chosen not to highlight this in my analysis as I believe it distracts from the content of audience responses, which is the focus of this work. Work that takes into account this demographic information may be beneficial in the future.

5. TJ's reference to "invisible dicks" refers to the ways in which some *mangaka* draw penises as barely visible or recognizable cylinders to conform to censorship laws.

6. Miyamoto Kano. *Rules* 1 Matsubunkan 2003: 30. scanlation via Liquid Passion http://hackthemain stream.com

7. Men who have sex with men (MSM) is a term used by social scientists to classify men who have sex with men, regardless of how they self-identify.

8. *New York Pride Guide 1994*, in Martin M. Manalansan, "In the Shadows of Stonewall: Examining Gay Transnational Politics and the Diasporic Dilemma," *GLQ* 2 (1995): 427.

9. Gary P. Leupp, *Male Colors: The Construction of Homosexuality in Tokugawa Japan* (Berkeley: University of California Press, 1995), 1.

10. Joseph Hawkins, "Japan's Journey into Homophobia," *Gay & Lesbian Review Worldwide* 7, no. 1 (2000): 36.

11. Ibid.

12. McLelland, Mark. *Male Homosexuality in Modern Japan: Cultural Myths and Social Realities* (Richmond, VA: Curzon, 2000).

Bibliography

Gudykunst, William B. and Bella Mody, eds. *Handbook of International and Intercultural Communication.* London: Sage Publications, 2002.

Hawkins, Joseph. "Japan's Journey into Homophobia." *Gay & Lesbian Review Worldwide* 7, no. 1 (2000): 36.

Leupp, Gary P. *Male Colors: The Construction of Homosexuality in Tokugawa Japan.* Berkeley: University of California Press, 1995.

Manalansan, Martin. "In the Shadows of Stonewall: Examining Gay Transnational Politics and the Diasporic Dilemma." *GLQ* 2 (1995): 425–438.

McLelland, Mark. *Male Homosexuality in Modern Japan: Cultural Myths and Social Realities.* Richmond, VA: Curzon, 2000.

Miyamoto, Kano. *Rules* 1 Matsubunkan 2003:30. Scanlation via Liquid Passion http://hackthemainstream.com.

Price, Shinobu. "Cartoons from Another Planet: Japanese Animation as Cross-Cultural Communication." *Journal of American and Comparative Cultures* 24 (2001): 153–169.

Sabucco, Veruska. "Guided Fan Fiction: Western 'Readings' of Japanese Homosexual-themed Texts." In *Mobile Cultures: New Media in Queer Asia,* edited by Chris Berry, Fran Martin and Audrey Yue, 70–86. Durham, NC, & London: Duke University Press, 2003.

13

Raping Apollo
Sexual Difference and the Yaoi Phenomenon
ALAN WILLIAMS

As a 25-year-old gay, white male living in Seattle in 2009, I purchase from my local bookstore the occasional manga about male-male romance and sex—a "yaoi" genre authored and drawn almost exclusively by women in Japan. Over the years, this genre has greatly influenced my fantasies regarding male beauty, love, and passion. As an aspiring novelist, I turn to the genre as I develop my own plotlines and characters. Yet, how am I to imagine myself alongside the majority of yaoi fans—straight females—most of whom are Japanese? Is such an imaginary naïve, egocentric, ethnocentric, sexist? Or does the genre, in its current transnational form, speak to aspects of human desire that are, in fact, beyond a single gender and culture?

In her 2008 dissertation "Reading and Living *Yaoi*: Male-Male Fantasy Narratives as Women's Sexual Subculture in Japan," Mizoguchi Akiko illustrates how she "'became' a lesbian via reception, in adolescence, of the 1970s 'beautiful boy' comics, the precursors to yaoi" (vi). That a woman would become a lesbian through a male-male genre makes plain the need to think beyond most structuralist arguments about yaoi and its fandom. By setting the boundary of who is within a particular subculture, the scholar (or fan, or "aca-fan") not only neglects those on or outside that boundary, but also pigeonholes and homogenizes those inside the boundary. This boundary-setting has political, pedagogical and ethical consequences that are not always apparent.

In this chapter I will examine competing narratives in recent studies of yaoi, pointing to where these narratives reach their ethical impasses. The concept of *sexual difference*, as expressed particularly by feminist philosophers Rosi Braidotti and Elizabeth Grosz, helps think through these impasses. By the end of this essay, I hope to have developed a framework in which I can imagine myself as a yaoi fan—a framework that is respectful of the ways yaoi remains a distinctly Japanese and female genre.

Yaoi as Political

Arts educators Brent Wilson and Masami Toku in their "'Boys' Love,' Yaoi, and Art Education: Issues of Power and Pedagogy" (2003) write:

> Should the dojinshi subculture be brought into [the arts] curriculum? ...
>
> Herein lies the problem. Dojinshi and its yaoi and boys' love components flourish because they are subversive, beyond control, and because they stand in opposition to conventional societal norms. To put these forms of youth visual culture in schools would probably rob teens of the pleasures that surround their creation and consumption: when we require students to do and make what they themselves have elected to do

on their own becomes no longer their own. Moreover, when the subversive is sanctioned it loses its social transformative functions. Surely, schools should not be in the business of assisting students to create dojinshi. They don't need help [under "Yaoi, Boys' Love and Art Education," paras. 7–8].

Wilson and Toku note that this does not mean that arts curricula can simply ignore yaoi, because "to do so leaves an intolerable critical void" (para. 9), as "surely, teenagers must learn to read semiotically and interpret critically the visual culture they create. Surely they must be taught to question things such as the forms of gender identity that are constructed within yaoi" (ibid.).

The irony Wilson and Toku point out is that yaoi cannot be "broached" (ibid.) in the schools that house its present and future consumers and producers due to yaoi's "inappropriateness" (ibid.) as seen by most educators and adults.

> Might it be the case, however, that the less problematic forms of visual culture created by youth might stand in for the unacceptable types? If boys' love provides the means for females to explore gender roles, then perhaps sanctioned forms of visual culture might provide the vehicle through which students could practice reading signs in the unsanctioned forms of youth culture which exist beyond schools [para. 10].

The assumption here is that unless a youth is already politically minded or outside the heteronormative norm, the youth will simply enjoy the genre and not question it. In Mizoguchi's account, the subculture has seen political "results" in the sense that (a) politicking and educating have had an effect within and without in the last forty years (that is, the genre does not exist in a social vacuum), and (b) the exploration of gender and social roles by yaoi fans has resulted in "liberation" for some fans. Mizoguchi writes:

> [I]t is only natural that an increasing number of characters have started to act on their own will, that is, the women fans' free will, rather than the yaoi formula that reflects male-centered heteronormativity.
>
> Of course, the yaoi formula[e] themselves were created by yaoi women fans and they reflected what the fans had internalized. As their sexual fantasies were and mostly still are played out across the bodies of the male characters that assume fixed top (male)/bottom (female) roles and thus seem to imitate heterosexual romance, the fans' fantasies seem to and do reinforce heteronormativity. But at the same time, because such fantasy narratives have been repeatedly created and received by women, some fans have come to fully possess such heteronormative assumptions as their own and fully live them out as their own, so to speak, by playing *both* roles in a women-only discursive space instead of regarding them as an unquestionable given. As a result, some women fans have overcome heteronormative assumptions (albeit in an unconscious matter in many cases) [2008, 372–73; emphasis added].

Thus, a classroom setting where "critical" tools are imparted to the student seems in service of a politics in which the yaoi subculture *cannot be trusted* to produce results *quickly enough*. An unconscious overcoming, in the eyes of the teacher, ought to be made conscious. Within their previously cited essay, Wilson and Toku write:

> The perspectives, positions, tastes, and orientations seem to exist in a frightening rhizomatic flux. Yaoi appears to reinforce conservative gender roles while simultaneously providing models for liberating roles. The choices are there and the readers and writers may, consciously or unconsciously, choose this, or that, or the other model — or their combinations. What are the consequences of being double-minded, playing with double-edged-ness, possessing double-pleasures, double-troubles? Perhaps this is an instance about which Jacques Lacan[1] writes — of "the incessant sliding of the signified under the signifier." He claimed that no anchoring of particular signifiers to particular signifieds is possible [under *Reading Signs of Signs*," para. 5].

Within a sexual difference framework, this Lacanian double-mindedness is redefined as "good." As Rosi Braidotti writes: "The feminist project is no longer described only in terms of willful choice, but also in terms of desire, that is to say un-willful drives. Consequently political passions, and the political analysis of affectivity that accompanies them, emerge as a central issue" (2000, 305). She further writes: "What the feminism of sexual difference wants to *free* in women is ... their desire for freedom, justice, self-accomplishment and well-being: the subversive laughter of Dionysus as opposed to the seriousness of the Apollonian spirit. This political process ... does not aim at the glorification of the feminine, but rather its actualization or empowerment as a political project aimed at alternative female subjectivities" (306; emphasis added). Elizabeth Grosz expands this to include all feminist theory: "Feminist theory is not the struggle to liberate women, even though it has tended to conceive of itself in these terms (if this is its function, it has failed miserably!); it is the struggle to render more mobile, fluid, and transformable the means by which the female subject is produced and represented" (2005, 139).

For many readers, what Braidotti and Grosz are suggesting might be a new way of thinking of feminist empowerment. For gender theorists and feminist sociologists who are already aware of "sexual difference" I am perhaps "opening a can of worms" (see Foster 1999, to get a sense of the multiple contentions here[2]). Yaoi is a valuable site for this theoretical battle to play out, as it "does not represent any person's 'reality,' but rather is a battlefield where straight, lesbian and other women's desires and political stakes clash and representations are born" (Mizoguchi 2008, vii).

Feminist philosophies of sexual difference postulate a *materiality of difference* underpinned by a fundamental binarism: the "masculine" and the "feminine" (hence, the label "sexual")—or, in Nietzschean terms, the Apollonian and Dionysian, order and chaos. This binarism is contested by some as a re-essentializing of the sexes (and an undue focus on "sex"), but such a critique is like setting Apollo (man) next to Apollo (woman-as-man-conceives-of-her), when, in fact, the Dionysian or the "feminine" element is that which is *yet to be*. This chaotic element is taken as the point of departure, which imagines each woman and person as "a multiplicity in herself: she is marked by a set of differences within the self, which turns her into a split, fractured, knotted entity, constructed over intersecting levels of experience" (Braidotti 2000, 303). "Sex" is just one way difference is and can be articulated (other ways include class, race, sexual orientation, and so on).

The title of this chapter, "Raping Apollo," is to imply that as we imagine yaoi and its subculture as a conversation between the "masculine" (or dominant structures in society) and the "feminine" (subversive not-yet-structures), Apollo is satisfyingly being raped by Dionysus. This rape is acceptable only because it is in service of a utopian love between Apollo and Dionysus, the juxtaposition of violence and devotion as seen in many yaoi texts. Rape vis-à-vis utopian thinking is perhaps one characteristic of yaoi texts that might compel educators like Wilson and Toku to want to give critical tools to their students. If we leave political expediency up to unconscious desire, then our material realities seem quickly reduced to an optimistic outlook on life (difference as utopia, where rape is actually a really good romp in the sheets) versus a pessimistic outlook (difference as dystopia, where rape is rape and clearly unethical). How can we trust unconscious desire to do the necessary political work in the world?

Braidotti and Grosz assert something grander about desire than whether or not it can be trusted. Desire *is* doing political work, whereas the willful political work we do in service of *singular* realities (the empowerment of "women" generally or the empowerment of "gay people" generally) is actually more harmful than it seems. As Braidotti writes: "[T]he utopian dimension of sexual difference inaugurates a visionary mode of thinking where the poetic and the political intersect powerfully" (305). Here we might read "poetic" as Dionysian laughter (chaos) and the "political" as Apollonian seriousness (order). Both are necessary to create and sustain change: chaos begins change and order sustains it — not the other way around.

Imagine, for example, the teacher "getting at" yaoi through other visual culture and how this would, in some ways, delimit yaoi as a subversive art form. There are no "critical" tools a teacher can provide without somehow deducting from the "feminine," "uncritical" or "subversive" that is yaoi. Is it the case that subverting heteronormativity at a macro level is worth delimiting yaoi? Sexual difference posits that there is no way to subvert heteronormativity "at a macro level." Besides, isn't the existence and sustainment of yaoi and its subculture *already* a subversion of heteronormativity? What more can the teacher provide?

Wilson and Toku write:

> [Boys' love, yaoi, and the *dōjinshi* in which they are found] are a sign of disputed power in the realm of art education and youth visual culture. They are signs of the larger global visual culture of youth which art educators and youth both share and do not share. If pedagogy is the sharing of power by students and teachers— and we think it should be — then shouldn't forms of visual culture studied in school be a topic for negotiation among educational authorities, teachers, and students? Indeed, we believe that this is one of the most important issues for students and teachers in countries throughout the world to negotiate and resolve [under "Yaoi, Boys' Love, and Art Education," para. 10].

While I agree with the sharing of pedagogy in the classroom, I am curious as to what the teacher might offer politically that the yaoi community does not already itself offer.

Consider Mizoguchi's discussion of how the manga *Sex Pistols* (Kotobuki 2004) might be talked about within the yaoi community in Japan:

> The story requires that everyone, regardless of gender ... play either a mother or a father in a relationship, which reinforces a heterosexual/heteronormative framework and thus can alienate anyone who has not engaged or does not plan to engage in reproduction. But at the same time, based on an understanding that the "boys' love" genre resists, or at least problematizes, existing heteronormative assumptions, *Sex Pistols* is an especially powerful work....
>
> A comment such as ... "I think it's a great work. All the characters are so attractive. But, I just can't stand that everything resorts to making a child and a marriage," "Well, yeah, but isn't it natural?" are made freely among the fans. If we recall that such fundamental discussions about reproduction, romantic relationships, marriage, and family are usually avoided as "too serious," especially among women of different marital statuses, sexual orientations, educational and political backgrounds, it seems reasonable to call the contemporary yaoi community an effective arena for feminist discourse, even though only *one* artist has proclaimed herself as feminist so far [2008, 378–9; emphasis added].

The feminist work being done here is that of multiple feminisms or the construction of multiple realities. The appropriate role of the teacher in this work is debatable.

Yaoi as Non/Heteronormative

As we just saw, the overcoming of heteronormative thinking for some fans has partly been the result of the yaoi subcultural space itself. This space, for Mizoguchi, is a "lesbian" space where women can participate in "collective virtual sex regardless of their sexual orientation" (2003). I read this "virtual lesbianism" not as a pigeonholing of yaoi fans as "queer" but as an articulation of a cultural phenomenon that is "not/queer." Braidotti has a pointed critique on what she sees as the feminist turn toward lesbian/gay/queer pedagogies that "[have] spelled the end of interest in heterosexuality as a possible field of transformation or becoming" (2003, 59). She writes: "Classified and filed under the somewhat hasty label of hetero-'normativity,' the idea of heterosexual desire [has] declined within feminist theory, in favor of either polysexual becomings or different variations around the theme of homosexual or queer desire" (ibid.). Mizoguchi's "virtual lesbian" is highly inclusive of the heterosexual yaoi fan, given that most yaoi fans identify as heterosexual.

In his "Girls and Women Getting Out of Hand: The Pleasure and Politics of Japan's Amateur Comics Community" (2004) Matthew Thorn makes a move into queer territory:

> There can be little doubt that both the artists and readers who are drawn to boys' love and yaoi are unhappy with mainstream norms of gender and sexuality. And while they speak fondly of *otoko no sekai* (world of and for men), and seem to prefer masculinity over femininity, yaoi artists and writers show contempt for "straight" masculinity, just as they scorn standardized femininity.
>
> ... Perhaps the reader can thus understand why I characterize this genre and its fans as "queer." The women and girls in this community may never display their dissatisfaction with mainstream norms of gender and sexuality in front of their more conventional peers, but they give expression to it in the liminal space of the "event," and every time they read or draw or write a story in this genre [179].

Is Thorn's homogenization of yaoi fans as "queer" similar to Mizoguchi's homogenization of yaoi fans as "virtual lesbians" (or "not/queer")? Thorn states that he is using the term "queer" as defined by Alexander Doty "to question the cultural demarcations *between* the queer and the straight ... by pointing out the queerness of and in straights and straight cultures, as well as that of individuals and groups who have been told they inhabit the boundaries between the binaries of gender and sexuality" (176; emphasis added). At first sight, it does seem that Thorn is imagining yaoi fans similarly to Mizoguchi.

Where Thorn and Mizoguchi depart from one another is in how they bracket yaoi fans' queerness. For example, Thorn writes:

> [W]e must acknowledge that even in Japan the majority of women do not find yaoi or boys' love particularly appealing. One person I have interviewed about yaoi and slash is an American woman with a singular biography. Once a great fan of slash, she discovered yaoi and was so drawn into that genre that she went on to learn to speak and read Japanese fluently, and now works in Tokyo as a professional editor of commercial yaoi anthologies. She feels strongly that an attraction to both slash and yaoi is "hardwired"; if you've got it, you can't avoid it, and if you don't, it's meaningless to you. This is essentially what Sakakibara[3] argues, though in different terms, when she claims that yaoi fans are "gay men born in women's bodies." Although traditional, essentialist notions of gender were debunked by feminism, feminist formulations of radical constructionism have themselves come under serious scrutiny. Nature and nurture may condition one another in complex ways, and it may be that notions like a "gay man in woman's body" (or "lesbian in man's body"), and indeed the concept of "transsexuality" are awkward attempts to describe manifestations for which we still lack adequate analysis [181].

Now consider the following by Mizoguchi:

> The reason yaoi fans can comfortably discuss their sexual desires in as assertive a manner as gay men in a society where women are conditioned not to behave as subjects of sexual desire is that, in the mind of the fan, she is merely talking about her favorite representation, not discussing her own sexuality [2008, 332].

Obviously, Mizoguchi's prose comes from a place of certitude as she considers herself an insider, notwithstanding that she did not "return to the genre [until] 1998" (53). But more important than this certitude is what she does with it: her discursive "virtual lesbian" *remains* discursive as a facet of its virtuality. Thorn's discourse is one of "substantiation" or getting to the bottom of the essentialism/constructionism debate so as to conjecture "what's really going on."

Sexual difference problematizes the theoretical work being done at both the center and periphery of a cultural site and the affectivity this work has on intersubjective understanding. Grosz stresses that the way we think about intersubjectivity ("insider" versus "outsider") is tied to the way we differentiate between time and space, predicated upon the patriarchal divorcing of the mind from the body (see Grosz 1994). In a nutshell, the mind and body inform each other such that the past is a virtuality from which multiple futures can be conceived and performed. The present is the threshold for these competing futures. Essentialist discourses are unduly homogenizing, whereas constructivist discourses overlay a "constructed" mind over an "essential" body (15–17). Grosz writes: "[T]he question of time, and of conceptualizing women's closer alignment with temporality, is crucial to the struggles of sexual difference, insofar as the feminine has remained largely associated with space, place, containment, and habitation, while having its becoming — its interiority — its transformations in time ... curtailed and contained" (2005, 177). Trying to substantiate "polysexual becomings" (such as "gay men born in women's bodies") can be avoided if we privilege difference as it is articulated at the moment of its articulation: minds and bodies in communication. Like the teacher, the appropriate role of the cultural anthropologist in this work is debatable.

Yaoi as Transnational

Surely, there are forces of "evil" outside the yaoi subculture (and I use the word "outside" precariously in light of Grosz) that require willful and deliberate politics to combat. In his "*Yaoi Ronsō*: Discussing Depictions of Male Homosexuality in Japanese Girls' Comics, Gay Comics and Gay Pornography"[4] (2006), Wim Lunsing alludes to such "evils":

> [The] discussions taking place on BLB [boy loves boy] manga are irrelevant to the majority of the readers, who simply enjoy what they read. Moreover, the recent popularity of BLB manga in China and Korea shows that their impact is not limited to audiences who grew up in a Japanese cultural context. It is to be hoped that BLB manga will remain beyond the scrutiny of the new Japanese law against child pornography and that Korean government efforts to ban the genre will be thwarted, since they are a form of art and art should be free [para. 34].

With yaoi's lawful existence threatened, a scholar might be moved to argue for the moral "good" of its continued lawfulness, such as Mark McLelland does in his "The World of Yaoi: The Internet, Censorship and the Global 'Boys' Love' Fandom" (2005).

Yet, in their 2007 article, "The International Yaoi Boys' Love Fandom and the Regulation of Virtual Child Pornography: The Implications of Current Legislation," Mark McLelland and Seunghyun Yoo write:

> Existing research into the yaoi fandom has been carried out primarily from literary and cultural studies perspectives. However, the behavioral effects of yaoi are surely of inter-

est as well to legislators, anthropologists, behavioral scientists, health care professionals, and psychologists. Yaoi, as an important form of sexual expression for many young people internationally, needs to be studied for both its positive and negative effects among the fans (including the negative effects of the law's pathologization of the genre). Research should also include yaoi's behavioral effects, if any exist, on adolescents' and young adults' psychological and sexual health. Such research would not only establish foundations for understanding yaoi but also inform legislation regulating both virtual child pornography and the sexual fantasies of young people [102].

When a scholar takes a political stance with regard to a cultural group, the scholar should always be explicit of the ways in which that group is homogenized for the purposes of political expediency (see Mohanty 2003). Here, the homogenization is that of yaoi fans as "youth" for the purposes of circumventing the "law's pathologization of the genre." Bearing in mind Mizoguchi's work (a "literary and cultural study" from an adult insider embedded in an adult-and-youth subculture), the rest of what McLelland and Yoo are promoting seems like maintenance of the patriarchal gaze. Whereas Wilson and Toku as educators are willing to share pedagogies with their students (that is, the teachers' and students' temporalities held as epistemologically equivalent in the classroom), I have serious reservations that "legislators, anthropologists, behavioral scientists, health care professionals and psychologists" would share as much.

Of course, this returns us to the crux of the debate between sexual difference theorists and those one might call "pragmatists." It is not my intention to dismiss *en masse* the political work being done by the scholars I have cited, nor is it my intention to make sweeping generalizations about entire disciplines or professions; the outsider is not always "bad" and the insider always "good." Rather, my aim is to reappraise further political work by insiders and outsiders alike. Braidotti writes: "This reappraisal of difference is proposed as a political practice, which coincides with the critique of a humanistic understanding of subjectivity in terms of nationality, self-representation, homogeneity, and stability. This view of the subject is questioned in the light of its dualistic relation to otherness" (2000, 302). In imagining the political steps we might take in light of yaoi's transnationalism (with regard to law, health, and autonomy), how much can we afford to make generalizations about yaoi fans without doing them an injustice?

McLelland and Yoo write:

> More research is needed in Anglophone and other cultures about yaoi content, its fandom, and its potential behavioral effects so that realistic ratings and legislation can be developed. As Angelides[5] argued, "We ought to be conducting studies that are not driven solely for a search for 'difference' or 'deviant' identities, but by the desire to appreciate ... diversity." The yaoi community, constituted as it is of primarily female fans from a wide range of cultures and backgrounds and conjoining as it does male homosexuality with youthful sexuality, has much to teach about human sexuality, the sexual fantasies of women in particular, and the impossibility of conjoining sexual fantasy to the limited range of sex and gender roles currently endorsed by mainstream society.
>
> ... The process of identification involved in the production and consumption of yaoi is thus obviously very complex, not only differing according to the sexual orientation of the reader but also being affected by various factors in the context of different yaoi language communities [101].

The language here sounds nice—but in practice, if we really want to "appreciate diversity" and "recognize complexity," then we must work as closely to the Dionysian as possible. Deviancy becomes diversity only at the expense of having its interiority contained.

Yaoi as Homophobic

On his blog "comics212.net," Christopher Butcher wrote in 2006:

> A community is defined by who it excludes, and the yaoi community seems to think
> that it doesn't include gay men. Sure, their reasoning is benign on the surface and it's all
> very *nice*, but honestly? It's false, entirely false, and it's only going to become more and
> more so as ... manga published in North America expands and the genre penetrates the
> public consciousness [under *A Few Comments About The Gay/Yaoi Divide*].

Yaoi offers an appealing formula for storytelling that has spawned iterations of the genre
in multiple locations worldwide. Any study of "American yaoi for gay men created by gay
men" or "Korean yaoi for females by females" or some other iteration would require attention to geographic specificity. But is there a voice to be had by the non–Japanese and/or
non-female fan who already feels at home with the genre in its Japanese and female form?
At the beginning of this essay, I asked: "Where do I fit in?"

The male fan is not included in Mizoguchi's detailed account because he is empirically absent in the Japanese yaoi subculture:

> [M]any Japanese gay men do not care very much about women and women's culture,
> including yaoi, and gay male readership constitutes a very small minority of yaoi read-
> ership. I want to stress this because ... the impulse to discuss, and even evaluate, yaoi in
> relation to gay men's reactions is very prevalent [2008, 184].

This is to suggest that non-gay males are even more empirically absent.

However, Mizoguchi writes at length about the "debates" in 1990s Japan (179), debates
that echo in America a decade later. Satō Masaki, a gay activist (who made the debates larger
than life), was obviously not representative of *every* gay male (181); in fact, he was "atypi-
cal" (182) and he homogenized yaoi fans as "asocial" (189) and apolitical. In his article,
"*Yaoi Ronsō*," Lunsing writes that Satō attacked yaoi as "creating and having a skewed image
of gay men as beautiful and handsome and regarding gay men who do not fit that image
and tend to 'hide in the dark' as 'garbage'" (2006, para. 14). Satō further compared yaoi
fans to "'dirty old men' ... who watch pornography [where] women engag[e] in sexual
activities with each other" (ibid.). Considerable response to Satō followed, taking various
forms, such as "yaoi was never meant for gay men," "yaoi is liberating for women," "yaoi
is indeed pornography," and "manga that targets gays isn't realistic either."

Interestingly, Lunsing lumps Satō and Mizoguchi together. In 2003, Mizoguchi gave
a lecture titled "Homophobic Homos, Rapes of Love, and Queer Lesbians: Yaoi as a Conflicting Site of Homo/Hetero-Sexual Female Sexual Fantasy." The following is from an abstract
of that lecture:

> [C]ontemporary yaoi texts contain five unrealistic and homophobic tropes involving
> rape as an expression of love, "straight" status for a male protagonist in a gay relation-
> ship, fixed top/bottom roles that correspond with the protagonists' masculine/feminine
> roles, and obligatory anal intercourse.... [T]he recent appearance of likable lesbian char-
> acters does not contradict the overt homophobia [2003, sec. 187].

Lunsing states that "in Japan, discussions of BLB manga tend to focus on particular
features of [only] some manga" (2006, para. 27) and that ultimately:

> Critiques such as those of Satō and Mizoguchi entail the risk of leading to the establish-
> ment of norms on how male homosexuality must be depicted, which would result in a
> normalised, stale representation of male homosexuality. Obviously, this would be utterly
> un-queer and contrary to the performative acts in which identity and activity are not

related in a linear manner—a characteristic of Japanese sexualities. Many Japanese gay men appear to use depictions of gay men that are not (meant to be) positive and supportive, by seeing them as performances that can in turn enhance their own lives [para. 34].

Lunsing is thus arguing for a description of the genre such that it would not be considered homophobic, whereas Mizoguchi is arguing for an articulation of the genre in which the *subculture* ceases to be. Still, there is much to make sense of here with regard to homophobia and liberation for these two scholars.

Let us consider the content of Lunsing's argument. On the one hand, the expediency of identity politics—that is, accurate portrayals of what it means to be "gay" for the sake of self-determination of only some gay males—does not necessarily outweigh the importance of maintaining a "queer" outlook as it pertains to good art and good storytelling, especially since many gay males (wherever they are in the world) enjoy the genre and find it liberating. In other words, he is cautioning against a "homonormative" reading of yaoi. On the other hand, Mizoguchi is a lesbian. She is experiencing homophobia in the ways *her* sexuality is not articulated in a female discursive space. Concerning the yaoi texts themselves, Mizoguchi writes:

> [H]omophobia works as a prop that enhances the thrill of the romance.... When yaoi protagonists say, "I'm not gay, I just love you," they are also saying that those gay men who love other men for their bodies are creeps. This simple sentence, "I'm not gay," repeated before and after the romance is consummated, works as a twofold operation of homophobia [Mizoguchi 2008, 134].

Lunsing seems to recognize the necessity of grounding queerness, but he positions himself as a cultural anthropologist who regards participatory experience as "valuable data" (Lunsing, 2006, para. 3):

> [I]nitially BLB manga were an important innovation in the otherwise asexual genre of shōjo manga. Love between boys was a means for women to reconsider, or even to begin considering, their own sexuality. It mattered less that the stories concerned boys than that they concerned sex.... Some women to whom I spoke could hardly stop talking about the "cute" boys in such depictions. They evidently identified strongly with the characters.... To me it seems that more have an actual interest in cute men/boys [para. 30].

So, if yaoi is just about "cute boys," it can't possibly be homophobic? I know I'm grossly oversimplifying Lunsing's argument, but Lunsing does consider Mizoguchi's examples of homophobia in yaoi texts to "lack the power to convince" (para 27). Since when was the goal of an analysis of perceived homophobic texts ever to "convince" those who do not perceive homophobia in some "greater" context? The other issue here is that Lunsing glosses over Mizoguchi's context as a lesbian in the subculture (or seemingly her position in the subculture altogether). The question of yaoi as homophobic was always beyond pitting the gay male fan against the straight female fan if we consider the lesbian fan.

At this current juncture yaoi is ridden with homophobic potential. Yet, given that there is no single "gay" interpretation of yaoi, firmly steering the genre and its subculture away from "homophobic" discourse makes little sense. As Mizoguchi writes:

> The complex and powerful ways in which the yaoi community is functioning as a lesbian and feminist space have happened precisely because of women fans' freed desires, and the extent the genre has changed in the past ten years in the direction of becoming more lesbian (gay) and feminist, that is, in the direction of ultimately making the fans' lives easier, suggests the huge potential of their fantasies [2008, 384].

Whereas Mizoguchi does not speak of sexual difference in the same terms that Braidotti and Grosz do,[6] I cannot help but think that her work on yaoi and its fandom is the ideal case study.

No doubt, as the genre continues to gain popularity worldwide, it will become an important site for future feminist theory-making.

Have I reached my framework? I think it was waiting for me all along. The heterogeneous group known as "yaoi fans" does not have a single standpoint, politics, or location, except that they all enjoy yaoi. My voice as a gay, white male in Seattle is valuable as long as I don't use that voice to trample on the ways others enjoy, and will enjoy, the genre.

Imagining those who "will enjoy" yaoi is key. As Rosi Braidotti points out: "Desire is active in that it has to do with encounters between multiple forces and the creation of new possibilities of empowerment. It is outward-directed and forward-looking, not indexed upon the past of a memory dominated by phallocentric self-referentiality" (2003, 57). Pedagogies of sexual difference privilege this future imaginary, because politics of sexual difference question every instance of homogeneity. I can only hope that future studies of yaoi take this raping of Apollo by Dionysus as seriously.

Notes

1. Wilson and Toku cite Jacques Lacan, *Écrits* (London: Routledge, 1977), 154.

2. The contentions that Foster lay out are too numerous to expand upon here, but the underlying issue seems to be that sexual difference has remained highly theoretical/mythical (and therefore privileges a certain way of conceptualizing difference), whereas gender theory and feminist sociology have been more material and applicable. My hope is that this essay counters that argument.

3. Thorn cites Sakakibara Shihomi, *Yaoi genron: yaoi kara mieta mono* (An Elusive Theory of Yaoi: The View from Yaoi) (Tokyo: Natsume Shobo, 1998).

4. *Yaoi ronsō* ("yaoi dispute").

5. McLelland and Yoo cite Steven Angelides, "Paedophilia and the Misrecognition of Desire," *Transformations*, no. 8 (2004), http://www.transformationsjournal.org/journal/issue_08/article_01.shtml.

6. For example, Mizoguchi states that she thinks "quick, clear-cut feminist activism is an impossible dream to begin with" (2008, 380).

Bibliography

Braidotti, Rosi. "Sexual Difference Theory." In *A Companion to Feminist Philosophy*, edited by Alison M. Jaggar and Iris Marion Young, 298–306. Malden, MA: Blackwell, 2000.

_____. "Becoming Woman: or Sexual Difference Revisited." *Theory, Culture & Society.* 20 (2003): 43–64.

Butcher, Christopher. "A Few Comments About The Gay/Yaoi Divide." comics212.net, posted August 18, 2006. http://comics212.net/older/2006_08_01_archive.shtml (accessed December 15, 2008).

Foster, Johanna. "An Invitation to Dialogue: Clarifying the Position of Feminist Gender Theory in Relation to Sexual Difference Theory." *Gender & Society.* 13 (1999): 431–56.

Grosz, Elizabeth. *Volatile Bodies: Toward a Corporeal Feminism*: Bloomington, IN: Indiana University Press, 1994.

_____. *Time Travels: Feminism, Nature, Power.* Durham, NC: Duke University Press, 2005.

Kotobuki Tarako. *Sex Pistols* 1–5. Tokyo: Biblos Be Boy Comics, 2004–2006.

Lunsing, Wim. "*Yaoi Ronsō*: Discussing Depictions of Male Homosexuality in Japanese Girls' Comics, Gay Comics and Gay Pornography." *Intersections: Gender and Sexuality in Asia and the Pacific*, 12 (2006). http://intersections.anu.edu.au/issue12/lunsing.html (accessed December 15, 2008).

McLelland, Mark. "The World of Yaoi: The Internet, Censorship and the Global 'Boys' Love' Fandom." *Australian Feminist Law Journal* 23 (2005): 61–77. Repr., http://ro.uow.edu.au/cgi/viewcontent.cgi?article=1152&context=artspapers (accessed December 15, 2008).

McLelland, Mark, and Seunghyun Yoo. "The International Yaoi Boys' Love Fandom and the Regulation of Virtual Child Pornography: The Implications of Current Legislation." *Sexuality Research and Social Policy* 4 (2007): 93–104.

Mizoguchi, Akiko. "Homophobic Homos, Rapes of Love, and Queer Lesbians: Yaoi as a Conflicting Site of Homo/Hetero-Sexual Female Sexual Fantasy." Abstract of paper presented at the annual meeting of the Association for Asian Studies, New York, March 27–30, 2003. http://www.aasianst.org/absts/2003abst/Japan/sessions.htm (accessed December 15, 2008, under section 187).

_____. "Reading and Living *Yaoi*: Male-Male Fantasy Narratives as Women's Sexual Subculture in Japan." Ph.D. diss., University of Rochester, 2008.

Mohanty, Chandra. *Feminism without Borders: Decolonizing Theory, Practicing Solidarity*. Durham, NC: Duke University Press, 2003.

Thorn, Matthew. "Girls and Women Getting Out of Hand: The Pleasure and Politics of Japan's Amateur Comics Community." In *Fanning the Flames: Fans and Consumer Culture in Contemporary Japan*, edited by William W. Kelly, 169–87. Albany, NY: State University of New York Press, 2004. Repr., http://matt-tho rn.com/shoujo_manga/outofhand/index.php (accessed December 15, 2008).

Wilson, Brent and Masami Toku. "'Boys' Love,' Yaoi, and Art Education: Issues of Power and Pedagogy." In *Semiotics and Visual Culture: Sights, Signs, and Significance*, edited by Deborah L. Smith-Shank. Reston, VA: National Art Education Assoc., 2004. Preprint http://www.csuchico.edu/~mtoku/vc/Articles/toku/Wil_Toku_BoysLove.html (accessed December 15, 2008).

14

Hidden in Straight Sight

Trans*gressing Gender and Sexuality via BL

ULI MEYER

Dedicated to the Memory of
Eve Kosofsky Sedgwick (1950–2009)

Introduction

BL and its more explicit subgenre yaoi are usually defined as same-sex male romances or erotica written "by women for women." Moreover, since the protagonists are male, it is generally assumed that BL fans are straight women. If, however, they are straight women, then what is it about BL that *ladies' manga,* or other straight erotica by women for women, cannot provide?

Takemiya Keiko, the author of *Kaze to ki no uta,* the first *shōjo* manga that contained gay male sex, explains BL's success like this:

> I'm surprised at how large it's become. The fact surely tells us what women "really" think. Somebody once said to me, quite memorably for me, "*Yaoi's* great because you can adopt both roles." Women's notion of gender may already have crumbled away.[1]

> Through boy's love, it is possible to express dual personality (feminine and masculine) that is involved in human beings.[2]

If Takemiya is right and the appeal of BL is that the reader "can adopt both roles" and also express a "dual personality (feminine and masculine)," it can be argued that BL involves some kind of transgression of sexuality and gender.

The taking of "both roles" or the gender transgression by *shōjo* manga fans/authors has often been discussed in a context of female oppression or of women as "negative" or lack.[3] I will show that by comparing the practices and texts of BL fandoms to other sexually/gender transgressive subcultures, it becomes evident that BL is not (just) about compensation but that it resembles a distinct sexual/gender subculture.

The yaoi *me* (literally, the "yaoi-eye") or yaoi *megane* ("yaoi glasses") that the BL fan utilizes to read straight or homosocial context as homosexual is comparable to other ironic and destabilizing reading practices of sexual and gender minorities, as exemplified in practices of drag queen culture, camp or "perverse reading." BL fans' preoccupation with gay men can be understood better in context of the practices of girlfags and transfags, i.e., female-born persons who eroticize and identify with gay men.

By identifying with one or more of the gay male characters in a manga, the fans/artists cannot just take on a traditionally male gender role, but a traditionally male sexual position, which allows them to experience themselves, among other things, as penetrator (*seme*) and a male counterpart (*uke*) as penetrated. Thus, the transgression of sexuality and gender in BL can be quite literal, enabling its readers/creators to identify or feel with the male characters on a physical level, in a process I call "creative transvestism." The transgressions of sexuality and gender of fans/artists are reflected on a textual and visual level in the evolution of the genre and in its conventions and techniques, while the literalness of the gender transgression is expressed in BL fandom practices such as *dansō kei* cosplay (female fans dressing up as male characters) and yaoi online role-playing.

Dhaenens et al., have suggested that film theory would gain by taking into account that so-called straight audiences might be familiar with practices such as slashing, and by employing a truly queer approach: "Ultimately, transgression of the boundaries between queer reading and slash fiction indicates the need to violate disciplines, which is exactly what a queer would do."[4] Jenkins has shown that Sedgwick's work on the homosocial/homosexual continuum in "Between Men" (1985), a foundational work of queer theory, can be easily adopted to understand slash.[5] Likewise, I suggest that both BL studies and queer theory would gain from working more closely together.

Modern "Western" thinking holds that sex, gender and sexual orientations are inborn, unchangeable and organized in dichotomies such as man-woman, male-female, gay-straight, lesbian-gay male, transsexual-cissexual (i.e. non-transsexual), etc. Discussing both BL and slash within that framework is especially difficult because they present us with a world where the boundaries of sexual orientation and gender are in flux and sometimes nonexistent: A world in which straight characters can suddenly turn gay (Captain Tsubasa yaoi, Kirk/Spock slash), characters swap social gender and even physical sex on a regular basis (Oscar, Ranma), and nothing can be taken for granted where sex and gender is concerned.

"Queer" in the modern sense stands not just for lesbian and gay, but for all forms of sex/sexuality/gender expression that do not conform to the conventional heterosexual model of genital relations between an active cis-man and a passive cis-woman. Queer theory scrutinizes the naturalness and stability of all modern categories of sex/gender/sexuality and so offers a more appropriate framework for discussing the worlds of BL and slash.[6]

Transgressing boundaries and violating disciplines myself, I will employ an eclectic approach that reflects my own eclectic background in the arts, academia and queer and transgender activism, thus analyzing the sexual and gender transgressiveness of BL on the level of techniques, contents, and fandom practices.

YAOI ME— *The Gaze of the Rotten Girl*

Yaoi started in the late 1970s as *dōjinshi*, or manga created and self-published by fans, by taking existing texts of male homosociality and turning them into homosexual ones. For example, an innocent boys' football manga such as *Captain Tsubasa* (1981) is transformed into a gay erotic text where the male characters have sex with each other. In its early days, yaoi was seen as part of the larger genre of *aniparo*, anime parody.[7] *Dōjinshi* strongly resemble "Western" fanfiction, and *yaoi* shares many similarities with slash. Like slash authors, yaoi artists use existing characters of pop culture who often live in homosocial environments or relationships (the star ship captain, the cop, etc.) and pair them as gay male couples. Referring to Sedgwick's study of homosociality in English novels of the nineteenth century, *Between Men* (1985), Jenkins argues that the technique of slashing is about bridging the disruption in the continuum of male homosociality and homosexuality[8]: "To draw the "homosocial" back into the orbit of "desire," of the potentially erotic, then, is to hypothesize the potential unbrokenness of a continuum between homosocial and homosexual — a continuum whose visibility, for men, in our society is radically disrupted."[9] The same might be said about the technique of yaoi.

But yaoi isn't just about rewriting texts. Some authors have noted a phenomenon called yaoi *me* (yaoi eye) or yaoi *megane* (yaoi glasses), a way of looking at the world through yaoi eyes.[10] The avid fan starts to see homosexual dynamics everywhere: between fellow students, pop stars, even politicians. This is mostly a case of projection (though a strong "gaydar" might play a role as well). But yaoi fans aren't delusional. They know that not everybody is gay — the yaoi gaze goes further than that. It consciously draws boys and men into the orbit of the fan's desire, turning them into objects of voyeuristic pleasure. The female voyeur subversively submits the male object of her gaze to a "forced homosexualization": Some men find this disturbing, as they still associate homosexuality with humiliating effeminacy and penetrability.

In recent years, Japanese yaoi fans have coined the term *fujoshi* to describe themselves. The original term 婦女子 (*fujoshi*) means a respectable lady. By smuggling the homophonous kanji 腐 for *fu* (rotten) into the word, the original meaning gets ironically reinterpreted, twisted and depraved, reflecting the way in which the *fujoshi* depraves respectable texts.

Fujoshi 腐女子 now means "rotten girl," showing that BL and specifically yaoi is still thought of, however (self) ironically, in terms of depravity and innocence. For girls and women, production and consumption of sexual texts is still considered extremely odd. Girls are brought up with the expectation that they are somehow less sexual than boys. The "innocent" artwork and design of most *shōjo* manga (girls' manga) reflects this. In comparison, many *shōnen* manga (boys' manga) are full of openly sexual, very physical imagery, while girls' manga frame references to sexuality in symbols and "emotions." Boys' manga would never get away with the degree of über-"innocence" that girls' manga display. It would look suspicious because "everybody knows" that boys are sexually active, but "everybody" still pretends that girls aren't.

In this way, girls who are involved with sexually explicit manga fandoms are caught in an "assumed innocence." And because nobody expects these "nice girls" to be sexually explicit, they can play with people's assumptions and expectations about them. The term *fujoshi* illustrates this dichotomy between assumed innocence and depraved interior beautifully.

On a different but comparable level, by eroticizing boys and men, BL fans are caught in an "assumed straightness": their interest seems "only natural." The fact that they are eroticizing *gay* men and acts is often ignored by commentators. By a similar logic, until recently, female-to-gay-male transsexuals (and male-to-lesbian transsexuals) were denied hormones and treatment: "They told me that I must not really be transsexual. After all, they thought, if I just wanted to sleep with men, why go to all the trouble?" says a female-to-male transsexual.[11]

BL fans might be women who are interested in men, but they are far from being straight. They are *reading* the world with yaoi eyes and have become perverse readers. Sedgwick explains, "The reading practices founded on such basic demands and intuitions had necessarily to run against the grain of most patent available formulae for young people's reading and life — against the grain, often, of the most accessible voices even in the texts themselves. [This is] becoming a perverse reader[...]. And this doesn't seem an unusual way for ardent reading to function in relation to queer experience."[12]

Lipton describes his own reading practices and that of other queer youth, noting that they "decode texts against the mainstream, heterosexual grain.[...] Some directly sought to alter the intended meaning of a text [and] bend interpretation from a heteronormative meaning. These readers could find homosocial/sexual content present in almost any text." Another group "negotiated" with a text or character. And a third group placed the reader in the role of the "detective. These readers insist their queer reading is directly embedded within the text by the author and their job is to find the hidden messages...."[13]

A subversive gaze that *reads* or *re-reads* a seemingly innocent or "normal" environment is common for marginalized groups. The ability to *read* a person or context, to recognize them as belonging to the marginalized group or culture, to see what is invisible or hidden, is a by-product of the necessity to *pass*. Most marginalized groups practice some kind of *passing*, or trying to not be noticed as part of the marginalized group. A person of color might try to pass as white; a Jewish person in 1930s Germany might try to pass as "Aryan," and so on. Often, the person doesn't even try to pass but is just assumed to be a part of the dominant group: a lesbian might be assumed to be straight, as long as she doesn't come out.

Transvestites and transsexuals are especially involved in the dichotomy of passing and *reading*. To avoid discrimination, a transsexual might try to pass as a cis-person, or non-transsexual. *Reading* a transsexual means seeing that he or she is not a cis-person, but a transsexual. And other transsexuals are the best "readers": it takes one to know one.

Reading is a necessity, for when members of minorities are *passing*, how are they to recognize each other? How can they form communities and subcultures and share the knowledge and cultural products that reflect their experiences? They need to develop an additional sense to *read* hidden clues and hints. This is why members of marginalized groups can look at the world and see things that others don't see. They have specialized knowledge, and knowledge is power. If queer people "know" that this actor or that politician is "one of us," even if (or especially if) that person is not "out" or even if the person is actually straight, it allows them to navigate the world with more power and with more fun.

On a textual level, the *reading* that a *fujoshi* does is not identical, but very closely related to the active process of *reading* subtexts, and *reading* of queer subtext *into* straight texts, that queer people have always done when consuming and producing cultural products. For example, an active form of *reading* Hollywood films was performed not only by the queer audience but also by the queer people who worked in the film industry, so that many of the subtexts didn't have to be *read into* the text — they were actually there and had only to be discovered by those in the know: "You got very good at projecting subtext without saying a word about what you were doing," says screen writer Gore Vidal about his work on *Ben-Hur* (1959), which contains a consciously gay subtext in the relationship between Ben-Hur and Massala.[14] Nowadays, HoYay! (from: Homoeroticism Yay!) fans of television shows have become "detectives," or experts at spotting the subtext.

But *reading* is not just a technique to discover the traces that other members of the minority have left. It can be used to actively *read into* or *queer*, and thus appropriate, a straight text. Completely "innocent" words, cultural products, even persons can be appropriated this way.

Reading can become a weapon: the drag queen who calls a male cop "girl" simultaneously mocks, subverts, and appropriates him. He gets drawn into her queer world, a world where he is suddenly the member of a minority.[15]

Camp, another queer subcultural technique of parody and subversion that utilizes the techniques of passing and reading, "'piggybacks' on the dominant order's monopoly on signification."[16] Perkovitch shows that this is "what any minority's parody does, but camp always tends to inflect its own gendered and "unnatural" aspects in such a way that the dominant order's signification can also be seen as constructed, or itself other than natural."[17]

Yaoi started as *aniparo*, anime parody, mostly of boys' manga. Today, yaoi and BL in general still contain many parodic elements. The yaoi *me* subverts, re-interprets, and appropriates straight male contexts. It could be argued that BL not only "piggybacks" on the dominant order's monopoly of signification but that it shows that the dominant order's significations, such as gender roles and roles of sex and sexuality, are constructed and not natural.

BISHŌNEN— *The Male Object of the Gaze*

BL offers almost archetypical voyeuristic pleasure, as does its accompanying merchandise: manga, anime, feature films such as *Boys Love* (2006), and yaoi computer games allow the fan to gaze at gay men and gay sexual acts without interruption or personal involvement. Creating *dōjinshi*, of course, allows for an even more active type of voyeurism, in that the artist actually dictates the sexual activity. Kamm has shown that yaoi has an explicitly sexual function for some German and Japanese fans.[18] Hashimoto found that about thirty percent of the Austrian and Japanese cosplayers she interviewed (who were also yaoi fans) had sexual fantasies relating to yaoi.[19]

BL is a medium that fetishizes and objectifies male characters as *bishōnen*, beautiful boys. Their slender bodies are displayed, often in erotic or sex scenes, for the pleasure of the mostly female voyeurs. BL artwork emphasizes the "feminine" qualities, such as expressive eyes, harmonious features, hairless skin, and sometimes beautiful outfits of the *bishōnen*.

BL idealization and fetishization of male beauty is most extreme in the *uke* characters. In the sexual scenes of BL, it is mainly the body of the *uke* that is displayed. He is shown as passive, penetrated, and in the throes of passion, a passion that is derived from receptivity. His arousal and sexual reactions are the focus of the sex scene, in much the same way that women's reactions are the focus of straight pornography. In plots that contain violence or rape, the *uke*'s pain and agony are sadomasochistically fetishized.

Voluntary or *forced sissification*, that is, dressing up male characters in women's clothes, is a staple cliché of BL manga. *Forced sissification* is also a common BDSM technique, including forcing the submissive partner to wear female clothes, do "female" chores such as housework, and so on. It seems that many BL fans/creators enjoy and fetishize the *sissification*, or male-to-female transgendering, of BL characters and real-life persons such as pop stars; in a technique that resembles that of drag queens who call straight men "girl," in BL boys and men get simultaneously subverted and appropriated as sexual objects.

It is often assumed that straight female readers of yaoi generally identify with the *uke*, the "passive" character in a sex scene, meaning that *seme/uke* relationships reflect heterosexual dynamics. This is clearly not always the case. I have talked to several fans and done some informal surveys at yaoi forums and groups in Germany and the United States, and many (at least one-third) said that they identify with the *seme*. In yaoi online and computer games, *seme* characters are often played by women. The point of view in sex scenes is either voyeuristic or from the *seme* to the *uke*, allowing readers an easy identification with the *seme*.

In explaining yaoi's success, Takemiya said, "Yaoi's great because you can adopt both roles."[20] As yaoi is mostly about sex, it seems doubtful that she meant this in a purely metaphoric sense. Yaoi allows its female readers to experience themselves as penetrating *seme* and the male partner as penetrated *uke*. If part of the gender transgression and attraction of yaoi and more generally BL is related to active female sexuality, the other part has to do with passive male sexuality.

That switch of sexual roles in real life is described in an essay by Susie "Sexpert" Bright, a well-known author on sexuality. She describes her own experiences with a sexual technique called BOB (short for bend over boyfriend) or *pegging*, using a dildo and harness to penetrate her male lovers anally[21]:

> The first time I ever asked a man if I could fuck him he said absolutely not. After that, I met a few men who definitely liked it, and even guided me to feel inside for their prostate gland (which felt like the tip of a nose). But after they came and cried out and loved every minute of it, I noticed a decided lack of conversation. They were embarrassed that I'd found some secret part of them. I sensed that if I insisted on talking about it, the taboo would get worse.[22]

Bright mentions a "secret" or "taboo" that seems to be related to male penetrability. When Sedgwick discusses the "continuum between homosocial and homosexual — a continuum whose visibility, for men, in our society is radically disrupted,"[23] she connects it to "the extent to which men's sensibility, like women's, had already been structured around rape."[24] It could be hypothesized that Bright's taboo and Sedgwick's disruption have similar roots, both protecting men from penetration and potential rape.

It has been argued that slash and BL are about equality, about women wanting equal relationships with men. Equality in that context refers to social and emotional equality, but in BL and slash, that equality seems to be more literal and physical. It is about the availability of both sexual roles for women and men, not just about euphemistically "active" and "passive" roles, but about who penetrates and who gets penetrated.[25] The question of who gets to fuck whom has political repercussions, of course. But on a more personal and physical level, it allows for interesting insights for both men and women: Bright describes how a male lover didn't understand why she wasn't in the mood to be entered every day. When he later was penetrated by his new girlfriend who was "insatiable," he confessed, "'I'm hiding,' he whispered to me one afternoon, 'and I'll never challenge you on this one again! I had no idea what it was like to be the one who's always there for the taking.'" Bright's description of actively penetrating a man sounds a lot like yaoi's queer mix of the romantic and the sexual:

> I would like more women with male lovers to know the pleasures of ravishing their husbands and boyfriends [...] because it's a deep emotional pleasure to be the one who holds the world in her hands, so to speak — to be on top and going inside. When a man is vulnerable to you in that way, he's not only having physical pleasure from his prostate, he's also giving himself to you in such a completely open way that it can't help but be intensely — dare I use the word — *romantic*, in an ultimate, far-out, upside-down kinda way.[26]

BARAZOKU — *Transtextuality and Transvisuality*

After Hagio Moto introduced gay male love to *shōjo* manga in 1971, the first manga to actually show gay male sex was Takemiya Keiko's *Kaze to ki no uta* (1976, Song of Wind and Trees). Thorn reports that "there were nine years between original conception and approval for publication, because she refused to remove or fudge the sexual aspect."[27] That would place its conception around the year 1967, in a decade when knowledge about queer subcultures was starting to become available for everyone, triggering a wave of recognition and self-awareness in many people and eventually culminating in the Stonewall riots, the moment of history that started the modern gay rights movement. The material that became available was often from the U.S. or Europe, feeding into already existing Japanese ideas about the "West": the Japanese terms *seiyō* and *Ō-bei* describe in an act of "reverse orientalism," a "conflated and sometimes eroticised Euro-American cultural sphere."[28] Thus, the "West" easily becomes the stage for queer sexualities and genders in a similar way as "Western" audiences like to believe in the exotic genders and sexualities of the "East."

Welker has shown that the authors of early BL, or *shōnen-ai,* were heavily influenced by the gay male cultures of late nineteenth and early twentieth century Europe.[29] Equally, it is said that Ikeda Ryoko was inspired for the European setting of *Berusaiyu no bara* (1972, The Rose of Versailles) by a European source, Stefan Zweig's biographic novel *Marie Antoinette* (1932). This heavy borrowing from Western sources has shaped BL and transgender manga on many levels. While modern BL has more contemporary or Japanese settings than the manga of the 1970s, titles with European or pseudo–European settings, such as Higuri's Yū's *Ludwig II* (1996), still abound.

Some European customs were imported to Japan during the nineteenth century and were preserved or revived there when they were already obsolete in Europe: the language of flowers or the character system of blood types, both a recurring convention of *shōjo* manga, have that origin. Obsolete symbols from early European queer subcultures were also preserved: around 1900 the color green was associated with male homosexuality, so much so that Oscar Wilde and his circle were said to wear green carnations to recognize each other. In manga, the color green seems to indicate homosexuality, as well. It is prominent in the *Kaze to ki no uta* cover artwork, which sometimes even depicts the characters with green hair. In the story arc of the *Sailor Moon S* anime series (1994–1995) that introduces Haruka and Michiru (a butch/femme or female-to-male transgender/femme couple), the eyes of an obsessed girl turn green before she attempts to kiss a girl. Michiru's green hair seems to mark her otherwise "normal" feminine beauty as queer.

Haruka, the butch or female-to-male transgendered sailor warrior, is Sailor Uranus, which indicates her homosexuality or "male soul" (and not just by the pun on "your anus"). The German Karl Heinrich Ulrichs (1825–1895 CE), who founded the earliest gay rights movement in about 1862, coined the then extensively used term "Uranier" (Uranian) for gay men and lesbians. He believed that a gay man was a female soul trapped in a male body and that a lesbian was a male soul trapped in a female body. The term referred to the eighth and ninth chapters of Plato's symposium, where homosexuality is associated with Aphrodite Urania, the heavenly Aphrodite, daughter of Uranus, who was born from severed body parts of her father.

In a similar way, the violet, a European flower symbol for lesbianism in early twentieth century Germany, has made its way into Japanese popular culture. In 1928, Marlene Dietrich sang her first hit with a female partner about what two girlfriends do together ("*Wenn die beste Freundin*") while both were wearing bouquets of violets. The pansy is part of the Violet family and both flowers are said to resemble female genitalia, while the color purple or violet has been associated with lesbianism. In Japan, the violet, or *sumire*, is the emblem of the Takarazuka Revue that was founded in 1913. In Takarazuka, all male roles are played by women, the male impersonators called *otokoyaku*. In its early years, the Takarazuka fandom, too, was associated with lesbianism.[30]

The Japanese practice of using nineteenth century European flower symbolism for a character or an atmosphere can be traced back to the girls' novels of Yoshiya Nobuko (1896–1973), a highly successful author who lived in a lifelong "marriage" with a female partner. In her *Hana monogatari* (Flower Tales, 1916–1924 CE), she used a different flower name for the title of each story, symbolizing the character of the different heroines.[31] In 1925, Yoshiya started publishing a magazine under the title *Kuroshōbi* (Black Rose).

In *shōjo* and BL manga, flowers often interpret a character or indicate gender or sexuality. Welker has discussed the meaning of the rose as a symbol for (male) homosexuality in early *shōnen-ai* at length. In 1976, the first male/male sex scene to appear in *shōjo* manga was shown as a copulation of two roses in *Kaze to ki no uta*.[32] While in the traditional European flower language of the nineteenth century the meaning of the rose was love, in manga it has come to stand for (male) homosexuality. This symbolism originated in gay male Japanese subculture. It came to prominence in 1971 with the founding of Japan's first gay magazine, *Barazoku* (Tribe of Roses), although the symbol itself had been in use for some time before that. It could be speculated that the rose became a symbol for male homosexuality via a pun on *rosette* (French for "little rose"), which is a common German, maybe European, slang term for the anus. It might have replaced the traditional Japanese and Chinese flower symbol for the anus, the chrysanthemum.[33]

By calling her 1972 classic manga about a female-to-male transvestite *Berusaiyu no bara* (The Rose of Versailles), Ikeda invited associations with Japan's gay male subculture. These associations strongly resonate throughout the manga and anime. For example, in the surreal opening sequence of the anime version of *Berusai no bara*, the nude figure of Oscar is revealed in a bondage-like pose, wrapped in long piercing thorns, reminiscent of a series of photographs of the queer author Mishima Yukio called *Bara Kei* (Ordeal by Roses, 1963) that had been republished in 1971.[34] The photos show the author in different stages of nude bondage, covered by roses, or as a modern St. Sebastian, tied to a tree and pierced with arrows.

Brought up as a boy and turned into a personal guard to Queen Marie Antoinette of France before getting involved in the French Revolution, Ikeda's hero/ine Oscar is also firmly placed in a queer European context: the unusual first name evokes Oscar Wilde, and Marie Antoinette was rumored to have been a lesbian.[35]

Sedgwick writes, "'common sense' about homosexuality involves two contradictory gender models: forms of the inversion trope (in which a gay man represents 'a woman's soul trapped in a man's body' and so on) that see queer people as uniquely situated *between* genders; and forms of the trope of gender separation, under which it only seems common sense that people of the same gender [who have a lot in common] [...] should bond together also on the axis of sexual desire...."[36] These two opposite perceptions of gay people as inverts, *Uranier,* and members of the "Third Sex" who are a mixture between female and male; or as homosexuals, that is, feminine women or masculine men who prefer people who are "the same" (homo) as themselves, evolved in nineteenth century European gay activism and were adopted by early sexology.

Interestingly, the two perceptions can still be found in many queer manga. Inversion or "Third Sex" is ever-present in the forms of sissified boys, male-to-female transsexuals, female-to-male transvestites, "intersexuals," and characters who change sex or gender for diverse reasons. The idea of a "Third Sex" merges with traditional Japanese ideas that interpret transgender as some kind of "reincarnation accident" (see, for example, the *Torikae-baya monogatari*, a Heian-period (794–1185 CE) classic about a sister who behaves like a man and a brother who behaves like a woman). This merging of European and Japanese ideas is exemplified in *Princess Knight* (*Ribon no kishi*, 1954) in which an unborn child, intended to be a girl, swallows a male soul by accident, the born child becoming quite literally a male soul trapped in a female body.

The homosocial topos is used in virtually every BL text in the form of a homosocial setting such as the boys' school, yakuza, or other all-male environments. A third topos of homosexuality, pederasty, was present in nineteenth century discussions and crops up regularly in BL manga, often in the form of an abuse theme. Manga such as *Kaze to ki no uta* combine both topoi: the love story between Serge and Gilbert is set in a boys' school; Gilbert was abused by his uncle/father, and he also dates older boys.

The homosocial boys' school setting with its juvenile friendships has been used regularly by European authors to thematize homoerotic attraction. Novels such as Achille Esse-bac's *Dédé* (1902) or Roger Peyrefitte's *Special Friendships* (1944, *Les Amitiés particulières,* literally, particular friendships) frame their taboo subjects in the context of adolescent boys' friendships and an environment without girls, in which a little boy/boy attraction seemed almost "innocent," a mere phase.

These boys' school romances are stylistic predecessors of BL manga, specifically of early *shōnen-ai*. In fact, Hagio Moto was inspired to write the first published *shōnen-ai* manga *Juichigatsu no gimunajiumu* (November Gymnasium; 1971) and *Tōma no shinzō* (Heart of Thomas; 1974) after watching the film version of *Les Amitiés particulières* (1964).[37]

Taking an existing homosocial genre or text, in the case of European authors the conventional boys' school novel, and sexualizing it, is a technique that is strongly reminiscent of the writing technique of early yaoi and BL in general. But while the European authors used subtle homosexualization of the homosocial to avoid prosecution, yaoi consciously transgresses the boundary between the homosocial and the homosexual for sexual titillation and subversion. Texts that use a similar clash between the innocent and the forbidden to beef up the sexual impact can be found in the literature of nineteenth-century European gay subculture, e.g. *The Priest and the Acolyte* (1894) by John Francis Bloxam.

It could be argued that Hagio's *Tōma no shinzō* was one of the first manga to be rewritten yaoi-style when her friend Takemiya used a similar, but sexually explicit plot for her 1976 *Kaze to ki no uta*. Both *Tōma no shinzō* and *Kaze to ki no uta* are about boys who were abused and at first reject the love of a fellow student. The intertextual communication between these manga can be easily explained by the friendship of their authors, who lived together for a time, but it is far from uncommon. Aoyama sees "intertextuality as central to manga and novels, and shōjo readers as adept at catching such references."[38] By referencing to and re-interpreting existing texts, yaoi itself is a highly developed form of intertextuality.

While the central technique of yaoi and BL in general is to *read* homosocial texts as homosexual, another type of *reading* or re-interpretation can be found in BL: the reading of female as male and vice versa. Hagio reported that she planned her manga *Juichigatsu no gimunajiumu* and *Tōma no shinzō* to be a female version of *Les Amitiés Particulières*. Welker has discussed how a lesbian reading of *Tōma no shinzō* is facilitated by the feminine look and ambiguously drawn nude bodies of the characters, some names, the way they are placed between unambiguously male and female characters, and so on.[39] As I have shown before, in an interpretation that resembles early European interpretations of homosexuals as "Third Sex" or inverts, Takemiya associates BL with gender transgression and "being both" genders: "Through boy's love, it is possible to express dual personality (feminine and masculine) that is involved in human beings."

If the sex/gender of *shōnen-ai* characters is ambiguously drawn, allowing them to be *read* as male, female, or both, manga and anime in general use several devices to represent or conceal the sex/gender of its characters. The grammatical structure of the Japanese language allows for a subtle or not-so-subtle verbal trans-gendering or un-gendering of a character. In anime, male characters are often spoken by women who are trained to sound like men, resulting in an ambiguous voice-over. The choice of the *seiyū*, or voice actor, often adds an additional layer of meaning to an anime: in the *Card Captor Sakura* anime series (1998), Yukito, the tender boyfriend of Sakura's brother, is spoken by the popular Megumi Ogata, the same *seiyū* who voices Haruka/Sailor Uranus in *Sailor Moon*, thus connecting the effeminate gay man to the female-to-male transvestite.

When Haruka was introduced in *Sailor Moon*, her androgynous look and masculine hobbies, together with her "male language," let her *pass* as a boy in the eyes of other characters and of the audience. Many manga and anime use similar devices to consciously misguide the audience for a long time, or even create characters that can't be properly read as either male or female.

The combined use of content, language, artwork, naming, style, voice actors, cross-references, and so on to provide a manga and anime with several layers of meaning that interpret and re-interpret each other goes far beyond simple intertextuality. Aoyama sees it as an example for what Genette calls *transtextuality*, which includes, for example, *paratextuality*, e.g. the relation between the text itself and its title, preface, dedication, illustration, etc.[40]

As manga and anime are visual media, one might suggest that they make extensive use of some sort of "*transvisuality*," allowing texts to communicate with each other and with themselves on a visual level. The devices of transtextuality and transvisuality play a major role in the gender transgressiveness of manga and anime.

Fujimoto has called *Princess Knight* (1954, *Ribon no kishi*, literally the knight with the ribbon) by Osamu Tezuka the first transgender manga.[41] But Fusanosuke Natsume, Matt Thorn, and others have shown that it has at least one precursor, Matsumoto Katsuji's *Nazo no kurobā* (1934, *The Mysterious Clover*), a short manga about a Scarlet Pimpernel- or Zorro-like girl.[42] Both Zorro and the Scarlet Pimpernel led double lives as effeminate men and as freedom fighters: it seems appropriate that a masculine fighting girl leads a similar double life.

In *Princess Knight*, Tezuka's hero/ine with two souls, a male and a female one, certainly struck a note with the audience and was followed by a large number of similar series featuring female-to-male transvestite hero/ines, including the classic *Berusaiyu no bara*. A lot of *Princess Knight*'s suspense is derived from the villains' attempt to find out if Sapphire is "really" a boy or a girl. In her first scene in the anime series, she is followed and attacked by three villains:

> "Why are you attacking me?"
> "We want to know if you're a boy or a girl"
> "Who wants to know?"
> "If this potion hits you it turns blue if you're a boy and purple if you're a girl."

They shoot a white substance from the tips of their swords but don't hit her. During the whole series, there is strong pressure on her to let go of her masculinity, her boy's soul, but she refuses until the end. Both *Princess Knight* and *Berusaiyu no bara* offer a "logical" explanation for the hero/ine's transvestism: Their respective fathers brought them up as boys for reasons of succession. However, both hero/ines display a strong "male soul" all of their own, leading lives as military men.

The gendering power of the "father" is alluded to by the *Princess Knight* musical (2006). In a case of ironic casting, the musical stars former Takarazuka *otokoyaku* Kaoru Ebira, a female actor who specializes in male roles and is expected to live in a male gender role to some degree. Ebira, in the role of a "Christian" God Father with a flowing white beard, angrily punishes some angels for mischievously feeding the unborn Sapphire a male soul. In an amazing moment of literal gendering, the transvestite God holds Sapphire's glowing, blue male and pink female souls in her/his hands.

Picking up the transvestite theme where *Princess Knight* left off, *Berusaiyu no bara* takes a closer look at the inverted hero/ine's sexuality. Ikeda's Oscar strongly resembles a real person, Julie (or Julia) D'Aubigny, called La Maupin (1670–1707 CE), a female-to-male transvestite who was brought up as a boy by her father, the secretary to the master of horses for King Louis XIV, and who later became the lover of a fencing master. S/he was a famous duelist, an opera singer, and was involved with a young woman. In 1835, Théophile Gautier published the novel *Mademoiselle De Maupin*, which he loosely based on D'Aubigny's life. Passing as Théodore de Sérannes, Maupin becomes the prototype of the erotic androgyne, with men and women falling in love with her/him.[43]

And, like Maupin's, Oscar's double-gendered identity opens up multi-gendered possibilities: Girls fall in love with him/her in a mixture of idealized heterosexuality and butch/femme lesbianism. Her love for her servant André is part reminder of her female anatomy (including heterosexual expectations) and part gay male fantasy.

The smooth switch from one gender to the other, and from one sexuality to the other, is facilitated by the visual permeability of the original manga: both Oscar and André have long flowing hair and feminine, idealized faces, but wear male uniforms. Oscar can be clearly read as male: s/he is thought to be a man by the characters who meet her. When Takarazuka started to stage the manga as a musical in 1974, the transgender potential of the series was fully realized and a new layer of meaning was added. As all the roles were played by women, André was played by a woman, an *otokoyaku* or male-role-specialist. In an interesting casting decision by the revue, the woman Oscar is always played by an *otokoyaku,* as well. These decisions classify the male character André as "the same" as the female-to-male transvestite Oscar, either feminizing André or masculinizing Oscar. On a visual level, then, the love story can be interpreted as between two butch lesbians, two female-to-male transvestites, between two men, or any combination of these.

Ikeda herself takes the lesbian interpretation to the next level in her manga *Onīsama e* (1975, *Dear Brother*), recasting the likenesses of Oscar, André, and Marie Antoinette in an all-female girl's school story. Oscar and André are turned into the female butches *Saint Juste* and *Hana no Kimi*. From there it is only a small step to an unabashedly lesbian reinterpretation in *Revolutionary Girl Utena* (1996/1997 *Shōjo kakumei utena*), which combines plot elements of *Berusaiyu no bara*, *Onīsama e* and even *Kaze to ki no uta*. It recycles the school setting of early *shōnen-ai* and *Onīsama e,* has duels like *Berusaiyu no bara* and includes an Oscar-like female-to-male transvestite as the bodyguard of the sexually abused, capricious "Rose Bride" Anthy, who strongly resembles *Kaze to ki no uta*'s Gilbert.

The *Utena* plot of a hero/ine protecting an abused girl but falling in love with a dark prince, while taking part in ritualized duels in a school, has recently been reinterpreted as

After School Nightmare (2004, *Hōkago hokenshitsu*), which unites lesbian, heterosexual and transsexual/intersexual narratives, while a gay male plot is present in the subtext.

The Takarazuka musical version also facilitated a gay male reading of *Berusaiyu no bara* that was already a potential in the manga: Fujimoto lists Oscar and André with other male/male couples of BL.[44] BL not only *reads* homosocial texts as homosexual, but, by reading female characters as male, it re-interprets straight texts, as well.

The fact that *Patallirō!* (1979), a satire on early *June*-type BL manga, uses likenesses of Oscar and André in the roles of male/male couples suggests that they had been read as a gay male couple by a larger audience, so much so that they had become clichés that could be satirized: the André-type is recast as the dark, brooding, long-haired "*bishōnen* killer" Bankoran, and the Oscar-type in the role of diverse blond, effeminate, androgynously clad, but deadly *bishōnen*: Thatcher's death in the *Patallirō!* anime (1982) consciously satirizes Oscar's death in the *Berusaiyu no bara* anime (1979). Thatcher dies on the street in Bankoran's arms amid tumbling rose petals. The end song sequence ("Beauty is a Crime") of *Patallirō!* constantly refers to the opening song sequence of *Barusaiyu no bara*. The song's lyrics speak of a black rose and the need to be wrapped by thorns while showing images of Maraich (an Oscar-type *bishōnen*) and a silhouette of the *seme/uke* couple among roses, their long hair blowing in the wind. The scene clearly references the opening scene of the *Berusaiyu no bara* anime, which contains a white rose, a song about having "a fate of roses," and a silhouette of Oscar wrapped in thorns, his long hair blowing in the wind.

Welker has suggested that in early *shōnen-ai*, the *bishōnen* represents the queer girl.[45] This transformative process, which took place during years from *Berusaiyu no bara*'s publication in 1972 to *Patallirō!*'s publication in 1982, renders the transvestite hero/ine indistinguishable from the *bishōnen*.

Manga and anime depict complex forms of transvestism: a form of "double drag" is central to the plot of another re-interpretation of the *Berusaiyu no bara* theme, the anime *Chevalier (Le Chevalier D'Eon)* (2005). This double drag trope is not new or unique to Japan. It can also be found in the original staging of Shakespeare's *As You Like It*, when a boy actor played the girl Rosalind who played the boy Ganymede. In Gaultier's novel *Mademoiselle de Maupin*, the hero/ine Maupin, who is passing as Théodore, plays Rosalind in a staging of *As You Like It*. A more modern example for this type of drag is the musical *Victor/Victoria* (USA 1982, a remake of *Viktor und Viktoria*, Germany 1933): a woman dresses up as a man who dresses up as a woman.

Set in pre-revolutionary France, *Chevalier (Le Chevalier D'Eon)* features an effeminate young hero being transformed into his sister, who used to dress up in male clothes and was masculine: the man dresses up as a woman who dresses up as a man.

The pair of siblings who have reverse gender roles is reminiscent of the *Torikaebaya monogatari*. The main character of *Chevalier* is, in fact, based on another queer European, the real Chevalier D'Eon, a famous male spy who lived as a woman (1728–1810 CE).

The opening scene of the anime series (2006) illustrates the intertextual and intervisual communication between *Chevalier* and *Berusaiyu no bara*: a short scene wherein the brother practices sword fighting with his sister, who is wearing male clothes, references a similar training scene between the young Oscar and André in the first episode of the *Berusaiyu no bara* anime. In the last scene of the *D'Eon* opening sequence, the brother exits the screen amid the ruins of a revolutionary France, now transformed into a spitting image of his sister/Oscar.

The "revolution" is a recurring topos of transgender and intersex manga and anime that can be followed from *Berusaiyu no bara* to *Revolutionary Girl Utena* to *The Day of Revolution* (1999, *Kakumei no Hi*), a manga about an intersexual boy who turns into a girl.

If in manga such as *Kaze to ki no uta* or *Berusaiyu no bara*, the queer girl or female-to-male transvestite, is indistinguishable from the *bishōnen*, in *Chevalier*, an anime that is aimed at a male or mixed audience, the queer boy is indistinguishable from the masculine woman and the female-to-male transvestite.

JUNE— *Girlfags, Transfags, BL Fans*

Thorn notes, "In her book *Yaoi genron* (1998), Sakakibara Shihomi, herself a popular *yaoi*-style novelist, describes herself as a gay man in a woman's body (a 'female-to-male gay' transsexual). S/he suggests that this condition may be quite common among fans of this genre and may in fact be the reason for its existence."[46] Sakakibara's contention is strengthened by the fact that BL fans used early BL magazines such as *June* or *Allan* to express their gay male identification. Welker shows that mostly "female" readers sent in letters, personal ads, and photos in which they staged themselves as beautiful boys. They described male-male desire, "sometimes tinged with fantasy, sometimes with sadness and accompanied by an appeal for understanding or solidarity." In the personal ads, these types of readers were looking for other beautiful boys, be they male- or female-bodied.[47]

BL is a medium with many gratifications that can be interesting for different people, even for straight men.[48] It certainly can provide voyeuristic pleasure for straight female identified readers. The BL fandom is too large and too diverse to serve only one purpose. But Thorn notes,

> Nonetheless, we must acknowledge that even in Japan the majority of women do not find yaoi or boys' love particularly appealing.[...] She [an editor of yaoi] feels strongly that an attraction to both slash and yaoi is "hardwired"; if you've got it, you can't avoid it, and if you don't, it's meaningless to you. This is essentially what Sakakibara (1998) argues, though in different terms, when she claims that yaoi fans are "gay men born in women's bodies.[49]

In Japan, women with an intense interest in gay male sexuality and culture seem to have existed before the invention of BL: two of the founders of the BL genre, Hagio Moto and Takemiya Keiko, got "hooked" on "that stuff" by a mutual female friend who was "an expert" on gay male texts and erotica, such as Hermann Hesse's *Demian* (1919) and the film version of *Les Amitiés particulières*.[50]

But this is not a purely Japanese phenomenon. As early as 1920, Magnus Hirschfeld (1868–1935 CE), the foremost German sexologist, documented: "bisexual [bisexual in the sense of "double-gendered"] women, who love feminine men and masculine women, who have [...] quasi homosexual relationships with the men" and: "A female student of that category, who had many male characteristics in her appearance and character, but was completely "normal in the sexual sense," because she had erotic feelings only for men, who once told me, and quite accurately, she "felt like a homosexual man" [my translation].[51]

The terms "girlfag" and "transfag" were coined during the late 1990s in the U.S. to describe persons who were female-assigned at birth and who feel an intense fascination for and identification with gay men.[52] In 2000, the GirlFags group on Yahoo! was founded, which today has about 3,000 members. The group's intro reads:

> Girlfags are women who are very attracted to gay/bi men; females who identify with gay
> male culture.... Famous [self-identified] girlfags include Carol Queen, Jill Nagle and
> Ann Rice. [*sic*] Do you fantasize about watching or playing with multiple gay/bi men...?
> Would you smile to see (watch) your boyfriend kiss another man (or much more), fos-
> tering your own lust...? ... Some girlfags feel like a gay or bi man in a woman's body....[53]

In 1997, Bagemihl compared slash fans to fag hags and female-to-gay-male transsexuals: "There is nothing new about women identifying as gay men or eroticising and idealizing sexual relationships between men. In fact, striking parallels to the sentiments expressed
by many female-to-gay male transsexuals can be found in two unlikely areas: 'fag-hagging'
and K/S [Kirk/Spock] 'slash' fanzines."[54] Bagemihl uses the older term "fag hag" in a similar sense as girlfag. He quotes a fag hag: "A straight man can look good to me but ... when
I know a man is gay, when he's picked up some of the gay male cultural tricks and man-
nerisms, I don't know, it just turns me on.... Since I was 19 or so I've fantasized about being
a beautiful boy in a loving relationship with a man."[55]

Comparing this statement to a quote by a female-to-gay-male transsexual, Bagemihl
shows how closely they resemble each other: "My first sexual fantasies were of a man hugging and caressing a boy and of men kissing each other.... What made gay men more sexually attractive than straight men? Simply the fact that they were aroused by other men."[56]

The difference between girlfag and transfag seems to be one of degree rather than quality. A person might strongly identify with and even as a gay man, while still maintaining
a female identity. Sedgwick wrote about herself, "In among the many ways I do identify as
a woman, the identification as a gay person is a firmly male one, identification 'as' a gay
man."[57] And several years later, "Probably my own most formative influence from quite
an early age has been a viscerally intense, highly speculative (not to say inventive) cross-
identification with gay men and gay male cultures as I inferred, imagined, and later came
to know them."[58]

Lou Sullivan (1951–1991), the founder of FTM International, an organization for
female-to-male transsexuals, initially identified as a "heterosexual female transvestite who
was sexually attracted to gay men."[59] He later transitioned from female to male. When still
living as a woman in a relationship with a feminine bisexual man, Sullivan wrote in his
diary:

> But the role [Mick] Jagger played [in a film] turned me on so—I could identify with a
> bisexual male, that's how fucked I am that I had possibly the most satisfying sex contact
> with Jim that nite [*sic*] I've ever had. There's so much written about all kinds of sexually
> weird people but a female who imagines herself as a bisexual male is way beyond any-
> thing I've ever read. And so how do I cope with myself?[60]

Members of sexual or gender minorities such as girlfags or transfags are often isolated
and, like Sullivan, fear that they are "the only one" who have such feelings. The letter columns
of early BL magazines such as *June* served similar purposes as later Internet venues such as
the GirlFags group on Yahoo!, in that they helped like-minded souls to connect. It could be
argued that these BL magazines were hosting a subculture in the making. Like the fans of
June who consumed gay male manga, Sullivan voyeuristically consumed a product of popular culture, in this case a film featuring gay or bisexual men. And like the *June* fans who
wrote about their gay male desires, Sullivan identified with a man who is attracted to men.
Both took measures to change their exterior to fit their interior identification: the *June* fans
dressed up as *bishōnen* and Sullivan began to wear male clothes, thus beginning a process
that would eventually result in the decision to change his body from female to male.

When attempting to put their sexual fantasies into practice, both girlfags and transfags who have not physically transitioned to male are confronted with the same problem: gay men are generally not interested in them. The GirlFag group intro says, "We'll face the difficulties of having an orientation that seems designed to engender frustration." And: "We'll talk about what it means to be a girlfag, try to figure out how girlfags can meet the boyfag (or girlfag) of their dreams."[61]

In personal ads, the *June* fans who felt they were gay *bishōnen* sometimes were looking for other female-bodied *bishōnen*. While Welker interprets their desires in the context of lesbianism,[62] I believe that reading them in a context of girlfag or transfag desire is more precise: girlfags and transfags are both attracted to gay men, but girlfags can be attracted to other girlfags. In the same way, transfags often date other transfags. This practice overlaps with, but is not exactly the same as, butches dating butches (or *tachi* dating *tachi*, in the Japanese context). The expression of a temporary or constant male identification is of central importance in such relationships, which can be a way to overcome the problem that "gay men don't date girls." The relationship is not just a vehicle or cover for a lesbian relationship, nor is it only a queer space for experimenting with nontraditional sexuality. It is, first of all, a safe and understanding environment in which the participants can actually be seen as male, acting out their masculine gender and often their perception of their own physical body as male on the level of sex and sexuality.

But even if girlfags/transfags date bisexual men or find a gay man who is interested, the problem is not fully solved. By having sex with him, they "turn him straight" and he might lose a great deal of his attraction for them. If they are male-identified, they might feel like Sakakibara: "She is therefore never happy, even if a man whom she loves, would love her. She wants to be loved as a boy."[63]

If the girlfag/transfag dresses in male clothes and manages to pass as a man, the moment when "her" "true" sex is discovered triggers what I would call the "gay transvestite's dilemma": while a relationship with a women would confirm the masculinity of the transvestite, a relationship with a man seems to "prove" his/her femininity. *Princess Knight* and *Berusaiyu no bara*, both texts with female-to-male transvestite protagonists in love with men, are obsessively trying to solve this dilemma: How can the transvestite have a sexual relationship with a man without losing her/his own masculinity?

As mentioned above, the first episode of the *Princess Knight* anime shows male villains who squirt a white liquid from the tips of their swords. When the liquid touches the transvestite hero/ine, it will reveal her/his "true," that is, genital, sex. Likewise, Oscar is feminized by her/his making love with André. S/he constantly oscillates between masculine and feminine, painfully trying to integrate both. A similar story is told by *After School Nightmare*: the "intersexual" or female-to-male transsexual main character is torn between his/her male identity and his/her love for a man.

DANSŌ KEI— *From Theory to Practice*

To solve these problems, Sakakibara uses her art as a way to live her sexual and gender identity: "Her creative work is the only possibility to fulfil her libido...."[64] She is not the only professional author who is using a mechanism I call "creative transvestism." The gay-male-identified Sedgwick wrote, "For very simply a sudden urgency to write narrative poetry, after my twelfth birthday, was coextensive with, was the same as, one or another plot of male homosexual revelation. Lawrence of Arabia, David and Jonathan, *The Man from U.N.C.L.E.*, Roger Casement, the Round Table, an avant–Girardian reading of Jules and Jim...."[65] Poppy Z. Brite (b. 1967), another gay-male-identified author who mostly writes about gay men, describes an even more traumatic experience of the same sort:

> The urge to be placed in context nearly killed me. ... [it] caused me to expose and embarrass myself in hopes of finding a peer group that didn't exist.... What's embarrassing is the naivete [*sic*] with which I believed readers would take my explanations at face value. "Oh, she's really a gay man! That explains everything!" ... I was completely unprepared for the people who thought my sexuality was some kind of promotional gimmick.... I thought I was ready to be called a "fag hag" with "penis envy," but I wasn't.... All I'd really wanted was for my readers, particularly my gay readers, to have a better shot at understanding why I wrote the things I did. With a few exceptions, though, the gay press ignored me.[66]

Writing about the autobiographies of female-to-male transsexuals, Jay Prosser explains that the subject's autobiography can sometimes "re-present" the body as a fantasized self, the self that they wished they could be through the transformation of clothes, appearance, and speech.[67] Barbara Guest offers a similar view of lesbian author Bryher: she "acted out her desire to be a boy in the historical fiction for which she is best known...."[68] Taylor concludes: "The desire to be a boy is collapsed into the wish to write, and literature becomes an erotic stimulus."[69]

The gay-male-identified painter Carrington (1893–1932 CE) drew herself/himself as a boy, transforming the body at least on paper.[70] Creative transvestism through visual arts can be a potent tool of identification: BL as a visual medium allows for a smooth identification of artist and fan with the male characters by providing an "involved" point of view and characters that look not so much like cis-men but like boys or female-to-male transgendered people in the early stages of transition. Interestingly, in international queer communities, it is common to refer to female-to-male transgendered people (ftm) as *boyz*, and many ftm say that they don't identify so much as men but as boys. As during the early years of taking testosterone, the ftm goes through a second puberty and looks (and sounds) like an adolescent boy, this seems only appropriate.

In "virtual reality," a process similar to creative transvestism can be observed in the form of people *cruising* the Internet or engaging in online role-playing games with a gender identity that differs from their everyday gender. Another example would be female-assigned persons who write gay male pornography under a male pseudonym for a gay male audience. This fairly common practice has been described by Patrick Califia who has written gay male erotica under a male pseudonym before transitioning from female to male.[71] I know of two female-to-gay-male identified German authors who live as women but are thought to be gay cis-men by their mostly gay male readers.[72]

Like putting on drag, creative transvestism is a technique that is not just available for transsexuals, but for everyone. The trans-gendered identification of manga fans and authors might last for the short moment of the romantic or sex scene, or for a lifetime.

Mulvey has argued for film theory that female spectatorship necessarily involves female-to-male "transvestism," as the female spectator needs to take the male point of view to be able to enjoy the male-centered narrative.[73] But she analyzed mostly male-produced mainstream cinema. BL differs from more conventional texts in several points: it is female-authored and consciously addressed to a mostly female audience. Moreover, while commercial BL is printed by male-dominated publishing houses, audience participation in the form of surveys and polls is invited and influences the content. And BL still has strong roots in and connections to amateur manga (*dōjinshi*) that is produced without any interference of "patriarchal" publishers. There is no structural need for female fans of *yaoi* to take a male point of view dictated by male artists.

Still, the term "transvestism" seems appropriate for BL writing and reading techniques. It was first coined by Magnus Hirschfeld in 1910, describing the act of cross-dressing and/or a part-time or full-time identification with the opposite sex. Hirschfeld's transvestites could be male or female, lesbian, gay, straight, bisexual, or asexual. They could be sexually aroused by transvestism or not. They could wish a physical change or not. A "transvestite," then, is a person involved in any of the above experiences.[74] The German term *Transvestismus* (transvestism) seems to have been in use in pre-war Japan as *toransuvechichisumusu*.[75] Hirschfeld's "Transvestismus" is pretty close to today's umbrella term "transgender," but as opposed to "transgender," it emphasizes the "act" of changing gender, not the internal "identity," making the change available for everyone.

While creative transvestism allows for male identification on a virtual level, cosplay takes the next step, in that it actually involves the body of the fan/artist. The readers of *June*, by sending in photos in which they staged themselves as beautiful boys, and describing their gay male desires, crossed the line between the literary and the literal. Their practices are indistinguishable from those of male-to-female transvestites who send photos of themselves in female attire to traditional transvestite magazines, describing their gender and sexual identifications, which are often lesbian.

Thorn notes that female-to-male cross-dressing yaoi fans have many similarities with male-to-female crossdressing fans of "Beautiful Girl" manga with mostly lesbian content:

> Nothing illustrates this fluidity of identification more vividly than the image of a man cross-dressed as a favorite heroine standing in line to buy a pornographic amateur manga featuring that same heroine. If, as Sakakibara argues, yaoi fans are gay men in women's bodies, then it might be fair to suggest that many fans of amateur "Beautiful [lesbian] Girls" manga are, as it were, lesbians in men's bodies, and not simply run-of-the-mill misogynists.... To accept, uncritically, [yaoi fans] as good, and reject, uncritically, [Beautiful Girl fans] as bad, would be a mistake. In a sense, the two genres mirror each other, and speak to the desires of those who, by choice or circumstance, do not fit neatly into society's prescribed norms of gender and sexuality.[76]

The "Beautiful Girl" cosplayers that Thorn describes strongly resemble the male equivalent of girlfags and transfags: guydykes and transdykes, i.e., male-assigned persons who eroticize and identify with lesbians and sometimes transition from male to lesbian.[77] Like the male-to-female transvestites who identify as lesbians, the "Beautiful Girls" cosplayers and guydykes/transdykes are often seen as "perverts," even by BL fans. The willingness to interpret the "male" behavior as a sexual perversion, while BL fandom or girlfags/transfags often go unnoticed, reflects the degree to which male sexuality is taken seriously and female sexuality is not.[78]

Certain cosplay fandoms, like the *visual kei* fandom, are strongly associated with female-to-male transvestism, or *dansō kei* (male dress style). *Visual kei* is a highly successful visual style of Japanese pop music that has roots in the style of androgynous and transvestite musicians like David Bowie. *Visual kei* bands usually consist of boys wearing make-up or female attire who are considered to be sex symbols. *Visual kei* fandom is closely connected to *yaoi* fandoms, with fans drawing *dōjinshi* imagining gay sexual relations between their favorite stars. The bands are fully conscious of that fandom and cater to it. At cosplay events, *visual kei* cosplayers who dress up as their pop idols mix with manga cosplayers.

But can *dansō kei* cosplaying be interpreted in a context of gender transgression and sexuality? Hashimoto answers the question with a partial yes, that cosplaying is a fetishistic activity.[79] In her study of female Austrian and Japanese *visual kei* fans who are also *yaoi* fans, Hashimoto made an interesting observation: While a certain percentage of the Japanese fans said that dressing up as another gender was part of the appeal of cosplaying, none of the Austrian fans said so. That is in itself is remarkable for a fandom that consists almost solely in female-to-male cosplay. While it could be argued that the *visual kei* stars themselves are wearing partial female drag, and thus the female fans are wearing female or feminine attire, too, the Japanese fans seemed to be aware that they were dressing up as men. The Austrian fans equally referred to the stars as sexy men, not as women or genderless beings. Then, how can this curious divergence be explained?

Japan has a strong, living tradition of public transvestism that is only partially associated with the pornographic or pathological. Japanese grow up with knowledge of male-to-female crossdressers in classical theatre and in the media (Bandō Tamasaburō, Peter, Akihiro Miwa, and several contemporary transgendered pop stars). Equally, they know about the Takarazuka *otokoyaku* and perhaps female-to-male cross dressing in classical theatre and dance, not to mention gender-bending in manga and anime.

By contrast, transvestism and crossdressing in German-speaking countries is almost completely associated with the pathological, the ridiculous, or the sexual. Transvestite artistic traditions that were alive until the Weimar Republic (1918–1933), reflected in feature films such as *Ich möchte kein Mann sein* (Germany 1919, "I Don't Want to be a Man") or *Viktor und Viktoria* (Germany 1933), were extinguished by the Nazi regime. After that, until very recently, male-to-female transvestites were seen only in the context of medical pathology, prostitution, or (very) lowbrow entertainment.

And most importantly, female-to-male transvestites were virtually invisible. Apart from a certain tradition in classical opera that is only known to opera goers, female-to-male transvestism was just not done. The very existence of female-to-male transsexuals was denied by many scientists, so much so that until about five or six years ago, the general public didn't know of its existence. Female-to-male transgendered individuals report again and again that even people who had heard of the existence of male-to-female transsexuals didn't know that the "other direction" was possible.[80] This is slowly changing, as during the last five years or so three celebrities have publicly transitioned from female to male, and information is available from the Internet. But it is still a very exotic topic. In this context of nonexistence, it makes sense that the Austrian fans don't reflect on the implications of their cross-dressing.

Another fandom with a lot of female-to-male cross-dressing is the Harry Potter *dōjinshi* fandom. The Harry Potter boom was as strong in Japan as it was in Europe and the U.S. The Harry Potter books seem to lend themselves to easy slashing, as there is a whole generation of international Harry Potter fans involved in online slashing. In Japan, the slashing naturally happens in the form of *dōjinshi*. With its boarding school setting, school uniforms, and boys' dormitories, the Harry Potter books resemble early *shōnen-ai*. The atmosphere of juvenile "innocence" and homosociality inspires authors to a diverse and often "polymorphously perverse" range of couplings, including students, teachers, relatives, and magical creatures. The fandom is strongest with male/male slash but has popular straight and lesbian couplings, too. At cosplay events in Germany and Japan, groups of girls in school boy uniforms, wearing the colors of the different Hogwarts houses, are a common sight.

Dressing up as a *bishōnen* for a day isn't enough for many fans, who are involved in online role playing games where they take on the roles of *seme* or *uke* characters over long periods of time. Some even impersonate these characters when they meet in real life, mixing the virtual with the real to a degree that they become indistinguishable. The mostly female teenage BL fans of a German manga group I used to attend regularly played *yaoi* role playing games. After play sessions, I witnessed recurring dialogues such as: "*HA! Ich hab dich gestern abend ge-*raped!" "HA! I have *raped* [English in German original] you last night! [in the context of the role playing game]." The dialogues were followed by scenes of bonding, cuddling, holding hands, and so on.

By coining and repeatedly using the "English" term *rape*, the German *yaoi* gamers show the importance they place on appropriating the role of penetrator and perpetrator, while at the same time removing it from real-life rape, which would be associated immediately if they used the German word. By saying "I" instead of "my character," they show that their characters are not just a gaming device for them, but a point of identification.

Are these girls who impersonate boys who have sex with boys and cuddle with each other lesbians or gay female-to-male transsexuals? Are they straight because they are girls who like boys? Are they straight female-to-male transsexuals because they take a male role and interact with a girl? Thorn has described the multiple sexual possibilities of the *cosplay* related crossdressing he witnessed in Japan, echoing the multiple sexual possibilities of the transvestite hero/ine of manga and anime:

> One occasionally witnesses eroticized teasing, particularly on the part of cross-dressed cos-players, who will make suggestive comments to or fondle fellow participants of either sex, who are usually happy to play along. When cross-dressing is involved, there are always multi-layered heterosexual and homosexual tensions. When a woman dressed as a man makes a pass at another woman, she is "playing at" heterosexuality, but the fact that she is biologically a woman creates an obvious homosexual element. If the other woman is herself dressed as a man, then the two are "playing at" male homosexuality, yet there is also a suggestion of female homosexuality, since both are biologically women, and, because each woman is ostensibly reacting to the performed "masculinity" of the other, there is a heterosexual nuance, as well. Similarly, when a woman dressed as a man is flirting with a man dressed as a woman, there is a double-reverse heterosexual element, yet, again, since each is reacting to the performed gender of the other, there is also a suggestion of homosexuality.[81]

What is true for female-to-male crossdressers is similarly true for male-to-female crossdressers. In Germany, boys in female cosplay attire are a regular if rare sight. While in Japan some male-to-female cosplayers were surprisingly old and strongly resembled sexy drag queens with "hyper" female attributes, in Germany, only adolescent boys can get away with serious female drag. Older cosplayers always frame it in a humoristic context. I have seen boys in fetishizing make-up and half nudity, often in chains, at the Leipzig annual cosplay convention. Tamer versions of the "boy-in-chains" can be seen at the monthly cosplay meeting in my area. The thirteen-to-sixteen-year-old Northern German female fans I have described enjoy going shopping while walking a male or female fan who is impersonating an *uke* on a leash, even when they are not wearing costumes.

In Japan, this blurring between the virtual and the real is taken further by so-called cosplay cafés. The customers are served by waitresses and waiters who are dressed up as manga characters, and often the interior design of the café recreates the settings of manga. Cosplay cafés that cater to yaoi fans and to fans who are interested in female-to-male transvestite cosplay are part of a larger Japanese tradition of host bars, *dansō kei* bars, and *onabe* bars in the entertainment industry. The heterosexual host bar provides female customers with beautiful male company for the evening. Similarly, cosplay butler cafés employ beautiful young men who spoil their female customers. Butler cafés such as Café Edelstein actively try to recreate the atmosphere of a BL manga, in that it pretends to be a boys' school and its uniformed hosts play the roles of school boys: "'I'm in the flower arrangement club,' whispers one girlish, long-haired waiter at the cafe, looking up from the book of German poetry he is reading."[82] Places as Café Edelstein allow the customers to physically intrude into the all-male fantasy world of BL and interact with it.

Dansō kei bars, or bars for female-to-male transvestites who are sometimes lesbian-identified and sometimes male-identified, originated in the 1960s. For the time around 1967, at least thirteen *dansō kei* bars for lesbians were documented in Japan. The bars seem to have been associated with the *otokoyaku* of Takarazuka and the Shochiku revue, e.g., one bar's name was *Zuka*.[83] As there seems to be a large clientele of "straight" women who are interested in dating *otokoyaku*-like transvestites, since 1973 there have been several so-called *onabe* bars that satisfy that need. The hosts are *onabe* (butches or female-to-male transsexuals).[84]

In the more recent *otome* or *dansō kei* cosplay cafés, the hosts are female-to-male transvestite *bishōnen* who can be rented for the evening. By providing a semi-real environment in which the transvestite hosts can interact with their customers as *bishōnen,* the cafés allow the hosts to live almost full-time as male without transitioning physically. If the customers wear male costumes themselves, they can engage with the hosts in a male/male constellation, bringing BL to life.

Conclusion

Women and other female-assigned people who eroticize and identify with gay men seem to exist internationally, but the commercialization of these desires and identifications is a uniquely Japanese phenomenon so far. A feature film such as *Tonari no 801 (yaoi) chan* (*My Neighbor Yaoi-chan*; Japan 2006), which humorously dramatizes the relationship between a boy and a *yaoi* fangirl, is as yet unimaginable for Europe or the U.S.[85] There are a few "female" authors such as Poppy Z. Brite or Mary Renault who have made a career from writing gay male novels for a mainstream market, but it is impossible to know how many such books might have met the fate of the German novel *Die Kunst der Bestimmung* (*The Art of Definition*, 2003) by Christine Wunnicke, a highly praised historical novel with a gay male theme. Although distributed by a major publisher, it couldn't be marketed properly because book agents felt uncomfortable recommending it.[86]

Things are improving, however. Recently, Floortje Zwigtman, a Dutch female author of juvenile books, received a far more positive response to her trilogy *Een groene bloem* (*A Green Flower*), about a boy prostitute of the Oscar Wilde circle, containing explicit sex scenes. Its first part, *Schijnbewegingen* (2005, planned English title: *Tricks of the Trade*), was called "Best Book for Young Adults 2005" in the Netherlands and received important awards for juvenile books all over Europe.[87] And in 2006, I talked to a German publisher of manga who, at the time, was still unbelieving that the Japanese success of BL could be repeated in Germany. Since then, however, BL titles have become some of the highest-selling manga in the German market.

While BL has been a factor in the creation of East Asian popular culture for some years, slash is only now beginning to influence Western commercial pop culture: *Torch-*

wood (2006), a spin-off of the British TV series *Dr. Who*, with its bisexual, immortal hero Captain Jack Harkness, has been created by an out bisexual television producer and script writer, Russell T. Davies. Davies was also responsible for the British original of *Queer as Folk* (1999). To reach a larger audience than gay men, *Torchwood* is aimed at women, who presumably have formed a large part of the *Queer as Folk* fan base as well. The *Torchwood* episode "Captain Jack Harkness" (2007), written by Catherine Tregenna, has a distinctly "slashy" feel. Since the success of the film version of *Brokeback Mountain* (1997/2005), another female-written, gay male text that was highly successful with women, producers might begin to be more open to gay male-themed projects.

While lesbian themes are already acceptable within conventional plots aimed at a major audience (e.g., *Buffy* or *Xena*) gay male plots are still considered problematic. Lesbians are sexy for many men who might be repulsed by gay men, due to the taboo on male penetrability. As the media are still male-dominated, major gay male characters and plots are scarce. By contrast, in East Asia, the commercial success of BL seems to have caused an increase in gay male- or transfag-themed feature films and television series aimed at a mostly female or mainstream audience, including *He's the Woman, She's the Man*, and the sequel *Who's the Woman, Who's the Man?* (both Hong Kong 1996), *Bishōnen* (Hong Kong 1998), *Boys Love* (Japan 2006), *Love of Siam* (Thailand 2007), *Bangkok Love Story* (Thailand 2007), *The First Shop of Coffee Prince* (*Coffee Prince*) (television series, Korea 2007) , and *Hua Yang Shao Nian Shao Nu / Hanazakari no Kimitachi e* (both television series based on the manga *Hana no Kimi*, Taiwan 2006 and Japan 2007). These films and television series make use of well known BL plots and devices.

Even though there seems to be a core group of gay-male-identified BL fans/creators, BL fandom cannot wholly be contained within transsexuality or the girlfag/transfag phenomenon. Instead, it reveals the perverse or queer sexuality of its "straight" fans/creators. Thorn says that Alexander Doty, in *Making Things Perfectly Queer* (1993), uses the term queer "to question the cultural demarcations between the queer and the straight ... by pointing out the queerness of and in straights and straight cultures."[88]

BL not only points out the queer sexuality but also the queer gender of its so-called straight female fans/creators. Like the green yaoi-monster in the film *Tonari no 801 (yaoi) chan* that pops out of the zipper in the *fujoshi*'s back whenever she thinks about yaoi, and leaves only a female shell behind, the queerness of BL fans pops out of what is only a shell of conventional straight femaleness.

Notes

1. Deb Aoki, "Interview Keiko Takemiya," http://manga.about.com/od/mangaartistswriters/a/Keiko Takemiya_2.htm (accessed August 12, 2009).

2. Masami Toku, "Interview with Keiko Takemiya, January 22, 2003," http://www.csuchico.edu/~mto ku/vc/interviews_full/Interview%20w_Takemiya.html) (accessed August 15, 2009).

3. Björn-Ole Kamm, *Fujōshi — Nutzen und Gratifikation bei Boy's Love Manga in Japan und Deutschland* (forthcoming master's thesis, University of Leipzig, Germany, 2008), 3. See also Björn-Ole Kamm, Introduction to: *Fujōshi — Nutzen und Gratifikation bei Boy's Love Manga in Japan und Deutschland*, http://www.b-ok. de/download/fujōshi_kamm_v1_1.pdf (accessed April 23, 2009).

4. Frederik Dhaenens, et al., "Transgressing the Boundaries of Screen Studies, Representations, and Slashing the Fiction of Queer Theory: Slash Fiction, Queer Reading, and Audiences," *Journal of Communication Inquiry*, Volume 32 Number 4, October 2008, 335–347, http://jci.sagepub.com/cgi/content/abstract/32/4/335 (accessed May 10, 2009), 346.

5. Henry Jenkins, *Textual Poachers* (New York: Routledge, 1992), 202.

6. Dhaenens et al., "Transgressing the Boundaries."

7. Kamm, *Fujoshi*, 29.

8. Jenkins, *Textual Poachers*, 202.

9. Eve Kosofsky Sedgwick, *Between Men* (New York: Columbia University Press, 1985), 2.

10. Kamm, *Fujoshi*, 33ff.

11. Sullivan, quoted in Bruce Bagemihl, "Surrogate Phonology and Transsexual Faggotry: A Linguistic Analogy for Uncoupling Sexual Orientation from Gender Identity," in *Queerly Phrased, Language, Gender, and Sexuality*, ed. Anna Livia and Kira Hall (Oxford: Oxford University Press, 1997), 385.

12. Eve Kosofsky Sedgwick, *Tendencies* (Durham: Duke University Press, 1993), 4.

13. Mark Lipton, "Queer Readings of Popular Culture," in *Queer Youth Cultures*, ed. Susan Driver (Albany: State University of New York Press, 2008), 168.

14. *The Celluloid Closet*, dir. Rob Epstein, Jeffrey Friedman (1995), DVD (Pro-Fun Media, 2004).

15. Paul Baker, *Fantabulosa: A Dictionary of Polari and Gay Slang* (London, New York: Continnum, 2002).

16. Moe Meyer, quoted in Mike Perkovich, *Nature Boys: Camp Discourse in American Literature from Whitman to Wharton* (New York: Peter Lang Publishing, 2003), 7.

17. Perkovitch, *Nature Boys*, 7.

18. Kamm, *Fujoshi*, 280.

19. Miyuki Hashimoto, "Visual Kei Otaku Identity — An Intercultural Analysis," *Intercultural Communication Studies* XVI: 1 2007 (University of Vienna, Austria), 95, http://www.uri.edu/iaics/content/2007v16n1/10%20Miyuki%20Hashimoto.pdf (accessed July 10, 2009).

20. Aoki, "Interview Keiko Takemiya."

21. A sexual practice with a long history, if one is to believe the Roman poet Martial (40–104 CE). In his poem *To Philaenis*, he satirized a woman: "Abhorrent to all natural joys/ Philaenis sodomizes boys." Anon. translation in Stephen Coote, *The Penguin Book of Homosexual Verse* (London: Penguin Books, 1986).

22. Susie Bright, "Move over, Ken, it's "Bend Over Boyfriend," Salon.com, http://dir.salon.com/story/health/sex/col/brig/1998/05/22/nc_22brig/ (accessed August 10. 2009).

23. Sedgwick, *Between Men*, 2.

24. Ibid., 193.

25. See also Jenkins, *Textual Poachers*, 198, about multiple identifications.

26. Bright, "Move over, Ken."

27. Matthew Thorn, "Girls And Women Getting Out Of Hand: The Pleasure And Politics Of Japan's Amateur Comics Community" (2004), 185 F 4, http://matt-thorn.com/shoujo_manga/outofhand/index.php#back8 (accessed August 10, 2009).

28. James Welker, "Beautiful, Borrowed, and Bent: 'Boys' Love' as Girl's Love in *Shojo Manga*," *Signs: Journal of Women in Culture and Society* 31:3 (Spring 2006): 841–70, 846.

29. Ibid., 863ff.

30. For a discussion of the historic lesbian context of the Takarazuka fandom, see Jennifer Robertson, *Takarazuka* (Berkeley: University of California Press, 1998).

31. Tomoko Aoyama, "Transgendering *shōjo shosetsu*" in *Genders, Transgenders and Sexualities in Japan*, ed. Mark McLelland, Romit Dasgupta (London and New York: Routledge, 2005), 55.

32. Welker, *Beautiful, Borrowed and Bent*, 859ff.

33. Gregory M. Pflugfelder, *Cartographies of Desire: Male-Male Sexuality in Japanese Discourse, 1600–1950* (Berkeley: University of California Press, 2000) 164 and 85N164.

34. First edition 1963 under the title *Death by Roses*, republished in international edition as *Ordeal by Roses* in 1971.

35. See Terry Castle, *The Apparitional Lesbian* (New York: Columbia University Press, 1993).

36. Sedgwick, *Tendencies*, XIII.

37. See Matthew Thorn, "The Moto Hagio Interview (2005)," http://www.matt-thorn.com/shoujo_manga/hagio_interview.php (accessed August 10, 2009). See also Nancy, "Poe no ichizoku," "Hagio's Interview "Hatachi — 20 Years Old" (translation) http://ponoichizoku.blogspot.com/2007/04/hagios-interview-hatachi-20-years-old.html (accessed August 20, 2009).

38. Aoyama, quoted in Welker, *Beautiful, Borrowed and Bent*, 864.

39. Welker, *Beautiful, Borrowed, and Bent*, 846ff.

40. Aoyama, "Transgendering *shōjo shosetsu*," 56.

41. Quoted in Kamm, *Fujoshi*, 25.

42. Matthew Thorn, "The Multi-Faceted Universe of Shōjo Manga" (2008), http://www.matt-thorn.com/shoujo_manga/colloque/index.php (accessed May 5, 2009).

43. Jim Burrows, "The Adventures of La Maupin" (1995–2008), http://www.eldacur.com/~brons/Maupin/MaupinIndex.html (accessed July 14, 2009).

44. Welker, *Beautiful, Borrowed and Bent*, 852ff.

45. Ibid.

46. Thorn, "Girls And Women Getting Out Of Hand."

47. Welker, *Beautiful, Borrowed and Bent*, 856, 857.

48. See Kamm, *Fujoshi*, 2008.

49. Thorn, "Girls And Women Getting Out Of Hand."

50. See Thorn, "The Moto Hagio Interview" and Nancy, "Hagio's Interview."

51. Magnus Hirschfeld, *Die Homosexualität des Mannes und des Weibes* (Berlin: Louis Marcus Verlagsbuchhandlung, 1920), 206.

52. See Carol Queen, Laurence Schimel, ed., *PoMosexuals* (San Francisco: Cleis Press, 1997).

53. GirlFags Yahoo! Group, "Introduction," http://groups.yahoo.com/group/GirlFags/ (accessed April 4, 2009).

54. Bagemihl, "Surrogate Phonology," 386.

55. Quoted in Bagemihl, "Surrogate Phonology," 387.

56. Ibid.

57. Sedgwick, *Tendencies*, 209.

58. Ibid., 14

59. Quoted in Leslie Feinberg, *Transgender Warriors* (Boston, Mass.: Beacon Press, 1997), 144.

60. Diary of Lou Sullivan (January 13, 1971), quoted in Corinna Genschel Erstrittene Subjektivität: Diskurse der Transsexualität, *Das Argument* 243 43/6, 2001: 821ff, http://www.linksnet.de/artikel.php?id=553 (accessed August 10, 2009).

61. GirlFag Yahoo Group, "Introduction."

62. See Welker, *Beautiful, Borrowed and Bent*. See also James Welker, "Lilies of the Margin: Beautiful Boys and Queer Female Identities in Japan" in *AsiaPacifiQueer,* ed. Fran Martin, Peter A. Jackson, et al. (Urbana and Chicago: University of Illinois Press, 2008).

63. Hashimoto, "Visual Kei Otaku Identity," 92.

64. Ibid.

65. Sedgwick, *Tendencies*, 208.

66. Poppy Z. Brite, "Enough Rope," http://www.poppyzbrite.com/rope.html (accessed August 2009), first published in: *Crossing the Border: Tales of Erotic Ambiguity*, ed. Lisa Tuttle (London: Indigo Books, 1998).

67. In Clare L. Taylor, *Women, Writing, and Fetishism 1890–1950* (Oxford: Clarendon Press, 2003), 51.

68. Ibid., 62n.17.

69. Ibid., 63.

70. Jane Hill, *Dora Carrington* (München: Knesebeck, 1995), 31.

71. Pat Califia, "Identity Sedition and Pornography" in *PoMosexuals* ed. Carol Queen, Laurence Schimel (San Francisco: Cleis Press, 1997).

72. Personal conversation with publisher, 2008.

73. For a discussion of film theory and manga, see Welker, *Beautiful, Borrowed and Bent*, 844.

74. See Magnus Hirschfeld, *Die Transvestiten* (Berlin: Verlag Pulvermacher, 1910).

75. Beverley Curran and James Welker, "From the Well of Loneliness to the akarui rezubian: Western Translations and Japanese Lesbian Identities," in *Genders, Transgenders and Sexualities in Japan*, eds. Mark McLelland and Romit Dasgupta (London: Routledge, 2005), 65–80.

76. Thorn, "Girls and Women Getting Out of Hand."

77. For more information about guydykes and transdykes, see Queen, Schimel, *PoMosexuals*; Markisha Greaney, "A Proposal for Doing Transgender Theory in the Academy," in *Reclaiming Genders: Transsexual Grammars at the Fin de Siècle,* ed. Kate More, Stephen Whittle (London: Cassell, 1999); Uli Meyer, Almost Homosexual — Schwule Frauen, Schwule Trans*Gender (GirlFags/Trans*Fags), in *Liminalis* 1, 2007 http://www.liminalis.de/artikel/Liminalis2007_meyer.pdf (accessed August 15, 2009).

78. Meyer, "Almost Homosexual."

79. Hashimoto, "Visual Kei Otaku Identity."

80. My observation in German-speaking queer and transgender communities since 1988.

81. Thorn, "Girls and Women Getting Out Of Hand."

82. Sophie Hardach, "Sexy Comics Feed Japan's Role Play Boom," *International Business Times* (March 4, 2008), http://www.ibtimes.co.in/articles/20080304/comics-japan-role-play-boom.htm (accessed August 10, 2009).

83. For a short history of *onabe* and *dansō kei* bars, see James Welker, "Telling Her Story: The Japanese Lesbian Community 1971–2001: Selections From '*Komyuniti No Rekishi*' 1971–2001: *Nenpyō To Intabyū De Furikaeru.*" (master's thesis / annotated translation, University of Sheffield, UK, 2002).

84. A documentary about *onabe* bars: *Shinjuku Boys,* dir. Kim Longinotto, Jano Williams (1995), DVD (20th Century Vixen).

85. The title is an allusion to *My Neighbor Totoro*, the well-known anime about a friendly monster.

86. Personal communication with a publisher, 2008.

87. Floortje Zwigtman, *Ich, Adrian Mayfield* (Hildesheim: Gerstenberg Verlag, 2008). The Foundation for the Production and Translation of Dutch Literature, "Floortje Zwigtman — Tricks of the Trade" http://www.nlpvf.nl/docs/Zwigtman_Schijnbewegingen_scr.pdf (accessed August, 10, 2009).

88. Quoted in Thorn, "Girls And Women Getting Out Of Hand."

Bibliography

Aoki, Deb. "Interview Keiko Takemiya." http://manga.about.com/od/mangaartistswriters/a/KeikoTakemiya_2.htm (accessed August 12, 2009).

Aoyama, Tomoko. "Transgendering *shōjo shosetsu.*" In *Genders, Transgenders and Sexualities in Japan,* edited by Mark McLelland, Romit Dasgupta, 49–64. London and New York: Routledge, 2005.

Bagemihl, Bruce. "Surrogate Phonology and Transsexual Faggotry: A Linguistic Analogy for Uncoupling Sexual Orientation from Gender Identity." In *Queerly Phrased: Language, Gender, and Sexuality,* edited by Anna Livia and Kira Hall, 380–401. New York: Oxford University Press, 1997.

Baker, Paul. *Fantabulosa: A Dictionary of Polari and Gay Slang.* London, New York: Continnum, 2002.

Bright, Susie. "Move over, Ken, it's 'Bend Over Boyfriend,'" Salon.com, http://dir.salon.com/story/health/sex/col/brig/1998/05/22/nc_22brig/ (accessed August 10. 2009).

Brite, Poppy Z. "Enough Rope," http://www.poppyzbrite.com/rope.html (accessed August 2009).

Burrows, Jim. "The Adventures of La Maupin" (1995–2008), http://www.eldacur.com/~brons/Maupin/Maupin Index.html (accessed July 14, 2009).

Califia, Pat. "Identity Sedition and Pornography." In *PoMosexuals: Challenging Assumptions about Gender and Sexuality,* edited by Carol Queen and Laurence Schimel, 87–106. San Francisco: Cleis Press, 1997.

Castle, Terry. *The Apparitional Lesbian.* New York: Columbia University Press, 1993.

Coote, Stephen. *The Penguin Book of Homosexual Verse* London: Penguin Books, 1986.

Curran, Beverley and Welker, James. "From the Well of Loneliness to the akarui rezubian: Western Translations and Japanese Lesbian Identities." In *Genders, Transgenders and Sexualities in Japan,* edited by Mark McLelland and Romit Dasgupta, 65–80. London: Routledge, 2005.

Dhaenens, Frederik, Van Bauwel, Sofie, and Biltereyst, Daniel. "Transgressing the Boundaries of Screen Studies, Representations, and Slashing the Fiction of Queer Theory: Slash Fiction, Queer Reading, and Audiences." *Journal of Communication Inquiry,* 32(4) (October 2008): 335–347, http://jci.sagepub.com/cgi/content/abstract/32/4/335 (accessed May 10, 2009).

Feinberg, Leslie. *Transgender Warriors* Boston, Mass.: Beacon Press, 1997.

Foundation for the Production and Translation of Dutch Literature, The. "Floortje Zwigtman — Tricks of the Trade," http://www.nlpvf.nl/docs/Zwigtman_Schijnbewegingen_scr.pdf (accessed August, 10, 2009).

Genschel, Corinna. Erstrittene Subjektivität: Diskurse der Transsexualität, *Das Argument* 243 43/6, 2001:821ff, http://www.linksnet.de/artikel.php?id=553 (accessed August 10, 2009).

GirlFag Yahoo Group. "Introduction," http://groups.yahoo.com/group/GirlFags/ (accessed April 4, 2009).

Greaney, Markisha. "A Proposal for Doing Transgender Theory in the Academy." In *Reclaiming Genders: Transsexual Grammars at the Fin de Siècle,* edited by Kate More and Stephen Whittle. London: Cassell, 1999.

Hardach, Sophie. "Sexy Comics Feed Japan's Role Play Boom," International Business Times (March 4, 2008), http://www.ibtimes.co.in/articles/20080304/comics-japan-role-play-boom.htm (accessed August 10, 2009).

Hashimoto, Miyuki. "Visual Kei Otaku Identity — An Intercultural Analysis," *Intercultural Communication Studies* XVI: 1 2007 (University of Vienna, Austria): 87–99. http://www.uri.edu/iaics/content/2007v16n1/10%20Miyuki%20Hashimoto.pdf (accessed July 10, 2009).

Hill, Jane. *Dora Carrington.* München: Knesebeck, 1995.

Hirschfeld, Magnus. *Die Homosexualität des Mannes und des Weibes.* Berlin: Louis Marcus Verlagsbuchhandlung, 1920.

_____. *Die Transvestiten.* Berlin: Verlag Pulvermacher, 1910.

Jenkins, Henry. *Textual Poachers.* New York: Routledge, 1992.

Kamm, Björn-Ole. "Fujoshi — Nutzen und Gratifikation bei Boy's Love Manga in Japan und Deutschland." (Forthcoming master's thesis, University of Leipzig, Germany, 2008).

Lipton, Mark. "Queer Readings of Popular Culture." In *Queer Youth Cultures,* edited Susan Driver, 163–179. Albany: State University of New York Press, 2008.

Longinotto, Kim & Williams, Jano (Directors). *Shinjuku Boys,* DVD, 20th Century Vixen, 1995.

Masami, Toku. "Interview with Keiko Takemiya, January 22, 2003." http://www.csuchico.edu/~mtoku/vc/interviews_full/Interview%20w_Takemiya.html) (accessed August 15, 2009).

Meyer, Uli. "Almost Homosexual — *Schwule Frauen, Schwule Trans*gender* (Girlfags/Trans*Fags)." In *Liminalis1,* 2007 http://www.liminalis.de/artikel/Liminalis2007_meyer.pdf (accessed August 15, 2009).

Nancy. "Hagio's Interview "Hatachi — 20 Years Old." http://ponoichizoku.blogspot.com/2007/04/hagios-interview-hatachi-20-years-old.html (accessed August 20, 2009).

Perkovich, Mike. *Nature Boys: Camp Discourse in American Literature from Whitman to Wharton.* New York: Peter Lang Publishing, 2003.

Pflugfelder, Gregory M. *Cartographies of Desire: Male-Male Sexuality in Japanese Discourse, 1600–1950.* Berkeley: University of California Press, 2000.

Queen, Carol & Schimel, Laurence (Ed.). *PoMosexuals.* San Francisco: Cleis Press, 1997.

Robertson, Jennifer. *Takarazuka.* Berkeley: University of California Press, 1998.

Sedgwick, Eve Kosofsky. *Between Men.* New York: Columbia University Press, 1985.

_____. *Tendencies.* Durham, NC: Duke University Press, 1993.

Taylor, Clare L. *Women, Writing, and Fetishism 1890–1950.* Oxford: Clarendon Press, 2003.

Thorn, Matthew. "Girls And Women Getting Out Of Hand: The Pleasure And Politics Of Japan's Amateur Comics Community," 2004, http://matt-thorn.com/shoujo_manga/outofhand/index.php#back8 (accessed August 10, 2009).

Thorn, Matthew. "The Moto Hagio Interview (2005)." http://www.matt-thorn.com/shoujo_manga/hagio_interview.php (accessed August 10, 2009).

Thorn, Matthew. "The Multi-Faceted Universe of Shōjo Manga," 2008, http://www.matt-thorn.com/shoujo_manga/colloque/index.php (accessed May 5, 2009).

Welker, James. "Lilies in the Margin: Beautiful Boys and Queer Female Identities in Japan." In *AsiaPacifiQueer,* edited by Fran Martin, Peter Jackson, et al. Urbana and Chicago: University of Illinois Press, 2008.

_____. "Telling Her Story: The Japanese Lesbian Community 1971–2001: Selections From '*Komyuniti No Rekishi*' 1971–2001: *Nenpyō To Intabyū De Furikaeru*" (master's thesis/annotated translation. University of Sheffield, UK, 2002).

_____. "Beautiful, Borrowed and Bent: 'Boys' Love' as Girl's Love in Shōjo Manga." *Signs: Journal of Women in Culture and Society,* 31(3) (Spring 2006): 841–70.

Zwigtman, Floortje. *Ich, Adrian Mayfield.* Hildesheim: Gerstenberg Verlag, 2008.

Glossary

These words are specific to the Japanese-derived context of boys' love and yaoi in the West; some of them have application to slash, fan fiction, and Internet terminology in general. Popular boys' love and yaoi fandoms have terminology not included here. Alternate usage is in parentheses following the main entry.

aca-fan. "Academic" + "fan," a term to describe a fan who may have a scholarly interest in a fandom, or a scholar who may be a fan. The word was coined by Henry Jenkins, who was moderator of the ACAFEN-L academic mailing list in the mid–1990s, and has been since popularized by him as the title of his blog, "Confessions of an Aca-Fan," which he started in June 2006. See **fan.**

alternate universe (AU). Fan work whose character(s) are depicted in settings other than occurred in canon. See **OOC.**

anime—Japanese-origin animation; the term became widespread in the U.S. in the late 1980s and early 1990s.

aniparo—"Anime parody," in which anime characters are used in humorous situations.

archive. Generally, a collection of fan stories and/or artwork and scanlated works made available on the Web. See **archontic** and **scanlation.**

archontic. The intertextual relationships at the core of literature. Expanding on Jacques Derrida's "archontic principle" as the "internal drive of an archive to continually expand," Abigail Derecho proposes "archontic literature" as a description for fan fiction to allow it to be conceived as an ethical project that opposes notions of hierarchy and property, and in lieu of words such as "appropriative," for its connotation of taking or theft, and "derivative," for its connotation as being lesser than the primary text.[1]

beta. To read and comment on, or proofread, fan fiction before the fan publishes it.

biseinen—Beautiful young man or young men.

bishōnen—Beautiful boy(s). The topos of the beautiful boy as a sexual object for men in Japanese discourse dates from at least the *Heike monogatari* (Tale of the Heike; ca. thirteenth century CE). It is seen in popular fiction in the twentieth century, deployed to serve against "civilizing" Western discourses. An example is the widely read story *Shizu no odamaki* (The Spool of Hemp), first published by high school and university students, then commercially up to about 1916. See *nanshoku.*

BNF. "Big Name Fan," a fan who is known by other fans in her/his fandom(s).

boys' love (BL)—Fan and commercial works depicting pre-adolescent, adolescent and/or young adult males in homoerotic relationships, transgressive of Western and Japanese notions of masculinity, heteronormativity and homonormativity. In Japan, the roman characters BL are used more often than the loan words "boys' love" (and the Japanese equivalent thereof, "*bōizu rabu*") as a rubric for the category in, e.g., bookstores and on television. Hervé Brient writes that "BL" appeared in Japan in the middle of the 1990s, rapidly replacing "*june*," "*shōnen-ai*" (in part for its connotation of pedophilia) and "yaoi" (which had become linked to the activities of the *dōjinshika*).[2] In English, "yaoi" is a more popular term than "boys' love." See *june, shōnen-ai* and **yaoi**.

butler café. Cafés in Japan where the waiters dress as European butlers to serve tea and pastries to a mostly female clientele. There is also a café in Tokyo, the Café Edelstein, where Japanese male waiters dress as European prep school *bishōnen*, and at Yaoi-Con, the Café Verführen, where Western female waiters dress as *bishōnen*.

canon. Facts known in fandom established by an original manga, anime, movie, book, or television show or series. See **fanon**.

Comic Market (Comike, Comiket) — A fan-created and -run market for the sale of *dōjinshi* and other products centered around manga, anime, video games and other media. Comic Market is held twice a year in Tokyo. From roughly 700 attendees at the first event in 1975, Comic Market grew rapidly. Since 2007 it has attracted more than 500,000 people over three days. Boys' love *dōjinshi* is exhibited in halls totaling $16,940m^2$. Over the past thirty years, approximately seventy-one percent of circle participants (*dōjinshi* artists) and fifty-seven percent of attendees were women.[3]

con. (1) Fan gathering for meeting each other as well as people who produce commercial products bought by fans, exchanging ideas in fandoms, displaying and/or selling fan created works, cosplay, etc. Boys' love-related cons in the United States include Bishie Con, Yaoi-Con, and Yaoi North (held at Anime North). See **Yaoi-Con, Yuricon**. (2) In Japan, as a suffix: complex, indicating an obsession.

cosplay — A portmanteau of "costume" and "play" to describe activities associated with dressing and acting like a character in anime, manga, or videogames, often at cons.[4]

crossover. Fan work(s) with characters from more than one fandom. See **fan**.

disclaimer. A statement usually at the top of a fic or on the index page for a fic series or in an archive that disclaims ownership of the characters. It may also warn of things some readers may consider controversial (e.g., for boys' love or slash: non-con, AU, a character death, or a very young or old character). Sometimes disclaimers will include a plot summary, a dedication, acknowledgments of beta readers and other content. See **paratext**.

dōjinshi (dj) — Fan-created literature, most often manga, encompassing magazines, books and other media. BL *dōjinshi* are sold at the Comic Market and at smaller comic markets in other cities in Japan as well in stores such as those in Tokyo's **Otome** Road. Their distribution in the U.S. has been limited to a few cons and mail order.

dōjinshika (*dōjinka*, djka) — Fans who create *dōjinshi*.

drabble. Fiction of 100 words.

fan (fanboi, fanboy, fangirl) — In boys' love, an aficionado of Japanese derived cultural products depicting adolescent young males in homoerotic relationships. See **boys' love**.

fandom. Fans and their activities, often specific to a canonical work or series, e.g., the fandoms around *Fullmetal Alchemist, Harry Potter,* and *Weiß Kreuz*.

fan fiction (fan fic, fic) — Fan-written fiction that uses characters, premises, or other material drawn from other, usually canonical, fictional works such as manga, anime, television shows, books, movies, etc., or from reports about real people. See **real-person slash**.

fanon. Fan-created elements of plot, character details, etc. that have become widely accepted by other fans. See **canon.**

fan service— Artwork or scenes inserted in a canonical manga, anime, or in other products, that in boys' love depict canonical characters in a homosocial / homoerotic context.

fansub. Anime that has been translated and subtitled by fans, generally without permission by the copyright holders.

fanzine (zine)— A fan-created magazine, generally a small-sized collection of fan fiction, art, articles, reader comments, etc. Distributed via postal mail and at fan conventions.

femslash (femmeslash). Fan works depicting homoerotic relationships between or among female characters.

fujoshi— Lit., "rotten woman." Female fan(s) of boys' love manga, anime and/or video games; a pejorative term that has been taken as positive by some fans. See ***otaku.***

GloBL. A term coined by *mangaka* Tina Anderson that combines "global" and "BL" to indicate the spread of BL, both in translated and original forms, across the world.

gosurori— Gothic Lolita fashion. See **Lolita fashion.**

graphic novel. A collection of manga stories, often by one author, translated and printed as a paperback book marketed in Western regions.

hentai— Pervert; abnormal sexuality; sexual perversion. Used by Western manga/anime fans to describe sexually graphic content.

hurt/comfort (h/c). A topos in fan and other fiction in many cultures wherein one character cares for another in pain or distress. It is often used as a way to bring them closer, literally and figuratively. In boys' love and slash, h/c is also a way to add a homoerotic dimension to an otherwise ostensibly homosocial relationship.

J-pop. A genre of Japanese music, some of whose band members present an androgynous appearance and who may be considered slashable, either as RPS or fictional characters. See **real-person slash.**

june. A popular descriptive word for the first commercial magazines treating male-male homoerotic themes and marketed to women. "*June*" became eponymous with what would become boys' love manga. *Comic Jun*, founded in 1978, published eight issues. In January 1979 it was renamed *June*, at that time becoming dedicated exclusively to stories about male homosexuality. It was published monthly until April 1987. *June DX*, a related magazine, was published bimonthly between 1984 and 2004. It was replaced by *Comic June*, which is still published.[5] Today in Japan and the West "*june*" refers to an early type of boys' love manga.[6] See **boys' love.**

lemon, lime. Scenes in fan fiction describing sexual acts between or among characters. "Lemon" implies an explicit description of an overtly sexual act such as intercourse or masturbation; "lime" a less explicit description.

lolicon (*lolikon, rorikon*)— Lolita complex, obsession with young adolescent girls in manga, anime and related products, after Vladimir Nabokov's novel *Lolita*. See **Lolita fashion.**

Lolita fashion (*Loli*)— In Japan, usually young women (not girls) and some young men who dress in cute, childlike and modest fashions. The Lolita aesthetic of hyperfeminine and hypercute characteristics, writes Theresa Winge, creates a visual form of resistance against the dominant culture, providing the subculture and its members with agency and identity and allowing *Lolis* to extend themselves into spaces and ways otherwise unavailable to them. One of the most popular Lolita genres is Gothic, which combines Goth, *kawaii* (cute), and Victorian dress.[7] See ***gosurori, lolicon.***

manga — Comics, generally published as magazine(s) with a collection of story chapters from different series within a broad genre such as boys' love. Manga are pervasive in Japan. Variant names in other languages include *manhua* (Chinese) and *manhwa* (Korean).

mangaka — Manga artist, cartoonist.

Mary Sue (Marty Stu). An idealized fan-fiction character modeled after the author. Often disparaged by other fans.

M/M. Male/male; see also **slash.**

mpreg. Fanfiction or artwork in which one or more male characters becomes pregnant.

nanshoku — Male-male love, implying an age-discrepant relationship, most often between an adolescent and a young adult or adult. "*Wakashudō*" (*wakashu* [youth] + *dō* [way]), for the "way of loving youths," may have been more commonly used during the Edo period (1603–1858 CE). *Nanshoku* was a sexual option available to most men and was widely practiced in most regions in Japan for more than a millennium. It left one of the largest repositories worldwide of material on male-male sexuality before the twentieth century, such as fiction and nonfiction books, kabuki or *bunraku* drama, and artwork such as prints, paintings, and folding screens. See ***bishōnen.***

non-con (n/c). Fan art or fiction depicting non-consensual sex act(s), where one or more characters has sex with other character(s), despite the latter's inability or refusal to consent.

one-shot. A work of fiction that stands alone; one that is not intended to be part of a series.

OOC. "Out of character," in which a fan's representation of a canonical character has him or her acting in ways other than generally accepted portrayals in canon or fanon. See **alternate universe.**

original character. A character created by a fan for his/her fic or artwork. Original characters may be part of an otherwise canonical fan work. See **Mary Sue.**

otaku — Fan(s) of manga, anime and/or video games; a pejorative term that has been taken as positive by many fans. Azuka Hiromi gives "*otaku*" in a Japanese context as males generally between the ages of eighteen and forty, whose culture became a mass social phenomenon in 1995–96 with the boom of interest in the anime series *Shin seiki evangelion* (*Neon Genesis Evangelion*).[8] In a 1989 moral panic "*otaku*" was extended to all amateur manga artists and fans irrespective of sex.[9] In a U.S. context, *otaku* may be female or male, and *otaku* status can be seen as "cool" among fans even as it has negative connotations among some.[10] The U.S. anime/manga and Asian popular culture convention Otakon calls itself "the convention of the otaku generation."[11] See ***fujoshi.***

***Otome* Road.** *Otome* ("maiden"), a nickname for the Higashi Ikebukuro district of Tokyo in which there are bookstores selling BL *dōjinshi*, manga, video games, CDs, DVDs, posters, cards, calendars, and other items, as well as the Swallowtail butler café. Billboards on buildings and sign-boards on the street advertise the stores' BL products with illustrations of *bishōnen* in homoerotic contexts.

OTP. "One true pairing," a fan's ideal pair of characters within a canonical work to be slashed.

OVA — Original Video Animation, a direct-to-video anime. The term came into existence with the release of *Dallas* (1983). Sometimes referred to as OAV (Original Animation Video).[12]

paratext. Elements around a text, such a story's length, its headers, and comments about it. Kristina Busse writes that "fannish reading practices ... create a paratextual apparatus of its own," and this "shapes how people engage with the [canonical work] they're invested in."[13] Gérard Genette, et al., characterize paratexts as an "'undefined zone' between the ... inward side (turned toward the text) or the outside (turned toward the world's discourse about the text)," and, quoting, Philippe Lejune, "'a fringe of the printed text which in reality controls one's whole reading of the text.'"[14]

plot bunny. An idea for a story, artwork (or element therein) to which the writer or artist feels impelled to give expression.

PWP. "Plot, what plot?" Fanfiction, usually stories, with a prominent emphasis on sexual activity, often in a humorous context, usually to the exclusion of additional plot. Sometimes given as "porn without plot."

real-person slash (RPS). Homoerotic fanfiction in which one or more characters are a real-life actor, celebrity, musician, politician, or other prominent person. See **slash.**

scanlation. The combination of "scan" and "translation" to indicate manga scanned from a printed copy and translated into a Western language, the translated text digitally inserted in place of the Japanese characters. Usually refers to work carried out by fans without the permission of the publisher.

seme— A male character in boys' love who is older, taller and more experienced than the *uke*. From "*semeru*," a verb meaning "attack, assault."

shōjo— Girl(s).

shōnen— Boy(s).

shōnen-ai— Boy(s) love. Although no longer used by fans in Japan, fans in the West may use the term to describe "light" boys' love stories that emphasize romance and contain little if any explicit sex. See **boys' love.**

shota— Generally used in the West to describe boys' love products featuring prepubescent (not yet adolescent) male(s).

shotacon— In Japan, "Shōtarō complex," an obsession with prepubescent male(s) in manga, anime and related products.

slash, slash fiction. Homoerotic stories, poetry, artwork, and video about male characters from television programs, movies, and books as well as about real people. Slash is distinct from boys' love, although fans may engage with both genres. Slash has flourished as an amateur art form in the UK, the U.S., and other Western regions since the late 1960s or early 1970s, roughly contemporaneous with Japanese boys' love and predating BL's adoption in the West. No early connection has been shown between slash and BL, but the origins of both may have been influenced, writes Matthew Thorn, "by a global questioning of gender and sexuality."[15] One of the key differences between the two genres may be the age of the media characters and of the fans creating erotic works about them. "Slash" is used as a verb by boys' love as well as by slash fans to describe creating a homoerotic situation for characters. See **real-person slash, slashable.**

slashable, slashy. A character or situation that may lend itself to being depicted as homoerotic.

squick. Content of a boys' love, slash, or other work that discomfits the reader or viewer to some degree. Also used as a verb, as in "Sorry, I didn't mean to squick you."

tankōbon — Lit., "special book; separate volume." Used to describe a collection of chapters in a single series after having been published in manga.

TPTB. "The Powers That Be," the intellectual property owner(s) of the characters being slashed, often corporations or other profit-making entities.

uke — A male character in boys' love who is smaller, shorter and less experienced than the ***seme.*** A "pushy *uke*" is an *uke* who acts aggressively towards the *seme.*

WAFF (fluff). Warm and fuzzy feeling(s). Fan fiction focusing on romance.

WIP. Work-in-progress: a story, series or a visual work not completed.

yaoi — Acronym of "*Yamanashi, Ochinashi, Iminashi,*" or "no climax, no point, no meaning." A spoof is "*Yamete, Oshiri ga Itai,*" or "Stop, my ass hurts." "Yaoi" was coined by a group of amateurs who titled their 1979 *dōjinshi Rappori yaoi tokushū gou* (*Rappori*: Special Yaoi Issue). They created the acronym because their work was a collection of scenes and episodes with no overarching structure. The story features two youths in a suggestive but not explicitly sexual relationship. See **boys' love.**

Yaoi-Con. A convention of yaoi and boys' love fans held yearly in and around San Francisco, California since 2001.

yuri — Anime, manga, fanfic and fan art featuring same-sex female relationships. Unlike boys' love, which is primarily by and for girls and women, yuri appears as a major theme in manga and anime for male and female readers; the approach and tone, however, are noticeably different depending on intended audience. The derivation of the word is not clear. One explanation, unproven, is that "yuri" derives from many characters depicted the genre being named Yuriko.

Yuricon. A convention of yuri fans held in the United States every other year since 2003. Its location varies.

Notes

1. Abigail Derecho, "Archontic Literature: A Definition, a History, and Several Theories of Fan Fiction," in *Fan Fiction and Fan Communities in the Age of the Internet: New Essays*, ed. Karen Hellekson and Kristina Busse (Jefferson, NC: McFarland, 2006), 61–78.

2. Hervé Brient, "Une petite histoire du yaoi," in *Manga 10,000 images: Homosexualité et manga: le yaoi* (Versailles, France: Éditions H., 2008), 10.

3. Comic Market Preparations Committee, "What is the Comic Market?" (Tokyo, February 2008), http://www.comiket.co.jp/info-a/WhatIsEng080528.pdf (accessed August 13, 2009), 21.

4. Theresa Winge, "Costuming the Imagination: Origins of Anime and Manga Cosplay," in *Mechademia* vol. 1, *Emerging Worlds of Anime and Manga*, ed. Frenchy Lunning (Minneapolis, MN: University of Minnesota Press, 2006), 65.

5. Brient, "Une petite histoire," 8–9.

6. Frederik Schodt, *Dreamland Japan: Writings on Modern Manga* (Berkeley, CA: Stone Bridge Press), 1996.

7. Theresa Winge, "Undressing and Dressing Loli: A Search for the Identity of the Japanese Lolita," in *Mechademia* vol. 3, *Limits of the Human*, ed. Frenchy Lunning (Minneapolis, MN: University of Minnesota Press, 2008), 47–48, 50, 57, 62.

8. Azuka Hiromi, *Otaku: Japan's Database Animals*, trans. Jonathan E. Abel and Shion Kono (Minneapolis, MN: University of Minnesota Press, 2009), xv, 117N1.

9. Sharon Kinsella, *Adult Manga: Culture and Power in Contemporary Japanese Society* (Honolulu: University of Hawai'i Press, 2000), 128–9.

10. Susan Napier, *From Impressionism to Anime: Japan as Fantasy and Fan Cult in the Mind of the West* (New York: Palgrave Macmillan, 2007), 131.

11. Otakon, "About Otakon," http://www.otakon.com (accessed August 14, 2009).

12. Gilles Poitras, "Contemporary Anime in Japanese Pop Culture," in *Japanese Visual Culture: Explorations in the World of Manga and Anime,* ed. Mark W. Macwilliams (Armonk, NY: M.E. Sharpe, 2008), 54.

13. Kristina Busse, "Paratextual Commentary as Writer Response Theory" (paper presented at the Society for Cinema & Media Studies, Philadelphia, PA, March 7, 2008). http://www.kristinabusse.com/cv/research/scms08.html (accessed August 14, 2009).

14. Ibid.

15. Matthew Thorn (personal communication with Mark McHarry).

About the Contributors

Yamila Abraham founded the publishing company Yaoi Press in 2004. Over the last five years she's overseen the publication of forty-five boys' love titles including graphic novels, comic books, and art books. Abraham has successfully licensed Yaoi Press titles into seven foreign languages. She has been a speaker or guest of honor at more than 150 anime fan conventions. Abraham is a prolific writer with over a dozen graphic novel works in print with four different publishers. Her most popular series to date are *Winter Demon* and *Dark Prince*.

Neal K. Akatsuka is an undergraduate at the University of Hawai'i at Manoa and expects to earn his B.A. in anthropology in 2010. He is currently working on an honors thesis in Tokyo on the Japanese public reception of genetically modified food, with a focus the construction of consumer epistemologies at this particular intersection of food, science, and culture in late capitalism. His research interests also include gender and sexuality in popular culture.

M. M. Blair is currently in the doctoral program at the University of British Columbia. She received her M.A. in Japanese literature from the University of Colorado at Boulder in 2009. Her thesis is "Love, Hate and Translation: Boys' Love Manga in Japan and America." Her undergraduate education was at the University of Washington, where she received degrees in Japanese literature and in drama in 2007.

Hope Donovan had only one logical career path, given a double major in English and drawing: comics. Having attained this goal through legitimate employment editing Japanese and Korean manga as well as developing original series for TOKYOPOP, Hope fulfilled her dreams by editing one hentai, one yuri, and one yaoi series simultaneously. She has contributed short manga to *Happy Yaoi Yum Yum* (Yaoi Press) and *Yuri Monogatari* (ALC). Hope currently is a freelance manga editor, English adaptor, layout artist, and creator.

Alexis Hall graduated from Hampshire College in 2007 with a bachelor's degree. She subsequently spent two years in Fukuoka, Japan, teaching English to junior high school and elementary students. Alexis hopes to pursue further study in the Japanese language and fan cultures in the future.

Mark John Isola, who earned his Ph.D. in literature from Tufts University, is an assistant professor at the Wentworth Institute of Technology in Boston. His interests include American literature, critical theory, new media studies, yaoi, GLBT studies, and AIDS literature. He has published journal articles in the *Nordic Journal of English Studies*, *Bad Subjects*, and *eSharp*, and has also contributed to multivolume collections on GLBTQ literary culture. He has been selected to chair panels and present papers at national-level conferences of the Modern Language Association, the American Literature Association, and the Popular Culture Association/American Culture Association.

Antonia Levi is a professor of Japanese history with an interest in the globalization of Japanese popular culture. She is the author of *Samurai from Outer Space: Understanding Japanese Animation* and numerous articles on Japanese animation (anime) and graphic novels (manga). Her Ph.D. is from Stanford University, and she has taught at Amherst College, Loyola-Marymount University, Whitman College, and Portland State University. She is now retired and writing a murder mystery about anime and manga fans.

Paul M. Malone is an associate professor of German in the Department of Germanic and Slavic Studies at the University of Waterloo. He is the author of *Franz Kafka's* The Trial: *Four Stage Adaptations* (Peter Lang, 2003), and has also published on performance theory and German drama and film. Other published interests include popular culture themes such as rock musicals derived from Goethe's classic *Faust*, German influences on Japanese anime, and film adaptations of the works of contemporary German queer comic book artist Ralf König.

Mark McHarry is an independent scholar. In addition to contemporary and Edo-period Japanese culture, his interests include the works of Fernando Vallejo and modern Latin American literature. He has contributed to *LGBT Identity and Online New Media* (Routledge), *Mechademia, Queer Popular Culture: Literature, Media, Film, and Television* (Palgrave Macmillan), the *Encyclopedia of Erotic Literature* (Routledge), *Dictionary of Literary Biography* Online (Thomson Gale), *Journal of Homosexuality, Z Magazine, Alternative Press Review*, and *Gay Community News*. He is currently researching the life of author-inventor Hiraga Gennai and his place in the *ukiyo* (floating world).

Uli Meyer is a freelance author and artist from Germany. After studying painting, Japanese, and anthropology, s/he has published extensively on gender in popular culture. S/he lectures about queer and transgender characters in manga and anime at film festivals and universities. As a painter, s/he is interested in the depiction of the objectified male. Contact: picoscript@yahoo.de.

Dru Pagliassotti is a professor in the communication department of California Lutheran University. She has published research on the Western reception of boys' love manga in *Participations: Journal of Audience & Reception Studies* and *Intersections: Gender and Sexuality in Asia and the Pacific* and maintains YaoiResearchWiki.Com for scholars with similar interests. Pagliassotti is also a fantasy and horror novelist and blogs at DruPagliassotti.Com.

Kim Senior is a senior lecturer at RMIT University, Melbourne. She publishes in pedagogy, feminist research methodologies, and arts-based educational research. She teaches in teacher education, lecturing in educational philosophy, and popular culture in education. In the near future she hopes to realize a desire to not only write about manga, but author one.

Marni Stanley teaches English and women's studies at Vancouver Island University in Nanaimo, British Columbia. Her academic research and publication areas include nineteenth century women travelers, television, cinema, and graphic narrative.

Tan Bee Kee graduated from the National University of Singapore with an honors degree in English literature. Currently, she is an M.A. research candidate in the Department of Japanese Studies, National University of Singapore. Her thesis, from which this article was adapted, is "Unauthorized Romances: Female Fans and *Weiss Kreuz* Internet *Yaoi* Fanfiction." She is a long-time observer of Japanese popular culture/youth subcultures. A former student of Edwin Thumboo and Kirpal Singh, Tan has published poems in *No Other City: The Ethos Anthology of Urban Poetry*, the journal *Singa 30, SilverKris* magazine (Sept 2000), *onewinged: a selection of works by young writers in Singapore* as well as *Love Gathers All: The Philippines-Singapore Anthology of Love Poetry*.

Mark Vicars is a senior lecturer in literacy at Victoria University, Melbourne. His research is located within the New Literacy Studies reflecting on literacy, language, and identity practices. An overarching concern, in his work, is to understand ways in which individuals use language and literacy. He is particularly interested in intercultural literacy and informal literacy practices as a means of practicing identity and of making sense of the world.

Alan Williams is a master's degree candidate in cultural studies at the University of Washington–Bothell. His interests include writing, game design, religion studies, feminist theory, martial arts, and yaoi. He's the author of *Ockham's Razor*, a novel.